Law for Small Business

FOR DUMMIES

A Wiley Brand

by Clive Rich

FOR DUMMIES

A Wiley Brand

Law for Small Business **For Dummies**®

Published by: **John Wiley & Sons, Ltd., The Atrium, Southern Gate, Chichester,** www.wiley.com

This edition first published 2016

© 2016 by John Wiley & Sons, Ltd., Chichester, West Sussex

Registered Office

John Wiley & Sons, Ltd., The Atrium, Southern Gate, Chichester, West Sussex, PO19 8SQ, United Kingdom

For details of our global editorial offices, for customer services and for information about how to apply for permission to reuse the copyright material in this book, please see our website at www.wiley.com.

For general information on our other products and services, please contact our Customer Care Department within the U.S. at 877-762-2974, outside the U.S. at 317-572-3993, or fax 317-572-4002. For technical support, please visit www.wiley.com/techsupport.

Wiley publishes in a variety of print and electronic formats and by print-on-demand. Some material included with standard print versions of this book may not be included in e-books or in print-on-demand. If this book refers to media such as a CD or DVD that is not included in the version you purchased, you may download this material at http://booksupport.wiley.com. For more information about Wiley products, visit www.wiley.com.

A catalogue record for this book is available from the British Library.

ISBN: 978-1-118-97046-1; ISBN 978-1-118-97045-4 (ebk); ISBN 978-1-118- 97044-7 (ebk)

Printed and Bound in Great Britain by TJ International, Padstow, Cornwall.

10 9 8 7 6 5 4 3 2 1

MIX
Paper from
responsible sources
FSC® C013056

Contents at a Glance

Table of Contents

Introduction

Small companies are often described as the engine room of the country's economy. The UK has over five million of them. They represent over 99 per cent of all companies in the UK, employ two-thirds of its workforce and deliver almost half its revenues. Yet they often find affordable, understandable legal advice hard to find. That's one of the reasons for all the anti-lawyer jokes:

> 'What do you get when you cross a lawyer with the Godfather?'
>
> 'An offer you can't understand'.
>
> 'How do you get a group of lawyers to smile for the camera?'
>
> 'Get them to say "Fees"'.

But I'm being unfair. Many people feel that there's no such thing as an anti-lawyer joke – they're all true.

Joking aside, this perception of lawyers as being expensive, difficult to understand and generally unhelpful is a serious problem for small companies, which encounter legal issues every step of the way: when they're setting up; employing staff or consultants; dealing with their intellectual property; contracting with customers, suppliers or distributors; dealing with disputes; or selling up. Yet research carried out by the Legal Services Board shows that almost half of the small companies in the UK don't use a lawyer to deal with these issues. They prefer to go it alone and take risks with their revenues, margins, profits and exit values by not taking care of their legal business properly.

Of course, many good, decent, helpful lawyers are available, but the traditional law firm structure probably doesn't cater very well for small companies and their needs. Law firms like to have regular clients that they can regularly bill for large amounts, to support their own partnership and overhead costs – but small companies don't need legal advice the whole time and are usually strapped for cash. Law firms like to take their time to consider thoroughly all the issues – but small companies are always in a hurry. Law firms like to give extensive advice and usually hedge their bets ('on the one hand you can do this, on the other hand you must consider that') – whereas small companies just want the essentials of the problem described to them and want to be told the answer.

As a result, a mismatch exists between what small companies need in the way of legal advice and what's available to them.

About This Book

This book gives small companies an easy-to-use guide to the law: it's highly practical and covers most of the typical situations in which small companies need legal help.

The book loosely follows the likely trajectory of a small company from set-up and start-up, to launching the business, growing the business and exiting. It maps the legal challenges that come up along the way, providing tips and analysis to help small companies solve them.

I have a caveat, of course (well, it is a legal book after all). Reading this book is helpful, but it can't be the same as taking legal advice. As a general handbook, it doesn't cover all circumstances, and other special features may apply to you and your case. If in doubt about your situation, talk to a lawyer – good ones are out there, I promise.

Foolish Assumptions

Small companies embrace a wealth of talented, committed, passionate individuals and contain some of the country's brightest minds. These people are often too innovative or driven to be contained by the boundaries of a more conventional larger corporation. They don't have a lot of time for (and aren't interested in) long-winded legal explanations that have nothing to do with their practical problems.

I assume that you're bright, in a hurry and looking for practical legal help written in plain English. I also suspect that you may have had a previous disappointing experience with lawyers – because they were too expensive, too slow or spoke a language only they understand. Why do I suspect this? Because the Legal Ombudsman received over 76,000 complaints about law firms in the last three years! I know that I may need to overcome your scepticism about the value of legal advice.

You've taken a great first step by buying this book. Now my responsibility is to show you that it's useful and make sure that you enjoy using it – so that it doesn't end up unused on the shelf.

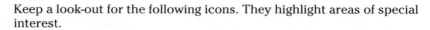

Icons Used in This Book

Keep a look-out for the following icons. They highlight areas of special interest.

This icon points you to a little gem that makes things easier or helps you get more from the book.

I could almost put this icon on every page, but these bits are super-crucial to keep in mind.

I make a real effort to avoid legal terms, but where insider words and phrases are so important that you need to know what they mean, I indicate them with this icon.

When you see this icon, you're steering through dangerous waters; I don't want you capsizing or even getting your feet wet.

Maybe not essential or riveting stuff about the law, but the text by this icon gives you a deeper understanding of the material.

Beyond the Book

Running your own business can get lonely, but you aren't alone. The legal tips and knowledge you gain from this book are sure to stand you in good stead throughout the life of your business.

In addition to the main text, I also provide several exclusive extra articles online at www.dummies.com/extras/lawforsmallbusinessuk. They include tests for your knowledge on intellectual property, contracts, keeping your business safe and raising funding. Plus, I provide ten tips to pull the rug from under the bullies of the negotiating world. I also share some essential legal pointers to keep in mind at all stages of your business in a handily-contained Cheat Sheet at www.dummies.com/cheatsheet/lawforsmall businessuk – something you can print off to decorate your office with, if you so desire (perhaps not, but you may want to file it somewhere for ease of reference).

Also, you need to find a lawyer or law firm you can feel comfortable with to help you through the inevitable legal issues involved in building a successful business. Don't try and deal with the challenges on your own if they're beyond your experience or expertise. Good, practical, affordable lawyers are around if you look for them. A little spent with the right lawyer at the right time can avoid far larger costs or expenses later.

Don't forget to get your lawyer involved in an issue early rather than waiting for a crisis to develop. Good lawyers can help you shape a strategy that avoids a problem developing and so save you money in the long run.

Where to Go from Here

I set out this book so that you can dip into any part, chapter or section that you need without reading the rest. Of course, you're welcome to read it from cover to cover, but if you don't have the time or inclination, this book is ready-made for cutting to the chase and getting straight to the legal subject that concerns you.

The law is a big subject and I can't discuss everything, but I definitely cover a range of issues that I know come up regularly for small companies. Search the theme of each part and chapter to find what you want. For example, if you're facing an urgent issue with getting your firm's software sorted, move straight to Chapter 9. If you need to hire some help in your firm and you're unsure of the difference between contractors and employees, read Chapter 5 before you make any mistakes you come to regret.

Good luck with your venture, and if you're sceptical about the usefulness of lawyers, I hope that this book changes your mind.

Part I

Getting Started with Legal Requirements

getting started with

law for small business

In this part . . .

- Discover the right business structure for you.
- Set up your chosen legal structure.
- Work out the kind of funding (and funder) you need.
- Navigate your way through the various types of funding agreement.

Chapter 1

Starting Your Legal Journey: Business Structures and Initial Research

In This Chapter

▶ Deciding on the right legal structure for you

▶ Checking various business registers

S o, you have a big idea for a business: maybe you've created a prototype for a machine that removes the overpowering aroma of gorgonzola or invented a cost-effective method of transporting irritating celebrities to another solar system. Perhaps you've created a *minimum viable product* (an initial version of your product that's good enough to test in the market) – and identified one or more individuals you want to work with. The sunlit peaks of entrepreneurial success lie before you. Exciting times!

Although I'm reluctant to draw cloudy shadows over this sunlit image, I have to point out that legal dangers lurk for the unwary new business owner, which can ruin your enterprise before you even start. Therefore, you need clear, comprehensible legal information from the initial start-up, through business growth and especially with disputes and serious problems (turn to Chapters 15 and 16, respectively, when you feel ready to think about that). You wouldn't start your business without a business plan, and I suggest you have a legal plan too.

For example, before you can get going as a small and medium-size enterprise (SME), you have to decide what business structure you want for your undertaking. Fortunately, along with some considerations for when you're registering your business, that's exactly the subject I cover in this chapter! Along the way, this chapter also acts as your guide to the rest of this book, which can continue to help you when you're ready to trade overseas (travel to Chapter 13), expand into other adventures (see Chapter 17) or sell your company for a well-earned cushy retirement (saunter with sand between your toes to Chapter 18)!

Deciding on Your Trading Structure

You can choose one of the following three main trading structures for a commercial business:

- ✔ Sole trader
- ✔ Partnership (including a limited liability partnership)
- ✔ Limited liability company

Each structure has different characteristics and distinct advantages and disadvantages, which I describe in this section. (When forming a charity you have some other options, but I don't cover that subject in this book.)

If you want more information, jump to Chapter 2, which talks you through the legal formalities of each type. For funding ideas and legalities, slip a coin into the slot and dispense the info in Chapters 3 and 4.

Going it alone: Sole trader

A *sole trader* arrangement is essentially a 'one-man band' where the business owner is self-employed and in effect *is* the business. Sole trading is one of the oldest and most traditional models of business ownership and has been used widely throughout many industries. A significant increase in the number of people setting up businesses as sole traders has occurred due to the sense of independence it brings. As a sole trader you have complete control over the business and can run it in any manner you choose.

This structure is also popular because of the ease with which you can combine it with other employment. On the other hand, personal liability attaches to you if the business gets into any difficulties.

Advantages

Here are some of the advantages of sole trading:

- ✔ **Autonomy and control:** The sole trader is truly independent and is in full control of the business and how it's conducted and any earned profits. You can therefore fully realise and develop your vision for the business without interference. Great!

✓ **Low administrative burden:** The lack of a formal setting-up structure makes for a cost-effective process requiring less paperwork. Usually, you don't need specialist legal or accountancy advice.

✓ **Less statutory obligations:** The Companies Acts don't apply to sole traders, and you have no requirement to file annual accounts or fulfil the other administrative burdens that fall on limited companies (see the later section 'Protecting your liability: Limited company' for details).

✓ **Flexibility:** As a sole trader, you can make decisions quickly because you don't need to consult anyone. Similarly, you can implement new decisions or ideas instantly.

✓ **Personal reputation:** A sole trader can build up an invaluable rapport with customers as the 'face' of the business.

✓ **Privacy:** Personal details of the sole trader, including address and profits, aren't in the public domain, because you don't have to register with Companies House (flip to the later 'Checking Companies House' section for more details).

✓ **Great for testing a new business idea:** Setting up as a sole trader is an inexpensive way to determine whether your business idea has true potential before you leave full-time employment.

If you're an employee of someone else though, check that you aren't breaching your employment contract by, for example, potentially competing with your employer or using confidential information.

✓ **Earning potential:** You retain any profits earned as the sole trader and (after tax) don't have to share them. When you've got your cake, you can eat it all yourself!

✓ **Ability to adapt:** If you begin your business as a sole trader, you can transition it into a limited liability company (see the 'Protecting your liability: Limited company' section later in this chapter) if it expands to a sufficient degree. No bar exists to *incorporating* the business at a later date by turning it into a limited company.

Disadvantages

Life as a sole trader isn't all sweetness and light. Here are some of the difficulties you can face:

✓ **Personal liability:** As a sole trader you can be held personally liable for losses suffered by the business, because no distinction exists between your personal and business assets. This disadvantage is a real 'biggie' – don't underestimate its significance. If you're a sole trader, you can end up funding the losses of the business out of your own savings, pension or house. Ouch! For this reason, you need to get your official Terms and Conditions (T&Cs) sorted to minimise your liabilities – check out Chapters 6 and 12 for your website T&Cs and other customer contracts, respectively, whatever business structure you choose.

✔ **Status or prestige:** An inherent snobbery exists regarding the sole-trader arrangement. Whether justifiable or not, sole traders are perceived as being less professional in nature and lacking professional credibility. Certain larger companies adhere to a strict policy of only dealing with limited companies.

✔ **Sole burden of responsibility:** A sole trader must operate as a 'jack of all trades'. Whether you have an aptitude for a particular area or not, you're required to fulfil *all* aspects of the business, such as administration (invoicing, filing, replying to customer queries and complaints) and finances (tax and National Insurance), as well as carrying responsibility for the core business's operation. Life can seem like a daily triathlon, followed by a decathlon, followed by a marathon.

✔ **Financial support or funding:** Sole traders have to rely on their own personal credit rating when seeking financial support. Potential lenders don't look on them favourably or as a secure option, which can cause difficulties in getting loans, a mortgage or investment for the business. (Chapter 3 has loads of great tips for early-stage funding).

✔ **Modest profits:** The effort you have to expend to achieve a profit can be burdensome when you're working on your own: achieving a good work–life balance can be difficult, particularly in the initial stages of the business. Your domestic partner may have something to say about this aspect, even if you're happy with it.

✔ **Unprotected business names:** No statutory protection exists for business names of sole traders, because they don't have to be registered with Companies House, unlike limited companies (flip to the later section 'Checking Companies House'). Protecting your name is therefore more complicated (see Chapter 8 under the heading 'Enforcing Unregistered Trademarks').

✔ **Less social security benefits:** A sole trader isn't entitled to the same social security benefits as employees. Sole traders are classified as 'self-employed' and so the amount of National Insurance they pay is usually lower than an employee has to pay. Therefore, if your business as a sole trader gets into trouble and ceases to trade, you can find that you have less entitlements built up to access unemployment assistance and less contributions towards your state pension.

✔ **Insurance:** As a sole trader, you usually need public liability insurance if you deal with members of the public. Plus, if you take on even one employee, employer's liability insurance is also necessary. These kinds of policy can be harder for a sole trader to get than a limited company or partnership – a double whammy given your risk of being personally liable for the losses of the business.

✔ **Harder to exit:** If a sole trader wants to sell the business *(exit)*, no shares are available to sell because it's not a company. All that's really available is the trading book and reputation you've built up as a sole trader. These aspects can be hard to quantify and still harder to sell, because they're wrapped up in your personality and history.

Collaborating with a colleague: Partnership

The *partnership* model of business is a vehicle in which two or more self-employed individuals are linked in a collaborative business structure with a view to making profits.

These arrangements have existed traditionally in the provision of professional advice services, such as law and accountancy firms. But whatever your sector, if you're working with someone collaboratively to make profits, the law may classify you as a partnership even if you don't think that you're one! In the past these *General Partnerships* haven't enjoyed the benefits of limited liability, and so the partners can be liable for their share of any debts of the partnership. Worse still, because the law says that partners are liable for the debts of the partnership 'jointly', you can be liable for the partnership debts of other partners as well as your own share of the partnership debt. Holy bank balance, Batman!

The law applying to partnerships has been significantly altered with the introduction of the concept of Limited Liability Partnerships (LLP) as regulated by the Limited Liability Partnerships Act, 2000. The LLP is a hybrid between a General Partnership and a limited liability company and offers its members protection from liability for partnership debts and partnership contractual liabilities, while retaining the flexibility of the partnership model. The formation of an LLP, however, involves a greater administrative burden than a traditional General Partnership.

Advantages

Setting up as a partnership provides a number of advantages. Here are the pros for a General Partnership:

✔ **Simplicity:** Relatively simple and straightforward to set up, and doesn't require a high level of administration or formality.

✔ **Low costs:** No great overheads involved.

✔ **Privacy:** No requirement to register a General Partnership's details publicly (as with limited companies) – a distinct advantage because no competitor can access potentially valuable company information.

Now I cover the advantages for both types of partnerships:

- ✔ **Only two people required:** You need only two partners to start and can introduce new ones without difficulty. This arrangement can make decision-making easier than in a limited company (see the later section 'Protecting your liability: Limited company') where numerous shareholders may be involved.

- ✔ **Partnership of equals:** Each partner brings a unique set of skills to the business, allowing a well-rounded and balanced business to develop. A partner with a particular aptitude can focus on a certain part of the business while the other partner concentrates on the disciplines where she's stronger. This type of collaboration allows for greater flexibility in the running of the business.

- ✔ **Professional requirement:** Some professional bodies and associations require that those trading do so via the partnership model: for example, accountancy and engineering firms. Setting up as a partnership enables you to operate in these sectors of business.

Here are some advantages of an LLP compared to a General Partnership:

- ✔ **Each partner enjoys limited liability against the partnership's debts:** Liability is limited to the amount of capital a person agreed to contribute as part of the partnership agreement – which can be as little as £1 if the partnership doesn't need capital to run itself. This is a big advantage over a General Partnership.

- ✔ **The LLP name can be protected:** The requirement to register an LLP partnership name ensures that no other company can register the same business name.

Finally, here are some advantages of an LLP over a limited-company structure:

- ✔ **LLPs retain the organisational flexibility and tax benefits of the traditional partnership structure:** They're easier to set up and run than limited companies and the profits earned aren't subject to corporation tax, which applies to limited companies.

- ✔ **No memorandum or articles of association and no holding of LLP meetings required:** You don't need to register the LLP agreement or formulate director or share agreements, as with a limited company.

Disadvantages

Lawyers are fond of saying 'on the one hand this . . . on the other hand that', which can be irritating for clients who just want to be told the right answer.

(No wonder that one U.S. President is reputed to have requested in exasperation that he only have to deal with one-armed lawyers, who might give him a single answer!) On the other hand (er, sorry), partnerships entail some genuine disadvantages, and so I look at some of those here:

✔ **No limited liability:** A General Partnership (of the traditional, non-LLP kind) has no limited liability. All partners are held personally and jointly responsible for the debts incurred by the partnership. If a partner enters into a contract that's not in the best interests of the partnership, it's binding on all the partners, for better or worse.

✔ **The 1890 Act applies if no partnership agreement is entered into:** Most General Partnerships are based on a deed of partnership agreement with specific provisions on how the partnership is to be run, in order to avoid the application of this Act. Given that the Act dates from Victorian times, you can imagine that it may have unintended consequences in a modern business environment – after all, it dates from a period when poorhouses were commonplace and so was eating offal!

For example, under this old-fashioned Act:

- **A partner can't *retire* (that is, leave the partnership):** If one partner decides to leave, or dies, the partnership has to be dissolved and the assets divided up.

- **A partner can't be expelled:** Again, the partnership has to be dissolved and a new one created.

- **All profits are shared equally:** All partners share equally in the profits irrespective of the amount of time or effort they devote to the business.

✔ **Consensus is required:** All decisions made require agreement by all partners unless the partnership agreement says otherwise. As such, the decision-making process can become slower and more protracted.

✔ **Shared goals and values are required:** Partners may not possess the same vision for the business and can have differing aims and ideas. Because control is shared, this situation can create difficulties in the running of the business.

✔ **Lopsided partnerships:** All partners may not apply themselves equally to the diligent operation of the partnership, but may still attempt to direct and manage the business (and take a pro-rata share of any profits). If efforts aren't rewarded justly, resentment and hostility are likely to grow.

✔ **Lower social security benefits:** A partner is entitled to less social security benefits than an ordinary employee. Because the partners are self-employed, they'll have made fewer contributions than employees of a limited company (for example, National Insurance contributions). Therefore, they have less access to social security benefits such as unemployment assistance and may also have a lower state pension.

- ✔ **Less obvious ownership and funding opportunities:** Generally, all existing partners must agree that someone new can become a partner, and so limited flexibility exists for creating additional ownership opportunities. The partnership structure is also less suitable on the whole (compared to limited companies) for raising finance, which is why most of the capital from partnerships tends to come from the partners themselves. Chapters 3 and 4 discuss your funding options and associated legalities.

- ✔ **Limited Liability Partnerships:** Though not as onerous as for a limited company, the administrative burden is much greater for an LLP than for a General Partnership. Registration with Companies House is required, as is the filing of annual accounts and returns and any changes to business names, addresses or members. Penalties may be imposed for late filing and, unlike some soccer referees, Companies House is always happy to award a penalty (see the later section, 'Checking Companies House'). I look at these formalities in Chapter 2.

Protecting your liability: Limited company

One of the fundamental principles of company law, which applies to limited companies, is that a company has a separate *legal personality* from its *members* (shareholders). The company has its own rights and obligations: it has a right to sue and be sued in its own name, to own property and it isn't affected by the death or insolvency of an individual member (unlike a partnership). This principle is known as the *veil of incorporation*.

Sounds very mysterious I know (after all, you don't hear about the 'cloak of isolation' for sole traders or a sacred chalice from which partners in LLPs have to drink to seal the deal!). But veil of incorporation just means that any liability incurred by the company is limited to the company and doesn't extend to its shareholders and directors.

The shareholders of the company are in principle only liable to the extent of the nominal value of their shares. The *nominal value* is the face value of the share (say £0.01 or £1.00 each) as opposed to the actual market value of the share if it were sold (which would hopefully be much higher). So that's why the principle is referred to as *limited liability*. If you have 50 shares worth £0.01, then all things being equal, your maximum liability for the company's debts is £0.50, even if the whole shebang goes up in flames and loses millions of pounds. What a relief. . . .

The concept of protection from liability provides one of the main motivations for forming a private limited liability company. This protection makes the limited liability company one of the most common types of trading structures for small and larger businesses.

Advantages

The protection from personal liability means that limited companies are the safest of the three types of business structure I discuss in this chapter. Here are some of the advantages of establishing a limited company in more detail:

- **Distinct entity:** A limited company is a discrete legal entity, completely separate from the people who run it. This arrangement provides security for company employees and members, because it exists beyond the life of its members. This setup is in stark contrast to the case of sole traders (read the earlier 'Going it alone: Sole trader' section) and General Partnerships, where no such separation exists (other than for the newer LLPs; see the earlier section 'Collaborating with a colleague: Partnership').

- **Limited liability:** Shareholders are liable only for any debt the company accrues according to the nominal value of their own shares. Their personal assets aren't at risk if the business gets into difficulty, which can occur with sole traders. I provide a number of tips to reduce your business risks in Chapter 14.

- **Clarity from the Articles of Association (the company's constitution):** These clearly set out the powers and responsibilities with which the company, the shareholders and directors must comply. I describe Articles of Association further in Chapter 2. The provision of a formal structure to trade under gives confidence and security to those involved and allows decision-making to take place relatively quickly and effectively and without undue difficulties.

- **Company name protection:** All limited companies are required to register a company name with Companies House (see the later section, 'Checking Companies House'). When registered, this name is protected from that date, though only as a limited company name – it doesn't have the same wider protection as a trademark (more on this important difference later in 'Looking into trademark registers').

- **Taxation benefits:** Limited companies are taxed only on their profits and, as such, aren't subject to the higher (personal) tax placed on sole traders or partnerships. The ability of members to pay themselves in the form of dividends rather than as a salary enables them to manage their tax liability and potentially save on National Insurance contributions.

✔ **Employee benefits:** A limited company can offer its employees an opportunity to purchase shares in the company (see Chapter 5), helping it to attract key personnel with an interest in the growth of the company. This benefit can also have positive tax implications for the company and employees. I provide more information on employees generally in Chapter 5 and on a company's responsibilities to them in Chapter 7.

✔ **Pensions:** Starting from October, 2012, companies have an obligation to establish an approved pension scheme, which provides greater benefits than ordinary self-employed pension schemes and provides tax savings for both parties. (See Chapter 5 for more details about complying with pensions law.)

✔ **Credibility:** Going through the incorporation process increases the perceived credibility of the enterprise in the marketplace. Many large companies have a policy of dealing only with limited companies.

✔ **Cost-effectiveness:** The initial cost involved in setting up a limited company isn't particularly high, because you can complete the whole process online.

✔ **Investment and funding:** If a company needs to raise capital it can do so by issuing new shares and differing types of shares. In order to attract outside investors, operation as a limited company is nearly always a mandatory requirement in order to be taken seriously. Chapter 3 covers finding funding partners and Chapter 4 delves into funding agreements.

✔ **Continuity:** A company ceases to exist only if it's formally wound up or struck off the Companies Registry at Companies House. If a shareholder or director wants to leave, retire or sell his shareholding, or he dies, procedures in the company's Articles or its Shareholder Agreement cover these events, and the company can continue regardless.

Disadvantages

The protection that you receive as a limited company doesn't come without effort: the requirement to pay attention to 900 sections and schedules of the Companies Act is enough reading to cure anyone of insomnia! In fact research shows that of the 229,961 hours that an average human spends sleeping in her lifetime, at least 10 per cent can be attributed to reading the Companies Act! Here are some of the problems:

✔ **Administrative burden:** The rules governing limited companies are more complex and restrictive in nature than those applicable to sole traders, General Partnerships or LLPs. A number of legalities are involved in creating and registering a new limited company: registration with Companies House; filing of annual accounts and returns; and arranging the payment of corporation tax, National Insurance, income tax obligations and possibly Value-Added Tax (VAT). Additionally, all limited companies must conduct an external audit of their accounts on an annual basis (unless the requirements of the small company exemption are met — see Chapter 2). All this paperwork takes up time, which is often the most precious of SME resources.

✔ **Ongoing costs:** Although limited companies are cheap to set up, the annual duty to file accounts and returns in a prescribed format means that you have to maintain proper financial records at all times. The ongoing nature of these statutory duties means that the cost of complying is significant and usually requires the appointment of an accountant or an accountancy service.

✔ **Privacy:** Information relating to the private company is on public file after it's registered, including information on the company's accounts, shares and directors. Although this transparency can be an advantage when seeking credit, the company has no control over who can access this information. If you browse the Internet you may be surprised to find numerous public databases with which you've had no contact featuring your company details.

✔ **Liability:** Companies come with limited liability, but that doesn't mean you're home free. Although courts have always been reluctant to make individuals controlling the company responsible for its actions, in exceptional circumstances the courts do 'lift the corporate veil' to get at those responsible for wrongdoing. Examples are when a company is being used primarily as a vehicle of fraud or if one company is simply acting as the agent of its (wrongdoing) parent company.

✔ **Director liability:** Statutory instances exist where members or directors of limited companies can be held personally responsible for their actions or liable for company debts. Directors can be personally liable under the Companies Act, 2006 if they breach any of their seven core responsibilities:

- To act within the powers conferred by the company's constitution

- To promote the success of the company for the benefit of its members

- To exercise independent judgement

- To exercise reasonable care and skill

- To avoid conflicts of interest

- Not to accept benefits from third parties

- To declare an interest in a proposed transaction or arrangement (which means, for example, that they must give notice of any benefit they may get from a contract the company is planning to enter into)

Directors can also be liable under the Insolvency Act, 1986 (if they're guilty of wrongful trading where they knew the company had no prospect of avoiding insolvency. They can also be guilty of fraudulent trading if they attempt to defraud creditors – this is a criminal offence).

Directors can also be liable under the Company Directors Disqualification Act, 1986 (a disqualified director who doesn't obey a disqualification order is liable for company debts incurred while so acting; this disobedience is also a criminal offence). Reasons for which directors can be disqualified include:

- Persistent breaches of the Companies Act relating to filing and accounts
- Committing fraud when the company is being wound up
- Engaging in fraudulent trading

Ignorance of the law is no excuse and so pay attention to these obligations. Realistically, you require professional help from an accountant and/or a lawyer to make sure that you don't trip up over any of these disadvantages. Limited Liability Partnerships (see the earlier section 'Collaborating with a colleague: Partnership') offer a good halfway house, because they're a bit easier to run than a limited company from a regulatory point of view. But a limited company, with the ability to create and allocate shares, offers broader opportunities to increase the number of owners and raise investment.

Researching Competing Company Names

You may have noticed (at least I hope you have!) that one or two other companies are trading out there. Selecting a name for your business that someone else is already using can land you in hot water.

Before registering or trading under a new company name, check the following registers to verify that the same name isn't already in use — they're free to access. They may look long and intimidating but are quite easy to search (and aren't nearly as long as the 158 verses of the Greek National Anthem, so think yourself lucky):

- **Companies Registry at Companies House:** `https://www.gov.uk/government/organisations/companies-house`

- **Trade Mark Registry at the Intellectual Property Office Registry:** `https://www.gov.uk/intellectual-property/trade-marks`

- **European Trade Mark Registry at European Union (EU) Registry on the Office for Harmonization in the Internal Market:** `https://oami.europa.eu/ohimportal/en/trade-marks`

You need to confirm that even *similar* names aren't in use, including any names that people can confuse easily with the one you want to use.

Your searches should also include verifying (by checking a domain name register) that the proposed name isn't in use as an Internet domain name.

Even after you've selected your name and begun trading, continuously review newly registered companies with Companies House and new applications in the UK and EU trademark registers to ensure that they aren't similar to your firm's. You can object to the Registrar of Companies House if you think that somebody else's limited company name is too like your own.

Similarly, when a trademark application is accepted in principle it's published in the *Trade Mark Journal* (https://www.ipo.gov.uk/t-tmj.htm), at which point you can *oppose* it (object) for three weeks (or three months in the case of publication of an EU Community Mark in the Community Trade Marks (CTM) bulletin: https://oami.europa.eu/ohimportal/en/where-is-the-bulletin). Your objection may not succeed, but it gives you the chance to nip potentially competing registrations in the bud.

Checking Companies House

The Companies Act, 2006 and the Company and Business Names (Miscellaneous Provisions) Regulations, 2009 set out provisions that relate to the use of business names. The provisions of this Act also apply to the following types of businesses:

- Individuals (sole traders) who trade under a name other than their own
- Partnerships that use a trading name that doesn't include the names of all the partners

A company generally can't use (either as a limited company name or a trading name) a limited company name that's already registered with Companies House. Nor may an LLP generally use a business name registered with Companies House. But if you find a name that's the same as the one you want to use, you may still be able to use a different suffix to distinguish it on the company register: for example, 'XYZ (Lawnmowers) Limited' to distinguish it from 'XYZ Limited'.

Restrictions apply on certain types of names. No company can use the following:

- Names that suggest a connection with Her Majesty's Government (such as 'Prime Minister's Rubbish Collection')
- Names that include 'sensitive' words and expressions (such as 'federation' or 'association')

- ✔ Names with words that constitute an offence (for example, a racist name)
- ✔ Offensive names (such as B*st*rd Limited, if you're under the surprising impression that would be an attractive name for your enterprise)

Even after your company has been incorporated, you can still be required to change its name in the first year if one of the following applies:

- ✔ Your name is 'too like' an existing name on the register.
- ✔ You provided misleading information at the time of registration.
- ✔ Your company's activities are misleading people into thinking that your products are actually produced by another existing company.
- ✔ Your name is too similar to a name in which someone else has *goodwill* (a reputation).

Research all these aspects before you start – you don't want to change your name after a year spent building a brand and spending money on marketing.

Looking into trademark registers

Registration of a limited company or LLP with Companies House (as I describe in the preceding section) *doesn't* automatically mean that your chosen name is definitely okay: it's only one piece of the puzzle. You can register your name with Companies House but still find that it infringes an existing trademark. The same situation can apply to sole traders' business names if they're using any name except their own personal name.

As a result, you also need to search the Trade Mark Register at the Intellectual Property Office to ensure that someone else hasn't already registered your proposed name or logo in the UK. The search doesn't cost you any money. A trademark registered under the Trade Mark Act, 1994 is protected from use in the *classes* (business sectors) in which it's registered. The owner has exclusive use of the mark and can bring an infringement action against any person who makes use of the trademark or a confusingly similar mark.

Take care when you're planning to use a business name (or logo) that's the same as or like an already registered name (or logo). If you're going to be operating in the same classes of business activity for which that trademark is registered, you can find yourself in trouble. Any infringement can prove very costly. An action brought for infringement of a trademark, even if unintentional, can result in your company being required to recall and destroy all business materials and even forfeit all profits made under that infringing business name or logo, in addition to an award of damages.

The Trade Marks Act, 1994 only applies to trademarks registered in the UK. If you have any aspirations to trade in the EU, you need to ensure that your proposed company name doesn't conflict with a same or similar trademark protected under EU law.

To do so, you need to check the EU Registry on the Office for Harmonization in the Internal Market website (what a mouthful!). This site oversees the European Trade Mark Register for marks registered in Europe: the CTM covers the whole of the EU and is valid in all 28 Member States.

For information on protecting your own intellectual property and using copyright and trademarks, move to Chapter 8. In fact, this book helps to protect your enterprise in all sorts of invaluable ways. For your software's protection, check out Chapter 9 and for looking after yourself when contracting over products or services, read Chapters 10 and 11.

Considering domain names

In order to ensure that you really are 'master of your domain', you also have to ensure that someone else doesn't already have the domain name that you want to use on the Internet.

You do so by checking a domain name registry, for example, Fasthosts (`https://www.fasthosts.co.uk/domain-names`), GoDaddy UK (`https://uk.godaddy.com/domains/domain-name-search.aspx`) or UK 123-reg (`https://www.123-reg.co.uk/domain-names`) to make sure that your domain name is free, *as well as* carrying out the checks in the two preceding sections.

If your particular suffix is taken (for example, '.com'), you may still be able to register other suffixes with that name (such as 'co.uk', '.org' or '.London').

Even if your domain name is free and clear, however, you're not out of the woods. If a business owns a trademark, it may be able to stop you using that domain name if it infringes its trademark – even if your domain name registration precedes its trademark registration.

This fact is often not very well understood: people can assume that if they have a domain name that precedes the date of someone else's trademark, they'll be okay. But no, they may very well *not* be okay. That's why, if you can, registering your business name as a trademark as well as registering the domain name is a good idea.

Chapter 2

Setting up and Running Your Business Structure: Legal Formalities

I know, I know – the terms 'legal' and 'formalities' sound off-putting. Place them together and you can feel like closing your eyes, sticking in earplugs and listening to almost anything – spoken hymns, running water, even Westlife. But – and it's a big but (and I cannot lie) – the information in this chapter is extremely important; please don't skip it.

Setting up your business structure is almost certain to be more complicated and time-consuming than you first think. Entrepreneurs usually want things done as quickly as possible, if not faster, but as my grandmother used to say 'Good and quickly seldom meet'. Sad, but true.

Perhaps I can reduce the intimidating nature of this subject a little by taking a cue from Ned Flanders of *The Simpsons* . . . here goes. In this chapter, I take a look at the 'legally-degally formaloroonies' required for each type of small business structure that I introduce in Chapter 1: sole trader, partnership (including a Limited Liability Partnership – LLP) and limited liability company. I walk you through the 'pro-diddles and con-diddles' of each type . . . diddly.

Nope, it's still boring stuff, but still absolutely essential.

Setting up for Life as a Sole Trader

Of the three types of small business structure, sole traders generally have less administrative and legal paperwork to contend with. But you still have to meet certain minimum requirements:

- **Registration:** You have to register as self-employed with Her Majesty's Revenue and Customs (HMRC) within three months of starting trading — or potentially face a fine. (I doubt Her Majesty has much to do with HMRC on a daily basis, and I'm sure she doesn't send herself a nasty letter when she's a day late with her VAT Return, but the official UK tax office still bears her name.)

- **Licensing:** You may need to obtain a licence before trading commences (for example, a licence from the local council to operate a stall at a regular street market).

- **Self-assessments:** You must pay income tax and National Insurance and conduct self-assessments each tax year. You also have to maintain records of income received to ensure that these assessments can be made properly and on time, and are supported by documentation. (As the saying goes 'Good accounting makes good friends'. I believe that accountants may have invented that saying.)

- **Business name:** If you decide to trade under a name that's different to your own personal name, you must display your own name as owner and an address, where documents can be served, on all your stationery. The Company and Business Names Regulations, 2005 lists restricted words that can't be used by any business, including sole traders. For example, you can't use the words 'limited' or 'ltd' after your business name.

- **Value-Added Tax (VAT):** You need to pay VAT if your earnings reach a particular threshold (currently £82,000). If that applies to you, you must register for VAT with HMRC and maintain business records of all transactions relevant for VAT for at least six years.

- **Business records:** No rule requires you to operate separate business accounts. But you must distinguish transactions relevant to the business from your personal spending.

For this reason, operating a separate business account is helpful.

Establishing and Managing a Partnership

If you decide to form a partnership, the road is steeper compared to being a sole trader (refer to the preceding section). I detail the legal formalities associated with setting up and operating a General Partnership and a Limited Liability Partnership in this section.

Creating and running a General Partnership

Setting up and running a General Partnership looks deceptively easy, but you need eyes in the back of your head to avoid mishaps (a bit like a scallop, which has up to 100 eyes on the fringes of its shell to protect itself from danger, and so rarely gets into trouble setting up a General Partnership).

Covering partnership basics

Here are the partnership essentials that you need to bear in mind:

- ✔ **Taxation implications:** The partnership itself *and* the partners are taxed via the annual self-assessment process and must pay income tax on any profits. Within three months of the partnership's start date, you must register it with HMRC (as must each partner).

  The partnership has to pay VAT if the partnership profits exceed a certain amount in any given year (currently £82,000). If your partnership employs people, you have to collect income tax and National Insurance contributions (NICs) for all those employees.

- ✔ **Partnership name:** Your partnership must decide under what name it wants to trade. You can trade under the names of all partners or a business name, though you can't include the words 'limited' or 'ltd'.

- ✔ **Partnership Agreement and necessary inclusions:** Make a *Partnership Agreement,* a comprehensive written agreement that all partners sign. Recording the terms of the partnership clearly from the outset helps avoid any potential for conflict at a later date. If a conflict does arise, that situation is much easier to resolve by referring back to a Partnership Agreement.

  If no such agreement is drafted and a dispute or unexpected event occurs, the provisions of the archaic Partnership Act, 1890 have to be applied – with its potentially clumsy consequences for all involved (flip to Chapter 1 for details).

Ideally, discuss difficult issues *before* the start of the partnership, when they're theoretical rather than arising in practice, and while you and all the partners are still getting along. A good setup at this stage bears fruit later on – but a bad tree doesn't yield good apples.

Even in cases involving existing relationships between people who're partners in a business (such as friends), you're much better off entering into an agreement in order to formalise the arrangement and safeguard the interests of both parties. In the absence of a clear agreement governing the partnership, disputes and arguments can end a friendship – or even a marriage.

Including key provisions in the Partnership Agreement

Here are some key elements for you to include in a Partnership Agreement:

- ✔ **Basic information:** Partners' names, the name and address of the partnership, the primary purpose of the business and accounting details, including the name of the accountants appointed to audit (inspect) the books of the partnership and prepare annual accounts.

- ✔ **Term of the partnership:** The date the partnership commences and how long you intend it to last, if the arrangement isn't permanent.

- ✔ **Investments and ownership:** You need to set out the amounts invested by each partner (called *capital*): no minimum requirement exists. The partnership members normally own the partnership in the same proportions in which they contribute capital.

The Agreement also needs to set out those assets or output that individual partners created, which fall within the partnership and so are owned by it (such as copyrights created by partners).

- ✔ **Profits and losses:** Include how profits and losses are to be shared and at what intervals. Provide for limited amounts to be taken out of the partnership (called *drawings*) by members in advance against their profit share, if that's agreed between the partners.

- ✔ **Division of responsibilities:** List a clear outline of duties and responsibilities and spell out whether the consent of all partners is needed before certain actions can be taken.

Unanimous consent is typically required for critical issues that are likely to affect all stakeholders – for example:

- • New partners joining the partnership

- • Hiring or firing of employees

- • Selling partnership assets by the partnership

- Taking on a substantial debt by the partnership
- Changing the Partnership Agreement
- Liquidating the partnership

Other issues can be decided by a majority decision. Also include the amount of time each partner is expected to put into the business, and whether or not he must work exclusively for the partnership and/or can't compete with the partnership business.

✔ **Dispute resolution:** Lay out how potential disputes are to be dealt with; for example, you can stipulate that mediation or arbitration must be used for all disputes to avoid having to sort them out in court. If you think this advice is overkill and that such arguments will never happen with your partners, remember the words of Danish physicist, Niels Bohr: 'Prediction is very difficult, especially about the future'.

✔ **Incapacity, death or leaving:** Describe what happens if a partner becomes ill or dies. Requiring all partners to take out life assurance is a good precaution. Cover what happens if a partner wants to leave the partnership (the official term is *retire*). You can specify that the person has to give a minimum notice period and (to create orderly exits rather than stampedes that might alarm customers) that no partner can retire within 'x' months of another partner retiring.

A leaving partner is paid out her share of the partnership assets at the point of departure (calculated based on the partnership accounts as of the year that she left). Customarily, a gap exists between the date of the calculation and the date of the payout (partly for cash-flow reasons and partly because the prospect of receiving a payout has a remarkable way of curtailing plans that the exiting partner may otherwise have implemented to compete with the partnership).

Also, set out the arrangements for introducing new partners and make clear that any new partner must sign up to (in the jargon, *adhere to*) the Partnership Agreement.

✔ **Insolvency:** Include a mechanism for how the partnership is to be liquidated if it becomes insolvent, including the division of partnership assets and payments to partners.

Forming and operating a Limited Liability Partnership (LLP)

In Chapter 1, you see that an LLP partnership differs from a General Partnership in that it's a distinct legal entity and limits the liability of members to the sum they invested. The hybrid nature of an LLP (part partnership/part company) means that – in addition to the items in the preceding section – certain sections of the Companies Act, 2006 also apply, making setting up and running an LLP a bit more complicated:

- ✔ **Registration:** An LLP must be registered at Companies House and include the following details: name, country of situation of the registered office, address of the registered office, and names and addresses of all members. The LLP issues a *certificate of incorporation,* as a formal record of the creation of the LLP.

  You must notify any change to the LLP's membership, names or addresses to Companies House.

- ✔ **Name:** An LLP can trade under the names of all the members, some of the members or a business name, though the name must end with 'Limited Liability Partnership' or 'LLP'. You must display the name on the office or place of business and on all business stationery.

- ✔ **Members:** An LLP needs at least two *designated* members, whose identity you have to notify to Companies House (these members can be *legal persons,* such as limited companies, as well as individuals). The designated partners have certain administrative responsibilities, as I detail under the 'Administrative duties' point later in this list.

  If a member of an LLP is a company that's wound up *(terminated),* or an individual made bankrupt or subject to a disqualification order as a director, he's prohibited from participating in the management of an LLP.

- ✔ **LLP Agreement:** An LLP Agreement isn't compulsory, but the Limited Liability Partnerships Act provides for a default Agreement that governs members' rights and duties if no specific LLP Agreement exists. The terms I refer to in the earlier section 'Including key provisions in the Partnership Agreement' are *all* equally applicable and should be expressly set out in an LLP Agreement. Creating an LLP Agreement gives you more clarity and protection than the default template of the LLP Act.

- ✔ **Administrative duties:** You must prepare and file annual accounts with Companies House and submit an annual return. You also have to conduct an external audit of accounts if your turnover reaches a threshold (above the current minimum of £5.6 million). Designated partners assume these administrative duties and are responsible for ensuring that the LLP complies with the legal and statutory obligations. They also have specified duties if the LLP becomes insolvent.

- ✔ **Taxation:** Under the Income Tax (Trading and other Income) Act, 2005, an LLP is treated in the same way as a General Partnership for tax purposes (see the earlier 'Creating and running a General Partnership' section). Members must register as self-employed and conduct self-assessments in order to pay income tax and NICs. If one of the members of the LLP is a limited company (rather than an individual person), however, corporation tax is payable by that company and also payable when the LLP is being wound up.

VAT also has to be paid if annual profits exceed a certain limit (currently £82,000) and an LLP must voluntarily register if this limit is reached. If the LLP has employees, it's responsible for operating a payroll and collecting income tax and NICs from employees, just like a General Partnership.

In addition to these requirements, the Finance Act, 2014 introduced significant changes to the taxation regime to add further complexity. Hurrah! A partnership member can now be taxed as an employee (which can involve paying higher rates of tax and paying tax earlier than under self-assessment) unless you meet one of three criteria.

To avoid being treated as an employee you must show the following:

- ✔ Your profit share is dependent upon the profitability of the whole business.

- ✔ You've had an influence on the decisions of the LLP.

- ✔ You've contributed capital equal to 25 per cent of your drawings from the partnership.

Considering a partnership conversion

The Limited Liability Partnerships Act, 2000 contains no statutory procedure for converting an existing 'old style' General Partnership into an LLP or for the conversion of an LLP to a limited company. However, if the needs of the business change, and this alteration is beneficial for taxation or operational reasons, completing the conversion process is relatively straightforward.

When converting a General Partnership to an LLP, the LLP has to be registered and a date set to transfer assets. Stamp duty (a tax on transfers of assets such as shares) isn't chargeable on this type of transfer, as long as the members of the LLP are the same as the original partners and they hold the assets in the same proportions.

In changing from an LLP to a limited company, you have to create a new limited company under the same name and then you can transfer assets from the old LLP to the new company. This change results in tax consequences in respect of the transfer of the business (perhaps capital gains tax is due on the gain that's taken place on the value of the assets transferred from the LLP to the new company). Also, tax consequences may arise in relation to taxing the new business in the future (the new company will be subject to corporation tax, as opposed to its individual partners being liable for self-assessment income tax).

Forming and Running a Limited Company

Make a fresh brew and grab a plate of custard creams, hobnobs and Bourbons. You need to build up your strength, because in this section you tackle the legal formalities of the toughest business structure: a limited company.

If you find yourself fidgeting like a cat on a hot roof while reading, stop and go for a bracing walk (or whatever cats do to chill out – swish your tail, stare out the window or lick your lips while watching a goldfish).

You need to take into account three major components when looking at the formalities governing companies: the Companies Act, the Articles of Association and the Shareholder Agreement.

But don't worry; take my hand (sorry about the chocolate – I took my own advice and chose a Bourbon) as I walk you gently through each one.

Grappling with the Companies Act

The Companies Act, 2006 specifies numerous responsibilities that you must carry out when setting up and operating a limited liability company. The regulatory body responsible for the registration and registry of all limited companies is Companies House. Also, don't forget that specific tax obligations apply to limited companies.

You *must* adhere to the various provisions of the Companies Acts as regards notifications and reporting. Companies can be fined for non-compliance, and not circulating notice of a resolution is a criminal offence. At the very least, when investors come to decide whether to put money into your company or buy you out entirely, they take a dim view if your compliance records are chaotic and have to be fixed retrospectively – it can reduce their valuation of your business.

You need to get to grips with it yourself or find someone, such as an accountant or lawyer, to do it for you.

Companies Act requirements

Here, then, are your Companies Act, 2006 responsibilities when setting up a limited company:

- ✔ **Name:** You must supply the company's business name to Companies House when registering (it must end in 'limited' or 'Ltd'). You must display the name at the company's registered office and disclose it on all business correspondence, documentation and websites.

- ✔ **Registration:** Every business setting up as a limited company must register with Companies House by submitting the relevant documents. Form IN01 contains the key details about your company, including registered office address, type of business being undertaken and details on directors and shareholders.

  A statement on share structure (sometimes called *share capital*) must accompany form IN01. You have to state the total shares taken by shareholders (called *subscribers*), including number of shares, type of shares, total nominal or face value of those shares and the amount paid for those shares *(paid up)* or to be paid *(unpaid)*.

- ✔ **Appointment and removal of directors:** You must have at least one director above the age of 16 for your company. Directors can't be undischarged bankrupts or otherwise disqualified from being a director. Each director must consent to act as a director and you must also provide that consent to Companies House.

  You have to supply the following details for each company director:

  - Full name and title, including former names
  - Date of birth
  - Country of residence
  - Nationality
  - Occupation (if any)
  - Usual residential address

  Directors can supply a different address for service of formal documents (if one exists), which can be the address that appears on the record for that director.

  The Act doesn't require you to appoint a company secretary, but if you do so that person must also consent to act in this role and must provide the details required in Companies House Form AP03.

- ✔ **Registers:** You must maintain statutory registers and keep them available for inspection, including:

  - A register of *members* (shareholders)
  - A register of directors and secretaries
  - A register of directors' residential addresses
  - Copies of all directors' service contracts

- Contracts relating to the purchase of shares

- Registers of charges (for example, any charges that lenders may hold over company assets, which they can activate to protect themselves if a company loan isn't repaid — sometimes called *debentures;* race to Chapter 4 for more about charges)

✔ **Records of resolutions and shareholder meetings:** Generally, companies can pass either *Ordinary Resolutions* (requiring those with more than 50 per cent of the votes to pass them) or *Special Resolutions* (requiring those with 75 per cent or more of the votes to pass them). Special Resolutions are only required for 'special events', such as changing the Articles or the company's name, or dis-applying pre-emption rights (see this chapter's 'Enjoying pre-emption rights' sidebar).

Shareholders must be given notice of proposed resolutions (often 14 clear days). Normally directors give notice of any resolutions, but shareholders owning at least 5 per cent of the shares can require the company to give notice of a resolution from them. If the required majority for any resolution isn't secured within 28 days of the resolution notice, the resolution can't be passed (it *lapses*).

You must keep minutes of every meeting and retain them for ten years.

✔ **Audits:** Limited liability companies are required to audit the annual accounts, unless they qualify as a small company and meet two of three mandatory criteria: annual turnover must not be above £6.50 million; annual balance sheet assets not more than £3.26 million; and number of employees not more than 50. A small company that meets two of these three tests need not file its 'full' accounts; it's only obligated to file its balance sheet (which is much simpler and summarises its assets, liabilities and capital at a particular date).

Larger limited companies must provide a profit and loss account, a balance sheet, and accompany these accounts with a directors' report.

✔ **Directors' duties:** In addition to those duties imposed on company directors by the Companies Act, 2006 (which I describe in Chapter 1), directors also have other specific duties covering the company's accounts and administration matters. If you're a director, you have to make sure that the company submits annual accounts, an annual return (form AR01) and annual corporation tax returns (CT600). You must also ensure that the company promptly notifies Companies House of the following:

- Any changes to the details of directors or the company secretary already lodged at Companies House

- Any changes to the company's registered address

- Any allocation (sometimes called *allotment*) of shares

- Any changes to the company's share capital

✔ **Special Resolutions:** Penalties can be imposed for the late delivery of accounts and returns. Foul! Whether or not a company secretary is appointed, as a director you're still ultimately responsible for ensuring that the company fulfils these administrative duties.

✔ **Taxation:** All limited companies are subject to corporation tax on annual profits. They must inform HMRC when the incorporation process has been completed and complete an annual corporation tax return. The rates of corporation tax have now been aligned to a single rate of 20 per cent and so you can't claim relief. You need to keep your business records for at least six years for tax purposes.

✔ **Tax:** You must make income tax and National Insurance deductions from employees' pay and in respect of your employees. You also have to pay employer NICs for each employee. Directors are liable for income tax, but may not need to pay NICs if income is taken in the form of dividends from the company and not as a salary. Like an LLP, a limited company is also liable for VAT if the annual turnover of the company is above a certain threshold (currently £82,000); you must register it with HMRC if this limit is reached.

Recent changes

The Small Business, Enterprise and Employment Act, 2015 introduces a number of changes that affect the law applying to limited company formalities. These new rules are due to come into force in 2016. At the risk of exhausting you with more formalities when you're already losing the will to live, here are some of the 'highlights' (if I can call them that):

✔ **Confirmation statements:** The annual return is to be replaced with an annual check and *confirmation statement.* The rationale behind this change is to make it easier to align the timing of the company's confirmation statement with its annual accounts date.

✔ **Directors' dates of birth:** The day of birth can be protected from public disclosure (to prevent identity theft or fraud).

✔ **Statutory registers:** You can elect Companies House to maintain your company registers. If you do, you can't use the provision of omitting the directors' dates of birth from being made publicly available. If you're a director, you have to decide whether you value slightly greater privacy or a lesser administrative burden!

✔ **Register of People with Significant Control:** The Act requires companies to keep a register of people with 'significant control' over the company (known as the PSC register). *Significant control* is defined as follows:

- A person holding 25 per cent of the shares or voting rights or a right to share in more than 25 per cent of the company's capital or profits

- An individual with the right to exercise, or who in practice exercises, significant influence or control over the company

Details listed on the PSC register for each significant person are to include name, service address, residential address, country of residence, nationality, date of birth and any restrictions limiting disclosure of such information. All companies are to produce such a register and to take reasonable steps to collect this information.

Don't worry if you're not a significant person for the purpose of the PSC. It doesn't mean that you've failed in life!

Creating Articles of Association

You have to register Articles of Association (Articles, for short) with Companies House, which set out how your limited company is to be run and rights between shareholders. Articles are like the instructions leaflet that comes with a new gadget and shows you how to make it work – and they're just about as interesting.

What Model Articles cover

The Companies Act, 2006 introduced a standard form of Articles called *Model Articles*. These have nothing to do with beautiful people strutting around on catwalks. They're called Model Articles because they apply by default to all companies incorporated on or after 1 October 2009, unless those companies register Articles of their own with Companies House. (Companies registered before 1 October 2009 may have an older version of the Model Articles called 'Table A'.)

Model Articles typically cover subjects such as the following:

✔ **Shares:** The Articles cover directors' powers to issue shares (or any restrictions on those rights where no authority is required, because the company has only one type, or 'class', of shares). The Articles also deal with different rights and restrictions attached to different types of shares. Normally, allotments of shares (allocations to shareholders) are supported by the passing of an Ordinary Resolution. The Articles include the obligation to provide a share certificate to each shareholder.

✔ **Board meetings and voting:** The Articles give directors wide-ranging powers to run the company day-to-day, stating that 'the Directors are responsible for the management of the company's business, for which purpose they may exercise all the powers of the company'. These powers include the following:

- Setting a minimum number of attendees (or *quorum*) for their own Board meetings

- Calling for Board meetings on reasonable notice

- Managing conflicts of interest in relation to voting on issues

- Making decisions at Board meetings (on a one person/one vote basis)

- Refusing to register a share transfer

The Articles contain similar provisions to cover the process for calling and running wider General Meetings of all shareholders, though nowadays private companies don't need to hold General Meetings (or indeed any company meetings) unless they want to change their auditors or remove a director (for which 28 days' notice to shareholders is required).

✔ **Dividends:** The power for the directors to recommend annual or interim *dividends* to shareholders (effectively, their proportionate share of distributed profits made by the company). The directors can also vote to *capitalise dividends* (turn them into extra shares instead of paying cash out).

✔ **Appointment, termination and rewarding of directors:** For example, the Articles spell out situations when a director automatically ceases to be one (such as if the person resigns, becomes incapacitated or is declared bankrupt). Normally, the Articles make provision for the Board of Directors to fill any casual vacancies or to appoint additional directors up to any maximum number, as may be specified in the Articles. The Articles may also permit the company to purchase and maintain insurance for the benefit of the directors, and allow directors to introduce director payments and reimbursement for their expenses.

If a Shareholder Agreement is in place (see the later section, 'Requiring and drafting Shareholder Agreements'), it can include extra provisions on the removal of directors, in addition to what's outlined in the Articles.

✔ **Changing the Articles:** Normally only allowable by passing a Special Resolution. Both the Special Resolution and the new Articles must be sent to Companies House within 15 days of being passed.

Adherence to the Articles is mandatory. If the Articles aren't followed, under Section 994 of the Companies Act a shareholder can apply for a Court Order on the basis that the company is acting in an unfairly prejudicial way to some or all its members. This approach is becoming a popular remedy for disgruntled shareholders . . . you've been warned.

What Model Articles don't cover

Model Articles aren't the perfect model, however, because they miss out some things. For instance, they don't deal with the following two rights:

✔ **Drag-along rights:** Designed to facilitate a sale by requiring all shareholders to sell their shares to a potential purchaser if a certain percentage of them (say, a majority) vote to sell to that purchaser. If this aspect isn't dealt with separately, under the Companies Act only shareholders with 10 per cent or less of the company can automatically be 'dragged along' in a sale.

✔ **Tag-along rights:** Protect smaller shareholders by giving minority shareholders the right to 'tag-along' with a sale of shares by the majority of other shareholders and insist that their shares are bought at the same time for the same price.

Model Articles also don't deal with the company communicating with its shareholders electronically. Making this addition is very useful, because it dispenses with the need to distribute company communications by post – which is inefficient and very costly, especially when you have a lot of shareholders. Dealing with notices to shareholders using a website notice and offering voting by email is preferable.

Enjoying pre-emption rights

Model Articles don't cover *pre-emption*. This provision means that if the company wants to issue new shares to a third party, those shares must be offered to the remaining shareholders first in proportion to their existing shareholding in the company. If, for example, a company wants to raise additional investment in return for new shares in the company, it must give the existing shareholders the right to purchase such shares first.

As a result, the existing shareholders have the opportunity to maintain the percentage level of their shareholding by buying their due proportion of the new shares, instead of it being diluted by the introduction of new shareholders owning the additional shares. The shares must be offered for a certain period and on the basis of the price set by the directors (the price per share at which the directors want to raise the new investment).

The same right of pre-emption also applies if an existing shareholder wants to sell her shares to a third party (or transfer those shares, for example, to a spouse or a company owned and controlled by the transferring shareholder or on the shareholder's death). Those shares must also be offered to the existing shareholders in proportion to their existing shareholdings.

The price is determined by the valuation mechanism set out in the Articles. For example, the price may be the one at which the selling shareholder proposes to sell her shares to a third party or (if no such price exists) a price set by an agreed mechanism for valuation (perhaps market value as determined by an auditor or maybe a pre-agreed fixed price).

If the existing shareholders don't want to buy all the available shares (in the case of a new issue), the shares can be offered to new shareholders at the same price as they were offered to existing shareholders. In the case of a proposed transfer, if the existing shareholders don't take up all the available shares, they can be offered by the selling shareholder to a third party at the same sale price at which they were offered to the existing shareholders.

Specific provisions in the Articles on pre-emption also provide a more flexible regime for pre-emption than applies under the default provisions on pre-emption for 'ordinary shares' set out in the Companies Act. If pre-emption provisions are drafted for the Articles and later it becomes expedient to dispense with them, pre-emption provisions can be waived or *dis-applied* by changing the Articles or voting through a Special Resolution to this effect.

Owing to such omissions, a separate set of Articles is usually drafted to meet the needs of the particular company and deal with these extra issues. Form IN01 allows companies to indicate whether they're adopting Model Articles in their entirety or with amendments, or whether they're adopting entirely bespoke Articles. Any such amendment or new Articles must accompany the company's application for registration.

Requiring and drafting Shareholder Agreements

If the preceding sections aren't cool enough for cats like you, and you're exhibiting signs of feline distress such as clawing at the sofa and bringing dead mice into the house, calm down. You now have the unrestrained joy of learning about Shareholder Agreements. Some people have a bit of a phobia about Shareholder Agreements, but don't worry, you won't feel a thing.

Shareholder Agreements are ones between shareholders that regulate relations and issues of control of the company between them. They're often entered into by larger shareholders (because they're the ones to whom issues of control are likely to be most meaningful). Some Shareholder Agreements, however, cover all shareholders, including smaller ones, with new shareholders being required to sign up to the Shareholder Agreement (enter into a *deed of adherence*) as a condition of their involvement in the company.

Unless all shareholders have to sign a deed of adherence, the risk exists that in putting rights and obligations in Shareholder Agreements you're only covering those shareholders who are signatories to that agreement – if smaller shareholders are excluded, they aren't covered. This is different from the Articles, which automatically cover all shareholders. On the other hand, if you *do* include all shareholders in the Shareholder Agreement you may be granting rights or imposing obligations on smaller shareholders that really only concern larger shareholders.

To make sure that the Shareholder Agreement and the Articles of Association are reconciled, include a clause stating that as between the signatories to the Shareholder Agreement if a conflict exists between the Articles and the Shareholder Agreement, the terms of the Shareholder Agreement prevail. This clause can require the shareholders to amend the Articles if such a conflict arises, to make sure that the Shareholders Agreement's terms govern, so that the two documents don't conflict.

That said, many companies have a separate Shareholder Agreement among all shareholders – and for good reasons:

✔ **Privacy:** Shareholder Agreements remain private, as opposed to the Articles, which can be viewed publicly after registration. (But if the Shareholder Agreement is mentioned in the Articles then the Shareholder Agreement *does* have to be filed at Companies House – so don't mention it in the Articles!)

✔ **Voting:** Any change to the Articles must be agreed to by a Special Resolution (requiring the votes of those holding 75 per cent of the voting rights). But you can alter a Shareholder Agreement simply by gaining the agreement of the signatories to it – it doesn't require a resolution to be passed.

Typically, you include these common features in your Shareholder Agreement:

✔ **Dividend policy:** Many Shareholder Agreements contain specific terms that must be complied with in relation to dividends and the way they're paid out. Provision can also be made for when a company doesn't have to pay a dividend.

✔ **Voting:** A Shareholder Agreement can specify in advance the way in which certain matters are to be voted on by the shareholders who are parties to the shareholder agreement. This provision can help to provide a more predictable structure for reaching decisions than in the Articles.

✔ **Confidentiality:** Shareholder Agreements tend to include a duty on all members to maintain confidentiality relating to company documents and sensitive information.

✔ **Business of the company:** Limited companies can generally undertake any commercial business that the directors believe is in the best interests of the company. A Shareholder Agreement can set out, however, the nature and extent of the company's business so that it can't be radically altered without the consent of the shareholders who are parties to the Shareholder Agreement.

✔ **Provisions regarding directors:** Shareholder Agreements may supplement the Articles by containing specific terms that the participating shareholders are to apply to the directors of the company. These terms don't bind the directors themselves (unless they're also shareholders), but bind the shareholders to making sure that the directors operate in a certain way or that decisions about directors are made in a certain way. Such terms can include provisions relating to:

  • Removal of directors

  • Payments to directors (sometimes called *remuneration*)

  • Role of directors

  • Limits on an individual director's authority

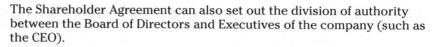

The Shareholder Agreement can also set out the division of authority between the Board of Directors and Executives of the company (such as the CEO).

✔ **Decision-making:** The management of the day-to-day business of the company is usually conducted by the directors under the Articles. A Shareholder Agreement can specify, however, that certain decisions can't be taken without a higher level of shareholder support before being approved. This restriction is often applied to decisions that may have a significant impact on the business. Alternatively, such controls may be a requirement of an investor to give special protection for her rights (for example, a minority shareholder may want to ensure that her consent is required for certain decisions).

Restrictions that favour shareholders may include, for example, a right of approval over the following such issues:

- Raising more investment *(capital)* that dilutes the existing shareholders

- Taking on loans

- Changing the nature of the business

- Issuing new shares

- Varying rights attaching to shares

- Selling the company

- Winding up the company

✔ **Information rights:** Shareholders have limited rights to information under the Companies Act, 2006 (they're only entitled to view annual accounts). Greater access to information can be set out in the Shareholder Agreement, allowing shareholders to monitor their investment on a more frequent basis.

✔ **Non-competing:** You can include non-compete terms. Called *restrictive covenants,* they're designed to prevent shareholders from competing with the company, and include 'non-solicit' terms to prevent shareholders poaching key staff or encouraging them to leave. These terms may apply during and for a limited period after when the shareholder owns shares in the company.

Restrictive covenants need to be limited in terms of geography, scope and duration. Restrictive covenants concerning shareholders are more generally enforceable compared to those relating to an employer – employee relationship, as long as you don't formulate the scope and duration too widely. See Chapter 5 for more details on restrictive covenants and how to make them enforceable.

- ✔ **Dispute resolution:** The Shareholder Agreement can provide for a variety of different options to deal with disputes between shareholders and deadlock situations, which can paralyse the company if not dealt with effectively. For example, a dispute resolution policy can stipulate that the parties must enter into arbitration or mediation.

I receive many enquiries from exasperated shareholders who've fallen out with their co-shareholder or co-founder and don't have a Shareholder Agreement. If they don't own more than 50 per cent of the shares and can't force through decisions, they're rather stuck.

In addition to the preceding items, the following provisions can make an appearance in a Shareholder Agreement as long as it applies to all shareholders (and a deed of adherence ensures this). If the Shareholder Agreement only applies to some shareholders, these provisions are better off in the Articles, which automatically apply to all shareholders:

- ✔ **Transfer of shares:** The Model Articles (refer to the preceding section) may only be suitable for smaller companies and not ones with complex ownership structures that want more stringent rules regarding the transfer of shares than Articles provide. Such details can be catered for in a separate Shareholder Agreement. For example, a Shareholder Agreement can include specific provisions regarding the issuing and transferring of shares and may be written to deal with different transfer scenarios, such as:

  - Bankruptcy of a shareholder or breach of the Shareholder Agreement by a shareholder (in which case transfer by that shareholder to the other shareholders is compulsory).

  - Certain permitted transfers for which pre-emption isn't required (for example, to a spouse or a personal representative of a shareholder who dies).

  - *Lock-down provisions,* which mean that shareholders aren't allowed to sell their shares for a particular period of time, so that the company knows it has a stable group of shareholders for that period.

  - The company granting a *security interest* over shares – for example, an interest in those shares in favour of a lender to secure a loan that the company receives (move to Chapter 4 to read more about security interests).

  - Provisions relating to the granting of shares to employees under an Enterprise Management Incentive scheme (whizz to Chapter 5 to understand how these schemes work).

- ✔ **Pre-emption provisions:** The Shareholder Agreement can provide more detail on pre-emption rights than the Articles, or give shareholders the right to dis-apply pre-emption provisions if they choose (see this chapter's sidebar 'Enjoying pre-emption rights').

- **Drag-along and tag-along rights:** These rights can be included in the Shareholder Agreement rather than in new Articles as long as it's a requirement that all shareholders (including new ones) have to sign the Shareholder Agreement (check out the 'What Model Articles don't cover' section, earlier in this chapter).

- **Good Leaver/Bad Leaver provisions:** The company wants to incentivise its key shareholder employees to stay (as do investors, who have a vested interest in the key players staying part of the team, including the founders). As a result, people include in a Shareholder Agreement provisions that encourage this result.

Good Leavers in a Shareholder Agreement include an employee and shareholder of a company who:

- Dies

- Becomes incapacitated through illness

- Is made redundant

- Voluntarily leaves, but only after a pre-agreed period of time

Any other leaving event is a Bad-Leaver event (boo, hiss), which includes cases where the shareholder employee:

- Leaves voluntarily before the end of the pre-agreed period of time

- Is dismissed for gross misconduct

- Is dismissed in other circumstances, as long as it's not a constructive or unfair dismissal

When a shareholder employee leaves, the person may be required to sell some or all her shares by these provisions, and you won't be surprised to hear that the Shareholder Agreement normally says that a Good Leaver gets a better price than a Bad Leaver. For a Good Leaver, the price may be the full market value of her shares – the top cats that get the cream. For a Bad Leaver, the price can be heavily discounted from the market price, so that the person ends up with only a fraction of her shares' market value – miaow!

If you managed to get through this whole chapter without a break, congrats: like any self-respecting cat you've earned yourself a long lie down, preferably on someone's lap.

Chapter 3

Choosing Your Funding Partner

- -

In This Chapter

▶ Considering your early-stage funding

▶ Sorting through the funding source options

- -

As ABBA put it decades ago (though sparkly pantsuits never really go out of fashion, do they. Oh, they do? Shame): 'Money, money, money'. The reality is that you need funding to get most businesses off the ground – and running them can be pretty darned expensive too. Whether you're thinking of starting out or looking for ways to grow your operation, you always have to consider the amount of money that you need to put in before dreaming about the money you can take out.

Here I lead you into the sometimes confusing world of business funding. It can be an arduous and frustrating process, but your enthusiasm for your great business idea can see you through. Plus you have something else on your side: this chapter's invaluable guide on funding considerations and sources.

Deciding What Level of Early Funding You Need

Although every business needs to look after its pennies, the ones that can survive for long without any external funding are relatively few in number. At the early stage you may need money for research and development (R&D), hiring your first employees, testing your early-stage product with customers *(beta-testing)* and initial marketing.

This initial finance (often called *seed funding*) doesn't normally exceed £500,000. But to raise it you definitely need a professional-looking *business plan,* which consists of a written narrative and a set of figures.

Your *narrative* covers the background to the enterprise:

- What's your big business idea?

- What problem does that idea solve?

- What product or service are you offering?

- What pricing is the product or service going to have?

- What's the *route to market* (for example, through physical retail sales, physical distribution, website sales or mobile distribution)?

- Is the product or service *protectable* (for example, do you have some intellectual property in the product or service that means that others can't copy it)?

- Who are the team behind the venture and what credentials do they have?

- What are the risks associated with the venture and how do you propose to manage them?

- What are the envisaged *exit options* for the enterprise (in other words how will you and your investors be able to sell the business for lorry loads of cash)?

- How much money do you require from investors and how is it being spent?

You need to back up your narrative with three years' worth of projected costs and revenues. Don't worry that many of the numbers in the plan are speculative – investors know that, but they take confidence from the fact that an entrepreneur has considered the costs and revenues as thoroughly and as realistically as possible.

Potential investors will be concerned, however, if the revenues are ludicrously optimistic and/or the costs look way too low. They know that achieving financial success normally takes longer and costs more money than an entrepreneur thinks or predicts.

You also need an effective *pitch* – a slideshow and/or presentation you can mail to investors or present in person, which brings your business to life for them and gets them excited about your opportunity.

Very often a business has little or no revenues at this stage, which limits the available financing options. At the start-up stage you normally just have future projections to work with. (I cover institutional funding – with private equity investors or venture capitalists who generally require a track record of performance and revenues before they invest – in Chapter 17, because it's more relevant after the business matures.)

If you require more information on writing your business plan or developing your pitch, as well as different sources of funding, you may like to check out *Business Plans For Dummies,* UK Edition by Paul Tiffany, Steven D Peterson and Colin Barrow (Wiley).

Selecting Your Choice of Finance

Plenty of funding options are available for early-stage businesses. You can get source funding from your nearest and dearest or from complete strangers and official organisations, such as the government and other public bodies. In this section, I look at some of the options, and evaluate their pros and cons with an eye on the legal consequences of choosing one route over another.

The best option for you depends on your personal financial situation, your business idea and, often, simply what you're able to obtain.

Working with friends and family

Raising finance through your nearest and dearest can obviously be an attractive option:

- ✔ **Keeping things simple:** Approaching a friend or family member is a relatively straightforward affair. You request financial assistance while providing assurances of repayment or comfortable returns on investment – all without subjecting yourself to the scrutiny of promoting your business to professional third-party investors.

- ✔ **Being involved with people you know:** If you choose to issue shares in your business in return for money (called *equity financing*), you may feel more at home selling those shares to a family member rather than a relatively unknown third party, and so keep the business 'in the family'.

- ✔ **Dealing with people you trust:** If funding is provided by borrowing money as a loan (called *debt financing*), a friend or family member can also appear to be a much more attractive choice of provider than a third party. Someone who knows and cares about you may be more relaxed about enforcing interest, repayment and penalty terms.

'Business is business', however, and so you need to bear these key points in mind about friends and family money:

- ✔ Never lose sight of the competing commercial interests of the future stakeholders in the business. Appreciate that the expectations of commercial success may be as elevated in the minds of friends and family as they are for the bank lender or the professional investor.

- ✔ Issuing shares to another person, whether friend or stranger, means parting with a share of your business, which means parting with a share of its control. If your objectives aren't aligned with those of an overzealous friend or family member, your plans for growth and development can be seriously hampered, particularly if the whole group of shareholders is small. The result can be frustration and discord on both a professional and non-professional level.

- ✔ Other feelings of angst can arise when borrowing money from a friend or family member. What happens if the loan can't be repaid? What does that do to your relationship? Friends or relatives can also surprise you by revealing a very different side of themselves when their commercial interests are at stake; if things aren't going to plan, you may find that it's more than the business that's in trouble.

- ✔ A personal relationship can affect your decision-making process adversely. Any desire to deliver a quick return on investment or to repay the debt of a relative or friend can cloud your business judgement, leading to rash decision-making. You may sacrifice a well thought-out medium- to long-term strategy in favour of turning a quick profit – which may or may not materialise.

Securing funding from grant agencies

Funding agencies award grants to start or develop new businesses.

A *grant* is an amount of money given (or *awarded*) for a specific purpose or project. Grants are mostly associated with governments or specific public bodies, but they're also awarded by non-public bodies – usually charitable organisations – and sometimes profit-making organisations.

The advantage of using a grant rather than taking a loan to fund part of a business is that the grant isn't normally repayable. Also, your business doesn't have to give away any shares in return for the investment.

Funding for innovation

Innovate UK (`www.gov.uk/government/ organisations/innovate-uk`) is a public body that regularly provides funding for initiatives in the field of innovation. Grants are awarded for a wide range of projects, including research and development in science, engineering or technology with the purpose of creating new products or services.

Amounts offered commonly range from £100,000 to £2 million, but greater and lesser grants are also available. You can also apply for any number of EU grants in technology and innovation – but expect the application process to be long and complicated.

The government is the obvious place to begin a search for a suitable grant. At the time of writing the government has 272 available grant schemes listed on its website: `https://www.gov.uk/business-finance-support-finder`. Many of these schemes are limited by geographic location, amount, size of company or industry sector. Under each listed scheme, details of the public body offering the grant, evaluation criteria and additional information is provided to enable you to verify eligibility and to connect to the website of the relevant body offering the grant.

Hundreds of options sounds great, but they represent a confusing maze of possibility. They can suck time from your business as you plough through the options and try to work out whether you're eligible: 'too much treacle and not enough custard' as my Uncle the Chef used to say.

For private grants, the Prince's Trust (focusing on young people) and the Wellcome Trust (focusing on health/science) are examples of well-known charitable organisations offering grants for business.

When considering government grants, bear in mind that your business is often required to add its own financing to the particular project eligible for the grant: called *matched funding*. This requirement is to make sure that you don't just rely on handouts, plus it provides reassurance for the lending agency – if your business can source an equal level of funding from another partner or the private sector, it's a less risky candidate for the grant of public money. Read the conditions of the grant carefully and ensure that where matched funding is needed, you have resources in place, or another source of funding available, to satisfy any financial requirements attached to the grant.

Flying without wings: Financing from angels

If you're seeking expert help as well as a cash investment in your business, you may want to look into funding from an angel investor.

An *angel* is an individual who provides finance to start-ups and (often) plays some further role in the development of the business. Usually an angel has some prior successful track record in business, which has generated funds that the angel can afford to invest.

Balancing angel pros and cons

Securing the backing of an angel investor can provide you with the following:

- **Experience:** You benefit from the experience and knowledge of someone who, essentially, invests in businesses for a living. These individuals specialise in helping start-ups and, having 'been there' before, can be an invaluable asset in getting your business up and running or helping it progress smoothly through the start-up phase.

- **Network:** Usually these experienced entrepreneurs have a network to bring to bear on your business, introducing you to other sources of finance, and contacts in marketing, sales, IT or accounting.

- **Longevity:** Provided that the business is moving in the right direction, angels may be in no hurry to withdraw their assistance, because their ultimate aim is to produce a fully functional and profitable business.

    When this situation happens, the business can attract the eye of further investors, which allows the angel investor to realise a substantial return on his investment from the eventual sale of his share of the business (otherwise known as an *exit*). To take a business to this point isn't a short-term venture, and so you can expect an angel investor to be involved in your business for around three to five years, depending on your rate of success.

The extent to which an angel investor seeks operational involvement in your business varies, which raises the crucial issue of how willing you are to bring in a third party and cede a level of control to him. Therefore, you need to understand the angel's expectations with regard to participation – and the angel needs to understand your way of working so that you can build a successful relationship.

I describe the terms of the funding arrangement to be put in place between you and the angel in Chapter 4.

Terms can only set a framework for the relationship. A crucial process that sits outside the contract is therefore getting to know the angel and discovering how the person views his role in the business, and deciding whether you feel that you can collaborate in a productive way.

Dealing with angels

When evaluating an angel investor, you also have to think about how much ownership of the business you're prepared to relinquish. Angels aren't necessarily that angelic as regards valuation. They often want to drive a hard bargain, knowing that you're reliant on their money to get going. You have to work out the maximum percentage of your shareholding that you're prepared to give away and the lowest offer that you're prepared to accept for those shares. If you don't have this clear in your mind when going into the negotiation phase, you may end up giving away more than you bargained for – which can be an unhappy start to this new business relationship that you may end up resenting later.

You also require patience when embarking on the process of finding money from angels and then agreeing terms with them (or indeed anybody else). The UK Business Angels Association suggests that two months is a fair estimate of the time required between agreeing to investment from an angel in principle and formally concluding the investment agreement; but the process can take up to four months.

Partly this delay is just because it can take angels a long time to make up their minds. Often the pitching process is quite arduous, with an initial presentation followed by a long series of questions and requests for further data. Some cynics, however, feel that occasionally angels delay deliberately, because they know that the longer they make you wait for a decision, the more you're spending your own money and the more desperately you're going to need their cash.

My experience is that in reality this process can take longer – say, six months from beginning to end. You have to be able to fund the period while raising money, and so you need to start early (so that you have enough existing reserves to fund the funding process). Equally, you need to make sure that you raise a big enough sum to allow you to fund debts accumulated during the funding process as well as for the future.

Sometimes you may want to access angels through a funding network or organisation of which they're members – for example, Angels Den (www.angelsden.com) and Angel Lab (www.angellab.co.uk). You can find many others who are members of the umbrella group, UK Business Angels Association (www.ukbusinessangelsassociation.org.uk).

These organisations enable you to pitch to many different angels at the same time, which may help you find just the angel(s) you need more quickly. They charge you something for making this possible – an upfront fee or a percentage (up to 5 per cent) of the monies raised, but this solution can be worthwhile because it saves on shoe leather and time. Endlessly scanning the skies by yourself for hopeful signs of heavenly investors can give you a pain in the neck!

You may also have to make some checks of your own on angels:

- ✔ Are they going to add any strategic benefit to the business apart from their cash?
- ✔ Do they have enough time to devote to you?
- ✔ Are they supportive or can you see them being a nagging distraction and a Moaning Minnie as your business proceeds?

Above all, work out whether angels really are good for the money, however much they brag about their financial resources. As Texans say, 'never mind about how big his hat is, how many cattle has he got?'

Angels increasingly pool their money and skills when investing in new businesses. If your intention is to secure a significant injection of capital, you may want to seek out 'angel networks' or syndicates and find out how the angels work together when investing in businesses. Frequently an individual within a syndicate or network represents the group and takes the lead in negotiations and further interactions with the entrepreneur and his business. But don't be afraid to ask about the composition of the network and the exact nature of their interactions with one another and with your business.

These investment groups can be helpful, because more funds are often available collectively than individually. But a group of four investors is likely to have five different opinions, which can slow down the investment process and mean that you have more queries, complaints and information to provide after the investment has taken place.

Obtaining tax relief for the angel

The availability of tax reliefs to investors in start-ups is often an important factor in their decision-making. Although obviously of more relevance to the investor than the business owner, bear it in mind when negotiating investment agreements, because it serves as an incentive to the angel to go ahead with the investment. These tax reliefs mean that the risk of providing funding is offset, in part, by the tax the angel saves under these schemes; they can be worth a significant amount of money.

The best-known investment tax relief schemes are the Enterprise Investment Scheme (EIS) and the Seed Enterprise Investment Scheme (SEIS).

Enterprise Investment Scheme

The EIS encourages people to invest in smaller companies, helping those firms to raise finance for higher-risk ventures. In its current form, the scheme offers investors the following reliefs:

- Income tax relief equal to 30 per cent of the value of the investment, up to a maximum relief of £300,000 (on a £1 million investment)

- No capital gains tax on any profit made on the sale of the shares

- The ability to set any loss on the sale of the shares against any income from the same, or the previous, year

- No inheritance tax on the value of the shares

To benefit from the 30 per cent income tax relief, the investor must hold the shares in the company for a minimum of three years and can't work for the company other than as an unremunerated director. Nor must the person hold more than 30 per cent of the share capital (or voting rights) in the company or be entitled to more than 30 per cent of the assets of the company on a winding up.

To qualify for EIS relief, all shares must be paid in full, be full-risk, ordinary shares (see Chapter 4 for a discussion on classes of share) and not carry any preferential rights to assets (as against other creditors) on a winding up of the company, or rights to a *cumulative dividend* (a right to be paid their share of dividends before any other shareholders). The company must have fewer than 250 employees and assets with a value of less than £250 million.

Seed Enterprise Investment Scheme

The SEIS was set up in 2012 and is similar to EIS, but the focus is on the first £150,000 of early-stage investment. Under SEIS, the investor can claim the following (even greater) reliefs on that investment:

- Income tax relief equal to 50 per cent of the value of the investment up to a maximum of £150,000 (with a limit of £100,000 per year)

- No capital gains tax on any profit made on the sale of the shares

- The ability to set any loss on the sale of the shares against any income from the same, or the previous, year

- No inheritance tax on the value of the shares

- Up to 50 per cent relief on any capital gains made on the sale of other assets to the extent that such gains are reinvested into your company (or into any other SEIS qualifying shares)

Under this scheme, the shares in the company must be held for a minimum of three years to qualify for the 50 per cent income tax relief and any capital gains relief on their sale. To qualify for SEIS relief, the company must have fewer than 25 staff and less than £200,000 worth of assets and be less than two years old at the date of issue of the SEIS shares. Like EIS, shares must be fully paid, ordinary, full-risk shares without preferential rights to assets on a winding up or rights to a cumulative dividend. The investor must hold no more than 30 per cent of the share capital (or voting rights) in the company and not be entitled to more than 30 per cent of the assets of the company on a winding up.

You can get pre-authorisation from HMRC that your company is EIS and SEIS compliant. Angels then look on you much more favourably and are more prepared to bless you.

Going mob-handed: Crowdfunding

If you don't want to give away too many shares (or *equity*) in your business, or you're concerned about maintaining control and influence over it, you can consider an alternative, relatively new phenomenon of raising finance. *Crowdfunding* involves raising finance through contributions, typically of low value, from a large number of people – usually (though not always) non-investment professionals.

Here's how crowdfunding works:

✔ Funding is raised through a crowdfunding website, which brings entrepreneurs seeking capital together with any member of the public interested in investing in a start-up.

✔ You create a profile on the crowdfunding website to pitch your business to visitors to the site. You set out details of how much money you're seeking to raise, timescales for investment, the value of the shares you want to sell and any other relevant information required to allow the investor to make an informed decision.

✔ The crowdfunding site plays its part in promoting the start-up by, for example, setting out details of tax reliefs available to investors and marketing the pitch to its investor network.

✔ The crowdfunding site takes a fee or a percentage of the funding raised for providing the funding platform. It can also assist with the process of issuing the shares, and maintaining details of shareholders and their respective shareholdings, as well as updating them in the future.

Considering the benefits

Crowdfunding has revolutionised the world of investment and brings a number of advantages:

- ✔ **Accessibility:** You can potentially reach thousands of investors in one go.

- ✔ **Speed:** Crowdfunding normally takes only a matter of weeks (often a limit of, say, eight weeks applies for your stay on the platform). This is often much quicker than other more traditional forms of finance. My own company has twice raised significant sums of money on Crowdcube (www.crowdcube.com) in less than a month.

- ✔ **Investors are eager:** During a period of low interest rates, non-professional investors can feel that they have little to lose by investing through crowdfunding sites, because they may ultimately gain more than if the investment money just sat in a bank earning a very low level of return. Investors can also have fun on these sites, making them feel like they're the kind of investor they see on television in *Dragons' Den* and *The Apprentice*.

- ✔ **Varieties of investment possible:** Although issuing shares in return for finance is the most common method of crowdfunding, you can also seek loans via these platforms in return for repayment with interest (for example, through Funding Circle – www.fundingcircle.com) or offer rewards instead of shares in return for funding (for example, through Bloom VC – www.bloomvc.com – or Richard Branson's Bank to the Future – www.banktothefuture.com).

- ✔ **Specialist investment possible:** An increasing number of crowdfunding sites are specialising in funding for specific sectors (for example, Kickstarter for creative funding – www.kickstarter.com).

Spotting the snags

Although crowdfunding is a useful way of obtaining finance if you're having trouble raising funds via more traditional means, certain drawbacks do exist:

- ✔ **Many investors:** The amount of capital raised by each individual is often very small, which means that you need a large number of investors to raise the required amount. Unless the site requires a minimum size of investment, you can find people investing as little as £10. As a result, your business can end up partly owned by a large number of shareholder investors (in the case of equity funding), each of whom has rights in the business – quite possibly including voting rights.

- ✔ **Complicated administration:** Having lots of investors means that obtaining approval for decisions requiring shareholder consent is more difficult and costly and administration of the business is more time-consuming.

- **Over-excitement:** The danger exists, when using crowdfunding, of losing sight of the amount of shares that you're giving away in your business. A particularly successful campaign can raise a substantial amount of money – more than you originally hoped for – but in the excitement of money pouring in you can also end up diluting your own shareholding to a greater degree than you anticipated. Therefore, you need to be clear on the maximum percentage of the business that you're prepared to give away from the start.

- **Additional parties involved:** Crowdfunding is conducted through a platform, which means that an additional party is involved in the process (the platform operator). As a result, the legal and logistical aspects of the funding are more complicated: you may be entering into an agreement with both the crowdfunding platform operator and the individual investors.

- **Lack of confidentiality:** During the investment process, your pitch and supporting business plan are up on the crowdfunding platform for all to see – including potential competitors, who may steal your ideas or strategy.

- **Regulation:** Crowdfunding has been a liberating experience for many entrepreneurs and investors, but no government wants people to have too much fun! An increasing concern is that investors on crowdfunding platforms, without the requisite skills and experience, may make investment decisions that they regret or can't afford, or that unscrupulous entrepreneurs can raise monies for their business and blow it on expensive cars and holidays – or just disappear altogether. Check out the nearby sidebar 'Regulating crowdfunding' for the regulatory details.

Regulating crowdfunding

Since 1 April 2014, crowdfunding has fallen under the regulated activity of 'operating an electronic platform in relation to lending' as set out in the Financial Services and Markets Act (Regulated Activities Order), 2001. Under the legislation, the platform operator requires authorisation from the Financial Conduct Authority (FCA), and individuals who lend through platforms are permitted to lend up to £25,000 to businesses.

On the equity crowdfunding side, authorisation from the FCA is also required. Offers of shares on the crowdfunding platform fall within the definition of a 'financial promotion', which is why FCA consent is required to regulate the activity. Therefore, crowdfunding platforms are increasingly insistent that businesses promoted on the platform go through quite a heavy degree of due diligence. Every claim in every pitch must be justified or backed up by evidence. So, increasingly, crowdfunding may not be as simple or speedy a process as it used to be for a business looking to raise finance.

Although crowdfunders can offer finance to your business in the form of a loan rather than through the purchase of equity in your business, the thought of owing money to lots of different people and having to pay them all back (with the addition of interest) can be a worrying proposition for a young business.

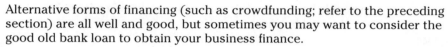

Sourcing loans the traditional way

Alternative forms of financing (such as crowdfunding; refer to the preceding section) are all well and good, but sometimes you may want to consider the good old bank loan to obtain your business finance.

With a bank loan:

- ✔ You have the advantage of knowing that you're using a tried and tested method of financing.

- ✔ You can choose from a number of long-established institutions.

- ✔ You can secure all the funding from a single lender and you just have to remember to make your monthly repayments.

- ✔ You don't have to give up any company shares in return for the funding, in contrast with equity financing such as funding from angels (see the earlier section, 'Dealing with angels').

Simple and easy, right? Nope. As you may expect, the theory isn't reflected in the practice. Since the global economic crisis, banks have become a lot more careful about lending, which means that even finding a bank willing to offer credit to your business is a high hurdle to overcome.

Traditionally, the '3 Cs' were important to a lender – your character, your commercial credibility and your creditworthiness. Now creditworthiness is really the name of the game. As is the case with angel investment (float your way to the earlier section 'Flying without wings: Financing from angels'), you have to present a robust business plan underpinned by strong business fundamentals.

If you're just starting out, you may well have particular difficulty securing funding. Unlike some other early-stage investors, banks are especially keen on seeing proof of a stable income stream, which you may simply not have had sufficient time to establish. In addition, complying with the terms of the debt agreement may also prove hard.

One thing you can be certain of when seeking funding from a bank is that the terms of the loan will be exacting and you'll be strictly held to them.

Releasing pension-led funding

Pension-led funding is a form of debt finance in which you use funds that you've amassed from a pension scheme to invest in your own business. A new scheme is set up and pension monies are transferred into the scheme. You then decide how to use this money and a scheme administrator releases the money to your business.

This form of funding works through the following two private pension schemes in which the beneficiaries of the scheme (the pension holders) can dictate how their pensions are invested:

- **Small Self-Administered Scheme (SSAS):** An SSAS is often considered suitable where a family business wants to create a pension scheme for its members together. They can then all make investment decisions regarding the investment of pension monies paid into the scheme (including into the business itself).

- **Self-Invested Personal Pension (SIPP):** A SIPP more often arises where an individual has an accumulated pension fund and wants to use the proceeds to invest in his own business.

The schemes release the finance by two main methods: they make a loan to your business or they purchase assets from your business and then lease them back to the business (called a *sale and leaseback*).

Both schemes are generally unable to invest in *tangible moveable property* – things that you can touch or move, such as equipment – without being subject to tax. But no similar restriction applies to *intangible* assets, such as intellectual property (IP; for example, the value of a brand, a computer program or an industrial patent – rush to Chapter 8 to find out more about IP). Therefore, you can sell intangible assets that your company owns to the pension fund or use them as security to secure the repayment of the loan from the fund.

Here are several advantages to this form of funding:

- **Control:** You retain control over the funding process, because you're not seeking funding from a third party who can place onerous conditions on you. Instead, you're releasing your own funds from a pension for the benefit of your business.

✔ **Low interest rates:** You may feel that with interest rates so low your pension fund is unlikely to be of much help to you when you come to retire (especially if the pot of gold isn't huge). Instead, you'd rather use the money purposefully now and hope to build your business assets with your pension funding.

✔ **Pension-building:** If an asset of the business is purchased or developed as a result of monies advanced from your pension fund, any success of the business results in an increase in the value of that asset. As a result, you're profiting from having provided funding to your own business.

✔ **Combination financing:** You can use pension-led funding in conjunction with other funding arrangements to secure additional funding. For example, if you've already taken out a secured loan with a bank, none of your IP is likely to have been used as collateral for the loan. Therefore, it can be a valuable asset against which to secure further funding and your bank may possibly consent (even if its secured bank-loan agreement gives it the right to say 'no' – the bank's favourite word).

Pension-led funding isn't all plain sailing for a number of reasons:

✔ **Risk:** In using your own pension funds for your business, you're placing your accrued funds at risk, instead of somebody else's. If the business fails the pension funds go with it, and that may well leave a hole later on in your retirement funding.

✔ **Cost:** Obtaining advice on the process and setting up the chosen scheme costs money. So does appointing an administrator to run the scheme; although not required it's highly advisable – not least because you have to register these schemes with HMRC.

✔ **Time:** The process can take anything from 6 to 12 weeks to set up on average, and so it's not that quick.

✔ **Funding limits:** You can't use all the value of the pension – restrictions apply on the value that can be released to the business in order to prevent pension owners being completely reckless with their pension monies.

✔ **Pay back:** Your business is required to pay back the amounts advanced over a period of time (often five years) at a commercial rate of interest, so that the pension fund can be replenished again to your benefit as its owner. This is all well and good, but means that your business must be able to afford the regular repayments over a long period of time. You're charged tax penalties if you fail to keep up these repayments.

Since April 2015, you've had the right (if you're over 55) to access your pension pot in one go, without using this sort of scheme. This arrangement sounds brilliant, but the tax implications can be quite scary. You can take the first 25 per cent as a lump sum tax free, but you then pay tax at your highest level of income tax on all the rest of the money. So if you have a £200,000 pot, you can take £50,000 tax free but may need to pay 40 per cent (or £60,000) in tax on the rest.

One way of mitigating this problem is to take small lump sums over a period of several years, instead of all in one go (in which case your taxable allowances each year can help you minimise the tax you pay on the rest). But this option may not be as attractive for your business as taking a larger lump sum now without tax implications, which is what these pension-led funding schemes can provide.

Chapter 4

Closing the Funding Agreement

. . . .

In This Chapter

▶ Finding out about funding formalities

▶ Entering into equity funding and debt financing agreements

▶ Completing the agreement

. . . .

*I*n Chapter 3, I discuss the main funding options available to your early-stage business. With that knowledge stowed away safely in your brain's pocket (eh?), here I turn to the practical issues involved with closing any funding agreement: what you have to sign in order to secure the money.

I describe negotiating and formalising the arrangements and the different kinds of investor agreements into which you enter in relation to various types of funding (broadly speaking, equity funding or debt financing).

If you get your funding, don't stand around admiring yourself like a cat with the cream. Spend it wisely, of course, but don't hang about – you're likely to increase your spending too, and when you have extra mouths to feed you can be amazed how quickly the money runs out.

Following Funding Formalities (Not for Fun!)

You need to observe a few formalities when closing a funding deal, such as considering confidentiality agreements, raising funds legally and ensuring that you have an investor agreement form. These items are for your protection, and so make that sure you take in the info I provide in this section; doing so may just help you avoid an unpleasant situation down the road.

Putting confidentiality agreements in place

When seeking funding from investors, you have to provide them with certain details about your business. They need to arrive at an informed decision about whether providing you with capital is a sound investment and is going to provide them with the returns they want.

Investors want to know the nature of the business, its actual or projected revenues, who your customers and suppliers are, what designs and logos you've developed, what your product looks like or what your services consist of and how they work, what assets you have in the business, your future plans for growth and so on.

These details represent a lot of sensitive information and require plenty of work on your part to prepare. If you're going to reveal this kind of information to a third party, you need to ensure that it's all legally protected against disclosure. You may decide that when you're dealing with an institution such as a bank, you're automatically protected by the relationship or its professionalism. But if you're dealing with angels (refer to Chapter 3) who review umpteen businesses a week, be careful about protecting what you reveal.

In order to protect your information (and before you disclose it to potential angel investors), always try to enter into a *confidentiality agreement*. Also known as a *non-disclosure agreement* (NDA), this formal agreement restricts the disclosure of information received by someone from you (other than in strictly limited circumstances – for example, if the recipient has to disclose it in a court of law). Within this agreement, you find the following:

- ✔ Restrictions on the use of the disclosed confidential information, to ensure that it's only used for a specified purpose (say, to allow a lender to decide whether to provide a loan to your business)

- ✔ Restrictions on the employees or other people with whom the lender can share your confidential information (usually on a 'need to know' basis)

- ✔ Terms relating to the return or destruction of the confidential information when the information is no longer required

Some people argue that confidentiality agreements are a waste of time, because they're hard to monitor and enforce. But I believe that they're a good deterrent against rampant disclosure and that you can make the signing of any agreement solemn enough to impact on the behaviour of those involved.

Some angels refuse to sign confidentiality agreements, because they see so many businesses that agreeing not to disclose certain aspects about them all is impractical. But if an angel refuses to give you the comfort of signing a confidentiality agreement, ask yourself why. It may just be a warning signal.

Promoting your fundraising legally

I'm sure that you're intimately aware of the provisions of the Financial Services and Markets Act, 2000 (the FSMA) and what it means for you when you're raising money. No? Okay then.

In essence, this Act governs financial services, and says that only a person authorised by the Financial Conduct Authority (the FCA – the regulatory body that oversees regulation of financial services) can invite another party to invest in a business. Funding institutions (such as banks, crowdfunding bodies or private equity funding organisations) secure regulatory clearance from the FCA. Individuals don't normally get such clearance and so they fall under the 'financial promotion restriction'.

The effect of this restriction is to prevent business owners from encouraging individuals to make investments they can't afford or duping them (for example, by sending them an overly optimistic pitch document). This protects vulnerable individuals from the dangers of buying a 'pig in a poke' by purchasing shares and other financial products when they shouldn't. (By the way, a pig in a poke was a cat disguised in a bag and sold in medieval times as though it was a much more valuable pig. The FSA wouldn't approve.)

Being certifiable!

A *high net worth individual,* for the purposes of the FSMA legislation, is a person with an annual income of £100,000 or who held net assets to the value of at least £250,000 throughout the financial year preceding the date on which you make the promotion.

A *sophisticated investor* is a person to whom at least one of the following applies:

✔ Has been a member of a network or syndicate of business angels for the last six months

✔ Has made more than one investment in an *unlisted* company in the last two years (a company not listed on a recognised stock exchange)

✔ Has worked, in the previous two years, as a professional in private equity or in the provision of finance to small and medium-size enterprises (SMEs)

✔ Has been, in the last two years, a director of a company with an annual turnover of at least £1 million

Exceptions to this rule do exist, however, and one of them allows a financial promotion to be made to a *certified high net worth individual,* a *certified sophisticated investor* or a *self-certified sophisticated investor.* In other words, people who have a high level of personal wealth or one of the permitted kinds of experience of the lending environment. Check out the nearby sidebar 'Being certifiable!' for more details.

When you're seeking investment from an individual (an angel or even a friend), get the person to sign a 'self-certifying letter' that states that she falls within one of the categories in the nearby 'Being certifiable!' sidebar. Get investors to sign this letter *before* you send your pitch, so that they can't complain that they were swayed by your silky presentation skills into providing that certification.

Drafting an investor agreement

If you're going to take in investment, you need an *investment agreement,* which sets out how much is being invested and on what terms that money is being invested.

If you're working with an institution such as a bank, grant agency or crowdfunding organisation, it provides you with its own form of documentation or terms. You must get a lawyer to review it. Really, you must . . . it's too important to simply deal with on your own, unless you have a lot of experience of such documentation.

Normally the institution tells you that the documentation is standard, but *don't* accept that explanation: it's often not true and frequently just a lazy way of ensuring that the lender doesn't have to do any work to defend its own documentation. Always question any 'standard' terms you're unhappy with, whether they relate to onerous repayment, scandalous rates of interest or ways of snaffling your shares on the cheap.

If you're dealing with an angel, a friend or a member of your family, he usually expects you to come up with the form of investment documentation. Again, you must use a lawyer to help you. I know that free versions are available on the Internet and you want to save money; perhaps you think that nothing could ever go wrong if you're dealing with a friend. Sad to relate, that's not the case. Drafting the document yourself or butchering some awful precedent you find on Google isn't a sensible way to save money. This is one of those occasions when you must get an expert to help you.

Tackling Share Investor Agreements: Equity Funding

The preceding section establishes the need for a formal investor agreement. Here I take a look at such agreements where the investment is made in return for shares. You need to be a bit of an octopus to negotiate these *share investor agreements* successfully, because they have numerous tentacles that spread in different directions at the same time. Here I describe six such tentacles of the share investor agreement. Keep an eye on your tentacles – you don't want them ripped off when shaking hands with those bankers!

Negotiating shareholdings

The most obvious aspect of formal investor agreements is shareholdings, and in particular the following:

- Calculation of the amount of shares that the investor wants to purchase
- Value of those shares
- Percentage of the business those shares constitute

In order to arrive at these figures, you need to attribute a notional value to the business as a whole. By this stage you've already presented investors with your business plan, including a statement of how many shares you want to issue and the amount that you're prepared to accept for that slice of equity. From this value you can extrapolate to produce your estimate of the value of the business as a whole. Friends and family, as well as crowdfunding investors, may well be happy to accept your valuation.

Savvy angel investors, of course, want to take more shares for less money when compared with your offer. They use their own knowledge to reach a figure, together with certain customary methods of valuation, and throw in a nice markdown, to enable them to realise a comfortable return on their investment. Some investors look for a 1,000 per cent return (that is, 10 times the value of their initial investment), and so they amend their valuations to best position themselves to achieve such a return.

Angels may seek to justify their lowball valuation by way of comparison to other investments they've made or know about, but bear in mind that, for most start-ups, valuation is a highly theoretical exercise because they have so little trading history. This benefits you in the sense that reducing your suggested valuation is harder by referring to existing precedents or financial models, but it also causes difficulty in persuading investors of your point of view, because your opinion is seen as subjective rather than objective.

Protecting against future dilution

This round of funding is unlikely to be your last: more funding requirements lie ahead. Your initial seed-funding round helps you through the first phase of your development life cycle. But unless your business takes off like a rocket after you invest this money (using it to achieve your initial goals), you may find yourself considering additional funding (called *series A* funding) to enable you to move on into the next phase of development. Maybe you now want to start mass marketing and producing your product, hiring more staff or moving into larger business premises. This round of funding may attract a larger investor, such as a venture capitalist (see Chapter 17).

You can follow series A funding with series B funding – and so on.

When you embark on any additional funding rounds, you have to give away further equity in your business, which means that your shareholding in the business becomes smaller *(diluted)*. Protecting yourself against dilution is very difficult.

That's not to say that conceding further equity to current or new investors is all bad. In addition to securing that extra money to propel your business forward, the extra investment helps you to increase the value of your own shareholding. At every stage, investors put money into your business based on what they feel it's worth. The further you move along the path of development, and the more trading history you have behind you, the easier investors find valuing your business highly.

Therefore, business owners are often prepared to give away increasing amounts of equity and see their shareholding diluted. Selling your business for, say, £10 million and taking £1.5 million of the sale price for a 15 per cent share is preferable to selling your business for a few thousand pounds and taking 100 per cent of the sale price: your slice of the pie is smaller if you take on further investment, but the pie is much larger, and so your slice can be tastier (I mean, worth more).

Despite this obvious benefit, still think carefully about further funding rounds and how much more equity you may want or need to give away to continue to drive the business forward: the more you give away, the less control you have. At less than 75 per cent of the shares you can no longer pass Special Resolutions on your own (refer to Chapter 2). At less than 50 per cent of the shares, you can be out-voted if everybody else gangs up against you.

The investor of course is looking at the issue of dilution from the other end of the telescope. If a further funding round occurs, the investor normally has the chance to put more money into the company in order to make sure that overall her percentage of shares in it stays the same (called a *pre-emption right* – check out Chapter 2).

Some investors try to argue that even if they don't want to put in more money in later rounds, their investment is so important to you that you ought to agree that it isn't going to get diluted in future – effectively, they want 'free' shares in any subsequent round to keep up their percentage of ownership. Of course, you should resist this unattractive option. Not only does it put you in a worse position, but also it may put off subsequent investors who object to the idea that previous investors are getting extra shares for nothing.

Conducting due diligence

Due diligence is the process by which a potential investor investigates your business before committing to an investment in it. Due diligence influences your business's valuation in the investor agreement.

The exact range of due diligence varies depending on the temperament of the investor and how advanced your business is (the more advanced, the more to check out). Therefore, you can expect due diligence to become more important in subsequent investment rounds and, of course, when you go to sell the company – I look at these points more closely in Chapter 18.

At the early stages, an investor may still want to check on the following areas, just to make sure that your business boat doesn't have any obvious holes:

✔ **Management:** In TV's *Dragons' Den,* the investors often comment on the impression the entrepreneur makes on them when seeking investment. Remember that you are, in essence, your business. Investors want to know about your skills, your background, what drives you and why you set up your business.

They also want to check that you have a talented team around you to help implement your dream and to make sure that you and your team are committed to the business contractually. They may want to check that you and your team have formal contracts or employment agreements with the business, and if you don't, they may require this as a condition of their investment.

Some angels feel that the three most important criteria for investment are 'management, management and management'; don't be surprised if it's a major issue for them.

✔ **Legal:** Angels may not trouble themselves with full legal due diligence, but they may well want to know the following:

- The current shareholdings are as you've described.

- Any contracts you've mentioned as being important are binding, clear and current.

- Intellectual property (IP) is properly registered or applied for, and who owns it (for example, trademarks, design rights or patents).

- Any required regulatory approvals have been applied for or granted (for example, from councils or industry bodies).

- The business isn't subject to any legal disputes or claims.

✔ **Financial:** Angels may not conduct full financial due diligence, but they're looking to see that:

- Your business plan stacks up.

- Your current accounts/balance sheet don't contain any debts (present or future).

- You're properly registered for, and don't owe any, tax.

If any problems are revealed after due diligence, the investor may try to beat you up on price, saying that the problem affects the valuation of the company and so it should get more shares for the same amount of money. To prevent this, you have to show that no problem exists, it's easy to solve or that its effect on the value of the business is minimal.

Minimising warranties

One way in which investors seek to limit their risk under the share investor agreement is by including warranties. A *warranty* is a statement or promise about some aspect of the business contained in the agreement, which, if found to be untrue, allows the investor to recover certain losses that flow from the false statement.

The business *and* you, as an individual, are required to be parties to the agreement. Therefore, you as an individual have to make warranties to the investor and can be individually liable for any losses arising from any breach of those warranties.

Angels may not be as aggressive about warranties as investors in subsequent funding rounds, because less money is at stake in the early stages. But you can expect them at least to want to see warranties in the agreement covering the areas of due diligence, so that the company and its owners fully stand behind their facts and figures by vouching for them in the written agreement. Many angels therefore seek to include warranties about the accuracy of the current shareholdings, management accounts, balance sheet, current contracts, debt, employee contracts, tax, disputes and so on.

I look at warranties and how to protect yourself against them in more detail in Chapter 18, but here are the basic rules to bear in mind:

- ✔ **Check the warranty is relevant:** Often blanket warranties are inserted that have no relevance to your business (for example, in relation to property leases in circumstances where in fact you share a workspace with others and don't have a lease). Cross these out.

- ✔ **Qualify the warranty:** Be careful not to provide a full warranty when you can't be certain that the statement is true, perhaps because it's beyond your control. When you're uncertain, qualify the warranty with the phrase 'So far as the warrantor is aware'.

- ✔ **Amend the warranty:** You can amend the wording so that the statement becomes one that you're comfortable making or to narrow the scope of the warranty's subject matter.

- ✔ **Limit your liability:** Cap the overall amount of your liability under the warranties so that it's proportionate to any realistic loss the angel may suffer from a breach and limited to what you can realistically afford.

  You can also limit the period following completion of the agreement during which the investor is allowed to bring a claim for breach of the warranties: say, to 12 months.

Remember – you're an octopus, and so you can always spray the investors in ink if they're making you twitchy (don't rely on that response though!).

Keeping operational control

Investors are keen to ensure that any activity of the business that can affect their eventual return is tightly controlled. With this concern in mind, they may well insist on inserting a basic term in the agreement stating that before certain decisions can be taken they require the consent of the investor (or a director appointed to the board to represent her interests). A list of these matters for which consent is required is often set out in a separate schedule at the back of the share investor agreement.

Depending on the nature of the matters included, this requirement can place a high degree of constraint on the business's operation. Although angels may not be as thorough as institutional investors in this regard, expect the list to cover the following decisions:

- Entering into charges that give third parties rights over the company's assets (take a look at 'Providing security for loans' later in this chapter for more on charges)

- Seeking additional funding from any other third party (because that may dilute the investor's shareholding or restrict her rights)

- Issuing new shares

- Increasing or reducing the share capital of the businesses

- Varying rights attaching to shares

- Significantly changing the company's business

- Winding up the company

You have the tricky job of balancing the investor's interests and concerns as a significant shareholder against the need to maintain flexibility in executing your business development strategy: don't let the need to get money in quickly seduce you into agreeing lots of controls. As the old saying goes, 'marry in haste, repent at leisure'.

You can negotiate these consent matters – for example, restrict the items on the list, try to get the word 'consent' reduced to 'consultation' or to 'consent, not to be unreasonably withheld or delayed'. Or you can try to get the consents to lapse after, say, one year, when you've proved to the investor that you're a worthy custodian of the business.

Dealing with different types of shares

When you incorporate your company, you normally have only one category of share: an *ordinary share.* This most basic share category usually entitles you to a vote at a shareholder meeting, a right to dividends and a right to a distribution of the assets on a winding up of the company (which I deal with in more detail in Chapter 16).

As long as the Articles (which I explain in Chapter 2) allow it, however, a company can have as many different classes of shares as it likes, and when investors apply (or *subscribe*) for shares in your business, they may well want to insist on having a class of share that provides them with specific rights. This is why companies usually give themselves in the Articles the right to issue different kinds of share – for example 'A' ordinary and 'B' ordinary shares. In such cases, one class can have more rights than another:

✔ One class may have priority when profits are distributed on a winding up.

✔ Holders of one group may have a right of veto/voting, which the other group doesn't have.

✔ One class may have the right to appoint a director, which the other class doesn't have.

✔ Shareholders of one group may have a right of pre-emption that another class doesn't have (Chapter 2 has more on pre-emption).

Many other types of share exist as well (preference, redeemable, convertible), but these tend to come up in later funding rounds with institutional investors (see Chapter 17). For now, bear in mind that angels may seek controls through the type of share they acquire as well as through express provisions in the investment agreement. Be mindful not just of how many shares you're giving away at what price, but also what type of shares and the rights that attach to them. Don't capitulate; negotiate!

Arranging Other Forms of Financing Agreements

Share investor agreements (the subject of the earlier 'Tackling Share Investor Agreements: Equity Funding' section) aren't the only form of financing agreement. As I describe in this section, plenty of other forms exist that vary depending on the source of the funding – bank loan agreements, crowdfunding agreements, grant agreements and pension-led funding agreements.

Don't be put off – these agreements aren't that complicated; you just need to keep your wits about you (like the common leech, which apparently has 32 brains and is brilliant at negotiating finance agreements when not sucking blood. No idea why leeches occur to me when discussing investors. . .).

Handling loan agreements

Debt financing (through loans) is more simple than equity funding (through shares; refer to the earlier 'Tackling Share Investor Agreements: Equity Funding' section) in the sense that your business isn't granting any ownership to the investor. The basic premise of the funding agreement from the investor's point of view, however, remains the same: minimise the risk and maximise the return.

Here are some points to look out for when you're negotiating this kind of agreement (they may seem harsh, which is one reason why bankers are so unpopular – they're perceived as living a fine life while making funding very difficult for everybody else. Hell, they're even less popular than lawyers right now. You may feel as though you're swimming with sharks as well as leeches!):

- ✔ **How much you have to repay:** Under a basic loan agreement, you borrow a fixed sum of money and have to repay that sum, with interest, (usually) via monthly repayments. Can you afford them?

- ✔ **Over what period you must repay the loan:** From your point of view, the longer the repayment period, the smaller the staged repayments are likely to be, but the more you have to pay in total. Different lenders offer varying combinations of repayment periods and interest rates, and they're looking for financial evidence of your ability to meet each staged repayment.

- ✔ **Early repayment provisions:** The default position is that a borrower has no right to repay a loan prior to the agreed repayment date, because any early repayment reduces the overall amount of interest payable on the loan. If you do come across a provision in the agreement that permits early repayment, it more than likely comes at a price – which can mean that you're no better off repaying early than repaying the amount over the full term. Try and get a clause that says no penalty for early repayment.

- ✔ **Fees:** Most lenders charge upfront fees as well as interest (for example, *arrangement fees*), which you have to factor in as a cost of doing the transaction with that lender.

- ✔ **Interest rate:** The lender has a minimum or *base rate* of interest that's linked to the base rate of the Bank of England (the rate at which banks can borrow money from the Bank of England) or the cost of borrowing from other banks (see the next bullet point). The base rate is calculated to cover the costs and risks associated with lending money while allowing it to provide competitive saving rates for investors. The rate of interest payable on the loan is a markup of this rate, the percentage of the markup being determined by a number of factors (such as the amount of the loan, the term, the risk factors perceived by the lender and the current market for lending rates).

- ✔ **Fixed or floating rates:** The interest that you pay on the loan can be set either at a fixed rate or a floating rate. A fixed rate of repayment doesn't change throughout the term of the loan, but a floating (or *variable*) rate loan adjusts over time according to changes in the underlying rate to which it's linked.

This underlying rate is frequently the London Inter-Bank Offered Rate (LIBOR), which is the interest rate at which London banks lend to one another. If this rate goes up, the rate of interest payable on your variable rate loan rises as well to represent the additional cost of borrowing for the lender. The frequency of any changes in the rate is agreed with you, but it can be altered on a 1-, 3-, 6- or 12-month basis.

Fixed-rate loans are more expensive, to compensate for the risk associated with fluctuating LIBOR rates, while a floating-rate loan is cheaper but contains the added risk of increased repayments.

✔ **Default provisions:** In order to guard against the risk of non-repayment of the loan (or *default*), the lender inserts a series of *events of default*. If these events occur, they allow it to call on you to pay the outstanding value of the loan immediately on demand, suspend your ability to take out any further money (if the loan is paid in several *tranches*) and enable the lender to enforce any security (see 'Providing security for loans' later in this chapter).

Events of default are the equivalent to lenders of a shark smelling blood, and so they're usually a cue for a swift attack on your business. Events of default commonly include the following:

✔ Failure to make any repayment on the scheduled repayment date

✔ Failure to comply with any term of the agreement

✔ Failure to pay interest on time or at all

✔ Any event that has a significant adverse effect on the business

✔ Any breach of a 'financial condition' set out in the agreement and relating to the financial status of your company (for example, breach of a condition about the value of your assets versus your liabilities)

Try to insert a provision allowing a grace period in which to remedy certain events of default before the lender has the right to take any action to recover its debt. Alternatively, try to include a clause saying that the event of default must reach a certain level of severity before the lender can call in the loan, so that a minor occurrence doesn't trigger repayment.

Taking care of convertible loan agreements

A *convertible loan* is one that provides the lender with a right to convert the outstanding amount of the loan into equity (that is, shares) in the business. The conversion may take place automatically, at a certain time or on the occurrence of a specified event (for example, the next round of fundraising), or it can be left to the discretion of the lender or the borrower as to whether to exercise this right. The option to convert can also remain open for the duration of the term.

If repayments become hard to make, the equity conversion can provide you with a 'way out', of sorts, from a difficult position. The flipside, of course, is that if the loan converts, you're giving away more shares in the business.

To ensure that the lender receives a sufficient amount of equity in exchange for the debt, it may try to insist on capping the valuation of your company for the purpose of the conversion (a lower valuation means a greater number of shares for the same amount of money). Or it may push to have the right to make the conversion at a discounted rate in order to achieve the same effect. Try to resist these attempts.

In return for granting the lender the possibility of trading the debt for equity in your business, you can seek more preferable terms than the ones granted in a simple loan agreement. These can include no early repayment fee and a lower rate of interest on the repayments.

Providing security for loans

In the event that all other protections that I discuss in the preceding two sections aren't enough to reassure the lender that its money is safe in your hands, it can resort to taking security over assets in order to underpin the loan. This approach gives it something of recognised value to fall back on in the event that you fail to repay the debt.

When a debt is *secured,* the lender has the right to receive back from you the value of an asset or assets owned by your company to cover the amount of the debt owed and any costs of recovering that amount, if the need and the right arise (the latter arises on the occurrence of certain trigger events specified in the written agreement).

Three basic types of security exist:

- **Legal mortgage:** The legal ownership of the asset passes to the lender, but your company retains the actual asset. The transfer of title is made on the condition that it's transferred back to you after full repayment has been made.

  A mortgage is the most secure form of security, and prevents your company from dealing with the mortgaged asset in any way, which can be a hindrance to the business.

✔ **Charge:** The asset and its ownership remain with your company, but the lender has a right to 'take over' the asset in order to sell it and retrieve the value of the outstanding loan.

Charges can be broken down into two types:

- **Fixed charge:** 'Attaches' directly to the charged asset and provides the lender with control of the charged asset. Your company can do very little with that asset while the charge is in place, which can be quite restrictive.

- **Floating charge:** Doesn't attach directly to the charged asset. Instead it 'floats' over the top of one or all your company's assets (sounds so harmless, doesn't it?). Usually, the asset or assets over which the floating charge is taken belong to a shifting class of asset; that is, those used in the ordinary course of the business and which therefore fluctuate from time to time. Examples of such assets are the trading stock of the business and receivable income from customers (called *book debts*).

  The whole point of a floating charge is that your company (as the borrower) retains control over the asset and is therefore free to make use of it as you choose without requiring any permission from the lender. Under the loan agreement, however, the floating charge can transform into a fixed charge *(crystallise)* on the occurrence of specified events.

  Certain events trigger this *crystallisation* by law (for example, when your firm ceases carrying on its business or when a lender appoints an insolvency practitioner over some of or all the company's assets). The lender also inserts other events into the loan agreement that trigger crystallisation, such as events of default (see the earlier 'Handling loan agreements' for details); for example, failure to pay back instalments of the loan or interest on time. The event of default operates to move control of the charged asset over to the lender, so that your company is no longer able freely to use and dispose of the asset.

You can see that from your point of view, a floating charge is preferable to a fixed charge. If you can avoid any fixed charges (and mortgages), you're less beholden to the lender and freer to deal with your assets as you conduct your business.

✔ **Guarantees:** Get out your cloves of garlic and lucky rabbit's foot, or chant whatever incantation you use to ward off bad spirits. Guarantees are evil. They're a separate form of security that lenders may demand and are particularly relevant in the case of start-ups, because your company may simply not have enough assets over which security can be taken. Yet the lender still wants assurances that the debt can be repaid if the business finds itself in financial difficulty, and so it turns to the business owner; that means you as an individual. Banks are particularly fond of this kind of protection.

The lender may seek protection from you in the form of a personal guarantee. Under this agreement the lender can call on you, the business owner, to honour payment of the borrower's (that is, the company's) debt under certain predetermined circumstances. The circumstances are likely to be the same or very similar to those that trigger an event of default under the loan agreement (non-repayment of loan or interest on time, the company ceasing to trade or entering into liquidation and so on). If the guarantee is triggered, you're responsible personally for repaying the loan – which can mean wiping out your savings, selling your house or even entering into bankruptcy.

Never enter lightly into a personal guarantee. If you're operating through a limited company, remember that one of the principal benefits of this structure is that your liability, as an individual, is limited to the extent of the nominal value of your shareholding in the business. In providing any kind of personal guarantee, you're effectively removing this benefit and exposing yourself to significantly greater liability. Entrepreneurs are the world's greatest optimists – but if you do take on such personal risk, ensure that you're comfortable with the level of that risk, and that your dependents can cope with it too. Don't think 'it can never happen to me'. It can, and lenders normally show no mercy when enforcing a guarantee.

I think I've been a bit unkind to lenders in this section. Though High Street banks can be inflexible, plenty of friendly lenders exist. Best to see whether you can find an SME-focused lender outside of the traditional banks. Organisations such as Credit4 (www.credit4.co.uk) and Funding Options (www.fundingoptions.com) are quick and empathetic to small businesses.

Tying up crowdfunding agreements

You can use crowdfunding (refer to Chapter 3) to raise money in exchange for shares (equity) or in return for a loan (debt-financing).

With both options, a crowdfunder charges you for using its funding service. Typically, the charge is a combination of an upfront fee and/or a percentage of the monies raised, and/or a further percentage or further fees for other services provided (for example, helping you with share formalities).

Take care that you look at these charges closely. They may not be negotiable, but they vary from platform to platform and should be part of your decision as to which crowdfunder to go with.

Equity raises

If you choose this option, your business signs up for Terms and Conditions with the crowdfunding site, which resemble the shape of the share investor agreements I discuss earlier in the 'Tackling Share Investor Agreements: Equity Funding' section.

The crowdfunding site accepts your valuation of your shares as long as it's consistent with other company valuations for similar raises and/or similar sectors. If the crowdfunding site doesn't agree with your valuation, it tries to negotiate your valuation down.

The crowdfunding site makes you sign Terms and Conditions prior to your equity raising, including a range of warranties about your business in relation to its state of affairs and viability. The crowdfunder also conducts limited due diligence to make sure that all the claims in your pitch are substantiated.

Some crowdfunding sites provide their own nominee shareholder to represent all the smaller individual investors. The nominee shareholder then enters into a subscription agreement with your company and may seek to secure consents or involvement in decision-making by your firm. If no nominee is provided, you may not have to enter into share investor agreements with every individual investor (which is a relief, because you may have hundreds of them). Instead, the crowdfunder makes the individual crowd investors agree to be bound by your Articles as a condition of their investment.

Loans

If you go for this debt-financing option, you sign up for something like the loan agreements I cover in the earlier section 'Handling loan agreements'. The crowdfunding site sets repayment terms, interest rates and default terms in its Terms and Conditions or in a separate loan agreement after the loan monies have been raised. Interest rates are in part set by reference to the perceived risk of lending to your particular company. Sites such as Funding Circle give themselves the option of taking the widest possible security over your firm's assets in order to secure the loan, including charges and possibly a personal guarantee.

Proceeding with grant agreements

A *grant* is effectively an 'award' for a purpose other than direct profit making (such as stimulating or accelerating innovation and promoting business and growth in the economy, in the case of government awards). But even a prize can come with strings attached. Here are some that can get you in a tangle:

✔ **Being in scope:** Grants are provided for a specific purpose or project, and so you have to ensure that your business falls within the scope of the criteria prescribed by the grantor. If you're unsure whether you qualify for the grant in question or you have any problems filling out any application forms, seek further information from the body making the grant, to help avoid any delay in the processing of your application.

Take care also to check the geographic requirements, because many grants are restricted to businesses operating within a specified city, town or county. My experience as a former assessor for Technology Strategy Board awards is that falling at the first hurdle is easy if you don't strictly follow the criteria for the grant concerned. Your application is simply dismissed as 'out of scope'.

✔ **Funding conditions and phasing:** One disadvantage of the grant method of funding is that you can be asked to match from other sources any funding the grantor offers (roll over to Chapter 3 for more details). In addition, you may also have to cover the total cost of the project upfront (that is, spend your half *and* that of the grantor) before being reimbursed the 50 per cent promised by the grantor. In such a situation, not only do you have to ensure that you have sufficient funds to match the value of the grant, but also you may need to find double the amount!

✔ **Meeting targets:** The grantor may insist that you achieve certain milestones to trigger or maintain funding. These targets relate to the purpose for which the grant was given (for example, in relation to product development if the grant was awarded for that purpose).

Try to get as much of the money as possible paid upfront, and make sure that these subsequent targets are realistic and achievable for you.

✔ **Supervising progress:** The grantor may well insist on supervising your work and require regular progress reports, updates and meetings to check that you're on track to fulfil the deliverables for which you obtained the grant. This aspect can be quite high maintenance, time-consuming and intrusive, but if you don't do it properly the promised grant monies can be withheld – or the grantor may demand repayment.

Try and ensure that any supervision you agree to isn't such a distraction that it stops you running the business properly.

Handling bureaucracy: Grant bodies are sometimes bureaucratic quangos with competing interests at their heart and confusing procedures, which may change as you go along. Winning the grant is only half the battle. Getting your hands on the money can be a lengthy process. Make sure that you have enough cash to ride that period out, together with

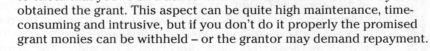

the patience of a saint for those occasions when you get a confusing, delayed or contradictory answer – consider modelling yourself on Saint Cornelius, Patron Saint of Earache.

Addressing pension-led funding arrangements

Pension-led funding is a complex arrangement that requires compliance with both pensions and financial services law. You must consult an independent financial adviser to talk through the funding process and ensure that you can legally proceed, before determining whether it's a suitable arrangement for you to undertake.

The business itself has to undergo a due diligence process, similar to that undertaken by angel investors (which I describe earlier in the 'Conducting due diligence' section). The reason is that under pensions law, any pension scheme that provides funding must ensure that the scheme stands to benefit from the investment, and that the assets being invested in are worth the money being advanced from the pension fund. Your financial advisor, or pension-led funding specialist, undertakes this due diligence and clears you to proceed with the funding arrangement. You then have to transfer your existing pension (and those of any other participating business partners) into a SIPP or an SSAS (which I define in Chapter 3).

The scheme has to be registered with HMRC and administered by trustees – normally members of the scheme for an SSAS – or by an appointed administrator for a SIPP. If the pension fund is making a loan, this is secured by a charge over the assets on which the loan is based in favour of the pension fund.

This space is so heavily regulated that you don't have much scope to negotiate any of these arrangements. Watch out for the following:

- ✔ **Affordability:** Can you afford the stipulated monthly repayments of the amount borrowed? If you can't, you may find that the scheme comes to an abrupt end and you have to repay the monies advanced from the pension fund, plus face tax penalties.

- ✔ **Interest:** Is the rate of interest on the amount borrowed acceptable? It's normally 1 per cent above base rate.

- ✔ **Provider payments:** What payments do you have to make to the provider helping you? This line of funding isn't cheap. You can incur payments for initial consultations and for obtaining a valuation, a percentage fee due on transfer of the funds, and administrative fees for providers to look after the scheme for you.

Finalising the Agreement

Whichever funding option you choose from the ones I describe in this chapter, the conclusion of any written agreement doesn't signal an end to the legal formalities. Oh dear me, no:

- ✔ **In relation to debt finance:** The lender wants to ensure that its interest in any mortgage or charge is registered (with Companies House) to provide it with rights to the security in the event of your default. Without that registration the lender can be in the same position as any of your other creditors if you default.

- ✔ **In relation to funding in return for shares:** You need to comply with a number of steps. If you use a crowdfunding source (refer to the earlier 'Tying up crowdfunding agreements' section) to raise your investment, you may find that it offers its services (in return for a fee) in helping you with some of these formalities.

This section is probably dull compared to a visit to Las Vegas or a night out at the Rio Carnival, but the following points are mighty important:

- ✔ **Shareholder consent:** You may need to pass an Ordinary Resolution to show the investor that you have the authority to issue more shares (equity-based crowdfunders insist on it). If you pass an Ordinary Resolution, it needs to be drafted, proposed (with appropriate notice to other shareholders) and passed (with the decision minuted). Or you may need formal written consent from other individual shareholders if they have some of the minority controls that I identify earlier in the section 'Tackling Share Investor Agreements: Equity Funding'.

- ✔ **Shareholder adherence:** You may need the new shareholder(s) to sign up to (*adhere* to) the existing shareholder agreement. If no standard adherence document is attached to the end of your shareholder agreement, you have to create one.

- ✔ **Changing Articles:** If you use crowdfunding arrangements, you may find that no formal process exists for adherence to the existing shareholder agreement. But crowdfunding investors are automatically bound by the Articles (including any updated version that the crowdfunder insists you adopt as a condition of allowing your company to be invested in – refer to 'Tying up crowdfunding agreements' earlier in this chapter). Such approval may require you to change your Articles to include modernised provisions. Angel investors may require you to do this in any event, to include in the new Articles provisions that favour them.

✔ **Companies House notifications:** If new shares are being issued, you need to notify Companies House – normally using Form SH01, which sets out the new share structure, including:

- The total number of shares in each class

- The nominal value of those shares

- The rights attached to each class of shares

- Whether the shares have been 'paid up' or (if not) the amount remaining 'unpaid'

✔ **Stock transfer forms:** If existing shares are being transferred in return for investment, you must get a *stock transfer form* executed. This standard form sets out the name of the company in which the shares are being traded, the number of shares involved, the sale price, the name of the current holder of the shares and the person to whom the shares are to be transferred.

✔ **Stamp duty:** If the investor pays more than £1,000 for her shares, she has to pay stamp duty on the amount paid (called the *consideration*). The current rate of stamp duty is 0.5 per cent of the consideration (rounded up to the nearest £5). You have to send the signed stock transfer form to HMRC within 30 days of the 'effective date of the transfer' (usually the date on which you sign the stock transfer form), together with the amount of stamp duty payable by the investor (if it hasn't already been paid). HMRC stamps the form as evidence of payment and returns it to the party that sent it.

No stamp duty fees are payable on an allotment of new shares – the duty only applies to share transfers.

✔ **Registering share changes:** After your business receives payment for the shares, it must formally approve the stamped stock transfer form if a transfer has been involved and (whether for a transfer or a new issue of shares) the registration of the new share owner as a shareholder *(member)* of the company. This approval is normally done via a Board meeting. Your business then enters the name of the new shareholder in the shareholder register (one of the corporate documents that a company is required to keep) along with the details of her shareholding and (in the case of a transfer) amends the previous details of the transferor.

✔ **Supplying share certificates:** Your company has to provide the new shareholder with a share certificate as proof of share ownership. For a transfer, you (or the transferor) send the existing share certificate to the company when executing the stock transfer form and a new certificate for the investor (the *transferee*) is issued within two months of the date of transfer. Similarly, on a new allotment of new shares, a share certificate is issued to the investor for her shares (and the same two-month limit applies).

Part II
Launching Your Business – Legal Essentials

Top Five Tips for Working with Staff

- ✔ Stay aware of current legislation – it changes all the time and the requirements on employers are getting tougher.

- ✔ Don't assume that just because you call someone a 'consultant' that's how the law or HMRC sees the person.

- ✔ Make sure that you have a written agreement with all your employees and contractors.

- ✔ Produce a staff handbook to avoid repeating all your policies in every contract – updating those policies is then easier.

- ✔ Take care when you employ temporary staff – engaging interns and using zero-hour contracts can be penny wise and pound foolish if not handled properly.

web extras

Check out the intellectual property quiz in the online article at www.dummies.com/extras/lawforsmallbusinessuk.

In this part . . .

✔ Understand the legal differences of 'employees' and 'contractors'.

✔ Get your online Terms and Conditions into shape.

✔ Meet your legal workplace responsibilities.

✔ Protect your intellectual property with copyrights, trademarks, patents and design rights.

✔ Ensure that your business software delivers what you want.

Chapter 5

Contracting Consultants and Employees

You can't do everything in your business all on your own. Even most sole traders need help from other people.

As I describe in this chapter, the most likely candidates to help you out are contractors that you engage to carry out projects for your business, non-executive directors (or NEDs) that give you independent advice and, of course, employees.

Creating Contractor Agreements

If you want to work with contractors, join the club. Over 4 million work in the UK and with traditional long-term employment opportunities reducing, you can expect more people to join the contractor bandwagon.

Taking the acid test: Defining contractors

No legal definition exists, but in practice *independent contractors* are people in business on their own account and who're responsible for deciding how that business is conducted. This description also applies to *consultants* and *freelancers,* but I use *contractor* to cover all such relationships in this section.

Contractor controversy

Many advantages exist for your firm and the contractor in having this relationship, including tax and National Insurance relief for both; it also frees you from a (vast) raft of statutory employment protection legislation.

But just because someone is labelled an independent contractor doesn't prove that he is one. You have to consider the facts of the relationship and the overall picture to decide whether such a relationship exists.

These types of arrangements have come under increasing scrutiny by the courts and Her Majesty's Revenue and Customs (HMRC) – in the context of the 'intermediaries' legislation or the Income Tax (Earnings and Pensions) Act, 2003 (or 'IR35' legislation; https://www.gov.uk/guidance/ir35-find-out-if-it-applies).

This Act seeks to prevent *disguised employment,* which is where you engage independent contractors through a service company in order to avoid the resultant tax and employment duties, when they are, in effect, 'employees'. A significant amount of overlap exists between the tests to determine a genuinely self-employed contractor and a contractor operating via a limited liability company for IR35 purposes, and so I combine them in this chapter.

Essentially, the status of the worker must be truly independent to be self-employed and to fall outside the scope of IR35.

Contractors whose contracts fail the IR35 tests can end up paying 12 per cent more in taxes than a similar employee earning the same wage. Furthermore, a contractor who can successfully claim that he's an employee can make a claim against a business for unfair dismissal as long as he has the relevant length of service (two years continuous service). You don't want that sort of thing happening to you.

When a contractor is a contractor

Here are some factors that HMRC takes into account when it investigates your engagements with contractors to decide whether you're really dealing with a contractor or an employee. Some of these may surprise you, but I see many so-called contractor agreements that wouldn't pass these tests:

- ✔ **No mutuality of obligation:** Independent contractors are able to 'pick and choose' the work that they undertake. When they agree to do work, they don't have to provide it personally and can delegate it. In effect, you have no obligation to offer them work and they have no obligation to undertake the work offered. If you offer continuous work, it indicates that the relationship is based on employment: it suggests that the contractor expects to be provided with future work. Giving a contractor a limited 'project' to perform, however, is okay.

'It's Been a Hard Day's Night', sang The Beatles, but if they were contractors that was only because they chose to work those hours. They were quite the experts on employment law, as you can discover throughout this chapter.

✓ **Substitution:** Contractors can select a substitute to carry out the work in their place. The contractor or his firm must meet the cost of sending a substitute. A right to substitute isn't likely to be genuine if the agreement requires the contractor to provide the service solely in a personal capacity. As far as you're concerned, who actually does the work doesn't matter so long as it's completed.

✓ **Control:** You should only control the outcome or end result of the particular project; the process of how the work is done has to be left solely to the contractor. If you exercise a high level of control over when, where or how contractors provide their services, it indicates an employer/employee relationship.

✓ **Use of equipment:** Self-employed contractors are expected to provide their own equipment and not rely on that supplied by you.

✓ **Alternative work:** Most contractors work on numerous different projects. A requirement to work solely or exclusively for one client is likely to signal an employer/employee relationship.

✓ **Financial records:** The way in which contractors are paid for services is important. Generally, a contractor invoices you when the service is completed and receives a fee rather than a payment resembling wages.

✓ **Separation of services:** Clear separation must exist between the services provided as a contractor and your business. The contractor should have no involvement in the running of your business and shouldn't be tied to your business (for example, by attending staff meetings, using facilities on a regular basis or going on your away-day team-bonding trips to build river rafts out of packets of crisps). The Beatles aren't talking about contractors when they sing 'All Together Now'.

✓ **Level of liability:** Independent contractors must maintain their own public liability insurance (against damage or personal injury to members of the public) and carry the risk if the work isn't carried out properly on a particular project.

✓ **Employee benefits:** Employees are protected by employment legislation and are entitled to receive statutory payments, and they also possess the right not to be unfairly dismissed (check out the later section 'Hitting the brick wall: Terminating employment'). A contractor engaged in a contract for services isn't entitled to receive these statutory payments or benefits. If the 'contractor' agreement says that the person does, it's probably not a contractor relationship.

✔ **Tax:** You aren't required to make deductions for tax purposes such as PAYE or National Insurance contributions (NICs) on a contract for services with an intermediary or personal contractor if the preceding tests are passed.

If HMRC undertakes an investigation, finds an employer/employee relationship and deems the contractor to be a disguised employee, all fees paid are then taxed as salary and you're liable for unpaid PAYE and NICs with the possibility of fines for late payment. Ouch!

The uncertainty surrounding the application of these tests by HMRC has prompted repeated calls for the abolition of the IR35 regime in its entirety. The government decided against abolition, however, and in fact the Finance Act, 2013 widened the remit. The legislation brings in more taxes – well, you aren't going to get mosquitoes voting for a reduction in their blood supply, are you? So these rules are likely to apply for the foreseeable future, meaning that you must be careful to avoid falling within their scope. No wonder The Beatles sang for 'Help'!

Drafting contractor agreements

As well as remembering the factors in the preceding section, when drafting a service agreement with a contractor you also have to create the right kind of commercial arrangement for you. Here are some additional commercial clauses you can include:

✔ **Defining the scope of the work:** Give details of the finished project or work. This clarity is commercially important for all parties. The contract doesn't have to specify *how* the work should be carried out though.

✔ **Agreeing confidentiality:** Include a confidentiality clause, because the contractor could be working for other clients within a particular sector ('Do you want to know a secret?'; make sure that your contractor keeps quiet about sensitive business information).

✔ **Securing intellectual property (IP):** State that any IP in work the contractor carries out belongs to you, and include the date from when this clause takes effect. Otherwise, contractors may end up owning any IP they create (jump to Chapter 8 to get more on IP).

Having a clause of this kind is another sign that the contractor agreement is genuine, because under an employment agreement you don't need to include such a clause (copyright in works created by employees generally belongs automatically to the employer). If you need any other rights in the contractor's work (for example, the right to edit, alter, distribute, sell, exploit), it's best to spell it out.

✔ **Payment of fees:** Ensure that the agreement states clearly how you pay the contractor's fees, at what intervals and how they're calculated: for example, whether it's a fixed sum per month/per project, whether a bonus is payable and if so on what basis, whether particular targets should first be met, and so on. The statement doesn't refer to holiday pay, sick pay or pensions, because the contractor's self-employed status means that's his responsibility.

✔ **Getting a commitment:** You can get a contractor to prioritise your work over other work he may have, but you can't include an exclusivity clause.

✔ **Agreeing the term:** Define the term of the contract. It can't be extremely long or on an indefinite or 'rolling' basis (those automatically renewed unless expressly ended by one of the parties), because that leans towards the existence of an employee relationship. The scope of the project should dictate the term.

You can include a clause that either party may terminate for any business-related reason with a minimum notice period. This clause can also allow you to terminate for poor performance.

✔ **Allocating risk:** State what happens if the project is late, or if faulty or infringing materials are delivered, and be clear on who's responsible for obtaining relevant insurance. These provisions are partly commercial in nature and partly go to the root of the relationship. The more the onus falls on the contractor to sort things out, the more likely the contract is to pass any scrutiny.

'Working 9 to 5': Employing People

A contract of employment between an employer and an employee is a legally binding document as long as certain conditions are met. The employee must accept your offer of employment and in return you agree to pay the person. The contract can be in writing, verbal or a combination of both. The contract contains expressed and 'implied' terms, and it can incorporate terms found in other documents (such as the employee handbook; see the later section 'Publishing policies and procedures in a handbook'). In general, the more senior the employee, the more detailed the contract. Plus, the contract is subject to a whole slew of employment legislation that I detail in Chapter 7.

This section sets out some of the main provisions of an employment contract. It contains a lot of references to statutes, because for some perfectly valid reasons employment law is heavily regulated – one reason why people are often keen to classify their relationship with each other as one of client and contractor instead (check out the earlier 'Taking the acid test: Defining contractors' section).

Including the right commercial terms

Here are some express terms that you ought to cover from a commercial point of view. If these make you anxious, don't worry – 'I Want to Hold Your Hand' as we go through them:

- ✔ **Job title and description:** Essential, because arguments can arise later if the role isn't tightly defined. I know this is difficult in a small and medium-size enterprise (SME) where everybody does a bit of everything, but employment wrangles often stem from a mismatch of expectations between employer and employee as to the employee's duties.

- ✔ **Term:** Includes the date on which the employment began and when it's expected to end. This term can be a fixed or a 'rolling' period (the term carries on unless either side terminates with the required notice period), or it may just continue indefinitely. You can state that the initial period of employment is subject to an evaluation by the employer, normally three months, which allows you to end the agreement quickly if the person just isn't working out.

- ✔ **Hours of work:** As The Beatles foresaw, 'Eight Days a Week' isn't permissible – I look at working time regulations in Chapter 7.

- ✔ **Location of work:** If you need an employee to travel to Outer Mongolia, you're better to spell that out from the start to avoid arguments if the employee expects to remain in your office in Hillingdon seven days a week. Provide for who makes travel arrangements, how expenses are to be claimed and so on.

- ✔ **Pay and benefits:** The rate of pay and intervals at which it's paid must be clear, as should any other benefits: for example, pension schemes, bonuses, private medical insurance and so on. Share options are dealt with in a separate share option agreement (which I discuss later in this chapter in the section 'Implementing options or other share schemes').

- ✔ **Holiday entitlements:** Define length and any rules about giving notice.

- ✔ **Confidentiality:** If an employee has access to any confidential information, include specific terms providing that he mustn't disclose or copy this information during or after employment. All employees owe an implied duty of confidence to their employer. A confidentiality clause is wider in scope and imposes a duty to keep your trade secrets under wraps along with specific information such as customer lists or know-how.

✔ **Notice periods and termination:** Spell out notice periods to be given before the agreement can be terminated. Also, because most disputes arise at this stage of the employment relationship, specify when you as the employer are entitled to terminate without notice (for example, for gross misconduct) and specific provisions relating to dismissal for poor performance.

If an employee is also a director, state that on termination he must automatically resign as a director so that you don't have to rely on the Articles or Shareholder Agreement to remove him from that role. With senior employees, you can include a 'gardening leave clause', requiring the person to stay away from the office but still remain employed during all or part of his notice. This ensures that a disgruntled senior employee isn't hanging around the office during the notice period, causing trouble. (The full title of the relevant Beatles song is 'All You Need Is Love, But It Helps to Have a Gardening Leave Clause'.)

✔ **Post-term restrictions:** These *restrictive covenants* restrict employees' activities after the end of their employment. They're particularly important in the contracts of senior employees, who're often in possession of confidential information about the business, have formed strong working relationships with key clients throughout their employment and may possess influence over other employees. They could use this information post-termination for their own benefit or for the benefit of a competitor. These covenants are a form of protection for you against such use, and can also act as a deterrent during and after employment to any employee considering such use.

A 'watertight' restrictive covenant that's definitely enforceable by a court doesn't exist, and so from a commercial point of view make your clauses as effective as possible. The courts strike a balance between the right of employers to protect their legitimate business interests and the right of individuals to use their skills for the benefit of themselves.

Courts don't allow covenants that 'unreasonably' restrict employees' right to earn. Here are some typical restrictions and factors that influence whether or not such covenants are allowed:

- **Non-compete:** This clause prevents a former employee from working for a competitor in a similar capacity or seeking to set up a competing business. These clauses tend to be the most onerous covenants, because they limit a person's ability to make a living for the duration of the restriction.

- **Non-poaching:** Not about rabbit hunting, this clause aims to prevent former employees from trying to take their ex-employer's staff to their new employment/business.

- **Non-solicitation:** Nothing to do with the activities of ladies (or indeed gentlemen) of the night, this clause imposes a duty not to approach an ex-employer's customers or prospective customers with a view to engaging in business with them.

- **Non-dealing:** This clause differs from non-solicitation and prevents former employees from dealing with customers or clients of the former employer when the customers initiate the approach.

For these kinds of clause to be enforceable, you require a legitimate business interest in need of protection and the protection sought can be no more than is reasonably necessary to protect that interest. The courts place the burden on the employer to prove that the restriction is reasonable. To meet this requirement, the court considers three main issues:

- **Duration of the restrictions:** Critical in deciding whether a particular covenant can be enforced. Common practice is for restrictive covenants to apply for periods of between 6 and 12 months (courts have upheld the right of employers to enforce restrictions on senior employees for periods of up to 12 months). Covenants in excess of 12 months are less likely to be enforced, other than in exceptional circumstances. If the employer invokes a gardening leave clause, it needs to deduct its duration from the length of the covenant.

- **Geographical scope:** Limit the geographical remit of the covenant to an area that's necessary in the circumstances. If a business is located primarily in the UK, don't bother seeking to impose a restriction that applies worldwide – such a covenant is too wide and unlikely to be enforceable.

- **Breadth of the restrictions:** Courts review the range of each individual restriction and the total number of restrictions. For example, a non-poaching restriction is more likely to be upheld if it applies only to the poaching of senior staff who've worked for the employer during (say) the 12 months preceding the end of the term than if it applies to all staff whether the employee knew or had any interaction with them while working for the employer. Likewise, a non-compete clause is more likely to be enforced if it relates to a tightly defined business sector than if it applies to 'all related sectors', 'all similar sectors' or simply 'all sectors'.

The courts also look at how damaging a breach of the proposed restriction would genuinely be to the employer, whether less onerous restrictions would have provided sufficient protection and whether such covenants are generally used within that specific sector.

Restrictive covenants are helpful in deterring ex-employees from damaging behaviour after they leave your business. They're also useful bargaining chips if an ex-employee wants to join another business and your restrictive covenants get in the way. Don't overdo it though: unenforceable restrictions don't achieve either of these objectives.

Being aware of implied terms

All employment contracts contain certain implied terms in addition to the more obvious expressed ones. These terms can be implied into a contract in a number of ways:

- ✔ By custom and practice
- ✔ By statute
- ✔ To reflect the presumed intention of the parties

For instance, an employee is subject to an implied duty of confidence and a duty to work with due diligence and care. An employer is under an implied duty of trust and confidence to the employee and a duty to take care of the employee's health and safety.

For a term to become implied by custom and practice, it usually needs to be long-standing and must have been followed without exception for a certain period of time (for example, the provision of a Christmas bonus each year for several years). Any term implied by custom also needs to be reasonable in the circumstances, fair and not arbitrary, and given automatically to all employees.

Publishing policies and procedures in a handbook

In addition to the contract of employment, many employers publish separate policies and procedures dealing with varying aspects of the employment relationship and make the contract subject to the rules set out in the employee handbook. This approach can be a practical and cost-effective solution for many small businesses, because employment law is ever-evolving with new regulations being introduced on a constant basis.

If you include policies on regulated areas in the contract, they can be more difficult to change at a later date. But containing these policies in a separate employee handbook allows you to update them at the same time for all employees. The handbook can make specific reference to matters such as health and safety, data protection issues, Internet usage and social media, disciplinary rules, poor performance, and any other relevant issues.

If you don't have your own staff handbook, and you don't want to go to the cost of creating your own human resources (HR) department, you can source one from a specialist who provides HR services on a consultancy basis.

Hitting the brick wall: Terminating employment

Many industry surveys highlight the fact that small businesses are more likely to end up before employment tribunals, most often in relation to claims of unfair dismissal. Any such claim can be extremely costly, disruptive and stressful for you. Therefore, have a clear set of rules about termination in place to help avoid such claims occurring and to help minimise losses if such a claim is unavoidable.

'The Advisory, Conciliation and Arbitration Service (ACAS) Code of Conduct: Disciplinary and Grievance Procedures' is no page-turner, but it's quite helpful (you can obtain a copy from the ACAS website: www.acas.org.uk). Although not legally binding, employment tribunals often take compliance with this code into account. Also, if you dismiss an employee without following this code, you face an increased risk of the dismissal being found unfair; plus, any compensation awarded can be increased by up to 25 per cent.

Employees have two key types of potential claim against their employers: wrongful and unfair dismissals. (I deal with other claims involving discrimination or redundancy in Chapter 7.)

Wrongful dismissal

A claim for *wrongful dismissal* arises due to a breach of the terms of the employment contract. If a contract is terminated properly, in accordance with its terms, a claim doesn't arise. These claims usually concern a dismissal where the termination isn't carried out in accordance with the employment contract. Here are some examples:

- ✔ Wrongly terminating a fixed-term contract before the end of that term.
- ✔ Failing to make a payment instead of notice where the contract requires it.
- ✔ Failing to give the minimum statutory period of notice if it's a contract without a fixed length.

> ✔ Failing to give 'reasonable' notice for a contract with no notice period. *Reasonable notice* is defined as a minimum of one week's notice after four weeks' service. This period increases to a minimum of two weeks' notice after completion of two years' service, and a further one week's notice for each additional year of service up to a maximum of 12 weeks' notice after 12 years' service. Got that? Good, I test you later!

Your only defences as an employer for a claim of wrongful dismissal are that you did give proper notice or that gross misconduct exists on the employee's part, which allows the employer to dismiss the person without notice.

Unfair dismissal

Employees can bring a claim for unfair dismissal if the employer doesn't have a valid reason for ending their employment. Generally, only employees who've worked for a certain period (a *qualifying period*) have a right to bring a claim for *unfair dismissal*. Under the Employment Rights Act, 1996, the qualifying period in order to be able to bring a claim of this kind is a minimum of two years' continuous service with the employer. If an employee has worked for you for less than this period of time, saying 'Hello Goodbye' is easier.

Certain dismissals however are 'automatically unfair' and can be brought regardless of the length of service, including where the claim relates to any of the following:

> ✔ The employee's trade union membership or activities

> ✔ The making of a protected disclosure under whistle-blowing legislation

> ✔ Following health and safety rules

> ✔ The employee asserting a statutory right

> ✔ Pregnancy or maternity leave

If an employee resigns in response to a very serious *(fundamental)* breach of his contract by you, he's treated as having been dismissed unfairly (known as *constructive dismissal*). Examples include:

> ✔ Unilaterally cutting an employee's pay

> ✔ Attempting to force an employee to resign

> ✔ Threatening to dismiss an employee if he doesn't agree to certain changes, such as to his job description or duties

> ✔ Varying the terms of employment without the employee's agreement

An employee claiming constructive dismissal must bring that claim without delay and show that he resigned due to the breach.

In order to defend a claim for unfair dismissal, you have to demonstrate that a 'fair reason' exists for the dismissal and that you followed fair procedures before the dismissal. Five potentially fair reasons exist:

- **Misconduct:** Claims concerning misconduct can give rise to automatic dismissal and often (but not always) involve extremely serious 'gross misconduct', such as theft, violence or wilful damage. Even in these cases, best practice is to follow fair procedures, such as those set out in the ACAS Code of Practice, or to at a minimum:

  - Carry out an investigation into the matter.

  - Hold a disciplinary hearing.

  - Make sure that you give the employee advance notice of the hearing in writing and provide full details of the alleged misconduct in writing.

  - Provide a number of warnings including an oral warning, a first written warning and a final written warning before dismissal, along with an opportunity to appeal. (Theft is an exception, because dismissal can be instant.)

- **Poor performance or lack of capability:** Dismissals regarding competency or ability to carry out duties aren't 'fair' unless the employer gives the employee a fair opportunity to improve. Here are some things you have to do to meet that standard:

  - Set out clearly in writing where the employee is falling short and provide fair targets to be met within a defined period.

  - State in writing the consequences of failing to achieve the required standards within that time frame.

  - Provide training or show consideration of redeployment to another role.

  - Make sure that what you expect of an employee is in line with what's set out in his contract of employment.

In cases of long-term illness and absence, refer to a doctor or medical expert before pursuing dismissal. If medical evidence shows that an employee is unable to return to work within a reasonable time frame, you can dismiss the employee fairly.

What's reasonable or fair also depends on the nature of the business and the position held by the employee; for example, a small business is less able to cope with continuing absence from illness. A short-term illness isn't grounds for fair dismissal. If a person has a disability recognised under the Equality Act, 2010, you must take care to ensure that, as the employer, you've met your obligation to make 'reasonable adjustments' to accommodate that disability before taking dismissal action.

✔ **Redundancy:** Here are a number of conditions to bear in mind before you can fairly make someone redundant:

- A genuine redundancy situation must exist, where a business or part of it is shut down completely, shut down at a specific location or the requirement for employees to do work of a particular kind has reduced or come to an end.

- You must use fair selection criteria when selecting employees for redundancy and the employees must be consulted about the reasons for their selection.

- You can take performance into account, but you have to use it in conjunction with other objective criteria, such as qualifications, attendance and disciplinary record.

- You must consider employees for redeployment in other areas if possible.

- The period of consultation should last between two and four weeks. You need to hold at least two meetings with each employee before any redundancies take place.

- Employees dismissed because of redundancy can be entitled to statutory redundancy payments if they have two or more years of service.

- If you're proposing to dismiss 20 or more employees within a period of 90 days, the Trade Union and Labour Relations (Consolidation) Act, 1992 provides that you have a duty to consult collectively with employee representatives.

- Dismissing an employee in connection with the purchase, sale or transfer of a business is usually unfair under the Transfer of Undertakings (Protection of Employment) Regulations (TUPE), unless you have a sound economic, technical or organisational reason.

✔ **Illegality:** You have legality issues with continuing to employ the employee in his current capacity. You may be permitted to dismiss employees if they can no longer perform their duties in a legal manner and no other suitable work is available for that employee. For example, if it becomes illegal to carry out a role without a qualification that they don't have.

✔ **Other substantial reasons:** To rely on one of these other reasons for dismissal, they need to be overwhelming, you must've looked at alternatives and no other appropriate option must exist in the circumstances.

Reasons that have previously fallen into this category include the following (again, you must employ fair procedures):

- Imprisonment of the person, which seems fair enough (as long as it's at Her Majesty's pleasure and not you locking a troublesome employee in a cupboard!)

- Irresolvable personality clash between the person and a co-worker

- Unreasonably refusing to accept a business reorganisation

Implementing options or other share schemes

If you're thinking that some of the preceding sections are a bit negative about employment, you'll enjoy this one because it's about something jolly and positive: incentivising employees with shares.

Enterprise Management and Incentive (EMI) option schemes

You can grant your employees options to acquire company ordinary shares in the future at an advantageous (low) price in accordance with the rules of your EMI scheme. In turn, the employees can exercise their right to acquire such shares at a later date by letting you know that they're doing so and paying that price.

This attractive alternative for many small businesses provides a means by which you can retain and attract the best employees without the expense of large salaries or bonuses. In return, employees have a personal interest in the growth of the company and are motivated to maximise their performance. These schemes may also provide many tax benefits for employees (and the employer too).

Here are six things you need to know about EMI schemes:

- ✔ HMRC administers the EMI scheme, and so you need to get an accountant to help you register the scheme there.

- ✔ No tax is payable when the option is granted for employees and the employer.

- ✔ To exercise the option, the employee must pay income tax on the difference between the market value of his shares at the date of exercise and the value of the price he paid. So, if the options were granted at a price that represented a big discount from the market value of the company at the time of grant, a larger amount of income tax is payable when the options are exercised.

✔ Both employee and employer need to pay National Insurance tax on the amount of the gain, if the shares are readily convertible into cash and were granted at a discount from their market value at the time of the grant.

✔ If the employee exercises the options and then goes on to sell his shares, he has to pay Capital Gains Tax (CGT) on the difference between the value of the shares sold and the value of the price he paid to exercise the options. This is generally more advantageous than paying income tax, because of a CGT allowance: beyond that allowance, CGT is only payable at 18 per cent (for a basic income tax earner) or at the higher 28 per cent rate (for a higher tax earner). Certain employees may even be eligible for entrepreneurs' tax relief and pay CGT at 10 per cent if they hold a sufficient number of shares (see Chapter 18).

✔ The company can deduct the cost of setting up and administering the scheme when calculating its corporation tax and any increase in the value of shares also attracts corporation tax savings.

You need to consider whether an EMI scheme is appropriate for your particular small company, because you have to meet and adhere to quite a number of requirements and a certain level of administration. I review this 'Long and Winding Road' now:

✔ **Qualifying company:** A company qualifies if:

- It's an *independent* trading company (it isn't a subsidiary of another company or under the control of another company) and its gross assets don't exceed £30 million.

- It carries on a qualifying trade within the UK (non-qualifying trades include banking, insurance, hire purchase, legal/accountancy services, property development, and dealing in shares, land or securities).

- It has fewer than 250 full-time employees.

✔ **Qualifying employee:** Employees qualify for the grant of an EMI option if they work for the company (or qualifying subsidiary of that company) for at least 25 hours a week, or 75 per cent of their working time (if less) is on the business of the company. A grant can be made to directors if they meet these requirements. Granting this option to non execs isn't usual, because they can't normally satisfy the working time commitment.

✔ **Qualifying options:** A number of conditions apply:

- The option must be in writing and list the date of the grant, number of shares the employee is being granted, the option price at which the employee can buy them and any performance conditions or restrictions on the shares. Options can be subject to performance conditions as long as they're clearly stated.

- Therefore, you can grant the options over shares to an employee in return for some tangible achievement for your business, such as achieving a unit-sales, revenue, profit or market-share target.

- You can stipulate that the options are granted and exercisable over time – for example, options granted annually over 'x' number of shares (thus giving an employee an incentive to stay on with the company). An EMI option must be capable of being exercised within ten years, however, because otherwise the tax advantage is lost.

- In practice, employees often exercise options just before the company is sold, because they know that they're going to be in funds after the sale takes place and so can afford the exercise price of their options and any tax due on exercise.

✔ **Limits on options:** An employee can't hold more than 30 per cent of the ordinary shares of the company or more than £250,000 in unexercised options at any time. The total value of all unexercised options granted by the company can't exceed £3 million.

✔ **Disqualifying events:** Such an event occurs if the company:

- No longer meets the independence test (that is, it becomes a subsidiary of or is controlled by another company)

- No longer satisfies the qualifying trade requirement

- Converts the ordinary shares that are the subject of the option into a different class of shares

A disqualifying event also occurs if the employee no longer satisfies the working time requirement or receives share options in excess of the £250,000 limit.

If a disqualifying event does occur, but the EMI option is exercised within 90 days of the event, the available tax advantages still apply.

✔ **Practical requirements:** One strict requirement is that all EMI options must be notified electronically to HMRC within 92 days of being granted. Failure to do so results in the loss of tax relief. All companies with an EMI scheme are required to register the scheme with the HMRC (with the Small Company Enterprise Centre, or SCEC) and submit an annual return in respect of the EMI option. Although you're not required to gain pre-approval of an EMI scheme, a company can seek advance assurance from the SCEC regarding authorisation to grant such options or regarding share valuation in order to provide tax certainty.

Unapproved option schemes

Sometimes you want to incentivise people you work with, but they aren't employees within the definition of an EMI scheme. Maybe they don't work the qualifying number of hours or maybe they're contractors or non execs. Or maybe your company doesn't qualify for the EMI scheme (for example, because it carries out one of the excluded trades).

If so, you can set up an *unapproved option scheme* (UOS) for these people. The taxation rules are in principle very similar but carry more flexibility: you don't have to fulfil the strict qualifying conditions for an EMI scheme and the scheme doesn't require HMRC advance approval (though you do have to report option grants to HMRC, as with an EMI scheme). That very flexibility means, however, that UOSs can potentially vary from company to company, and so definitely check out the structure of your proposed scheme with your accountant first, to ensure that it achieves all the desired tax consequences.

Complying with pensions law

If you think that the legislation regarding EMI schemes in the preceding section is complicated, wait until you start to read about pensions legislation. It's enough to make you 'Twist and Shout'.

Pension legalities

The new pension regulations involved are quite complex, which is unsurprising given the nature of the pensions system itself. Compliance for any business involves a significant financial and administrative burden, and I can hear you groaning at the thought of having to deal with all that. Too bad. If you don't comply, the Pensions Regulator has the power to issue 'compliance notices' directing the employer to take or refrain from certain actions in order to comply with the legislation.

Failure to comply can attract a fixed penalty notice or an escalating penalty. So, don't be 'The Fool on the Hill': get involved and make sure that you comply. Your accountant should understand the various rules involved in the new system, even if you don't.

To deal with your responsibilities, which arose as a result of the 2015 Pension Regulations, you have to address a number of things, as I detail here, which place an obligation on you to help fund your employee's pension. Any outstanding contributions must be paid within three months and, if still outstanding after this time, the employer is liable to pay both the employer and employee contributions.

To prepare, you should confirm your staging date (see the following list), review all employees to identify whether they're eligible, draw up policies for opting-out and in, and consider how to provide a qualifying scheme (for example, does a current scheme meet the requirements or would the government's default NEST option be more appropriate?). You may find that having all eligible employees enrolled in the same scheme is more cost-effective.

Here are some starters for ten:

- ✔ You now have a duty to enrol all employees in a pension scheme (called *duty of enrolment*). This new law applies to all employers with at least one employee, meaning that *all* SMEs need to comply.

- ✔ The Pensions Regulator has allocated all companies a *staging date* (between October 2012 and February 2018) and these new duties apply from this date (check out `www.thepensionsregulator.gov.uk/employers/staging-date.aspx`). As an employer, you can ask to defer enrolment for three months.

- ✔ You're required to ensure that eligible employees are enrolled into the pension scheme. The employee has no obligation to complete any form or to provide any information.

- ✔ Minimum employer contributions are 3 per cent of the employee's qualifying earnings from the staging date. You must register online with the Pensions Regulator within four months of your staging date and confirm that you've fulfilled this obligation.

This intervention is well-intentioned and designed to make sure that employees have some income protection for their old age and are less of a burden for the state.

I don't know about you, but I'm expecting to have to work until I'm at least 140, and so some of this seems a bit academic. Nonetheless, here are the main features relating to auto-enrolment:

- ✔ **Eligible job holder:** People working in the UK, over 22 years of age and below state pension age, and earning above a certain amount or *trigger* (currently £7,475) must be auto-enrolled. You have to inform all eligible job holders that they're being automatically enrolled and that they have a right to opt out. Directors with no contract of employment aren't eligible.

- ✔ **Non-eligible job holder:** People aged between 16 and 75 who don't meet the age/salary criteria. You have to inform them that they're entitled to enter a pension scheme, and if they take up this right, you must make contributions for them as if they're an eligible job holder.

✔ **Entitled workers:** People working in the UK under a contract of employment with the employer and earning less than the threshold. They can require you to allow them to join a pension scheme, although you aren't required to make contributions.

You have to monitor the status of all workers on an ongoing basis: an ineligible employee can become eligible if his earnings rise (or he reaches the age threshold) and you must then auto-enrol him.

✔ **Opt-out clause:** Employees can opt out of a scheme after one month. You can't encourage them to opt out or give financial incentives to encourage such opt out, or contract out of, limit or exclude any of your auto-enrolment duties. Employees can't suffer any detriment in their employment as a result of being enrolled.

✔ **Re-enrolment:** You must re-enrol all eligible employees who opted out after three years, to encourage them to reconsider their position.

✔ **Qualifying scheme:** All employers must enrol their employees into a qualifying pension scheme. Existing pension schemes can qualify as long as they meet the minimum standard for the level of contributions made or the level of benefit provided as set out in the Pension Act, 2008.

Defined contribution schemes

A bewildering number of pension schemes exist, but most likely to be relevant for a small company are *defined contribution schemes.* Here the employer and employee agree on a set percentage of the employee's earnings to be contributed by both of them to an individual pension fund. The fund then invests this amount to produce a retirement income.

Here are the features of defined contribution schemes:

✔ The employee gets a limited amount of tax relief on contributed income, which is credited to the employee's pension fund. A limited amount of employer contributions can be set against corporation tax.

✔ As I cover in Chapter 3, members can (since April 2015) draw down as much of their defined contribution pension pots as they want from the age of 55 onwards. Apart from their 25 per cent lump-sum, tax-free entitlement, tax is payable at their marginal rate on whatever they draw down (you can see other aspects of this new flexible regime at `http://www.thepensionsregulator.gov.uk/employers/your-step-by-step-guide-to-automatic-enrolment.aspx`).

✔ Employers favour these arrangements, because the pension outlay is controlled and gradual, the cost involved is known from the outset and the liability for how the investment performs is passed onto the employee.

✔ The amount of income payable from such a scheme depends on a number of factors, including the following:

- Amount employee and employer contribute

- Level of charges

- How well the investments made under the scheme perform

- Type of retirement income chosen and how it's taken

✔ Defined contribution schemes that are already in place may be used for auto-enrolment as long as the minimum contribution requirements are met. Total contributions for each worker must be at least 8 per cent of that worker's qualifying earnings. The employer must contribute at least 3 per cent.

NEST

If your firm has no qualifying existing pension scheme in place, as an employer you must set up a new scheme based within the UK or the European Economic Area.

Alternatively you can sign up to use the National Employment Savings Trust (NEST), which the government has established as a default option (see www. nestpensions.org.uk). It has a public-interest function and is obliged to accept all employers. NEST can also be used alongside other qualifying pension schemes.

Working with Non-Executive Directors

No review of people helping out your business is complete without looking at *non-executive directors* (non execs or NEDs), board-level advisors who aren't employees. Think of this section as 'The Joy of Non Execs' (groan).

Getting the best from your non execs

Non execs can be vital to any company but especially for small ones. Some people stereotype NEDs as old, retired fuddy-duddies in tweed jackets just looking for something to do and somewhere to go, which can pay them a few bob when they're not playing golf. Rubbish.

Non execs are often dynamic individuals with altruistic motives, and their experience can be really helpful. For all the cleverness of the tech age, the same problems come up in business again and again, and a wise NED can help you avoid making the same mistakes that other firms make repeatedly. Here are some benefits non execs can bring to your company:

- ✔ **Independence:** This is perhaps the main attribute NEDs bring, which allows them to evaluate the governance and performance of your company in a more detached and objective way.

- ✔ **Experience:** They generally possess a lot of prior business experience and are perhaps more skilled than you in the areas of due diligence, corporate governance, raising finance and problem solving. Your company can gain valuable and cost-saving advice by appointing the right NED when financial burdens may be high.

- ✔ **Expertise:** They may be skilled in a particular industry or sector and bring particular expertise from which you can benefit.

- ✔ **Network:** They may have a very good network of contacts to deploy on behalf of your company.

The role offers NEDs flexibility; many relish the opportunity to act as mentors and help a new company progress, while gaining helpful insights and perspectives that they can take to their own companies.

You and the NED must conduct a sort of due diligence before the role is taken up. The NED must become familiar with your company and probe enough to be satisfied that he can carry out the role effectively. You also must be satisfied that you're engaging a NED suited to the role who can commit sufficient time and energy.

The UK Corporate Governance Code (the 'Code') sets out the standards of good practice that apply regarding these types of directorships (see http://www.frc.org.uk/Our-Work/Codes-Standards/Corporate-governance/UK-Corporate-Governance-Code.aspx). The Code details the fundamental importance of independence and lists situations where independence may not exist – for example, where the director has been an employee of the company/group within the last five years or has had links with other directors.

At Board meetings the NED should constructively challenge other directors if necessary, help with proposals on strategy and satisfy himself that all financial information is correct. To do so, the person must constantly keep up-to-date with matters relating to the company in order to be prepared and to contribute effectively at these meetings.

Contracting with non execs

You need to confirm the appointment of a NED with a written agreement *(letter of appointment),* the key features of which are as follows (they're mostly mentioned in the Code):

✔ **Status:** A NED is a *non-employee* and receives a *fee* as opposed to a salary (though some may waive the fee for a while for start-ups). Non execs are expected to devote only part of their time to the advisory role.

✔ **Term:** State the period of appointment and termination rights. Appoint the NED for a specific term; the Code requires the person to be subject to re-election (normally once every three years for small companies).

✔ **Duties and restrictions:** Define these aspects, including confidentiality and exactly what else your company expects of the NED (for example, 'reviewing strategy presented by the company' or 'reviewing annual business plans').

✔ **Other interests:** The NED should notify you of any new appointments he wants to take on (for approval) and any new business interests.

✔ **Fees and expenses:** Make sure to set these out. The Code makes no specific reference to granting shares to a NED. A review conducted on corporate governance (Higgs Review) recommended that NEDs should have the opportunity to take part of their remuneration in shares. The Code does state, however, that remuneration can't include performance-related share options or elements, because such perks can undermine the requirement of independence that's so essential for a non exec.

✔ **Time spent:** Specify the minimum time that the NED is required to spend on your company's business and confirm that he can commit that amount of time to the role.

✔ **Induction:** Confirm that the NED is to receive induction and ongoing training.

✔ **Insurance:** Commit to providing insurance to NEDs.

✔ **Non-compete:** Although the NED isn't an employee, you can include an anti-compete clause (refer to the earlier section 'Including the right commercial terms') for the duration of the engagement and a period of time afterwards.

✔ **Attendance at Board meetings:** Include the requirement to attend your Board meetings in the letter of appointment.

✔ **Compliance with director's duties:** The Companies Act doesn't distinguish between the duties of non execs and other directors, and so both have the same responsibilities. Check out Chapter 1, but these obligations include the requirement to act within the powers conferred by the company's constitution and to promote the success of the company for its members' benefit. Confirm these responsibilities in the letter of appointment.

Chapter 6

Dealing with Your Online Responsibilities

....

In This Chapter

▶ Sorting your online Terms and Conditions

▶ Setting out the necessary policies

▶ Complying with online laws

....

*I*f your business has a website, you need to create Terms and Conditions (Ts and Cs) for it. They go together like fish and chips, eggs and bacon, Posh and Becks and England losing at football on penalties. Normally the Ts and Cs comprise a bundle together with these other documents that link to each other: Acceptable Use Policy, Privacy Policy and Cookies Policy.

I look at the four documents in turn, and show you why they're important and what they must contain. I also show you how specific laws affect everything you do in your business online.

Minding Your Ps and Qs in Your Ts and Cs

Terms and Conditions set out the contractual and legal relationship between the website owner (that's you) and the consumer or other users of the site (called the *User*). They also give you the opportunity to comply with a growing number of laws that regulate the conduct of business online.

Here are the key terms to include in your website's Ts and Cs (if you don't have a document like this on your website, finish reading this chapter, put the book down and go get some Ts and Cs done):

- ✔ **Introduction, or general information:** The Ts and Cs give basic information about whoever's running the site. For example, 'This "Website" is run and maintained by [. . . . .] registered in England and Wales [Company number] and whose registered office is at [. . . . .] and whose VAT registration number is [. . . . .]'.

  If you're a member of any trade body or regulated by any regulatory body you must set that out here too. This part of the Ts and Cs also needs to describe the products and services available from you.

  The Companies Act, 2006 requires you to specify your registered office address, company registration number and place of registration on your site. In addition, the Electronic Commerce (EC Directive) Regulations, 2002 complement the Companies Act by requiring you to provide the following information easily, directly and permanently to the User:

  - Name of the service provider (if that's different from the trading name, you must explain the difference)

  - Details of the service provider, including an email address

  - Details of any trade association or professional body of which you're part

  - Your VAT number

- ✔ **Rights of use and access:** This clause makes clear that if the User uses the site, the person is automatically bound by the Ts and Cs. The clause also sets out limitations on the User's rights of access, which go together like bees and honey:

  - A User is given only a temporary right to use the site and only in accordance with the Ts and Cs and for her own personal use. This right may be withdrawn without notice, and no liability exists if the website is unavailable at any time or for any period.

  - If a User is provided with an identification code or password, she must treat it as confidential and not disclose it to anybody else.

- ✔ **Contributions and uploading of material to the website:** The Ts and Cs say that any interactive features that allow a User to upload material to the site, or to make contact with other Users of the website (such as through chat rooms or bulletin boards), must comply with content standards as set out in the Acceptable Use Policy (which you link to from the Ts and Cs). For more on this Policy, check out the later 'Presenting an Acceptable Use Policy' section.

✔ **Disclosure:** You also give yourself the right to disclose the User's identity to anybody claiming that material uploaded is infringing their intellectual property rights or their right to privacy. You also retain a right to remove any material uploaded or posted by a User if the material doesn't comply with the content standards set out in the Acceptable Use Policy. You can't have Ts and Cs without disclosure and take-down rights – they go together like cheese and pickle.

✔ **Reliance on information posted:** To minimise reliance by the User on material you display on the site, the Ts and Cs contain a clause that any comments or other materials posted on the site can't be relied on as advice, and exclude legal liability for any such reliance by the User or anybody else the person informs.

✔ **Intellectual property:** Make it very clear that as between you and the User, you own all rights in the site, including all trademarks, logos, graphics, photographs, videos, text, images or software used to operate the site. The User isn't allowed to licence any parts of the site to someone else, or modify, copy, sell, download or use any parts of the site for her own commercial purposes without your permission.

✔ **Data protection:** Users must be informed that information is collected and processed about them in accordance with the Privacy Policy for the site (see the section 'Prepping your Privacy and Cookie Policies' later in this chapter) and a link is provided to that Policy from the Ts and Cs. In addition, by using the site the User consents to this collection and processing and promises that all information provided is accurate. Making Users aware of your Privacy Policy and obtaining their consent to data collection blend well together like strawberries and cream. (I'm getting pretty hungry now!)

✔ **Links to other websites:** You want to make sure that you aren't responsible for links that you provide to other sites, because you don't know what's on those other sites or their terms. Your Ts and Cs say that you don't endorse or recommend any links to third-party sites and they're provided only for informational purposes. No responsibility is given in respect of these other sites and you aren't liable for any loss suffered as a result of visiting such sites. A right to prevent or veto links to your site being made by Users is also included, because you may not want some links from sites you don't approve of.

✔ **Viruses, hacking and other offences:** You want to make clear that the site can't be knowingly misused by introducing viruses, Trojans, or other material that's malicious or technologically harmful. (*Trojans* are malicious software, not ancient soldiers who download themselves from wooden horses.) Unauthorised access isn't allowed to the site, server or to any database connected to the site. Any such actions are likely in any event to be a criminal offence under the Computer Misuse Act, 1990, but including this provision gives you a contractual right and reason to terminate the User's use of the site, and the right to report any such actions to the relevant law enforcement authority. It's a double whammy, like vim and vigour.

✔ **Variation:** You may well want to change the Ts and Cs as you develop the site or think of new products and services. Therefore, state that you can alter the Ts and Cs at any time and advise Users to check them regularly. You also say, however, that whether Users check the Ts and Cs or not, any such changes automatically bind them.

✔ **Disclaimer of liability:** You want to make sure that any grounds of liability are as narrow as possible, so that you don't have to defend yourself from claims by hundreds or thousands of Users. This may sound over the top, but the world contains a surprising number of argumentative people with too much time on their hands who enjoy making trouble if they can. So the Ts and Cs have a *disclaimer,* an often unwieldy clause (especially in United States Ts and Cs), containing a number of exclusions that go together like pickled herrings and indigestion (oh, excuse me):

- You provide all information on the site on an 'as is' basis and give no responsibility about the accuracy or validity of the information.

- You give no promise or 'warranty' in respect of any use of the site and its content, including for any mistakes or omissions you've made. You accept no legal responsibility for any loss or damage suffered by a User, including money, profits, data or reputation.

- Any reliance placed on the content of your site is at the User's own risk.

- You have to be careful to go no further than the law allows in excluding liability, and so the Ts and Cs don't exclude liability for death or personal injury arising from negligence (if that's physically possible from using a website), for fraudulent misrepresentation, or for any other liability that the law says can't be excluded or limited (see Chapter 12 for more details).

✔ **Jurisdiction and governing law:** If you're operating in the UK, normal practice is to say that all terms of the site are governed by English law. If a dispute arises with a User, the Court has to use English Law to resolve it (instead of the laws of some far-flung country where the User is based). You also normally say that any disputes can only be brought in English Courts. This stops a User going to Court in Timbuktu or any other region, where defence proceedings can be costly for you and the outcome and procedure uncertain.

✔ **Contact and concerns:** You usually give a contact email for when the User has any concerns about material appearing on the site.

Presenting an Acceptable Use Policy

An *Acceptable Use Policy* sets out the terms that all Users of the site must follow, such as specific standards for content they upload to it. As with the Ts and Cs of the preceding section, you need a provision at the start saying that by using the site, a User agrees to accept and be bound by this Policy.

Here are the terms to include:

- ✔ **Prohibited uses:** You insist that the site can be used only for lawful purposes and in particular that the User can't use the site to do a number of the unpleasant things (listed below), which go together like stink bombs and rotten eggs:

  - Breach any local, national or international law or regulation

  - Take part in unlawful or fraudulent activity

  - Harm or attempt to harm those under the age of 18 (minors)

  - Send, knowingly receive, upload, download, use or reuse any material that doesn't comply with the site's content standards

  - Transmit unrequested or unauthorised advertising (spam)

  - Transmit any data containing harmful viruses or Trojans or other harmful programs that may damage computer software or hardware

  - Reproduce, copy or resell any content of the site

  - Access, damage or disrupt any part of the site, or any equipment, network or software connected to the site

- ✔ **Interactive services:** If the site provides interactive services, such as chat rooms, bulletin boards, or comment or review facilities, these are made subject to a number of conditions and limitations on both sides:

  - You promise to provide clear details on interactive services, including information about the type of service available and whether it's reviewed in real-time, to make sure that nothing inappropriate is going on (such as bullying). This is called *moderation*. You also set out the type of moderation you carry out and details for contacting the moderator.

  - Although you take care to assess potential risks (especially in relation to minors), you make it clear that you have no duty to monitor or moderate any such interactive services, and you exclude legal responsibility for any loss that may arise from use not complying with the site's content standards.

  - Any use of interactive services by a minor is made subject to parental consent. If parents allow such use by a minor, you advise them to communicate the risks of using the site to their children.

▶ **Content standards:** The main purpose of the Acceptable Use Policy is to set out the standards that apply to all material contributed to the site. You don't want inappropriate material on your site for which someone may hold you liable. All contributions must be sugar and spice and all things nice, and in particular:

- Accurate (if facts are stated)

- Genuine (if opinions are expressed)

- Compliant with the law in the UK or any country from which they're posted

Contributions mustn't contain horrid things like 'snips (whatever they are) and snails and puppy dog tails', and in particular mustn't:

- Contain obscene, offensive, hateful or inflammatory material, or defamatory information that unlawfully damages someone's reputation

- Promote violence or sexually explicit material

- Promote discrimination based on race, sex, religion, nationality, sexual orientation, age or disability

- Infringe the intellectual property rights of any other person

- Be likely to threaten abuse, harass, upset, embarrass, alarm or annoy anyone

- Be used to misrepresent someone's identity or impersonate another person

- Help to commit or assist an unlawful act

▶ **Suspension and termination:** If a breach of this policy occurs, you give yourself the right to take actions that go together like 'shock and awe' to protect you and your site, such as the following:

- Implementing the immediate, temporary or permanent withdrawal of a User's right to use the site

- Implementing the immediate, temporary or permanent removal of any material or posting uploaded to the site by the User

- Issuing a warning to the User

- Commencing legal proceedings for reimbursement of all costs resulting from the breach

- Disclosing information about the breach to the appropriate law enforcement authority

- Taking further legal action or any other action that you think is appropriate – and excluding liability for any such actions taken because of breaches of the Acceptable Use Policy

✔ **Changes to the Acceptable Use Policy:** You point out that you can revise the Acceptable Use Policy at any time and that the User is automatically bound by any such changes.

✔ **Contact and concerns:** You give an email address for any concerns regarding material on this site – you don't want to appear unfriendly.

Prepping Your Privacy and Cookie Policies

A *Privacy Policy* sets out what data you collect (as the website owner) about Users and tells them how you'll use that data. Your *Cookies Policy* informs Users, logically enough, about cookies. Nothing to do with chocolate chip biscuits, these *cookies* are small bits of data sent from a website to a User's browser; they're stored in that browser and activate whenever the User is browsing your website. They recognise returning Users and maximise their experience of the site based on their browsing history.

All sites that collect personal data or use web cookies need to publish a specific Privacy Policy on their site. *Personal data* is data that can individually identify a living person or be used to do so in combination with other data that the collector of the data has: your name, residential address, email address and credit card data are obvious examples. A Privacy Policy informs Users about the processing of their personal data and exists to inform and reassure Users that any information they provide is used appropriately.

The Privacy Policy needs to be easy to find and available for review before visitors are required to submit any personal information about themselves.

Baking your Cookie Policy just right

Your privacy policy must provide users with clear and comprehensive information about the type of cookies being used and for what purposes. You need to include the following standard terms:

✔ **Consent:** Must be obtained before your website places any type of cookie on a User's computer. The method to obtain consent should include a link to your website's privacy and cookie policy. You must also detail whether third-party cookies are used.

✔ **Type of cookies:** Must be disclosed and should explain the purpose of and the type of data retrieved from each type of cookie. Distinguish necessary cookies (such as those for security) from analytical or performance-type cookies. You must also disclose whether the data collected is to be transferred or sold to third parties.

✔ **Opting-out:** Instructions that inform users on how to opt-out or disable cookies. Also include a statement on the implications of disabling cookies.

The legal reason you have to comply with these requirements is the Privacy and Electronic Communications (EC Directive) (Amendment) Regulations, 2011. Since this amendment, Users must be given information about cookies and must also give their consent for you to place them in their browser in the first place. No exact definition of consent is given, but it must involve some form of communication where Users knowingly indicate their acceptance: clicking an icon, sending an email, subscribing to a service or accepting via a banner displayed on the website. Implied consent can be enough if the User takes action to confirm consent after you make an attempt clearly to inform the User about the use of cookies on the website (for example, by choosing to continue to use the website or moving from one page to another).

The only exception to the consent requirement is where the cookies are 'strictly necessary' for a service requested by the User (for example, to provide online security or where a cookie remembers the goods that a User wants to purchase). Cookies that fall into the non-essential category are those used for analytical purposes to count the number of visitors to a website; those used by you on your site, third-party advertisers or affiliates of yours; or those used to tailor greetings to return Users or to display an optimised landing page.

This is why on many sites you visit you now find a specific pop-up message when you first arrive on the site (as well as a separate cookies policy) telling you that the site operates cookies and asking you to consent to that use.

Staying up close and personal: Including other Privacy Policy terms

Terms that businesses typically include in a Privacy Policy are as follows:

✔ The type of data being collected, including:

• Information that Users provide when they register with or visit the site

- Details of transactions carried out on the site

- Records of any correspondence with that User

- Information about what Users do when they visit the site

- Information about the User's computer, such as its IP address

✔ Why the data is collected, which can be for a number of reasons:

- Presenting the site in a way that suits that User's preferences

- Allowing access to interactive services on the site

- Telling the User about charges

- Combining one User's data with other Users' data in aggregated lists, which don't identify the User individually but help give a picture of overall behaviour on the site

- Telling the User about other related goods and services the site provides, in which she may be interested

✔ Whether you plan to disclose data to third parties and why. For example, you may want to do so for marketing purposes, which can be a valuable source of revenue for you. But in that case, you must say in your Privacy Policy that you won't do it without the User's consent and that the person can withdraw her permission whenever she wants. Data can also be disclosed to a buyer of your enterprise or to other companies within your group, to protect against credit fraud or risk, or if you're legally required to disclose it (for example, by the Courts).

✔ How and where the data is stored, and how it's kept secure. For example, explain that the data is kept in the UK (if that's true) and kept secure through, for example, encryption of payments. Qualify this, however, by saying that you don't guarantee the effectiveness of those security measures.

✔ How you deal with complaints or queries relating to personal data. For example, how the User can find out about, update or request the deletion of information you're storing about her.

✔ A warning that if the User follows links to third-party sites, those other sites may have their own (different) privacy policies for which you aren't responsible.

You have to comply with these requirements because of the Privacy and Electronic Communications (EC Directive) Regulations, 2003 and the Data Protection Act, 1998.

Privacy and Electronic Communications (EC Directive) Regulations, 2003

These Regulations deal with the transmission of 'unsolicited' communications to 'individual subscribers' for marketing purposes. The important elements are:

✔ **Requiring consent:** The subscriber must consent to unsolicited direct marketing (whether the marketing is delivered by email or SMS/text message). Here are two key rules:

- Rule 1 applies to all marketing messages sent by electronic mail, regardless of the recipient (a business or an individual). It says that (a) senders mustn't conceal or disguise their identity and (b) senders must provide a valid address for opt-out requests.

- Rule 2 only applies to unsolicited marketing messages sent by email to individual subscribers. It says that (a) senders can't send such messages unless they have the recipient's prior consent and (b) they must give the opportunity to opt-out.

✔ **Gaining consent:** Individual subscriber consent to receive such emails must be 'specific' and requires some positive action such as the ticking of an opt-in box. The opt-in must be 'clear and distinct' and allow individuals to see clearly what they're opting into when they tick such a box or provide their email address.

✔ **'Soft' opt-in:** You can treat subscribers as giving consent to receive marketing emails in circumstances where they haven't provided specific consent – for example, if:

- Their email addresses are obtained 'in the course of the sale or negotiations for the sale of a product or service'. An example would be an email address obtained from a User making a price enquiry or checking stock availability.

- The direct marketing is in respect of 'similar products and services only', which are those that subscribers would reasonably expect to receive.

- The subscribers have been given a simple means of refusing the use of their contact details for the purposes of such direct marketing at the time the details were first collected.

- The subscribers are given an opportunity to opt out in every subsequent email they receive.

Data Protection Act, 1998

This Act balances the rather incompatible needs or rights of Users for privacy of their personal details with the needs of organisations to collect and use such information for business purposes. It hopes to create a harmonious concoction of ice cream and tomato sauce (one of my favourite snacks).

Given the growth of online business and the use of increasingly sophisticated online marketing tools to track consumers' online habits, this law is becoming more and more significant. You can all too easily make a mistake and any non-compliance can cause headaches for you, such as fines or other regulatory enforcement, as well as negative public relations and damage to your brand if word gets out through social media that you abuse User data.

The Act regulates the *processing* of personal data, which includes obtaining, recording or holding the information. This definition has a wide meaning under the Act and covers almost any operation concerning data. Note the following terms:

- ✔ **Data subject:** The person whose data is collected.

- ✔ **Data controller:** The person who decides the purposes for which, and the way in which, any personal data is processed. This person has a duty to make sure that she processes personal data in compliance with the Act and must register with the Information Commissioner's Office at `https://ico.org.uk/for-organisations/register`.

I bet you didn't know that more people each year are killed by donkeys than die in aeroplane crashes. I bet you also didn't know that The Data Protection Act, 1998 sets out eight fundamental principles of data protection that you must observe at all times from the point of collection and throughout the subsequent processing of data. You can see that the Privacy Policy terms I discuss earlier in this section reflect a number of these principles:

- ✔ **Personal data shall be processed fairly and lawfully:** You must ensure clarity about the data that's being collected, why it's being collected and how it's used. Here are the two elements to this principle:

  - The processing must satisfy at least one of the following conditions: the data subject has consented to the processing, the processing is necessary for the performance of a contract, the processing is necessary for the 'legitimate interests' of the data controller, or the vital interests of the data subject, or the data processing is necessary to uphold the law.

  - You must provide individuals with certain information when collating data on them, which includes: the identity of the data controller(s) for the data; the intended uses for the data; and any other information necessary to enable the processing to be fair.

  More restrictive conditions exist for the processing of 'sensitive' personal information, including information about race, health, religion, politics, union membership or criminal offences.

✔ **Personal data shall be obtained only for specified and lawful purposes, and processed in a manner compatible with those purposes:** You must clearly state what the data is to be used for and any new purpose must be in line with the original purpose to be covered.

✔ **Personal data shall be adequate, relevant and not excessive in relation to the purpose or purposes for which it's processed:** You should only hold the minimum amount of personal data needed.

✔ **Personal data shall be accurate and, where necessary, kept up to date:** Although checking the accuracy of every piece of personal data received may not be practical, you need to take reasonable steps to ensure that it's accurate and not out of date.

✔ **Personal data processed for any purpose or purposes shall not be kept for longer than is necessary for that purpose or those purposes:** When data is no longer needed, you have a duty to dispose of it properly. You should carry out a review of the purpose(s) for which information is held and if the data is no longer needed for this purpose, you should securely delete it.

✔ **Personal data shall be processed in accordance with the rights of data subjects under the Act:** Individuals have a number of rights in their personal data and they may do the following:

- Make requests to those who process personal data about them for information as to what data is stored, what it's used for, the source of the personal data and recipients to whom it is or may be disclosed, known as subject access rights. (You can charge a fee of £10 and must give a response within 40 days of a request.)

- Object to processing likely to cause or that is causing damage or distress to them or someone else.

- Object to direct marketing.

- Veto automated decisions that significantly affect them.

- Take action to get their personal data corrected or erased.

- Seek compensation from data controllers for breaches of the Act.

✔ **Appropriate technical and organisational measures shall be taken against unauthorised or unlawful processing of personal data and against accidental loss or destruction of, or damage to, personal data:** Although a bit vague, the message is that you must hold personal data securely and the security must be 'appropriate' to the nature of the information and the harm that may result from improper use. In practice, limit rights of access to what's strictly necessary.

✔ **Personal data shall not be transferred to a country or territory outside the European Economic Area (EEA):** This principle is designed to prevent personal data being sent to countries with inadequate data protection regimes. It's especially relevant in the context of cloud computing, in which ascertaining where the data is being held is often difficult. You can get the User to consent to overseas transfer of the data (as I describe at the beginning of this section when listing the standard terms of a Privacy Policy) or you can keep personal data within Europe, because protections afforded in countries outside the European Economic Area (EEA; EU Member States plus Iceland, Liechtenstein and Norway) are generally not regarded as 'adequate' or sufficient to comply with the European rules.

Trading Places Online

The Internet is a beautiful thing that can be used for ugly purposes, which is why new and ever-expanding legislation protects Users from all types of real and potential threats from online traders. You need to become aware of these requirements, because serious consequences lie in wait for non-compliance, including fines or damages. Here's a selection of laws (I deal with ones that apply offline as well in Chapter 12):

✔ **Electronic Commerce (EC Directive) Regulations, 2002:** These Regulations apply to electronic sales to consumers and business-to-business. They state that all commercial websites offering Internet marketing, whether they're selling goods or services or not, must provide minimum information. These Regulations overlap with the Consumer Contracts Regulations that I describe in Chapter 12. Unlike those rules, however, these Electronic Commerce provisions apply to sales to either businesses or consumers.

The Regulations list additional requirements that must be provided during the course of an online transaction including:

- The technical steps necessary to conclude the contract
- Whether the seller will file away the contract and whether it will be permanently accessible
- How Users can detect and correct any errors prior to placing orders
- Acknowledgement of receipt of the order or payment by the seller
- The language used to conclude the contract

The Regulations also require email and service providers to ensure that 'any unsolicited commercial communication sent by electronic communication is clearly and unambiguously identifiable as such as soon as possible' (that's *spam* to you and me). The Regulations don't specify how such messages should be identified, and I deal with them more fully in the earlier section 'Staying up close and personal: Including other Privacy Policy terms').

✔ **Consumer Rights Act, 2015:** This Act provides for the first time that consumer contracts for digital content are a separate category of content and sets out statutory rights and remedies that apply to such contracts. Digital content applies to data 'produced and supplied in digital form' and includes products and services such as music downloads, films, software, computer games and mobile applications (apps). The definition also includes digital content largely or wholly stored and processed remotely, such as software supplied via cloud computing. Contracts to supply digital content to a User for a fee are covered as are contracts to provide digital content to a consumer free with paid goods or services.

Certain terms are implied in all contracts for the supply of digital content (whether you include them in the contract or not):

- The digital content must be of satisfactory quality.

- It must be fit for a particular purpose.

- It must meet any given description.

- You have the right to supply the content.

If these requirements aren't satisfied, a User has the following rights:

- The right to repair or replacement of the content.

- The right to a price reduction of an 'appropriate amount' up to the full price if repair or replacement isn't possible or you fail to repair within a reasonable time.

- An additional compensation mechanism where digital content causes damage to a device or other digital content owned by the consumer (for example, by a virus) if she can demonstrate that you didn't exercise reasonable care and skill.

- The right of a refund only applies where you don't have the right to provide the content. No right exists to reject digital content or to return it. Internet Service Providers and mobile phone providers aren't regarded as traders for the purpose of this legislation. No, I don't know why either.

✔ **Advertising standards and marketing:** All websites that contain advertisements must comply with the UK Code on Non-Broadcast Advertising, Sales Promotion and Direct Marketing (CAP Code; see www.cap. org.uk/Advertising-Codes/~/media/Files/CAP/Codes CAP pdf/The CAP Code.ashx). An advertisement must be legal, decent, honest and truthful and not mis-describe products or services. This Code applies to all UK-based business websites regardless of the sector or size of the business or organisation. The Code now covers businesses' own marketing claims on their websites and in other non-paid-for space they control, such as Facebook and Twitter. Therefore, you can no longer tweet that your sow's ear is really a purse in order to sell it. Looks like the end for the sow's ear business.

The Advertising Standards Authority (ASA) enforces the CAP Code, handles complaints and can order advertisers to take down or amend material that breaches the Code. It can also refer a case to the Competition and Markets Authority (previously the Office of Fair Trading) to pursue legal action against offenders.

✔ **Third-party advertising:** You need to be especially careful about the consent issue with bought-in lists of potential customers. Consent can be collected from an individual by a third party on another's behalf, as long as the third party makes it clear that the individual's details will be passed on. If you buy lists of those individuals without having obtained this consent, emails to those individuals may be unsolicited direct marketing emails and breach anti-spam rules.

✔ **Mobile applications (apps) and geolocation:** The use of location data on mobile applications is subject to clear rules about consent. You must obtain such consent in advance and provide any Users with the means to withdraw that consent.

Clarifying the Country of Origin principle

The Electronic Commerce (EC Directive) Regulations, 2002 introduce the *Country of Origin principle.* Providers of goods or services established in an EU Member State are entitled to provide their goods or services to any other Member State: for example, a UK-based business selling online to a customer in Italy. This principle means that providers of goods or services only have to comply with the rules of the country in which those service providers are established. Therefore, a UK-based website only needs to follow UK law, even if it sells into another Member State such as Italy.

Despite this, and with characteristic EU zeal for making everything as muddled as possible, the Regulations go on to state numerous exceptions to this principle – including contracts with consumer contracts. Therefore, if you plan to sell to an Italian consumer (rather than an Italian business), the *Country of Reception principle* applies, which means that you have to follow the law in the country you're selling into (in this case Italy). Confused? You will be. What's more, if you plan to sell to other European Member States, technically you must follow consumer protection rules in all Member States. Well done everybody. So much for a Single Market.

Note: You can't get around this for consumer contracts by agreeing in your Ts and Cs that 'English law' applies. Sorry!

Chapter 7

Staying Onside in the Workplace

In This Chapter

▶ Sorting out your commercial leases

▶ Knowing your obligations to employees

▶ Nailing your responsibilities to temporary staff

*S*ettle down with a mug of cocoa (okay, add a nip of something stronger if you insist) as I walk you gently through the law as it applies to your activities in the workplace.

I look at commercial leases for business premises – what to include, what to keep out and what to negotiate. I also review some of the legal obligations you have to comply with in your premises, such as how you treat employees and temporary staff – a tangled, sticky web of legislation.

Digging In: Obtaining Your Business Premises

Your home may be your castle, but your business premises are your trenches – the frontline of your battle to succeed as an entrepreneur. You spend most of your waking hours there, under a constant barrage from competitors, funding demands, unruly customers and fickle fortune. You want your trenches to protect you from whatever's coming at you – and to require low maintenance so that you can focus on winning ground in the competitive terrain around you.

When you're sourcing premises for your business, generally you have three main options:

> ✔ **Purchase the property freehold:** You own it outright. The purchase of premises requires significant investment and may not be a feasible option for you due to the difficulty of obtaining commercial mortgages for a small business.

✔ **Commercial property licence arrangement:** A short-term arrangement that's informal and less onerous in nature than purchasing and is mainly suited to the needs of new start-ups.

✔ **Commercial property lease:** This require careful consideration because it's often long and complex in nature and is routinely drafted in favour of the landlord. The rights and obligations imposed aren't easy to understand, and so they're a minefield to navigate.

I focus on commercial property licences and commercial property leases, because freehold purchases are usually beyond the financial reach of most small businesses.

Embracing commercial licences

A *commercial property licence* arrangement is particularly advantageous for a start-up business because it's flexible in nature and relatively straightforward. It provides an attractive option if your business is in its infancy and you can't predict your future needs or rate of expansion, and when you want to keep your overheads down. Also, commercial licences are inexpensive, quick to draw up and allow quick access to a property. They aren't subject to stamp duty and don't expose the business to the numerous duties and obligations that apply under a commercial lease (which normally lasts much longer; take a look at the next section).

A commercial property licence grants lawful permission to a person (the *licensee* – you) other than the owner (the *licensor*) to use the property. Unlike a property lease, it doesn't grant you any interest in the property.

In practice, licences usually allow you to use the property for a specific purpose and for a set period of time, normally six months. A licence usually gives both parties the right to terminate, which typically involves notice of one month. When the end date is reached, however, you must leave the property and can't renew unless the licensor wants to renew the contract.

That's it . . . because you have limited rights under a commercial licence and they don't last very long, they tend to be short and sweet.

Most licences don't allow subletting, transfers or alterations.

Wrestling with commercial leases

A business *lease* is a legally binding contract between the legal owner of the property (the *landlord*) and the occupier (the *tenant* – yep, that's you). If you fail to comply with the terms of the agreement you can face court action, and so watch out.

The language of leases is particularly prone to old-fashioned legal gobbledy-gook. Surely, a faintly humorous lawyer coined the phrase 'legalese' for complicated documents of this kind, which are anything but easy to understand.

The Code for Leasing Business Premises (www.leasingbusinesspremises. co.uk) helps you to understand appropriate and fair terms to include in a commercial lease, but nothing beats taking expert advice at the earliest stage possible to avoid your business premises resting on shaky foundations.

Here are the most common terms to deal with in a commercial lease arrangement, along with tips for getting the best out of any deal you sign:

✔ **Term or length of the lease:** In order to be economically viable for both parties, most commercial leases run for several years at a time. They're rarely granted for more than 25 years and in recent times the trend has been for considerably shorter leases, with the average now being around 8 years. Generally speaking, the longer the term of the lease, the more important having an exit strategy is – something to get you out of a jam if you want to stop.

Many leases, for example, contain a *break clause,* which allows the tenant or landlord to finish the lease early at an agreed date. A break clause is sometimes subject to harsh pre-conditions for the tenant – for example, if you commit even a minor breach of the lease, the landlord may have the right to refuse to accept the break.

The best scenario for you is that the only conditions attached to your right as a tenant to a break clause are the following:

- Service of prior written notice in accordance with the lease

- Being up-to-date with your rent

- Leaving behind no subleases

As a tenant your view of the agreed length of a commercial lease may be influenced by the amount of stamp duty land tax you have to pay. In general, entering into a commercial lease for a term of more than seven years at an annual rent in excess of £1,000 requires you to submit a Land Transaction Return to HMRC. Stamp duty of 1 per cent is charged to the tenant on the net present value of rent payable, unless the overall rent is lower than the current exempt threshold (£150,000 for commercial leases). The longer the term, the greater the potential for a higher stamp duty liability.

The landlord must register all commercial leases longer than seven years and all assignments of leases with more than seven years left to run with HM Land Registry under the Land Registration Act, 2002.

Ideally, make sure that you have a choice as to whether the lease is protected or excluded from the Landlord and Tenant Act, 1954. This Act says that tenants have a legal right to claim a new lease on the expiry of the old lease as long as they haven't breached the old one. The Act provides an exception if the landlord wants to sell, redevelop or move into the property. If the location of the premises is ideally suited to your business needs and the security of a long-term lease is important, negotiate for the lease to be a 'protected' one so that you have the right to a new lease at the end of the lease term.

You can exclude the protection of the Act from a commercial lease but both parties must agree to it. Therefore, a specified procedure involving the service of statutory notices and the swearing of a declaration needs to be followed to 'exclude' a lease from the Act.

Resist this option if you can. If you are going to forfeit the right of protection, negotiate other more favourable terms under the lease instead.

✔ **Rent:** Do some research yourself to make sure that you're paying a competitive rent. Sometimes you can get the first few months at a discount or even free if the landlord is keen to let the premises. Watch out for interest (and the rate of interest) due on unpaid rent or rent paid late. Sometimes landlords include an *escalation clause*, which imposes automatic increases in rent for inflation. Insist on a cap on the percentage of the increase to protect yourself from large increases if such a clause is included.

On top of the rent, the landlord may look to include additional wording to include VAT. Although commercial property is generally exempt from VAT, option to tax exists, and an owner can elect to waive the exemption and pay VAT if doing so makes commercial sense to him (for example, to recover VAT on refurbishment costs). After the option to tax is exercised, VAT must then be charged on any lease or sale. So you may have to pay VAT on your rent. (If VAT is payable, HMRC takes it into account when deciding whether you've exceeded the stamp duty threshold so that stamp duty is payable too. Sneaky, huh?)

✔ **Deposit:** If you're required to pay a deposit upfront, ensure that you're clear how long the landlord can hold any deposit, how the deposit will be repaid and whether interest is payable on it. Don't tip-toe around the sensitive area of the circumstances in which the landlord is allowed to keep all or part of the deposit, so that you maximise your chances of getting it back.

Try to include a pre-condition that the deposit is kept in an escrow account in case the landlord becomes insolvent.

✔ **Personal guarantee:** Sometimes landlords want one as security for the rent. If so, sprint to Chapter 4 for the perils of personal guarantees. Your business getting into trouble, you not being able to afford the rent and having to give up the lease is bad enough. If you and Elvis have left the building, the last thing you want is the landlord coming after your personal assets or your domestic home to recover money he's owed.

✔ **Rent review:** Clauses relating to periodic rent review are routine – but treat them with caution, because often you see an *upwards only* rent review. This kind of clause says that the new rent negotiated can't fall below the rent the tenant was paying before the rent review, even if market rates have fallen. Not great, and so ensure that rents can be lowered as well as raised.

Agree a date to review the rent so that you have some certainty as to when that's going to happen, and agree the method to determine the new rent (for example, whether it's going to be based on changes in the retail price index or based on rents available in the open market). A sensible move is to include provision for appointing an independent arbitrator if agreement can't be reached on the new level of rent.

✔ **Alterations and changes of use:** Commercial leases usually limit the use of the property to a specified purpose. As the tenant, you're responsible for ensuring that a proposed use complies with the lease and any current planning consent obtained by the landlord. Therefore, ensure that the *permitted use* specified in the lease is clear and wide enough to cover the purpose and likely development of your business.

Restrictions on signage and alterations are often included in the terms and any such changes normally require the landlord to provide consent. You can expect more flexibility for non-structural internal alterations and non-structural partitioning, and so agree that the landlord's consent in such cases shouldn't be unreasonably withheld or delayed. Landlords are very reluctant to agree to structural and/or external alterations.

✔ **Alienation rights:** Nothing to do with allowing space creatures to inhabit your premises (though I've never seen such a prohibition so if you can find some suitable aliens, feel free to give them office space). *Alienation rights* prevent you from assigning the lease or subletting the leased premises to someone else. Normally the landlord doesn't want to agree to you subletting or assigning your lease. From your point of view, though, doing so gives you much more flexibility.

Negotiate the widest range of permissions you can to ensure business flexibility. Expect the landlord as a minimum to require prior consent and to insist that the provisions of the Landlord and Tenant Act, 1954 don't apply to any sublets (so that anybody you sublet to can't insist on a renewal of the lease at the end of your term). Try to make sure that any clause on subletting doesn't limit you from subletting at a lower rent than the current rate you're paying.

A *sublease* transfers a portion of your rental rights to a third party for a temporary period – but you remain responsible for the subtenant's tenancy and the original lease still stands. So if the subtenant mucks up some obligation in the lease, you're responsible for that to the landlord.

Assignment involves passing on the lease to another business and formally ending your occupation of the premises. If landlords do permit an assignment, they may require you to guarantee the next tenant's performance of the lease, including payment of rent, which is known as an *Authorised Guarantee Agreement* (AGA). If you're asked to do this, alarm bells need to start clanging: you risk being directly responsible as a guarantor for the lease obligations until the *assignee* (to whom you pass the lease) assigns the lease to another party or the lease ends. As a Middle Eastern saying goes, 'If a camel gets his nose in the tent, his body will follow': don't open yourself up to this possibility.

Try and get agreement that the only precondition for assignment is obtaining the landlord's consent in writing. Failing this, secure agreement that any guarantee can be cancelled when certain conditions are met (for example, after an agreed period of time) – and check that the assignee is financially sound before you enter into any AGA.

✔ **Repairs:** As a tenant, you normally have an obligation to keep the premises in good condition, which includes redecorating or renewal of carpets and replacement of equipment. As far as repairs are concerned, landlords often include a *full repairing clause* in leases, which can be a big burden on you because it effectively requires putting and keeping the whole property in good repair at all times (including roof and foundations). As a result, you can become responsible for extensive repairs that are out of proportion with the length of time for which you're leasing the property and the condition of the premises.

Try limiting any repairing liability to 'internal only' obligations for repairing and decorating the interior. Also (whether the lease has full repairing or internal only obligations) restrict these to keeping the premises in no worse condition than at the commencement of the lease.

Hire an independent surveyor at the negotiation stage. A full survey inspection, complete with a formal photographic schedule of condition, verifies the condition of the premises. This report discourages the landlord from making any unjustified demands on you at the lease's end. Also, if disrepair is found to exist before you enter into the lease, you can limit your liability for repairs through an agreed *schedule of condition,* which records the condition of the property at the lease's commencement.

Clarifying the condition of the property at the outset is also helpful in preventing any unfair retention of deposits. As ever, 'diligence is the mother of good fortune' (just naming your daughter 'Good fortune' isn't enough!).

If you don't comply with your repair or decorating obligations, the landlord can serve a *schedule of dilapidations* on you (see what I mean about gobbledygook language in leases?). This notice requires you to put the property back into a satisfactory state of repair as required by the lease. A landlord can pursue a legal claim against you for breach of the lease if you fail to carry out the work, including potentially retaking possession of the property.

✔ **Service charges:** Normally an additional cost to the rent in multi-occupied properties with common areas (for example, for common area maintenance fees, maintaining car parks). Take a minute to check these charges. After all, what else can you usefully do in a minute? Well you could break the Guinness World Record for eating M & Ms blindfold with chopsticks (currently 20) or the record for most ice cream scoops thrown and caught (currently 25), but a more productive use of 60 seconds is probably to watch out for the following points:

- These charges tend to be a flat fee per year but can be expressed as a percentage of expenses, which gives you little control of your costs. A service charge cap is a good way of making sure that service charges don't get out of control during the lease.

- Make sure that you specify exactly what services the landlord is going to supply you with in return for these service charges.

- The landlord should only levy service charges for routine repairs and maintenance; structural repairs, including inherent defects in the building, must fall outside the scope of these charges.

- Agree only to pay a reasonable proportion of the cost of shared services.

- Require a clear estimate of the likely service charge costs for each year of the lease in writing in advance, and clarity on how the charges are apportioned and when payment is due.

- The landlord should provide you with an accountant-certified copy of service charge expenditure annually.

- Management fees for any managing agent carrying out the services should be reasonable and not based on a percentage of expenditure on services.

The Service Charge Code, 2011 provides a useful benchmark of how landlords and tenants should handle service charges in commercial leases.

✔ **Insurance:** Generally, a lease requires the landlord to arrange the building's insurance and you're responsible for your portion of the premium. You must check the terms of the insurance policy to ensure that the premium is competitive and represents value for money.

Make sure that the landlord is required to reinstate the premises in the event of any damage, such as fire or building collapse (or a takeover by those aliens you invite into the building). Also include a provision for rent reduction or termination if you can't occupy the property for any period. You're made responsible for insuring the plate glass of the property and your own contents insurance.

Define any uninsured risks and carry out a check as to who bears the risk for such events. Flooding, for example, is regarded as an uninsured risk. Responsibility for such risks should be shared.

Insurance policies sometimes contain *subrogation provisions,* which allow the insurer to 'step into the shoes' of the insured party and take legal action on behalf of the insured to recover the amount of the loss from the person causing the loss. For example, if you cause damage to the landlord's property through negligence, even though the landlord is compensated through his insurance policy, the insurance company can then pursue you – bad news. If it's allowed by the insurance terms, inserting a waiver of subrogation rights in the lease avoids this possibility. Without it, you can be responsible for costs and expenses well beyond the loss originally caused.

- ✔ **Forfeiture provisions:** You may remember doing 'forfeits' at children's birthday parties. Well, *forfeiture* of a lease involves similar losses but without the fun of the game – it means that you have to give up the lease, because you've done something wrong (for example, failing to pay rent or fulfil your repairing obligations). The landlord can lock you out of the building or obtain a Court Order entitling him to do so.

Restrict the list of forfeiture provisions to major causes (for example, persistent failure to pay the rent) and not a one-off blip. Make sure that you're clear on how and when forfeiture terms are activated. Include in the lease a reasonable opportunity to remedy any breach before the landlord can commence legal action or enforce forfeiture (try saying that with your teeth out).

- ✔ **Ancillary legislation:** Most leases require you to comply with loads of other statutes – for example, the Equality Act, 2010, the Town and Country Planning Act, 1990, the Control of Asbestos at Work Regulations, 2002 and the Health and Safety Act, 1974. Ask the landlord to confirm that the property complies with all such regulations before you enter into the lease so that at least you start off with a clean slate. I deal with the Health and Safety and Equality Acts in the later sections 'Staying safe: Health and Safety Act, 1974' and 'Performing a balancing act: Equality Act, 2010', respectively.

Coping with Your Workplace Obligations to Employees

When you've secured your workspace, all you need to do is fill it with happy, smiling workers and your troubles are over? Right? No! Those workers may be smiling now – they may even nod emphatically when you beam indulgently and remind them that 'a smile is the curve that sets everything straight' – but they won't be smiling for long if you don't comply with your obligations in the workplace.

In this section, I describe some of the legislative obstacles you have to negotiate on an everyday basis. Don't despair, though; you should still have time to do a bit of work each day after complying with all the requirements.

A number of complicated notice provisions exist under some of these Acts. To avoid driving you berserk, I exclude details.

Staying safe: Health and Safety Act, 1974

Under this Act, you have a duty to ensure that, so far as is reasonably practicable, you protect the health, safety and welfare of all your workers in the workplace. You must also take care of other people visiting the worksite – for example, customers or contractors. You need to strike a balance between the degree of risk in a particular workplace against the time, cost and difficulty of taking measures to avoid or reduce the risk.

Most small businesses tend to be low risk, but all firms with more than five employees are required to have written health and safety policies in place and to bring them to the attention of employees. You must also consult with trade union safety representatives on matters of health and safety in the workplace. A small business can satisfy this requirement by engaging in direct consultation with employees by email, at meetings, through notice boards and so on.

Employees have a duty not to put themselves or others at risk and to co-operate with the business's health and safety policy.

You must comply with The Management of Health and Safety at Work Regulations, 1999, which provide that employers with five or more employees must carry out a risk assessment. You have to assess the risks to the health and safety of your employees in the workplace and of anyone else who may be affected by their activity, so that necessary preventative and protective measures can be taken and put into practice.

Under the Workplace (Health, Safety and Welfare) Regulations, 1992, physical conditions in the workplace must meet minimum standards, including: lighting, provision of drinking water, temperature, rest facilities, ventilation, toilet facilities, room dimensions, cleanliness, maintenance of buildings and equipment, condition of floors and traffic routes.

If an accident or injury occurs in the workplace, you must report it to the Health and Safety Executive under the snappily named Reporting of Injuries, Diseases and Dangerous Occurrences Regulations, 2013 (RIDDOR). You must have employers' liability insurance in place against the risk of such accidents and injuries. I discuss this type of insurance in Chapter 14.

Performing a balancing act: Equality Act, 2010

The Equality Act applies to all businesses regardless of size and to all workers, whether full time, temporary or employed with or without a contract. It applies to all aspects of the employment process, including recruitment, terms and conditions of employment, training, promotions, dismissals, redundancies and retirement. Small firms such as yours aren't exempt and you may find compliance with this worthy legislation more burdensome than large organisations if you lack an in-house human resources structure or access to legal advice.

Discovering your obligations under the Equality Act

The Act provides that certain characteristics at work are protected from discrimination: age, disability, gender reassignment, race, religion or belief, sex, sexual orientation, marriage and civil partnership, and pregnancy and maternity:

- ✔ **Age:** People of all ages are protected against discrimination. In addition, the Employment Equality (Repeal of Retirement Age Provisions) Regulations, 2011 abolished the default retirement age of 65. The government recognised that people are going to work till they drop in future, and so an employer is no longer permitted automatically to retire an employee at 65. If you dismiss an employee above this age, the dismissal must be fair and reasonable, because otherwise it can give rise to a claim for age discrimination or unfair dismissal.

- ✔ **Disability:** People are *disabled* if they have a physical or mental impairment that has a substantial and long-term adverse effect on their ability to carry out normal day-to-day activities. The disability must have lasted or be likely to last 12 months. People with mental impairments are *not* required to have an impairment that's 'clinically well-recognised'. Those living with HIV, multiple sclerosis or cancer automatically qualify as disabled, without the need to establish any adverse effect on their normal day-to-day activities.

Asking questions about health or disability before offering an employee a job is unlawful. This prohibition is to prevent disability/health issues being used to reject a job application without first providing an opportunity for the candidate to demonstrate the necessary skills. Such questions are only permitted if they fall within narrow exceptions.

You have a duty to make 'reasonable adjustments' in the workplace to help disabled persons overcome disadvantage resulting from impairment. The cost of the adjustment, financial resources available to the employer and how much it improves the situation are taken into account in deciding whether the adjustment is 'reasonable' in a particular case.

✔ **Gender reassignment:** Transsexuals who start, propose to start or have completed a process to change their gender are protected against discrimination. They don't need to be under medical supervision to be protected.

✔ **Race:** Protection against discrimination in this area includes non-discrimination for colour, nationality, ethnicity and national origins.

✔ **Religion:** All religions (and the lack of one) are protected against discrimination (presumably including Jedi, which counted as a 'religion' in the last UK Census).

✔ **Sex:** Men and women are protected against discrimination. Specific protection is provided for breast-feeding mothers.

✔ **Sexual orientation:** Bisexuals, gays, heterosexuals and lesbians are protected against discrimination.

✔ **Marriage and civil partnership:** Married employees and those in civil partnerships are protected against discrimination.

✔ **Pregnancy and maternity:** A woman is protected against discrimination during the period of her pregnancy.

A number of types of discrimination exist:

✔ **Direct discrimination:** Occurs when a person is treated less favourably than another person because he possesses one of the above-listed, protected characteristics. Direct discrimination can occur by association – you can't discriminate against a person because he's associated with a person with a protected characteristic.

✔ **Indirect discrimination:** Occurs if a policy, practice or rule applies to everybody, but disadvantages a person with one of the protected characteristics. For example, perhaps everybody is incentivised to work in the workplace on a Saturday, but in practice this disadvantages staff whose religious beliefs prevent them working on Saturdays.

✔ **Harassment:** Includes unwanted conduct that violates someone's dignity or is hostile, degrading, humiliating or offensive to a person with a protected characteristic.

✔ **Victimisation:** Involves treating people unfavourably because they've taken action under the Equality Act or they've supported someone who's doing so.

✔ **Not paying equally:** You must pay men and women doing equal work the same amount and the same benefits. Even if pay and benefits aren't part of an employment contract, you can't discriminate against an employee because of gender. Any difference in pay must be shown to be due to a 'material factor' that has nothing to do with gender.

Defending claims under the Equality Act

You have a couple of defences open to you in cases of alleged discrimination:

✔ **Objective justification:** You may be able to show that the treatment or practice is a proportionate means of achieving a legitimate aim. For example, in relation to direct age discrimination, an age threshold imposed to meet health and safety requirements/comply with insurance standards can justify a policy of employing only people aged over 18.

✔ **Occupational requirements:** Perhaps you can show that only a person with a particular protected characteristic is suitable for the job (for example, in certain situations you may need to recruit someone from a particular religion or sex, such as employing a male customs officer to carry out searches on male passengers).

Keeping time: Working Time Regulations, 1998

These Regulations set out the basic limits on working time and rest periods for employees. Here are some things you need to remember about them:

✔ Employees can work for a limit of 48 hours a week and are entitled to 11 hours rest a day and a day off each week.

✔ An employee can 'opt out' of these time period restrictions but must do so in writing.

✔ On-the-job training, work carried out at home (with prior agreement of the employer), travel required as part of the job and time spent 'on call' at the workplace all constitute working time.

✔ You must keep records of time worked by your staff.

✔ Special rules apply for young people. Young persons (aged between 15 and 18) over compulsory school age may only work 8 hours a day and 40 hours a week, and can't opt out.

The Working Time Regulations also cover holiday pay (check out the later section 'Getting away from it: Holiday pay regulations').

Feeling under the weather: Statutory Sick Pay (SSP)

How are you doing? Ready for more legislation to comply with? You look a bit peaky. I'm sure you need a day off – if so, you may get paid for it.

The Social Security and Housing Benefits Act, 1982 introduced Statutory Sick Pay (SSP) for employees. Here are some key facts about it:

✔ All employees earning at least the National Insurance Lower Earnings Limit (currently £8,060) are eligible for SSP up to a maximum of 28 weeks.

✔ Statutory Sick Pay is paid only from the fourth consecutive qualifying day of sickness: absence from this day is known as a *period of incapacity*.

✔ The employee must provide you with evidence of incapacity for work for the first four to seven days in a self-certificate form, and for periods after the first seven days in a doctor's certificate.

✔ An employer can opt out if it operates its own sickness scheme, but payments must be at least equal to what would be received under the statutory provisions. An employer may offer a more generous scheme than SSP under the employee's contract of employment.

Small businesses can feel the effects of repeated or long-term sickness very keenly. Therefore, implement a policy around illness and standards that all employees must meet. Record all absences to help to deter unauthorised absences and detect genuine problems. (By the way, if someone works for you in the North Pole and claims time off for flu, you know he's making it up, because the region is too cold for flu viruses to survive.)

Paying up: National Minimum Wage (NMW)

The National Minimum Wage Act, 1998 says that employers must pay a minimum wage to all workers, including agency workers, those working part-time and workers on short-term contracts. This requirement applies to *all* businesses regardless of their type or size, and an employee can't agree to be paid less than the NMW.

Limited exceptions do exist, including the genuinely self-employed, those under school-leaving age, au pairs, volunteers and armed service personnel. Interns qualify if they're providing real work for the employer and don't fall within the 'work shadowing' category of NMW.

The four rates, which increase annually, are as follows from October, 2015:

- **For workers aged over 21:** £6.70 per hour
- **For workers aged 18–20:** £5.30 per hour
- **For workers aged 16–17:** £3.87 per hour
- **For apprentices:** £3.30 per hour

Failure to comply can result in the first instance in you being issued an enforcement notice, requiring you to pay the difference between what you paid and what the worker was entitled to under the Act. Further non-compliance can result in you receiving a penalty notice and financial penalties. The Small Business Enterprise and Employment Act, 2015 introduced even tougher penalties for underpayment of the NMW.

Getting away from it: Holiday pay regulations

If you've read this chapter from the start in order, you're probably ready for a break. Well, The Working Time Regulations (which I introduce in the earlier section 'Keeping time: Working Time Regulations, 1998') provide minimum requirements in respect of annual leave that you must provide to all workers, except the self-employed:

- The legal minimum is 28 days' paid leave each year (calculated on a pro-rata basis for part-time workers).
- Workers are entitled to take their leave from the start of their employment and it must be paid at the time it's taken – 'rolled up holiday pay'

(where holiday pay is paid as part of a daily rate for the job regardless of when it's taken) isn't allowed.

✔ Workers on sick leave continue to accrue their statutory holiday pay, and if they leave their employment and haven't taken all their annual leave entitlements, you have to pay them in lieu of this untaken leave.

✔ You can include in your employee's contract the process for granting annual leave (such as the amount of notice that must be given). The minimum notice that must be given is two days.

✔ When dealing with requests, treat all employees in the same way (you can't differentiate on the grounds the Equality Act covers; see the section 'Performing a balancing act: Equality Act, 2010' earlier in this chapter). Ensure that all employees receive at least their statutory leave entitlements during the year.

✔ No statutory requirement exists to include bank holidays in the 28 days or to provide extra pay on a bank holiday.

✔ You can provide more annual leave as part of an employee's contract if you want to.

✔ The calculation of holiday pay is already quite complicated and must now include pay for non-guaranteed overtime – overtime that you don't have to offer but which the employee is obliged to work when asked.

Stretching out: Flexible working obligations

All employees can apply for flexible working if they've been continuously employed for 26 weeks. Don't believe me? Well, The Working Time Regulations, 1998 say so.

Employees can make only one application per year and it must be in writing. Such requests can include asking to vary hours of work, times of work or places of work. You must consider all such requests in a 'reasonable manner' and only refuse when a clear business reason exists why you can't grant one. For example, if Ronald's job is to milk your cows on your farm, working from home wouldn't be very helpful.

You have limited legitimate grounds on which to refuse such a request:

✔ Additional costs

✔ Inability to re-organise work among existing staff

- Inability to recruit additional staff

- Change has a detrimental impact on the business's ability to meet customer demand, on quality or on performance

- Insufficient work

- Planned structural changes don't fit with such requests

Starting a family: Maternity leave and pay

A number of laws give protection to pregnant women and women on maternity leave, most notably the Employment Rights Act, 1996, the Maternity and Parental Leave Regulations, 1999 and the Equality Act, 2010. You definitely need a calendar to comply with these important requirements properly. You also need the 11 fingers of both hands to do some of the calculations (sorry, maths was never my strong point).

You can offer a contractual maternity scheme with benefits above the following statutory minimum benefits if you want:

- A pregnant employee is entitled to paid time off to attend medical appointments and must take two weeks' maternity leave starting on the day childbirth occurs.

- The employee can take 26 weeks' Ordinary Maternity Leave (OML) anytime from the 11th week before the expected week of childbirth and after the birth, followed by a further 26 weeks' Additional Maternity Leave (AML).

- After ordinary or additional maternity leave, the woman has a right to return to the same job, or, if that isn't reasonably practicable, to another job suitable and appropriate for her in the circumstances. An employee must give you eight weeks' notice if she plans to return before the end of OML or AML.

- All employment rights of the pregnant employee continue to be payable throughout this 52-week period (except wages – see the next bullet point). Normal holiday pay continues to accrue throughout the period of maternity leave and, dependent on the type of scheme in place regarding pensions, contributions may still need to be made.

- Statutory Maternity Pay (SMP) is money that the employer must pay to a pregnant employee for up to 39 weeks, provided that the mother satisfies all the following conditions:

  • Is pregnant at the 11th week before the expected week of childbirth

- Is in continuous employment for 26 weeks with the same employer, up to and including the 15th week before the expected week of childbirth

- Has average weekly earnings not less than the lower earnings limit

- Has given 28 days' notice to her employer

- Has produced a medical certificate from a doctor or midwife that gives the due date

- Has stopped work

Pregnancy and maternity constitute a 'protected characteristic' under the Equality Act (see the earlier 'Performing a balancing act: Equality Act, 2010' section). Discriminating directly or indirectly on this ground is unlawful. You need to take particular care during the recruitment process, in providing the same or other suitable jobs on the mother's return from maternity leave, and also in cases involving redundancy during maternity leave. Pregnancies involving surrogates are now also protected.

You also need to reassess health and safety policies in the workplace and take any reasonable steps to remove any extra risks when you're informed of a pregnancy.

Standing aside: Complying with other entitlements

Here are a number of other pieces of legislation that you have to follow in the workplace. Feeling a bit daunted? Never mind, every path has its puddle.

Paternity leave

'What about fathers?', I hear you shout over the sound of a screaming child. Under the Paternity and Adoption Leave Regulations, 2002, most fathers qualify for statutory paternity leave of one or two weeks plus pay, as long as they fulfil the following criteria:

- ✔ They've been employed by the same employer for at least 26 weeks by the end of the 15th week before the expected week of childbirth.

- ✔ They're the biological father of the child, or are married to or are the partner of the baby's mother (includes same sex partners).

- ✔ They have responsibility for the child's upbringing and want to take time off to care for the child or support the mother.

This leave is also available where a child is being adopted.

Dependents leave

Under the Employment Rights Act, 1996 all employees have the right to time off, which allows them to take 'reasonable' unpaid time off to deal with an emergency involving a dependent. Here are some examples:

- When a dependent person falls ill, or is injured
- Death of a dependent
- Unexpected disruption or termination of care
- Unexpected incident involving a dependent child at school

Given that this legislation applies to emergency situations, employees must notify you of the reason for the absence and how long they expect to be absent 'as soon as reasonably practicable'.

Parental leave

The Maternity and Paternity Leave Regulations, 1999 say that parents of either sex who have responsibility for a child aged under 18 are entitled to take up to 18 unpaid parental weeks. The employee must give you at least 21 days' notice and can take the leave only in blocks of one week and no more than four weeks per year. The right to return to the same job as before applies. Parental leave is only available to employees who have at least one year's continuous service.

Shared Parental Leave (SPL)

This new right is governed by the Shared Parental Leave and Leave Curtailment (Amendment) Regulations, 2015.

Mothers have a statutory entitlement of up to 52 weeks' maternity leave and to receive statutory maternity pay for up to 39 weeks (see the earlier section 'Starting a family: Maternity leave and pay'). Under SPL, she must still take the two weeks of statutory maternity leave after the birth, but after this she has an option to share the parental leave with the baby's father, her partner or someone living with her in an 'enduring family relationship' who'll share responsibility for childcare.

Parents can divide up 50 weeks (minus the two compulsory maternity weeks) less the period that the mother has spent on maternity leave and share up to 37 weeks' shared parental pay (39 weeks less 2 weeks' compulsory maternity pay) less the pay the mother has taken. (It sounds like one of those maths problems you used to do at school, doesn't it? 'If it takes 15 minutes to fill a bath with 20 litres of water, how long does it take Betty to drive a fork lift truck from Brighton to Falkirk – while blindfolded?')

This leave is available to qualifying adopters and parents in a surrogacy arrangement, and another entitlement for such parents is to take unpaid time off to attend two antenatal appointments.

Eligibility and notice criteria apply to qualify for SPL, but you need to be a NASA scientist to understand them, so I don't set them out here.

Pay requirements

Under the Employment Rights Act, 1996 you must give an employee a written itemised pay statement containing the following:

- ✔ Gross amount of the wages or salary
- ✔ Amounts of any variable and fixed deductions from that gross amount, and the purposes for which they're made
- ✔ Net amount of wages or salary payable
- ✔ Amount and method of payment of each part-payment (where different parts of the net amount are paid in different ways)

If you fail to provide a pay statement or provide a deficient one, say, with incorrect particulars, an employment tribunal can order you to reimburse the employee.

This Act also says that you're not allowed to make deductions from an employee's wages unless required by Statute, permitted by contract or the employee gives written consent. Lawful deductions include income tax and National Insurance contributions. Any unlawful sums must be repaid to the employee and can be enforced by an employment tribunal.

Data Protection rights

You must comply with the Data Protection Act, 1998 when *processing* (that is, recording, storing, using) data relating to your employees. I set out details of this Act in Chapter 6, so by all means nip there now – I'll wait.

Generally, an employee must consent to this data being processed. You need to formulate a specific employee policy regarding the use of such information or include such a clause in their contracts of employment. Also, you must make sure that this information is held securely and can only be accessed by a restricted number of employees.

Coming and Going: Working with Temporary Workers

Temporary working relationships are a valuable resource for new and expanding small businesses. They help you expand incrementally without adding greatly to the costs and complexity of running the organisation at times of fluctuation and great change. You can find that the regulatory environment concerning funding, corporate governance and so on is complicated enough, without triggering the need to comply with numerous employment regulations when the business may not have the financial or human resources to deal with such compliance.

You can have too much of a good thing though. Although in general temporary workers don't have the same rights as employees in the workplace, you still need to observe some 'dos' and 'don'ts'. The Health and Safety Act Requirements, the Working Time Regulations and the Equality Act all apply to temporary workers, as does the National Minimum Wage Act. The Immigration, Asylum and Nationality Act, 2006 also requires employers to check documents that prove the right of people to work in the UK, and to carry out follow-up checks. This aspect may be especially relevant if a business hires temporary staff, because the immigration authorities can regard their activities as 'work'.

Here I take a look at the various types of temporary worker and different aspects to remember for each group.

Agency workers

You often bring in agency workers (or 'temps') when you have a short-term need for extra pairs of hands – for example, for a particular project or seasonal work.

The agency is in effect the employer. But you have to make sure that all agency workers are treated equally to your other employees after the temp completes a 12-week qualification period. Agency workers can't 'opt out' of these provisions and are also entitled to any on-site facilities that you provide for your own employees.

To avoid the impact of the various regulations, limit the use of agency workers to a period of less than 12 weeks. Or you can use overtime for existing employees or self-employed contractors to avoid this problem. If the agency worker starts a new assignment that's substantially different, starts a new assignment with a different client or has at least a 6-week break, the 12-week rule doesn't apply.

Apprentices

An *apprenticeship* provides an opportunity for on-the-job training and for persons aged 16–24 to attain a nationally recognised certificate on completion. If you enter into a contract and its main purpose is to train the employee, in effect it's an apprenticeship contract. These contracts are usually for a fixed number of years and can't be terminated early other than for very serious cases of misconduct such as fraud.

 The new and more common arrangement is an *apprenticeship agreement* as described in the Apprenticeship, Skills, Children and Learning Act, 2009. The Act sets out a 'prescribed form' for this agreement: it must include the skill, trade or occupation for which the apprentice is being trained. This type of agreement is a 'service' agreement and may be more helpful to you, because terminating is easier in the event of misconduct on the part of the apprentice.

Interns

No legal definition of an *intern* exists, although certain elements tend to characterise the arrangement. Internships provide an opportunity for people to gain hands-on work experience, related to their area of study, and allow the firm to expand and add value to its day-to-day operations. This aspect is especially helpful for a small business, because it provides an effective way to take on bigger projects without increasing financial and administrative burdens.

 The main concern for a small business employing interns is whether or not they're classed as *workers*. If so, they're entitled to the National Minimum Wage (see the earlier 'Paying up: National Minimum Wage [NMW]' section). The use of internships has expended greatly in recent times, as have allegations that employers are using them illegally. Merely using the title of 'intern' or 'volunteer' or the fact that people are happy to do unpaid work can still mean that they're workers for the purposes of NMW. A *volunteer* exception to the NMW applies to those working for charities and voluntary organisations, but most interns work within commercial organisations, and so this exemption doesn't apply.

Interns are probably classed as workers for the purposes of NMW if one of the following applies:

- ✔ The person is providing real work to the employer that a paid employee can do.
- ✔ The person isn't free to come and go as he pleases.
- ✔ The person stays for the placement longer than a few weeks.
- ✔ The person has been offered future work, and is using his specific skills in carrying out work for the employer.

Cases regarding internships and breaches of NMW show that the Courts or the Employment Tribunal look at the reality of the relationship; the fact that no contract exists or no money is provided (except for expenses) can still mean that the intern is a worker.

To avoid an intern being classified as a worker, the person must fall within the *work shadowing* category of the NMW Act. This means that the intern is only observing or shadowing employees of the business and not undertaking work. In other words, you mustn't rely on the services of the intern.

Zero-hours contracts

The concept of a zero-hours contract hasn't yet been defined in law, leaving critics to say that these arrangements are abusive.

A *zero-hours contract* is a casual agreement where the employer isn't obliged to provide work and the employee isn't required to accept work; the employee is paid only for the hours he works and is usually required to work on short notice. In effect, no obligation exists on either side.

These agreements allow more flexibility in working arrangements for when you face a sudden increase in demand, seasonal changes, expansion into new markets or a need for emergency cover due to unforeseen circumstances. In 2014, the Office for National Statistics estimated that over two million zero-hours contracts were in place in the UK.

The main concern regarding these types of contracts is the use of 'exclusivity clauses', which restrict employees from working for other firms even if the employer has no hours to provide at a particular time. This clause effectively requires a worker to be available at all times with no guarantee of work or payment. The Small Business, Enterprise and Employment Act, 2105 has now banned this type of provision.

Employment tribunals have found that people on zero-hours contracts can be 'employees', if a pattern to the hours worked exists and this has remained the same for a particular period of time, with all the protections for the worker that status implies. In any event, zero-hours employees must be paid NMW rates for the hours they work and for any hours they spend hanging around in the workplace, waiting for work. In light of this, and the prohibition on the use of exclusivity clauses, explore all other options before settling on the use of zero-hours contracts.

Chapter 8

Protecting What You Own: Intellectual Property

Many things have business value for you (and I don't mean that signed photo of Warren Buffett on your desk as a good-luck charm). I'm thinking about your products, stock, machinery and staff – including you, of course, you great big bundle of talent. But one of the most valuable parts of your business is something that's often quite difficult to see or touch: your intellectual property.

Intellectual property refers to the output of your creativity. The World Intellectual Property Forum (the inelegantly named WIPO) refers to intellectual property as 'creations of the mind'. Your creativity can find expression in the creation of a brand, the design of a logo, the production of a film, the writing of software, the invention of a brand new technical process – even the creation of a unique smell.

Intellectual property rights are the rights you have to protect that creative outpouring (yes, that's right, even a special pong you create can give you intellectual property rights). These creations are sometimes called *intangible assets* to distinguish them from *tangible assets* (such as plant and machinery) that you can physically see or touch.

Here I look at the different types of intellectual property: copyrights, trademarks, patents and design rights. I describe what each one is, who owns it, why it's valuable and how you can protect it.

Defining and Using Copyright

Copyright is one of those expressions that everybody has heard of but is quite hard to define. You are, almost certainly, familiar with the copyright notices that you find on the inside of book covers and on LP and CD covers (sorry, that dates me a bit). You also recognise the familiar copyright symbol '©' that usually forms part of the copyright notice. So, what is a copyright?

Copyright is the right of a creator of a particular piece of work to prevent other people from reproducing or making use of that work. The law of copyright exists to make sure that if you're a creator, you can create value from your work by retaining control over its exploitation.

Recognising different types of copyright

The types of creative work that have copyright under English law are set out in a statute called the Copyright Designs and Patents Act, 1988 (or CDPA). These rights apply to *original literary works:* things in writing, such as books, poems, articles, plans and so on.

Literary works don't have to meet any particular standard of artistic merit to qualify for copyright. They just have to be written. Even if you detest the lyrics and tune to 'The Birdie Song', the writers still have a copyright.

As you can see, the definition of a literary work is wide and includes the following:

- **Computer programs:** Because their functionality can be reduced to a written form, even if that written form consists of 1s and 0s and other symbols that mean nothing to non-programmers.

- **Tables:** Not the kind you spill your dinner on, but an arrangement of columns or rows displaying data.

- **Compilations:** If you compile, say, newspaper articles or reports, you could be creating a copyright in the compilation of that data, which is separate from any copyright in the individual items that are part of that compilation.

- **Databases:** Such as registers of consumers, customers or corporate information, or even phone directories. To qualify, the data has to be arranged in a 'systematic or methodical way and individually accessible by electronic or other means'. So that probably rules out your weekly shopping list. . . .

Since 1997, a separate EU right for databases also exists, mysteriously called the *sui generis* right (a Latin expression meaning 'separate right'). Why they can't use English or one of the other four official EU languages to describe it, I don't know. In order to benefit from this right, you must have made a 'substantial investment in obtaining, verifying or presenting the contents of the database'. This phrase refers to the time and effort spent in finding data or materials that have already been created and verifying them and collating them, as opposed to any investment made in creating any new data or material.

✔ **Dramatic works:** Includes television screenplays, theatre scripts and documented dance routines. The key feature of such works is that they're capable of being performed in front of an audience.

✔ **Musical works:** Covers written songs, jingles, theme tunes or the background music to a computer game. Mere sounds are excluded, and so your singing in the shower doesn't count, however delightful.

✔ **Artistic works:** A catch-all that covers other creative outputs, including a graphic work (a diagram, drawing, cartoon or plan), photograph, sculpture, collage, work of architecture or artistic craftsmanship (including creative works of interior design).

✔ **Sound recordings, films and broadcasts:** Including those received by satellite and cable, radio broadcasts, and audio and video streaming services, or on-demand transmissions over the Internet.

✔ **Typographical arrangement of published editions:** The way in which words are arranged on a page. So any unique style of publication of a piece of work can be protected as a copyright work. An example would be a particular printed edition of a book by a publishing house. Another publisher that wants to reprint the work can't use the same style or layout as the original publisher.

Different types of copyright can exist within a single work. For example, a song may contain lyrics that are protected as a literary work while the music is protected as a musical work. A recording of that song attracts protection as a sound recording. Similarly, a video stream of a movie is protected as a broadcast, the movie itself is protected as a film and the script can be protected as a dramatic work. The 007 James Bond films have copyright in all these elements and have generated US$6 billion of revenues as a result – a lasting legacy that influences this chapter.

Creating copyrights

The law of copyright protects the *expression* of ideas but not the ideas themselves. To benefit from copyright, the work must be recorded in some way. This essential requirement is known as *fixation*.

No matter how much artwork or how many designs and products you dream up, any attached rights only arise after you commit them to paper or some other recorded form. So that great song you think of on the number 39 bus isn't a copyright until you write it down or record it.

In relation to literary, dramatic, musical and artistic works, and databases, only original works qualify for copyright protection. Therefore, you can't just copy someone else's work and pass it off as your own piece of creative work. You must have used your own skill, judgement and effort.

The test of originality isn't a high one to overcome, with works such as calendars having been deemed original. Copyright in films, broadcasts, sound recordings and typographical arrangements don't require originality, because they're always composed of other underlying works.

Owning copyright: Who do these rights belong to?

The general rule is that the first owner of copyright in the work is the author. This seems obvious for something like a book, but who's the author of a film or of a sound recording? The CDPA specifies who the author is in these and in other cases of uncertainty:

- **Sound recording:** The author is the *producer* – the person who made the arrangements necessary for the sound recording.
- **Film:** The authors are the producer and the principal director:
  - The *producer* is defined in the CDPA as the person who made the arrangements necessary for making the film.
  - The *principal director* is the person who has creative control over the making of the film.
- **Broadcast:** The author is the *person making the broadcast.*
- **Typographical arrangement of a published edition:** The author is the *publisher.*

The fact that the first owner of copyright is the author of the work is important in the case of commissioned works. You may believe that your business automatically owns the rights to a work you commission a third party to make – but not so fast, Mr Goldfinger. In fact, you have to specifically agree for a transfer (an *assignment*) of the ownership of the rights in the work to ensure that those rights belong to your business. Otherwise the third party is the author and therefore the owner.

So, if you commission a freelancer, consultant or contractor to write some software for you, or create some designs, make sure that you take an assignment of their work.

In one instance, the author *isn't* the owner of the copyright in the work she created: when she's an employee. Under the CDPA, where an employee makes work in the course of her employment, the first owner of copyright in that work is the employer (subject to any agreement to the contrary). However, because the rule relates only to work made 'within the course of the employee's employment', work that the employee does outside of her employment isn't automatically caught by the rule. What if the employee creates something not strictly related to her work in her garage over the weekend? Tricky.

For this reason, insert a term into the employment contract with your employees stating that copyright in *all* works created by the employee during her period of employment and in the course of her employment are owned by your business, regardless of when and where they were made.

Watch out for creating situations in which *joint ownership* of copyright arises (where more than one person has created the work). Joint ownership can be a problem, because the authority of all owners is required to exploit the rights to such work. This can be very difficult if the owners have different views on how their work can be used. No doubt you can envision the type of awkward situations that can crop up.

Protecting your copyright

Worried about how to protect your copyrights? No need; I've been expecting you, Mr Bond, and here are some tips. In the UK, the owner doesn't have to comply with any formalities in order to rely on copyright: under English law copyright arises automatically, with no need to register it with any regulatory body.

The same doesn't apply in all countries – for example, the US requires registration.

Therefore, you may be wondering why you see copyright notices in publications and what use the copyright symbol serves? In English law the © notice doesn't signify anything, but it's used for these reasons:

✔ It reminds others that the author (or other owner) has rights in the work and that any attempt to make unlawful use of that work may result in legal action being taken.

✔ It provides an automatic bar to a defence of 'innocent' infringement of copyright. If you don't know that the work is copyrighted, and have no reason to know, you can use it as a defence or to reduce the amount of damages you have to pay for infringement. But you can't make that argument if the work you infringe carries the © notice.

✔ It identifies the owner so that people know who to contact if they want to licence that copyright.

Infringing copyright

Copyright doesn't last forever, and the period of protection varies for different works:

✔ **Literary, dramatic, musical or artistic works:** 70 years from the end of the calendar year in which the last remaining author dies.

✔ **Films:** 70 years from the end of the calendar year in which the last principal director, author or composer dies.

✔ **Sound recordings:** 70 years from the end of the calendar year in which it was published.

✔ **Broadcasts:** 50 years from the end of the calendar year of broadcast.

✔ **Typographical arrangement of published editions:** 25 years from the end of the year of first publication.

✔ **Sui generis databases:** 15 years from first publication (the earlier 'Recognising different types of copyright' section has more details).

If you're the copyright owner in a piece of work, only you are permitted to do a number of specific acts during these periods of time; nobody else can do them without infringing your copyright. The CDPA sets out these infringing acts, which are divided into two general categories: acts of primary infringement and acts of secondary infringement.

Primary infringement

The six acts of *primary infringement* don't require knowledge of infringement or intention to infringe:

- ✔ Copying the work, including by downloading
- ✔ Issuing copies of the work to the public – for example, by selling it or distributing it
- ✔ Renting or lending the work to the public
- ✔ Performing, showing or playing the work in public
- ✔ Communicating the work to the public
- ✔ Making an adaptation of the work (for example, changing it in some way) or doing any of the above in relation to an adaptation

Authorising another person to do any of these acts is also a primary infringement of copyright.

Secondary infringement

Acts of *secondary infringement* require some knowledge by the infringer that the work is infringing and frequently apply to retailers or publishers.

These infringing acts include importing infringing copies of the work into the UK other than for domestic and private use; selling infringing copies; making, importing or selling equipment specifically designed to make infringing copies of copyrighted works; and knowingly transmitting infringing copies of the work over a telecommunications system such as the Internet.

Making copyright count

If you think someone is infringing your copyrighted work, you can take action to prevent it.

You can get your legal representatives to send *cease and desist* letters. These letters inform the suspected infringer that she's making use of the work without the authorisation of the copyright owner and demanding that this action stops, or the infringer risks facing legal action.

For 'online' infringements of copyright, another option is to write to the search engine provider or site hosting your material without authorisation, notifying it of the infringement and requesting the *take down* (removal) of the content from the offending host site. Many sites that use copyright extensively (such as YouTube) have well-documented procedures in their Terms and Conditions to help you do so. (I discuss online Terms and Conditions in Chapter 6.)

If you've already tried these approaches, or if the matter is very urgent, you can apply to the court for an *injunction* to prevent any further infringement of your work or to deliver to you any infringing copies of the work. This temporary order from the court stops somebody doing the infringing action immediately – get your skates on, though; if the court thinks that you've been too slow, it assumes that the matter is not urgent enough to grant you an injunction.

If you're aiming for *A View to a Kill,* you can bring a claim against the infringing party for *an account of profits* (to pay the money it made from the infringement to you) or for damages (for an amount that puts you in the financial position you would've been in if the infringing act(s) hadn't taken place).

If you obtain an injunction, it's reviewed during a subsequent trial for damages or profit accounting. If the court decides that you were wrongly granted an injunction, you may have to pay damages to the person you wrongly accused for her losses during the period of the injunction.

If you do decide to take legal proceedings, bear in mind the time and expense involved (flip to Chapter 15 for more on disputes). Also consider the effectiveness of litigation – especially if the infringement is a digital one. People can make floods of infringing copies at the push of a button and unless you have a lot of resources, infringers can be very difficult to trace and stop; you may be using a sheet of paper to halt a tsunami.

Demystifying Patents

A *patent* is a right to use and to exploit an invention on an industrial scale for a limited period of time (as opposed to a parent, who's someone you can use and exploit your whole life!). Patents can be divided into two broad categories: *product patents* or *process patents,* and they're governed in the UK by the Patents Act, 1977.

Traditionally, patents are associated with scientific inventions in fields such as aeronautics, pharmaceuticals or electronics, but their application is considerably wider. Huge amounts of time and effort are put into researching and developing new and potentially enormously lucrative technologies, including by small companies, and a patent can be a valuable way of protecting a return from that investment.

No doubt many of Q's ingenious inventions from the Bond movies would attract patents – the exploding pen, cigarette lighter and cheese and pickle sandwich – what, you don't remember that last one?

Knowing whether you can obtain a patent

Your invention must fulfil four key criteria to be granted a patent:

- ✔ **The invention mustn't be excluded under the Act.** These exclusions come in four sets:

  - Creations that are copyrights.

  - Discoveries, scientific theories or mathematical methods.

  - Presentation of information.

  - Schemes, rules or methods for performing a mental act, playing a game, doing business or computers programs are also expressly excluded as non-patentable.

  This last item is worth bearing in mind if your business is a technology enterprise – for example, building software. Generally, patenting computer programs isn't possible in the UK (though in other territories, such as the US, more scope exists for doing so).

- ✔ **The invention must be new.** The invention, or any information relating to it, mustn't have been made available to the public in any shape or form before the *priority date* (usually the date of filing of the patent application) in such a way as would allow a skilled person to work out the invention for herself.

  The formal expression is that the patent mustn't 'form part of the state of the art'. The disclosure of such information is known as an *enabling disclosure* (or *anticipation*). For example, the disclosure in a journal of details of your invention or any use of it in public could invalidate any subsequent patent application.

  Keep inventions *For Your Eyes Only* in the early stages. File an early application for your patent before word leaks out or you inadvertently blab about it in your excitement.

- ✔ **The proposed invention must involve an inventive step.** The invention mustn't be obvious to a person skilled in the area to which it relates. In other words, the invention must feature some real creative spark or ingenuity.

✔ **The invention must be capable of industrial application.** *Industry* is widely interpreted in this case and refers to any trade or manufacturing – whether for profit or not.

Registering patents in the UK

Here's the process for obtaining a patent, which typically takes up to four years until it's granted (if you're in a hurry, it may not be for you):

1. **Filing your application:** You must submit your application to the Intellectual Property Office (IPO) at `http://www.gov.uk/apply-for-a-patent` and include these elements:

   - A *request* for the grant of the patent.

   - A *specification* containing a description of the invention. The specification must be clear and complete and provide enough information for a skilled but uninventive person to be able to perform the invention. The idea is that if the inventor is to be granted a patent (a monopoly right to exploit the invention) in return the inventor must provide sufficient information to enable the invention to be further exploited after the patent expires. So, you do have to disclose details of your patent in order to get the protection in the first place. Some people feel uncomfortable about revealing such information.

   - A set of *claims* or numbered statements that define the requested boundaries of the rights granted under the patent – the areas of activity that the monopoly should cover, which you want to be as broad as possible.

   - An *abstract* of the invention, which is a basic summary of it.

   The application is a very complex document and you really need to get it right. I suggest that you employ a patent agent to draft it for you (and submit the application on your behalf).

   After the patent application has been filed with the IPO, you usually have 12 months to submit any further details.

2. **Requesting a search:** Following your request, the IPO makes an initial examination and assessment of the application, including searches of other published patents against which the application can be considered. The IPO usually issues a report within six months of receipt of the search request having been made.

3. **Publishing the application:** Usually done 18 months after the filing date, with the IPO following it up with further substantive investigation. It

then raises any further issues with you, informing you of any changes that need to be made to the application.

4. **Publishing the patent:** Wait for it . . . this usually takes another couple of years, after which a certificate evidencing the grant is issued to you as the patent holder. The patent is granted from this second publication date. Phew!

The patent is yours. Marvellous! Patents last for a period of up to 20 years, starting from the date of filing of the patent application (not the date of its grant). An initial 4-year period is granted and the patent is renewable each year after that up to the 20-year limit.

The cost of obtaining a patent starts from around £2,500 if you use a patent agent and can rise, depending on the complexity of the invention, to between £5,000 and £7,000. Some people see this as being quite expensive and take the view that they'd rather invest in more innovation to protect their lead in the market than investing in patents. But my advice is don't be Moneypenny wise and pound foolish – a patent can be very valuable for your business and its valuation.

If your application is rejected you have a period of time to alter it in line with the IPO's reasons for rejection and reapply. Failing that you have 28 days from the decision to give notice of an appeal to the court.

Registering patents internationally

The UK is only part of the picture. What if you want protection in other countries? At the moment, no European Union patent currently exists, but under the European Patent Convention (EPC) an applicant can obtain patents in member countries by following a single process:

1. **You make a single application to the European Patent Office (EPO) in Munich.**

   You can do so directly or through the IPO in the UK, listing the countries in which patent protection is sought (check out `http://www.epo.org/applying/basics.html`).

2. **The EPO conducts searches in a similar way to the IPO with UK patents (refer to the preceding section).**

   A single examiner considers the application, applying criteria set out in the EPC.

3. **The patent is granted.**

   You get a bundle of patents covering each requested country (rather than a single one covering several areas).

If your European application fails, you can appeal to one of about 30 different appeal boards depending on the sector of technology that applies to your potential patent.

The EPO's collection of granted patents lasts for 20 years from the date of filing of the application, though the process is somewhat flawed:

- ✔ The process is long, generally taking 3–5 years from filing. Never mind, *You Only Live Twice.*

- ✔ The process is very expensive, due in part to the fact that all patents must have their claims translated into English, French and German. The actual fees depend on the number of countries in which registration is required, with estimates of around €30,000 for a patent registered in eight countries as a rough guide – a significant amount of money.

  In addition, because the effect of the EPC patent is the same as granting patents in each relevant country, you have to conduct any legal action you take to enforce your rights under the patent on a national basis. In other words, you have to bring a claim in each country in which you have the benefit of the patent protection – another expensive and time-consuming exercise.

Unleashing the power of patents

When granted, a patent provides a monopoly right over your invention, covering all elements of the claims set out in the specification. You can use it exclusively or license it for money. With more than 20 million patents in the world generating over US$500 billion annually in licence fees, it's potentially a great source of value. (Small wonder that the latest 007 movie *Patents of Doom* involves a Bond villain stealing the globe's repository of patents and holding the world to ransom. Not really – but it would make a great Bond movie if you included enough explosions.)

You can also protect your patent as follows.

Others infringe your patent with these primary acts of infringement:

- ✔ Using a patented product or patented process
- ✔ Making a patented product
- ✔ Disposing of a patented product or offering to dispose of it
- ✔ Keeping a patented product

✔ Importing a patented product

✔ Offering a patented process for use in the UK, knowing that such use without the patent owner's consent is an infringement

An act of secondary infringement is to supply, or offer to supply, any person in the UK with the capability to put the invention to use, when the person knows, or should reasonably know, that the intended outcome is UK usage of the invention.

If your patent is being infringed, you have a number of options available to you to protect your invention, which are similar to those for copyright infringement (see 'Making copyright count' earlier in this chapter).

You can write to the suspected infringer with a copy of the patent asserting your rights and warning against infringement.

If you make any threats without justification, the accused can bring her own claim against you (called a *threats action*), including suing for damages for any loss caused by such unjustified threats.

If that doesn't work you can seek an injunction. You can seek damages or an account of profits, but this isn't available if the defendant argues successfully that she wasn't aware of the existence of the patent and had no reasonable grounds to believe that it existed.

You can help protect your patent by marking a patented product with its patent number or application number where possible; this serves to overcome the 'I wasn't aware' defence (adding the word 'patent' or 'patented' has no such effect).

Defendants also commonly try to argue that the patent itself isn't valid: surprisingly, the award of a patent isn't conclusive evidence of its validity. If a defendant can show that the invention is *not,* in fact, novel or the other requirements haven't been met, the infringement claim fails, and, what's worse, the patent can be revoked.

Litigating patent infringement claims can be extremely expensive due to the complexity of inventions. Apple and Samsung slugging it out in the US courts is one thing; a small and medium-size enterprise (SME) taking on this kind of cost and evidential burden is quite another.

The Intellectual Property Enterprise Court (`http://www.justice.gov.uk/courts/rcj-rolls-building/intellectual-property-enterprise-court`), a specialist UK court designed to handle intellectual property claims, offers some help with two claims processes:

✔ **Higher value process:** Damages recoverable for infringement are limited to £500,000 and recoverable costs of litigation from the other side are limited to £50,000.

✔ **Lower value process:** Damages are limited to £10,000 and recoverable costs awards are very restricted.

Marking Out Your Property: Trademarks

A *trademark* is a mark that a business uses to differentiate its goods or services from those of all other businesses. It's a badge of (trade) origin that tells the consumer 'this is my product' or 'these are our services'.

As the business sells more goods or services, more people become familiar with it and the trademark assumes greater significance and value. The golden 'M' of McDonalds, the blue Twitter bird and that ever-present apple out of which someone has taken a sneaky bite are all strong trademarks. So is the 007 trademark from the Bond films.

When you have a trademark registered, nobody can use that mark in your business sector without your agreement, and so it's a very valuable way of protecting your brand.

Exploring whether you can trademark

To protect your trademark in the UK, you can register it with the IPO. You don't have to, and you can still bring a claim against someone for unauthorised use of your mark if it's unregistered, but succeeding is a lot more difficult than if the mark is registered (see the later 'Enforcing unregistered trademarks' section).

In order to be able to register your trademark, it must meet the definition in the Trade Marks Act, 1994. The full definition is 'any sign capable of being represented graphically which is capable of distinguishing goods or services of one undertaking from those of other undertakings'.

Here are some things businesses can and have registered:

- ✔ **Designs, letters and numbers:** As long as they're distinctive, for example, the James Bond '007' mark, or Bond's favourite 'Martini' mark (whether shaken or stirred).

- ✔ **Slogans:** For example, Nike's 'Just do it' and Internet domain names.

- ✔ **Shape of a product or its packaging:** Think the triangular-shaped Toblerone chocolate bar or the Coca-Cola bottle.

- ✔ **Sounds:** Computer chip maker *Intel* has registered its short musical jingle consisting of four notes.

- ✔ **Smells:** As long as they can be represented graphically! For example, a tyre manufacturer has registered a floral fragrance in connection with its manufactured tyres – much more fragrant than the smell of burning rubber. The smell of freshly cut grass has also been registered in relation to tennis balls and the smell of bitter (beer) in relation to darts – 180!

- ✔ **Gestures:** For example, supermarket chain Asda trademarked the 'double-tap on a back pocket' from its TV adverts.

Plenty of potential marks, however, fail to qualify for registration:

- ✔ **Marks that lack any distinctive character or are purely descriptive of goods or services.** This is because the trademark is a monopoly and a monopoly can't be granted in something that's indistinguishable from the general use of the words involved. So 'Cookies' (for a name of biscuit) can't be registered on its own.

  Note that you can't get around this with a novel spelling of a general word like 'Cookeees' (bad luck), but combining two or more existing words, or parts of those words, can be registered if they're used in an unusual way (for example, 'Big Bear Cookeees' may be okay, as might Big Bear Cookies, unless you're making biscuits for large bears to eat).

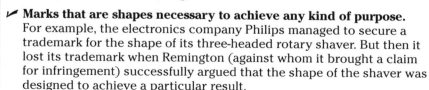

  When setting up your business, make sure that you think of a catchy name for it. As well as grabbing attention, the name is also more likely to be eligible for trademark registration.

- ✔ **Marks that are shapes necessary to achieve any kind of purpose.** For example, the electronics company Philips managed to secure a trademark for the shape of its three-headed rotary shaver. But then it lost its trademark when Remington (against whom it brought a claim for infringement) successfully argued that the shape of the shaver was designed to achieve a particular result.

✔ **Marks that aren't descriptive but provide substantial value to the goods.** For example, the design of the Dualit toaster failed to obtain a trademark, because the designer shape added *substantial value* to the product.

✔ **Marks contrary to public policy or acceptable principles of morality.** For example, if for some bizarre reason you wanted to register 'Fraudster' as your trademark, you'd fail.

✔ **You're registering the mark 'in bad faith'.** For example, if you have no intention of using it.

Also, if you try and register a mark that's identical or similar to any other registered trademarks that are used in relation to identical or similar services to yours, you get a *Dr. No* from the IPO.

A further restriction relates to well-known brands, even if they operate in a completely different area to your business. Any mark that's identical or similar to a mark of such a brand isn't allowed if its use would (without due cause) take unfair advantage of, or cause damage to, the distinctive character or reputation of the well-known mark. This rule is designed to prevent a business riding on the coattails of another business.

Registering trademarks in the UK

To register a trademark, you apply to the IPO, supplying details of your proposed mark at `http://www.gov.uk/register-a-trademark`.

Be careful with colours. If you represent your mark in one colour, the IPO assumes that you want protection for only that colour, unless you specify otherwise. If your mark is in black and white, you have to specify that these are your chosen colours, otherwise the IPO assumes that these shades aren't a feature of the mark.

You need to state the goods or services for which the mark is to be used. The registration applies only to the classes you request. The IPO uses the *NICE Classification* system, which separates goods into 34 categories and provides 11 classes of service to choose from (see `http://www.wipo.int/classifications/nice/en/ITsupport/Version20150101`).

As for patents claims, you may want to cover as many different classes of goods and services as possible to extend your protection as widely as possible. But the wider you cast the net, the more you risk others challenging you at the time of registration or later due to similarity to other marks in the classes you've chosen.

After you file the application, the IPO examines it to check that the registration requirements have been met, including conducting a comparison of the mark with other registered marks. Within 20 days of receipt of the application, the IPO sends you a report, setting out any objections to the application and providing a period of two months in which to address any issues raised in the report.

If the examiner is satisfied with the application in its current form, or following any required amendments, your application is published in the *Trade Marks Journal* where everybody can read all about it for a further two months. The IPO publishes this journal every Friday and it contains applications for UK trademarks and international applications that include the UK. During this period, anybody can oppose the registration by notifying the IPO in writing and setting out grounds for opposition. Any objections are usually dealt with in writing, although a hearing can be requested for representations to be made in person.

In the absence of opposition, or if any opposition is withdrawn or proved unsuccessful, the trademark is registered and you receive a certificate of registration. The whole process can be quite quick. With no opposition, it can take only a few months from start to finish – voila!

When registered, protection lasts for an initial period of ten years. Well, only *Diamonds Are Forever.* The trademark can then be renewed for successive periods of ten years upon payment of a renewal fee.

The fee for registering a trade mark is £170, plus £50 for each additional class requested. Alternatively, you can use the 'Right Start' application, in which the IPO drives the process of registration – for which you pay £100 upfront for an examination to be carried out and a further £100 if you go ahead with the registration. The £50 for each additional category also applies to this form of application.

Tackling international trademark registration

If you want to protect your mark or marks outside of the UK, you can register a *Community Trade Mark* (CTM) in Europe.

CTMs are administered by the Office for Harmonization in the Internal Market (OHIM), which is based in Alicante in Spain (`https://oami.europa.eu/ohimportal/en`). Through this organisation, you can obtain a single trademark registration that covers all 28 member states of the European Union.

Any trademark must meet the criteria set out in the European Regulations that govern trademarks in the EU, which are, essentially, the same as those in the UK.

You submit your trademark application to the IPO or directly to the OHIM. The contents of the application are the same as those of the UK application in the preceding section. You can make your application in any language, but it must also be translated into a second language: French, German, Italian, Spanish or English.

The OHIM searches against other CTM applications and registrations. It's looking for identical or similar marks and can refuse your application if the criteria aren't met. You can also request a search of the national registries of certain countries, on payment of an additional fee.

The OHIM then sends you a report. It sets out any objections to the mark, and you have two months in which to remedy any issues it raises.

If the application is refused, you may still be able to convert the CTM application into a national application.

If no objections are raised, or the objections are resolved, the trademark is published in the EU's official hugely popular daily *CTM Bulletin* in a mere 23 EU official languages.

After publication, people have up to three months in which to oppose the trademark application with written submissions to the OHIM. They can raise opposition only on the grounds of existence of an identical or similar earlier mark of a business providing identical or similar services (where a risk of confusion exists), or with a reputation where your use of the mark would take advantage of, or be damaging to, the other mark.

In the absence of objections, the mark is registered and you get a certificate. Registration is for ten years initially and can be renewed for successive ten-year periods.

A CTM application costs €900 if made online (€1,050 in paper form) and a supplementary fee of €150 is payable for each additional class of goods or services required in excess of the first three classes, So, covering all 28 countries in the EU isn't too expensive. Also, the process can be completed in around five months, which is pretty fast by EU standards.

Terrorising with trademarks

A trademark provides you with a monopoly right to use the mark in relation to the classes of goods and/or services for which it's registered. You can bring a claim for infringement for any unauthorised use of that mark – including for backdated infringements that occurred from the date of the filing of your application to the date of actual registration.

Someone else can't use, in the course of trade, any sign that's identical to the mark in relation to identical products or services. Nor can it use a similar mark in relation to the same or similar services where public confusion is likely. Nor can it use your mark in relation to any goods and services where your registered mark has a reputation and use of the similar or identical sign takes unfair advantage of, or is damaging to, the distinctive character or reputation of your mark.

You can seek to remedy trademark infringement in several ways, some of which I look at here. (They're similar to the remedies for breach of copyright and patent infringement: refer to the earlier sections 'Making copyright count' and 'Unleashing the power of patents', respectively.)

Before you bring a claim, you usually write to the offender, enclosing evidence of your registered trademark and requesting a halt to its use of the mark. You warn that if it doesn't stop, you have a *Licence to Kill* (well, permission to take action, at least), and you'd then commence formal proceedings against it. You must be careful though, because (as with patents) for some types of claim you can be subject to a *threats action* yourself if your claim is unjustified.

If that doesn't work, you can claim an injunction to prevent further use of the mark – an order to remove the mark from any goods or materials, or for the goods or materials to be delivered to you or destroyed. You can also claim damages for loss of revenues caused by the infringement or seek to recover profits the offender makes as a result of the infringement.

Some defences do exist to trademark infringement. For example, the defendant may say that your trademark should be revoked because it's misleading or has become a generic term and so is no longer distinguishable. Or she may argue that the trademark should never have been granted in the first place, because of another competing application or someone else with a general reputation in that name already. Also note that a competitor may use your name without this amounting to infringement if it's doing *comparative advertising* (for example, comparing the [lower] price of its goods with the [higher] price of yours).

To notify others of the registration of your trademark, you can place the '®' symbol, the letters 'RTM' or the words 'registered trade mark' directly after the mark. Like the use of the copyright symbol, doing so serves no formal purpose in the UK, but it's a practical measure to warn off potential infringers. Only use these symbols if the mark is registered; otherwise, you're breaching the Trade Marks Act, 1994 and committing a criminal offence by falsely representing that the mark is registered.

Enforcing unregistered trademarks

If your trademark isn't registered and somebody starts using that mark, you may still be able to bring a claim under the law of *passing off.*

Passing off is a *tort*. No, not a tart (or indeed a torte), but a legal wrong not based on any underlying contractual relationship between the parties concerned. Judges developed torts from case law (the *common law*) to try to make the world a fairer place.

In order to bring a successful claim against a third party for passing off, you have to establish three elements:

- ✔ **Goodwill:** The mark has a good name or reputation. In other words, what makes a customer return to the same service provider or repeatedly buy the same brand of product.
- ✔ **Misrepresentation:** For example, the public is led to believe, or is likely to believe, that the infringer's goods or services are yours.
- ✔ **Damage:** What you suffered as a result.

Check out the nearby 'We're talkin' chalk and cheese, guv, honest' sidebar, for a couple of real-life examples.

Passing one let alone all three of these tests is tough, and so register a trademark if you can: enforcing it is then much easier.

We're talkin' chalk and cheese, guv, honest

The three trademark passing-off elements came up in the *Jif Lemon case*. Jif Lemon packaged its lemon juice in a plastic lemon-shaped and sized container with a green cap. It brought a claim when a supermarket began selling lemon juice in a slightly larger plastic-shaped container with a red cap. The shape of the packaging wasn't protected by a registered trademark, but the claim was successful.

Misrepresentation arose when Asda used the slogan 'Pick up a Puffin' to advertise its Puffin biscuits. This slogan was similar to United Biscuits's famous 'Pick up a Penguin' slogan, used for Penguin biscuits. The courts decided that misrepresentation applied: people may believe that the makers of Penguin biscuits made Puffin biscuits (that's a lot of seabirds!).

Another common misrepresentation is representing that celebrities endorse a particular product when they don't.

If you can't register your mark, still use the letters 'TM' to notify that the mark is functioning as a trademark – it may put people off using it.

Understanding Whether You Have Design Rights

Although some elements of the design process can find protection under the law of copyright (such as design documentation and diagrams; refer to the earlier 'Defining and Using Copyright' section), copyright alone doesn't always offer you enough protection for your designs. For example, you can use *design rights* to protect the appearance of your product or its look and feel.

Design rights are an underused element of intellectual property rights because many people don't know about them. Aston Martin, makers of the famous James Bond DB7 car (which I really want for my birthday), recently sued a car manufacturer for allegedly stealing its designs.

Two types of design rights exist: registered design rights and unregistered design rights (for the latter, see the later 'Taking action to enforce unregistered design rights' section).

The Registered Designs Act, 1949 (RDA) provides protection for the whole or part of a design, including its texture, contours, shape, materials, colours or how it's ornamented. You can protect a wide range of products, including packaging, graphic symbols and individual elements that form part of a *complex product* (one composed of at least two replaceable component parts).

In order to be capable of registration, a design must meet these criteria:

✔ **The design must be new:** One not identical to any other design made available to the public before the *relevant date* – the date of application for registration of the design. If you willingly disclosed the design before applying for registration you risk making your application invalid unless (despite your disclosure) your design couldn't reasonably have become known to any specialist carrying on business in your sector in the European Economic Area.

✔ **The design must have individual character:** The impression that the design makes on a tradesperson in the field in which the design is used must be different from any impression made by any other design that already exists in the relevant field.

   ✓ **The design mustn't be dictated purely by the product's technical function:** If a product looks a certain way because it must do so in order to work properly (for example, a ceiling light fitting), the look of the product can't be protected as a registered design.

   A similar exclusion applies to parts of a product that must be designed in a certain way in order to allow the product to connect to something else so that it can work properly. For example, the part of a bicycle pump that connects to the valve in a bicycle tyre can't be protected, because it must be made to fit around the valve without allowing any air to escape (called the *must-fit* exception).

   ✓ **The design mustn't be contrary to public policy or accepted principles of morality:** Therefore, a design for torturing budgerigars is unacceptable – however sleek.

Registering design rights in the UK

A registered design provides you with an exclusive right to use the design 'and any design which does not produce on the informed user a different overall impression'. The initial period of protection is five years from the date of registration of the design. The registration can be renewed after that for further periods of five years each, taking the total length of protection under a registered design to 25 years. Renewal fees are £130, £210, £310 and £450 for each successive five-year period of renewal.

To register a design in the UK, you submit your application to the IPO (http://www.gov.uk/register-a-design/defer-your-registration). In the form, you set out what the design is and provide a representation of it, showing all relevant views of how it appears to the eye. You can also say whether you want to register the design straightaway or defer the application for a specified period of up to 12 months.

The latter option can be useful, because it provides more time to test-market the product, although you risk failing the test of 'newness' if you disclose your design too widely.

Unlike for patents and trademarks, the IPO doesn't conduct searches and examinations for novelty or distinctive character. Instead, the onus is on you to verify that these criteria are fulfilled and that you're not wasting your time in making an application for registration.

A fee of £60 is payable for a single design to be published immediately. The cost of a deferred design is £40. Following registration, third parties can apply to cancel the registration on various grounds, such as lack of novelty and distinctive character or that you aren't the rightful owner.

Aiming to protect design rights internationally

You can apply for a Registered Community Design (RCD) in the European Union. As with trademarks, you can apply directly to the OHIM (`https://oami.europa.eu/ohimportal/en/`) or submit through the IPO in the UK. If filing through the IPO, you can apply for several designs in one application, as long as the products to which the designs relate all belong to the same class.

Like the UK system in the preceding section, the application process doesn't include any formal examination of the design or include an opposition process. All that's required is that the application shows a design and that such design isn't contrary to public policy or morally questionable. The application is, however, still submitted to an examiner for this very purpose and to ensure that all paperwork is in order.

If the examiner finds any issues with the paperwork, you're notified with a tartly-named *deficiency letter* and normally given two months to rectify any problem. If no issues arise with the application, or following you rectifying any issues, the design is registered and published in the mass market daily *Community Designs Bulletin*. A certificate is then issued to you electronically (you can request hard copies).

To register a community design costs €230, (with each additional design requiring a fee of €115 up to ten designs and €50 for each additional design after that). An additional cost applies of €120 for publication, with a fee of €60 for the publication of each additional design up to ten designs and a further fee of €30 for publication of each additional design after that. A handling fee of £15 is charged by the IPO if the community design application is filed through it.

When registered, you have the exclusive right to use the design in all member states for an initial term of five years. You can renew the registration for further 5-year periods up to a total of 25 years. The renewal fees for each design are €90, €120, €150 and €180 for each successive five-year period of renewal.

Destroying with design rights

In the UK, a registered design is a monopoly right (like a registered trademark or patent). You don't need to prove that a third party had access to the design or was even aware of its existence to prove infringement.

Here are some of the things you can prevent with design rights (if you want to *Live and Let Die*), and how to enforce those rights:

- ✔ Section 7(2) of the RDA sets out a non-exhaustive list of infringing actions: making, offering, putting on the market, importing, exporting or using any product in which the design is incorporated, as well as stocking a product for any of these purposes.

- ✔ Section 7A(2) of the RDA sets out a list of permitted acts that are *not* infringing, including acts done privately and reproducing the design for teaching purposes.

- ✔ The remedies for infringement are similar to those available for breaches of copyright, patent and trademark rights (which I describe earlier in 'Making copyright count', 'Unleashing the power of patents' and 'Terrorising with trademarks', respectively).

As a safeguard to warn against infringement or protect against any claim of innocent infringement (for which more limited financial remedies are available), you can place the registered number of the design plus the words 'registered design' on the product carrying the design.

As with copyright, if an employee creates a design within the course of her employment, it's owned by the employer in the absence of any agreement to the contrary. But if you're commissioning a third party (including a consultant or freelancer) to create a design for your business, that third party owns the design and so you must have a signed agreement if you want that person to transfer ownership over to you.

Taking action to enforce unregistered design rights

A separate regime exists under English law to protect unregistered original designs. These unregistered design rights apply automatically – bet you didn't even know you had them! In the UK these rights arise under the CDPA that creates copyrights.

Unregistered design rights aren't as effective for a couple of reasons:

- ✔ The unregistered design isn't a monopoly right, and so coincidental independent production of an identical design isn't an infringement – you have to suffer actual, wilful copying.

- ✔ The period of cover is much shorter – 3 years in the EU and 10 years from when the articles using the design are placed on the market for the UK, or 15 years from when the design is first recorded in a document.

Chapter 9

Acquiring and Using Your Own Software

....

....

Computers seem to liberate and enslave people in equal measure. But whether you like them, loathe them or are just bewildered by them, computers are here to stay; in an age of ever faster technological change, your business is likely to need reliable software.

Computer software is necessary to create a website and/or an app, to develop a User Interface, to implement a sales process, to deliver digital goods and/or services, to process payments, to store and easily access customer information safely and to record all sorts of data from which you can compile reports on the performance of all areas of the business.

Many software manufacturers provide standard 'commercial off-the-shelf' software packages, but they're not always sufficient to address your business's specific needs. So you may need a professional to design and develop a program (or a suite of programs) especially for your business, providing a customised solution with all the functionality you require.

In this chapter, I look at the legal aspects of software development and – the key elements you need to consider in any agreement with a software developer. Read on to discover how to get the best out of your software agreements and create the 'perfect' software platform for your business, ensuring that the developer gives you software that's the 'bee's knees'. (I've never seen a bee's knees, but this euphemism for things being 'perfect' or 'remarkable' is just one of many such expressions from the Roaring 1920s in the US that you may be able to spot in this chapter.)

I work from the agenda of you as a client in this chapter. If you're on the opposite side of the contract, as a developer, simply reverse the 'Tips' and 'Remember' points so that they work for you.

Imagining Perfection: Software Design and Functionality

When you engage a software developer to design a program for your business, you have to tell the person what you want your program to be able to do. Think of it as being like loveable pocket-boss Bernie Ecclestone asking you to design the functionality of your perfect racing car. You want it to go from 0–100 mph in three seconds, turn right angles at the same speed, have almost zero wind resistance and so on. If it does, your car's the 'cat's pyjamas'.

Therefore, having a *specification* that covers the following of your software is essential:

- ✔ **Proposed functionality:** *What* the program will do.

- ✔ **Technical specification:** *How* the functionality will do what it's going to do. For example, if you're commissioning an app, the technical spec must specify that the app is technically configured for the appropriate platform. The developer takes the lead in coming up with this part of the spec.

- ✔ **Design specification:** What the functionality will look and feel like to the user. (By analogy, will your racing car be red or green, have yellow spots, or furry dice in front of the windscreen?)

Set out these requirements in writing as clearly as possible to minimise any chances of misunderstanding and, therefore, disputes at a later date.

Finding a software developer who can deliver the functionality and technical spec and who's also creative enough to deliver a beautiful, sleek design spec is quite unusual. You may have to split this task between two different specialists. If so, make sure to involve both in the specification phase so that the technical developer knows what designs the designer has in mind for the functionality, and the designer knows the limits of the functionality when crafting his designs.

Planning and Delivering Your Software

You may have envisioned a perfect program, but you also have to make sure that the contract covers the process of building, testing and delivering it to you. Spookily, that's precisely what I cover now.

I look at the traditional, linear process for development (called the *waterfall* methodology), in which specification is followed by development milestones and acceptance testing for each part of the project. This linear approach is 'safe' from a legal point of view, because it's underpinned by a specification that sets out exactly what you require from the developer from the outset of the project.

But a business can't always know (and explain) with any measure of certainty what it's looking for in a custom-made piece of software at the outset of the design and development process. Therefore, I also examine another, more flexible approach: agile development.

Creating timescales

Information technology (IT) projects are notorious for running over agreed deadlines. Some people say that developers are like builders – always running late, over-budget and blaming someone else for the delays. How cruel.

The reality is that supplier and customer are often to blame when delays happen. The best approach is to agree some timescales for the contract at the outset. If someone's designing and delivering a Formula 1 car for you (normally costing a mere $15 million), you definitely want to know when it's going to turn up.

Here are some tips on timescales:

- ✔ **Be realistic:** For example, you want the software delivered by a certain date to coincide with a business objective, and the developer may agree to that date just to get the work. But software design and development target dates are often unrealistic, which only leads to stressful disagreements later on, when the software is 'late'.

- ✔ **Agree something:** In the absence of any defined timescales within which to complete various parts of the project, chaos can ensue. If the agreement contains no required date by which the *full* program must be completed, the developer is merely required to complete the work within a 'reasonable period'. What's 'reasonable' in each case is a matter of opinion and therefore a recipe for disagreement.

✔ **Agree milestones:** Use a *project plan* to separate the development process out into various stages and set up what has to be delivered (a *deliverable*) by defined *milestone dates.* So, for example, you can define dates for the following:

- When the designs for the program must be completed

- When the development work must be done

- When supplier and customer testing must start and be completed, with time frames for fixing any issues that arise in the test phase

- When customer data must be migrated into the new program

- When the software must be fully operational in a real environment (the *go-live* date)

If a developer doesn't meet any deadlines set out in the project plan, he's in breach of the agreement and can be required to pay damages for any loss brought about by the delay.

Quantifying any such loss is a very difficult exercise. Instead of relying on this method of recovery, you can insert a provision in the agreement requiring that specific sums (known as *liquidated damages*) be paid to you by the supplier for failure to meet certain milestones. These sums are deductible from the developer's charges for the work under the project. The developer will want to say that any such delays must be because he's at fault (not because, for example, you delayed making decisions or providing information), so if you're the client be prepared for some push-back in this area.

Any sums payable for delays must represent a genuine estimate of the amount of money that you've lost because of the failure of the developer to meet the agreed timelines in the project plan. If the sum is just an arbitrary amount designed to punish the developer, as opposed to compensating you for your losses, it's termed a *penalty clause,* which isn't enforceable under English law.

Testing times

In building the program, the developer goes through a process of writing computer code, testing to see it works, noting any issues or errors *(bugs)* and then refining the code until he's happy that the software does what it's supposed to.

You want to be sure that the developer gets it right before you accept the product. It's got to be the 'cat's whiskers' or possibly the 'kipper's knickers' (yep, that really is a phrase from the 1920s). Therefore, you need a part of the agreement dedicated to a formal acceptance process under which *acceptance*

tests are carried out. After all, you wouldn't accept your brand new racing car without giving it a test drive first. You would? Remind me not to be your co-driver, ever.

You need to provide or agree these elements of acceptance testing:

✓ **Timeline:** For the acceptance testing (also set out in the project plan – refer to the preceding section).

✓ **Copy of the software:** So that you can carry out various tests to verify its functionality. In addition to choosing the *environment* in which testing takes place (that is, the hardware and software used to carry out the testing), *test scripts* have to be agreed to run the tests. These sets of instructions are fed into the program to see whether it functions in the correct manner.

✓ **Set of acceptance criteria:** Criteria, or sets of output, that have to be achieved in order for the program to pass the acceptance tests.

✓ **What happens if the software doesn't pass the acceptance tests:** The agreement often specifies that if any 'defect' is found in the software, you have a number of options:

• Make the developer remedy the defect at his cost and submit the software to you for a further round of testing within an agreed timescale.

• Accept the software in its current state, if it's still functional, but subject to a reduction in the purchase price.

• Use a third party to remedy the defect at the developer's cost.

• Reject the software and terminate the contract.

The developer may not be eager for you to have the last three listed options, and may try and insist that he has at least one further opportunity to remedy any defect first. He may also try to exclude from the scope of the defect provisions any defect that doesn't have any substantial impact on the functioning of software.

✓ **The members of the developer's team present during the testing:** In order to eliminate any allegations of incorrect testing or findings.

✓ **Recording of results:** A certificate is presented for you to sign evidencing successful completion of the tests. You should retain at least part-payment of the fees for the design and development work pending successful completion of the acceptance tests. You wouldn't give away all $15 million of the budget for your shiny new racing car before testing it, would you?

Changing times: Altering the specification

What happens if part-way through the project you want to change some aspect of the functionality of the program, or you want to add some features to it in order to make it even better and the real 'eel's ankle'?

Your requirements can change over time: perhaps the demands of the business alter, you think of a new essential feature or some extra programming steps are required to deliver the agreed functionality. (You may decide by analogy that your racing car needs a different hydraulic unit or a loud bicycle bell so that other drivers know when you want to get past them.) If you request any changes during the design and build phase, it can result in delay and additional cost on the part of the developer, which of course he wants to pass to you. Equally, you want to ensure that the developer doesn't use the change as a pretext for unduly lengthening the timetable, failing to meet agreed milestone dates and/or artificially inflating the price of the overall project.

For these reasons, you include a formal *change control procedure* in the agreement. Here's how it works:

1. **You inform the developer of any changes you want with a written *change request*.**

2. **The developer produces a document recording all information relevant to the proposed change, sometimes called a *change control note*.**

   Examples of the information in a change control note include: the reason for the change, the work involved in the change, details of any specification or an amended specification, a proposed timetable for carrying out the work and how much it will cost.

3. **You review this document, raise any issues in it with the developer and both parties sign off on it when they're happy.**

4. **You both amend any specification and project plan accordingly.**

Staying nimble: Advantages of agile programming

The *agile methodology* was developed to offer businesses a more flexible approach to development than the traditional linear technique. Instead of setting out precisely what's required at the start of the project, the parties establish only larger, overarching goals. The developer works towards these goals using a fluid process. Using a continual presentation/testing and feedback loop, he keeps refining the product until a complete solution is provided that fully meets your needs.

The result is a process of development that defines itself through its life cycle and responds to your new and changing requirements, which, in turn, are triggered by close participation in the development process (see www. scrumalliance.org – a network where you can find out more about how agile programming using the 'scrum' framework works).

Here's how agile development works:

1. **Create the vision via a scrum.**

   Not the rather dubious element of rugby in which 16 strapping young men put their heads between each other's legs. In a development scrum, a team of people from your side and the developer side works together, under the leadership of a 'ScrumMaster', to create a *product vision* – a short description of the requirements of the product and the attributes of the program that will be designed and built to meet those requirements. I suppose they could put their heads between each other's legs while doing so, but I've never witnessed it (perhaps they all waited for me to leave).

2. **Flesh out the vision with a *product backlog*.**

   This list of requirements is a bit like a functional specification, but it isn't fixed and can change throughout the life of the project. The requirements take the form of *user stories*, which are high-level outcomes rather than absolute requirements and are ranked in order of importance.

3. **Select user stories from the top of the product backlog, and work on them in sprints.**

   A *sprint* is a short period during which the developers design, build and then test a part of the overall program. The sprint is carried out according to the *sprint backlog*, which is a to-do list for the particular sprint. Each sprint can last from two to four weeks – about the same length of time it takes me to complete the 100 metres.

4. **Produce a fully functioning part of the program from the sprint.**

   If any defects are discovered in the work produced in the sprint, you can add any remedial work to the product backlog and carry it out later as part of another sprint. In the same way, if you decide that you want to amend or add to the functionality of any work completed under one sprint, those extra requirements can also be noted on the product backlog and implemented under another sprint.

Agile programming has a number of benefits compared to the waterfall approach:

✔ **Much more flexible process:** Changes can easily be absorbed into the development process without invoking a cumbersome 'change control' procedure. This helps perfect your software so that it's more likely to turn into the perfect 'caterpillar's kimono'.

✔ **Working software available sooner:** Separating the work into smaller contained sections allows development work to begin sooner and components of initial working software to be delivered quicker.

✔ **Detection of errors at an earlier date:** At the conclusion of each sprint, error detection eliminates the possibility of finding a raft of defects towards the end of the project, which may then all have to be dealt with in one go and severely impact timescales for the development work.

Note the following drawbacks of agile programming from a contractual point of view:

✔ **Difficult to tie developer obligations to particular stages of the project:** If an issue arises during a testing phase of a particular sprint, you simply note and deal with it at a later date. The same applies to any of your new customer requirements. As a result, imposing contractual milestone dates (and payments linked to them) is much more difficult.

✔ **Difficult to specify a 'delivery date':** The program is always in one sprint or another – development doesn't actually 'stop'.

✔ **No fixed specification at the beginning:** You only have a product vision, which also makes holding the developer accountable for delivery failures more difficult.

✔ **Less certainty as to how all the individual elements will function together:** Again, setting a bar for successful 'delivery' and a ceiling for payments in return for successful delivery is more difficult. You can imagine that designing a racing car in bits that you largely make up as you go along can create ambiguities as to how they all work together.

Protecting Your Software

When your software is designed and delivered, you need to take a number of steps to protect it, such as arranging maintenance and warranties and securing the source code. If you don't ensure that your software is the 'ant's pants', bad things can happen and make you as grumpy as a pantless ant!

Keeping it all shipshape: Deciding on maintenance and service levels

When the software is deployed in a live environment, you want to be sure that you can use it, that the developer will resolve any problems that subsequently arise and that any improvements you require (or the developer produces) can be made available. (You wouldn't be happy if the builder of your new racing car gave you the keys and then disappeared, so that you had nobody to call when it stalled first time out.)

Maintenance, training and support agreement

All these elements are dealt with in a *maintenance, training and support agreement.* You can include these three elements in the main developer agreement or conclude them in a separate agreement.

Here are some key elements of these arrangements:

- **Maintenance and training services:** Frequently supplied by the original developer, although third-party IT services providers can undertake them.

- **Training:** Involves agreeing how many sessions you're entitled to, who's going to give it, how long each session lasts, where the training takes place, exactly what it covers and how much it costs.

- **Scope of maintenance and support:** For example:

  - Are queries on how to use the program included in the maintenance/support services or do they only cover technical problems with the software?

  - Is on-site support included or does this incur extra costs?

  - Between which times will a support helpdesk be open?

  - How can the helpdesk be provided (phone, email)?

  - Does a distinction exist between simple issues and more complicated ones?

Usually, a helpdesk functions as the first port of call for customers experiencing difficulties with a software program, but typically it only provides solutions to basic errors with the software. More complex issues are handed over to engineers who attempt to come up with a solution. They may even need to escalate the problem to more experienced engineers, and so a tiered system of support is often put in place (first line support, second line support and so on) to cover issues of varying complexity.

Service levels of maintenance

In addition, the service levels are often attached to the maintenance agreement as a separate Service Level Agreement (SLA).

More serious problems take more time to resolve than less serious ones. Therefore, an SLA categorises faults into different categories of severity and provides different response and resolution times for each one. Here's the sort of thing you may see:

- ✔ **Category 1 fault:** Perhaps termed a 'critical failure' and defined as 'a failure in any major functionality of the software with a material impact on the business'.

- ✔ **Category 2 fault:** Perhaps a 'severe failure' where a significant problem exists with the functionality of the software that affects the business, but not in such a serious way as a Category 1 fault.

- ✔ **Category 3 fault:** A 'minor issue' that has little or no impact on the business and can be fixed in the next update of the software.

The different categories of fault are accompanied by the target timescales in which to respond or acknowledge the problem by phone or email, and then to provide a 'fix' or 'resolution' to it.

Calls or emails to the supplier (through the helpdesk) are logged and a receipt of acknowledgement is sent to you setting out the nature of the support request and the time the developer received it. Resolution times are then measured from the time stamped on the acknowledgement.

If service levels aren't met, the developer has to pay an amount of money to you to make up for the service level failure (called a *service credit*).

The parties set a time period over which service levels are measured, say, months or quarters. The amount of service credit is usually expressed as a percentage of the maintenance fees payable by you during the relevant period (for example, '5 per cent of the monthly charges'). A greater amount of money is payable for failure to meet a Category 1 service level to reflect the severity of the issue and of the service level failure.

Make sure that any service credit is a genuine representation of your loss (liquidated damages) rather than a 'penalty' (which is unenforceable; refer to 'Creating timescales' earlier in this chapter).

A developer often argues that if he has to provide service credits for failure to meet service levels, this should be the only financial remedy to which you're entitled. In other words, you can't sue for more than this amount even if the service level failure costs you more than the service credit. Resist if you're the client.

You may want to have the additional option of terminating the support services agreement if you experience a critical service level failure or a number of repeat failures of lesser consequence. The developer won't want this, and so you have two options:

✔ Allow for the possibility of termination where the total amount of service credits payable for service level failures passes a certain threshold, such as 25 per cent of the annual support fees.

✔ Set out a *remedial* (or *remediation*) process in the SLA that must be followed before the agreement can be terminated. The process is triggered by a certain number of service level breaches (say, three Category 2 or 3 service level failures within a three-month period).

The supplier is required to draw up a plan to present the results of any analysis of previous failures and agree to implement new measures to minimise the chances of such failure being repeated. This *remedial plan* is sent to you for approval, and if adopted, any subsequent service level failure (or set number of failures) results in you having a right to terminate the support services agreement.

Give yourself the right to terminate the agreement if any issue with the software that's more than a minor inconvenience can't be fixed within a specified period of time.

Developer arguments

Developers often look for other ways to soften their obligations to resolve any issues with the software – for example:

✔ Removing any liability for defects that don't materially affect your business.

✔ Removing any requirement to fix problems where the issue required input from you and you didn't provide it.

✔ Replacing any absolute obligation to fix software faults with a 'best endeavours' or 'reasonable endeavours' obligation. They argue that they can only do their best to try to remedy issues that arise, and that finding a solution to each and every problem may not be possible.

As the client, these changes muddy the water and risk future arguments about whether the developer is responsible for fixing problems. If you agree to them, you may find yourself feeling unhappy later, as though you'd got out of bed on the wrong side. (Apparently the Romans believed that getting out of the left-hand side of the bed was a sure portent of bad luck. And you thought the only thing holding back your enterprise was a lack of funding and the world's indifference to your genius!)

Promising the Earth: Agreeing warranties

In the development and maintenance agreements, you want to include promises or *warranties* from the developer about the program.

In the development agreement, you want a warranty that the program will function in accordance with the technical and functional specification. You also want assurances that the software doesn't contain any Trojans, worms or other malware that may damage your systems, and that the developer owns or has properly licensed all elements in the software (see the later section 'Making sure your software belongs to you').

Developers aim to limit the warranties as much as possible (and as client, you want to resist their attempts as much as possible). They may try to:

- ✔ Say that the warranties should apply only for a very limited period of time.

- ✔ Qualify warranties by saying, for example, 'as far as the developer is aware' the software contains no viruses, giving them a get-out (they can always say later that they 'weren't aware' of the problem).

- ✔ Exclude (in relation to any warranties on functionality) defects that arise as a result of any improper installation of the software by you, or use of incompatible hardware by you or modifications to the software you make. The problem is that this creates an argument about the source of the defects. They may also try to limit the remedies available for breach of warranty to correction of the defective software, rather than giving you any financial remedies.

In relation to the maintenance agreement, you need a warranty that the developer will comply at all times with its SLA obligations to you. You also want a promise that you won't be charged any support and maintenance costs for correcting a defect that's a breach of warranty under the development agreement. You don't want to pay costs for correcting something that shouldn't have gone wrong initially.

The maintenance agreement also needs a warranty promising you free delivery of any updates (minor improvements) and also free upgrades (major overhauls) to the software, which the developer creates for himself or other customers, so that you automatically benefit from improvements available for your software. This protection enables your software to continue being the 'gnat's elbow' (as a 1920s flapper would say).

The importance of source code

A third party needs access to the source code to maintain your software. *Source code* is the set of instructions that the computer must perform as written by the developer in his chosen programming language. It's written in human readable form and is of great value, which is why the developer guards it closely. Commercial off-the-shelf software (together with consumer software) is always provided in *object code* version, a machine-readable (binary) form of the software converted from source code using a program called a *compiler*.

Source code is written with the aid of programming tools and according to specific design methodologies. It's also accompanied by the developer's notes on how the program is put together. Without these further elements, converting object code into source code is very difficult, even for an experienced software engineer.

Keeping your software safe and sound: Escrow agreements

A legitimate concern for you is what happens in the event that the developer is no longer able, or no longer willing, to support the software. You don't want to have to abandon the software and start again with a new version, just because you can't maintain what you've got.

Ask the developer whether a third party can maintain the software if he can no longer do so, although any third party would need access to the software's source code (to see why, check out the nearby sidebar 'The importance of source code'). Unless you own the software, you don't have automatic access to that code.

One option in these circumstances is for the developer to place the source code in *escrow* in accordance with an escrow agreement. Here are some tips for concluding the 'perfect' escrow agreement (or the 'elephant's adenoids' as you might have called it in the distant past):

✔ Deposit the source code with a third party, known as an *escrow agent*, who safely keeps it with the intention of releasing it on the occurrence of specified events, as agreed between the parties.

The main trigger is the developer's insolvency. But also ensure that the refusal of the developer to provide support services, or its inability to do so for any reason, triggers release of the source code.

✔ Set out these events, and the rest of the escrow arrangements, in an *escrow agreement*, a tripartite agreement entered into by you, the developer and the escrow agent.

✔ Agree exceptions to the release of the source code if the developer's refusal to support the software is for a valid reason: such as you not paying any maintenance service fees or providing assistance or co-operation as required under the maintenance agreement.

✔ Deliver to the escrow agent at the same time as the source code any development tools, methodologies and other documentation explaining the source-code's composition.

✔ Require the developer to deposit any updates or upgrades to the program with the escrow agent to ensure that the source code is fully up to date.

✔ Include a requirement to test the source code in the escrow agreement to provide assurance to you that the product held in escrow is fully functional.

✔ Select as escrow agent a firm with experience of dealing with software code that you and the developer can trust to look after it.

✔ Record the name of the escrow agent in the development agreement (and the maintenance agreement if separate) and attach a copy of the escrow agreement to the development agreement.

Negotiate who pays for the escrow service. If you insist on the developer paying for these costs, watch out for any uplift in any licence fees or support fees payable to the developer to compensate for such outlay.

Many firms provide escrow services, though two well-known escrow agents are The NCC Group (`http://www.nccgroup.trust/uk/our-services/software-escrow-and-verification/escrow-agreements`) and Iron Mountain (`http://www.ironmountain.com/Services/Technology-Escrow-Services/Technology-Escrow.aspx`).

Considering Ownership and Cost Issues

Commissioning your own software doesn't come cheap. Ensure that you control the outlay and really do own what you think you're buying.

Making sure your software belongs to you

When you ask for a computer program to be specially made for your business, you may think that it automatically belongs to you. After all, if you spend $15 million building a racing car, you assume that you own every nut and lick of paint, right down to the go-faster stripes.

But software isn't quite so simple. In fact, several possibilities can exist:

✔ **The software is 100 per cent written for you.** In this case, you can go for ownership. That's the perfect answer . . . the 'bullfrog's beard' (some phrases going out of fashion isn't too surprising, is it?). So far so good, but bear in mind the following caveat.

The developer may want to reuse some of the newly developed code for future projects. The danger for you is that doing so can erode the competitive edge that you want the software to give you.

Include in the development agreement a specific provision assigning the rights in the software to you, because unless the person is your employee, the developer is assumed to be the owner of the software under the Copyright Act unless a specific assignment is made to someone else (refer to Chapter 8).

✔ **The software is 100 per cent written for you, but the developer won't agree that you own it.** If ownership isn't possible, you can propose that you own the software but that the developer is granted a *non-exclusive licence* to use it, subject to either of the following:

  • The developer can't grant licences to a third party who's a competitor to your business (you must specify in the developer agreement businesses you regard as competitors).

  • The developer can't grant *any* licence of the software without your permission.

✔ If the developer won't agree to either option, insist on having an *exclusive licence* yourself to use the software program in its entirety, so that no other person has the right to use the program as a whole.

✔ **The software includes elements written by people other than the developer.** This is quite common. Many software developers have written sections of code that are of universal application in software programs. Your developer is likely to be eager to reuse such lines of code where possible, to simplify the development work and save time in the process. Such use may comprise the simple incorporation of the code into the program, or can involve taking the code and adapting it to suit your requirements. The developer may also want to incorporate certain pre-written software modules that have been licensed by third parties. If this happens, you can still own the bits of software created just for you, but the position with third-party software isn't so straightforward.

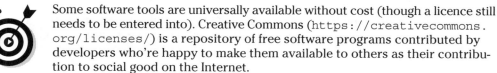

Some software tools are universally available without cost (though a licence still needs to be entered into). Creative Commons (`https://creativecommons.org/licenses/`) is a repository of free software programs contributed by developers who're happy to make them available to others as their contribution to social good on the Internet.

In any event, any outside software that the developer proposes to use must be expressly referred to in the development agreement, and the developer needs to secure any licences you require to use such elements as a condition of the development agreement.

Read any such licences in order to understand the nature and extent of any rights granted, and any limitations. For example, a licence may impose specific restrictions on the use of the software and any action by you not expressly allowed under the licence may be a breach of the licence terms. Typical restrictions involve the following:

- ✔ Prevent any copying, modifying or decompiling of the software
- ✔ Restrict usage to just one business (so you can't assign or license those rights to anybody else)
- ✔ Limit the number of people who can use the software or limit the number of machines on which it can be used
- ✔ Confine usage to a particular location

These issues can be a problem. For example, if you aren't allowed to grant rights in the third-party software to somebody else, what do you do if you want to outsource running of your software to another provider?

You also have to check whether such software can be supported by the developer (rather than the original creator) and set out how you can get access to updates and upgrades of that third-party software.

If your developer is planning on incorporating any third-party software into the program, you may want to check whether such a third party has any multi-party or multi-licensee arrangement in place with an escrow provider, with the name of each registered user of the software listed in the agreement, so that you can always get access to that software if you need to. Similarly, if the developer is using any proprietary standard software in your program, you can ask for your business to be noted on any multi-party escrow agreement it has in place with an escrow provider of its own. These precautions help you ensure that the inclusion of third-party software doesn't prevent your program being the 'cat's miaow'.

Agreeing the cost of the software

To commission 'the cuckoo's chin' of software development, you need to keep cost control and (in particular) cash flow uppermost in your mind.

More rights equal higher costs; if you want to own your software outright, taking an assignment from the developer, this approach is likely to cost you more than if the software developer retains title and you just take a licence off him. Your ownership is a better outcome in terms of giving you control over your software, but it comes at a price.

For this reason, you need to budget for your spend; software development meanders like a river and the costs can turn into raging rapids as the process twists and turns. Set a budget at the outset so that you have an anchor against which to measure your financial progress as the project develops. The following points help you to cap your software spend and the rate at which it flows out the door:

✔ **Set development milestones:** Set milestones and break the payment of costs down so that they're linked to the achievement of each milestone. Doing so puts you in a safer place than paying upfront or paying in timed stages (regardless of actual progress) or (worse still) paying an hourly rate for development. The latter leaves you horribly exposed and incentivises the developer to take more time.

Setting milestones *and* timescales for achieving them allows you to include delay deductions from the overall price if a milestone date is delayed.

Setting milestones is harder when you're using an agile form of software development rather than a more traditional waterfall process because, by definition, the scope keeps changing (refer to the earlier section 'Staying nimble: Advantages of agile programming'). However, you can still set a cap at the outset on the overall budget for which you expect the entire project to be delivered, and hold back as much as possible until final delivery. In this way, you don't provide an incentive for the developer to spend infinite amounts of time adapting and refining multiple elements of the software.

✔ **Watch out for extras:** Be aware of the following potential extras:

- If your chosen software includes elements your developer has licensed-in from third parties; unless each of those software elements is free, you then have to pay for the licence.

- Establish at the beginning which third-party owned software the developer is going to use and how much it's likely to cost.

✔ **Scope creep:** Even if you use the traditional waterfall approach to software development (refer to the earlier section, 'Planning and Delivering Your Software'), the original scope can still expand as you think of new elements that need to be added. Therefore, ensure that you have a robust spec at the beginning to keep as many subsequent developments as possible 'in-scope'. Having a rigorous change-control process enables you to work out the additional price of any subsequent changes before you commission them.

✔ **Bug fixes:** The potential exists for ongoing costs associated with error or *bug* correction. Bug fixes are as inevitable as flies round a picnic or bees round a honeypot (why do bees congregate around honeypots – they make the stuff anyway).

Having a tight specification enables you to argue that the developer provide bug-fixing free of charge, instead of being deemed a 'change' to the software for which he can charge additional amounts.

✔ **Training/software maintenance and support:** You have to pay ongoing costs for these services. The perfect response ('the clam's garter', as it was known in the 1920s) is to limit payments to an annual amount so that they're capped; or even better, to limit them to the lesser of an annual payment or an amount per hour (in case you use less of these services than you expected).

Don't agree to an amount per hour on its own or you'll be taken to the cleaners.

Maintenance charges are often subject to annual increases over the period during which the support is provided. The knack is to limit any such increase to the growth in the retail price index (RPI) as a cap (so that you pay the lesser of any percentage increase specified in the contract, or the increase in the RPI over the preceding 12 months).

Part III
Growing the Business – The Legal Blueprint

Top Five Tips for Selling Abroad

- ✔ **Do your local research.** Don't assume that because people can speak English, doing business abroad is the same as in the UK.

- ✔ **Pick the right business model for you.** Do you want to franchise rights, licence rights or enter into local joint ventures? More control over your local partner equals more rewards, but greater risk and time involvement.

- ✔ **Understand the local legal landscape.** If you're going to operate a local subsidiary, make sure that you have a grip on employment laws, tax laws and legalities relating to local ownership.

- ✔ **Make sure that you're up-to-date with local customs and duties requirements when exporting.** You don't want any costly foul-ups or delays.

- ✔ **Ask someone who's exported before if you're in doubt.** Exporting is a big priority for the UK, and so plenty of government resources are available for you.

I provide a quiz on licensing contracts online. Test yourself out now at www.dummies.com/extras/lawforsmallbusinessuk.

In this part . . .

✔ Grow your business by working successfully with product suppliers as retailer, distributor or licensee.

✔ Get a handle on the contractual risks, rewards, rights and responsibilities of working with service partners.

✔ Grasp the dos and don'ts of legal contracts with consumers.

✔ Meet the challenges confidently of working abroad.

Chapter 10

Cooking Up a Tasty Contract with Your Suppliers

. . . .

In This Chapter

▶ Producing retail product agreements

▶ Distributing products to other businesses

▶ Licensing contracts

. . . .

*V*irtually all your revenues come from arrangements in which you're the customer or the supplier, and both these relationships need agreements. The menu of possibilities for these arrangements is enormous, as is the menu of possible terms within each type of contract. In this chapter, I create some tasty morsels for you as I review the most common types of arrangement where someone supplies you, as a business customer, with its products. (As well as gorging on this chapter, you can check out Chapter 11, which deals with agreements where a supplier delivers you services.)

I use a recipe to analyse these types of agreement: *the 4 Rs.* These four aspects come up in every supply and business customer contract: they're a good way of classifying the ingredients of each one using a consistent method. All contracts have to cover the following 4 Rs:

- ✔ **Rights:** Granted by the supplier to the business customer, including any restrictions on those rights

- ✔ **Responsibilities:** Duties and obligations that each party is taking on in the agreement

- ✔ **Rewards:** Payment(s) the business customer has to make to the supplier for the products or services supplied by the supplier (royalties, advances, guarantees and so on)

✔ **Risks:** Allocation between the parties of risk for things that can go wrong (for example, faulty products, unlawful products, infringing products, unsold products)

Similar issues come up repeatedly in all supply and business customer agreements. I refer to such aspects once and then point you to the relevant section when the same issue arises with a different type of agreement. You can choose to take the full English Breakfast, gorging on all the suggested terms for every type of agreement, or stick to a calorie-controlled diet of the type(s) of agreement most common for you.

Introducing Product Agreements

To grow your business you need product agreements with the following parties, whether the products and goods are physical or digital:

✔ **Your suppliers:** They supply you with goods – in these arrangements you're the *business customer.*

✔ **Your customers:** Whether they buy, distribute or sell-on your own goods, you're the *business supplier* here.

I write this chapter from the point of view of you being a business customer supplied by someone else. But don't worry if your business involves you being a business supplier and supplying these products (for example, as a manufacturer, wholesaler or licensor): just reverse the 'Tips' and 'Remember' points for your benefit.

Product agreements include those where you're a business customer in the following arrangements:

✔ **A retailer to consumers:** Supplied by a manufacturer or supplier of already-finished goods (such as a wholesaler).

✔ **A distributor to other businesses:** Supplied by an owner of finished goods.

✔ **A licensee:** Supplied by a licensor who grants you the right to use the product under licence (say, audio visual content or artwork).

The licence agreement structure is particularly common where the licensor owns some intellectual property (such as a copyright, design right or trademark of patent) and you want to exploit it (dash to Chapter 8 for all about intellectual property).

Tasting Manufacturing and Wholesaler Contracts: Retailing Products

I use the 4 Rs here to look at agreements where you're being supplied by a manufacturer or wholesaler with goods to sell to consumers.

Getting it all: Contractual rights for retail products

Whether you're selling compression shorts to cyclists, batons to cheerleaders or ice to Eskimos, you need your contracts with your business supplier to cover as many rights as possible:

✔ **Extent of rights:** You want to obtain the most extensive rights possible – the full three-course meal rather than just a selection of starters. Make clear that you have *title* in the goods – in other words, that they belong to you, and you can do what you want with them, including exploiting the products through any sales channel (offline, Internet, mobile). You also want the right to alter and/or adapt the goods and/or include them in or with other products.

If rights are unavailable, perhaps the supplier has other conflicting agreements with other customers – in which case, you have to live with it for now. But negotiate that if any currently excluded rights become available to the business supplier, they automatically fall under your agreement.

✔ **Territory:** Define the extent of the territory in which you can exercise your rights. The supplier may be working with different partners in countries where you aren't present or not a big player, but if you have a retail capability outside your domestic territory, you want the broadest possible geographic reach. Negotiate an option to add countries to the territory over time, when you've proved yourself or as rights in other countries become available to the supplier.

Broadly speaking, after goods are put on sale in the EU with the consent of the owner, subsequent movement of goods to other countries within the EU must be allowed, and so your supplier can't prevent you from exporting within the EU. It would be unlawful, just as it should be to eat chips without tomato ketchup.

✔ **Exclusivity:** Are your rights exclusive or non-exclusive? If they're *exclusive,* nobody but you can be supplied with this product. (You wouldn't expect manufacturers of Louis Vuitton luggage to be allowed to supply that brand of luggage to anybody else unless Louis Vuitton agrees to it.) Often, however, the supplier wants only to grant you *non-exclusive rights,* and so you have competitors.

If you can't get exclusivity in all countries, you can add a variety of sauces to brighten up your dish. Perhaps you can get exclusivity in some parts with non-exclusivity in other parts of the territory. Or maybe you can have exclusive rights to one market sector, one set of customers or one set of channels to market (say, online or mail-order) that's your specialism, with non-exclusivity applying to other channels. Or perhaps you earn the right to exclusivity after a certain period of time or on the basis of agreed sales success.

✔ **Term:** Set out the length of your agreement's term, during which you can exercise those rights. In many cases, where you're dealing with a manufacturer or a wholesaler, the term of the agreement isn't a material concern: you simply go back and place orders whenever you need to. But if a term exists, your supplier may want a limited term in case you prove to be an unsuccessful sales outlet for the products. Ideally, you want the term to be as long as possible.

To organise this, the term can be for an agreed fixed period. Alternatively, you can agree that the term rolls on unless either side terminates with a written notice not less than 60 days prior to the end of the current year. This approach gives the term a good chance of continuing, because the supplier must be alert to the deadline and minded to terminate for the agreement to come to an end.

Taking responsibility: Contractual obligations for retail products

Whether you're retailing capes, capons or canoes, you need to allocate responsibilities between you and your business supplier so that everybody knows who's doing what:

✔ **Product:** In all cases you need to be clear about the specification of the product being delivered. You don't want to order a hamburger and end up with a nut salad. If you're being supplied by a manufacturer, you need to have given a clear manufacturing spec upfront with any design requirements, technical specifications, patent requirements and obligatory components that must be used. Include a contractual requirement for the product to be manufactured exactly in accordance with that spec. Also include that the product must be manufactured containing your trademark, logo or patent number, if that's required.

Add an ongoing responsibility to allow you to inspect the manufacturing facility so you can check that acceptable products are being produced. You may get resistance (just as when you ask to inspect a restaurant's kitchen), but knowing that your products are being made to your requirements is important for you.

- **Form of delivery:** How are the units going to be delivered to you: by truck, rail, ship? How are they going to be packaged and what containers are they to be shipped in?

- **When and where?** In all cases, don't forget to add where the products have to be delivered and when (just like ordering a takeaway). The delivery date may be critical to your operations, which is why you sometimes see a clause saying 'time is of the essence'. This phrase means that if delivery is late, it's automatically a serious breach of contract that may entitle you to reject goods or terminate the agreement.

- **Placing orders:** Delivery can be a recurrent process under the agreement rather than just a one-off (for example, you may need to place repeated orders for manufacture). If that's the case, you need clarity about the ordering process. For example:

    - With whom do you place orders in the supplier's organisation?

    - Does a minimum order quantity apply?

    - If you place an order, can you change your mind about the number of ordered units before delivery? If you do this in a restaurant, the waitress just rolls her eyes and brings you a new dish, but in industry you can be charged for the incorrect order.

    - Do orders have to be placed in writing and if so, is email sufficient, or does the order have to be placed in a prescribed 'purchase order' format?

    - How long after placement before each order has to be delivered by your supplier?

Reaping rewards: Contractual payments for retail products

Whether you're e-tailing bedknobs or broomsticks, you need to set out how much your business supplier is paid, and when and how it gets paid:

- **What's being paid?** Often for deals with a manufacturer, an agreed price per unit manufactured applies. For wholesale deals, a wholesaler price per unit is normally agreed, with possible discounts based on the volume of orders you place, or linked to the marketing commitments you're prepared to agree to.

✔ **Deductions from payments:** Can you deduct anything before you make your payments to the supplier? For example, if you're a retailer onwardly selling the product, having an allowance for a certain number of 'promotional' items is normal, for which you may not have to pay the supplier.

If you're a retailer, you want to be able to deduct the value of all items you weren't ultimately able to sell (called *sale or return*). Expect your supplier to choke on that provision in the agreement.

✔ **Changes in payments:** In the event of an ongoing supply of products, you don't want your supplier to increase prices during the term of your agreement, any more than you want your restaurant increasing prices during the middle of the meal. Ideally, therefore, the price stays fixed.

If you need to agree to price increases, make sure that they can only happen with adequate written notice (say 3–6 months) so that you can adjust your business plans accordingly (and if necessary raise your prices to consumers). You can also make sure that any price increases are limited to the rate of inflation shown by the Retail Price Index over the preceding 12 months.

✔ **Any extras?** You know how annoying it is when a restaurant adds 12 per cent service to your bill that you weren't expecting, and so flush-out any extra charges and know the maximum extent of your liability. For example, your supplier may intend to charge you for:

- Picking and packing goods off the shelves at the manufacturing facility to ship them to you

- Cost of shipment to you

- Cost of insurance when the goods are shipped to you

✔ **Any upfront payments?** You may be asked for an upfront payment of the manufacturing cost every time you place an order. Try to minimise it, so that the bulk of the price (say 75 per cent) is paid at the back-end, when you've received a satisfactory order. If buying stock from a wholesaler, payment normally follows 30, 60 or 90 days after the order.

Try to negotiate credit terms (how long you have before you need to pay) so that payment to your supplier coincides with your payment from your own customer. This is a very efficient use of cash.

Some wholesalers and manufacturers refuse to give you credit at the outset of the relationship – you have to pay 100 per cent of the order price upfront until you've demonstrated that you're a good payer. If that's the case, you need to make sure that you can bridge the cash flow gap between paying for an order and receiving funds from the consumer for those goods.

✔ **Audits:** Obtain rights to audit your manufacturer to check that it's not manufacturing extra units that aren't being supplied to you. Typically audit rights are exercised on reasonable written notice, not more than once per year, and by a professional accountant on your behalf.

Spreading the risk: Contractual precautions for retail products

You have to cater for a number of risks in any agreements of this kind. Thinking about them may be boring, but it's good for you, like eating all your vegetables:

✔ **What happens if something goes wrong with the products?** If you're given corked wine in the restaurant or cold food, you want to be able to send it back, don't you? Similarly, you want your supplier to take responsibility for the delivery of faulty products. The faults may be discovered at delivery or later, when one of your customers complains. The goods may not work or be consistent with the manufacturing spec. In either case, you want a rebate for the cost of the faulty products and/ or the supplier to replace them with products that work at its cost. Alternatively you want the right to offset the cost of the faulty products from subsequent orders you may place.

Try and get the supplier to pay for the cost of collecting, insuring and sending the shipments of faulty goods back to it.

✔ **What if someone sues you?** You may face many types of different claims in relation to the products, making your plate too hot to handle. Claimants may allege that:

- The exploitation of the goods is an infringement of their rights of ownership (for example, someone else owns the copyright, trademark or patent that the supplier is allowing you to use).

- The exploitation of the goods infringes some other right (for example, their right of privacy).

For this reason, suppliers usually agree to give you a promise (or *warranty*) that they own or have all necessary approvals or consents to grant you the rights that the agreement grants you, and that the goods don't infringe any third-party rights. If that promise proves to be incorrect, you can then sue the supplier for breach of contract.

If you face legal proceedings and consequent expenses as a result of such infringement, you want an *indemnity*, which is the right to deduct those costs from the cost of any ongoing payments to the supplier. Alternatively, you want the supplier to agree to reimburse you for all your costs associated with that claim (win or lose).

An indemnity is stronger than a warranty, because it requires payment back of all costs and losses on a pound-for-pound basis, whereas for a warranty the court restricts the amount of costs you can get back even if you win the warranty claim and receive damages.

✔ **What happens if the supplied goods breach a legislative requirement?** In any industry, the goods need to comply with laws or regulations. For example, they can't be obscene, *defamatory* (unlawfully lowering someone's reputation) or infringe consumer rights (see Chapter 12 for details). Also make sure that your suppliers comply with any applicable 'standards' that apply to their business. For a few examples, see the nearby sidebar 'Complying with legal regulations and industry standards'.

Name any specific legislation with which you need the goods to comply and then add a catch-all along the lines of the supplier ensuring that the goods comply with 'all applicable local, foreign, domestic and other laws and regulations'.

Complying with legal regulations and industry standards

Under the (Packaging Essential Requirements) Regulations, 2003, businesses that manufacture, use and import packaging must comply with the following requirements: minimise the amount of packaging used, and ensure that packaging can be reused or recycled and doesn't contain a high level of certain heavy metals (unless the parcel contains *Motorhead* CDs, of course). Companies handling more than 50 tonnes of packaging a year with a turnover of over £2 million must register with an environmental regulator or pay for the recycling of a certain amount of packaging waste.

Specific industry-sector legislation can also apply. For example, in the UK clothing has to comply with the fibre-content labelling regulations (showing what it's made from), country of origin labelling legislation (showing from where outside the EU it came), care regulations (showing how best to look after it – the maximum washing temperature and so on) and (in the case of nightwear) flammability standards.

The Waste Electrical & Electronic (WEEE) Regulations, 2013 (wee! tee-hee!) provides that producers who manufacture, rebrand or import electronic or electrical equipment such as household appliances, IT equipment or lighting equipment must register with an approved compliance scheme. These Regulations apply to all producers regardless of their size.

The British Standards Institution is the UK's national standards body. Although their use is voluntary, standards can help to increase efficiency, differentiate products and services and provide reassurance. For example, Quality Management (ISO 9001: 2008) is an internationally recognised standard for quality management systems. Many larger businesses and public bodies only contract with suppliers with ISO 9001 certification. This standard has four elements: management responsibility, resource management, product realisation and analysis and improvement of consumer satisfaction. Visit www.bsigroup.com for a full list of standards and applications for certification.

✔ **What if someone discloses your confidential information?** Normally, contracts have two-way commitments on non-disclosure of business information, know-how and trade secrets, which come to the attention of parties during the course of the agreement.

✔ **What if some unforeseen calamity occurs?** Usually, a mutual clause deals with unforeseen problems (sometimes obscurely called a *force majeure clause*). These problems have to be serious. Force majeure covers wars, strikes, riots, acts of terrorism, storms, floods, power outages and attacks by flesh-eating zombies (well, not that last one). The clause normally says that neither party can be sued if one of these eventualities impedes its performance and the term can be extended for the duration of such an eventuality and for a certain period of time (for example, up to six weeks).

✔ **What if someone breaches the agreement?** Normally contracts feature a termination clause for if either party commits a serious (or *material*) breach of its responsibilities under the agreement. If the breach can be put right, whoever committed it is given a 'cure period' of 14–30 days in which to put right whatever it got wrong. If it fails to do so (or the breach just can't be put right; for example, a breach of a promise of exclusivity can't be reversed), you can terminate the agreement on account of the breach.

✔ **What if someone gets into financial trouble?** I look at this aspect in more detail in Chapter 16, but suffice to say that normally a clause allows either side to terminate if the trading partner suffers a serious financial reverse. The list includes liquidation, bankruptcy, appointment of a receiver, appointment of an administrative receiver, winding up, not being able to pay creditors on time or making an 'arrangement' with creditors to defer or reschedule debts. I explain all these cheerful terms in Chapter 16, and so travel straight there if you can't wait to find out their morose meaning.

Chewing Over Distribution Contracts

In this section, the 4 Rs of rights, responsibilities, risks and rewards form the basis to look at agreements where you're supplied by an owner with finished goods in order to distribute to other businesses.

Bringing home the bacon: Contractual rights for distributed products

Whether you're distributing candlesticks, fiddlesticks or hockey sticks to other retailers, give yourself the widest definition of rights possible:

✔ **Extent of rights:** You wouldn't serve roast beef without roast potatoes and Yorkshire pudding. Similarly, if you have the rights to distribute goods, you also need the appropriate accompanying rights, such as to advertise, promote and sell them.

If the supplier wants to segment the market into a network of distributors, you may find that your rights are restricted to certain channels or customers, with the supplier retaining rights in these areas to supply other parties. If so, strive to make any restrictions as narrow as possible so that you have the maximum market reach.

Negotiate that your rights can broaden to other sectors or sales channels if you're successful with the initial offering for which you have rights.

The icing on the cake is to propose that you have an option to add additional products from the supplier to your range of existing products after a certain period or if you hit certain sales targets with your initial offering.

The cherry on the icing on the cake is to propose that you can add extra rights to your rights basket following consultation with the supplier, or on the basis of the supplier's approval (not to be unreasonably withheld, and assumed to have been given if the supplier doesn't say 'no' within a set period).

✔ **Territory:** The issues here are the same as in agreements for retail sale to consumers, which I describe in the earlier 'Getting it all: Contractual rights for retail products' section.

✔ **Exclusivity:** Your supplier may want to argue that exclusivity works in its favour (that you can only obtain this product from it and can't compete against it with other suppliers of the same or similar products).

This clause is asking for trouble – like agreeing only ever to eat at the same restaurant. Resist it unless the supplier is also prepared to agree reciprocal exclusivity with you (meaning that you're locked in to each other). Even then the arrangement is dangerous unless you can both terminate with short written notice.

- **Term:** Your supplier is likely to propose a limited term of, say, one year, if you're a distributor. In contrast, you want the term to be as long as possible – just as you always get more out of a leisurely meal than from a fast-food drive-through. Get your supplier to agree to an initial period with an option for you to extend the term at any point prior to the expiry of the initial period.

  Alternatively, get your supplier to agree that you have the automatic right to extend the term if you hit certain sales, revenue or shipment targets during the initial period of the term.

  In any event, ensure that your rights don't expire completely at the end of the term. If you're holding existing stock already supplied to you or that you've already manufactured, you want to be able to sell that stock for, say, another six months (called a *sell-off period*).

- **Licensing or assigning rights:** Can you pass on your rights to third parties? Ideally you need the freedom to appoint sub-licensees to exercise your rights (for example, in other countries) or even assign the whole agreement to somebody else (for example, if your business is restructured or sold).

  If the supplier is unwilling to agree to a right to sub-license or assign, make this right subject to consulting with the supplier, or subject to the supplier's prior written consent (such consent not to be unreasonably withheld or delayed).

  If you don't have the right to license and/or assign, or a prohibition applies to such activities, and you go to sell your business, you create a risk – like eating oysters in a month without an 'R'. The deal may turn out okay, but equally your proposed buyer may reduce the valuation of your business on the basis that your supplier(s) may have the right to terminate the agreement(s) concerned.

Playing it safe: Contractual obligations for distributed products

Whether you're distributing coals to Newcastle, pasties to Padstow or goats' cheese to . . . er . . . Cheddar, take the time to define the responsibilities on you and your business supplier:

- **Product:** Be clear on what's being delivered to you and its quality. Ask for samples to be delivered free of charge so that you can check – a bit like tasting the wine before you buy the bottle.

- **Format of delivery:** Make sure that the contract covers aspects such as products for distribution being delivered in certain pallet sizes or in certain quantities, or on certain days of the week to suit your distribution setup. They may have to contain certain packaging or markings (say, bar codes) to be suitable for sale by the customers to whom you distribute.

✔ **When and where:** You may have multiple distribution centres and require the product to be delivered a certain number of days before you, in turn, have to distribute it to your own business customers, so that you can deliver to your customers on time. Include any such requirements in the distribution agreement.

✔ **Placing orders:** Refer to 'Taking responsibility: Contractual obligations for retail products' earlier in this chapter for guidance on placing orders.

Your supplier may ask you to forecast your next 3–6 months of distribution orders in advance so that it knows how many units to have available in the warehouse. One way of avoiding committing yourself to a forecast is to require that in any event your supplier must keep not less than three months' stock available in its warehouse based on the ordering pattern of your preceding three months.

Sweeping success: Contractual rewards for distributed products

Whether you're distributing sweeties to Switzerland, coats to Croatia or poles to Poland, set out the agreed payment structure with your business supplier:

✔ **What's being paid?** For distribution deals, a fixed price payable per unit ordered may apply. You sell on to your own customers and make a margin based on the difference between the price at which goods are sold to you and the price at which you sell them to your customers. Alternatively, you may be allowed to take a percentage of the supplier's price to you (or your price to your own customers) as a commission, remitting the rest of your receipts to the supplier.

✔ **Deductions from payment:** You may be able to deduct the value of returns of product that you receive from your own customers, from the accounting that you have to pay the supplier. Perhaps you can send them back because they're faulty or your business customer has certain automatic or 'privileged' rights of return to you of a limited percentage of unsold stock. Your business customer wants a rebate from you for such products, and so you don't want to have to pay your supplier for goods in respect of which you aren't paid.

✔ **Changes in payment:** If you're paying a fixed price per unit, your supplier may want the freedom to raise that price during the term.

If you're under pressure to agree price increases, propose escalations at certain levels of sales success so that you know that any increase is covered by the extra margin you're making on the additional sales.

✔ **Any extras?** Make sure that you know of any hidden extra costs. For example, suppliers may want to charge you (as distributor) a commission for 'handling' your returns (whether they're faulty returns or not) as well as for any units they send you that aren't accounted for by your onward sales.

Some stock often gets lost en route to your own customers or in your own warehouse. Therefore, get the supplier to give you a shrinkage allowance of say 1 per cent of stock shipped per year so that you don't have to pay for stock that goes missing up to that allowance.

✔ **Any upfront payments?** You may be asked for a payment as an advance against the supplier's receipts from you under the agreement.

Calculate this sum carefully so that it represents a reasonable proportion of your expected receipts and therefore a manageable risk. Otherwise, the deal may turn into a complete Horlicks for you. (Are you surprised that this drink has become synonymous with unpleasant outcomes? Not me.)

✔ **Any other payment commitments during the term?** Sometimes suppliers insist that you commit to spending specified amounts per year marketing their distributed products, so that they know you're getting behind them.

Minimise such payments by amount or by restricting them to an initial period when you're proving yourself (say, the agreement's first year).

✔ **Any back-end payments?** Suppliers can ask you to guarantee in the agreement that during the term you'll sell or distribute a minimum number of units or generate a certain amount in revenue for it. If you fail to do so, at the term's end you have to pay the difference to the supplier between what was achieved and what you guaranteed. Don't over-cook any such guarantee or you may have to make a painful payment if the deal doesn't work out as you hope, especially if an advance payment applies too.

If you have to make a guarantee, agree that the term can extend automatically until you've earned back the guarantee payment.

✔ **Accounting for payments:** Distribution payments are normally made within 'x' days of the placement of a distribution order for stock. Alternatively (and better for you), they may be made monthly, within 'x' days of the end of the month, and covering your receipts from all orders for which you're paid that month.

You don't want to have to pay your supplier for goods for which you haven't received payment from your own customers, which means excluding 'bad debts' from your payment obligations. Your supplier, of course, has a different view and the compromise may be to agree a low maximum limit of bad debts you can deduct (amounting, say, to 1 per cent of revenues accounted to the supplier during each accounting period).

A good idea is to have a retention from accountings, which you can hold as a reserve against returns of product that come back to you later. That means you don't end up paying for stock for which you don't receive payment from your customers. This is a better use of your cash than paying for the goods initially and having to get a rebate for returns from your supplier later. You can release the return deduction back to your supplier over time, to the extent that it exceeds the amount of actual returns that are received over time.

✔ **Audit rights:** Your supplier is likely to want to audit your books and records to ensure that you don't under-account to it for your sales.

Insist that these rights are limited (for example, each accounting statement can be audited only once and is deemed accepted if not objected to within three years after it's received). If an error is found, make sure that the supplier pays for the cost of the audit – unless it's a big error. (A larger enough error to cause you to have to pay the audit costs instead would be one of more than 10 per cent of the sums on the statements examined or more than a certain amount, whichever is greater.)

Balancing the risk: Contractual precautions for distributed products

Flip to the earlier 'Spreading the risk: Contractual precautions for retail products' section for a discussion of allocating risk in distribution agreements. The issues are almost identical.

Tucking into Licensing Contracts

In this section, I use the 4 Rs to look at agreements where you license the rights to use products from a licensor.

Lapping it up: Contractual rights for licensed products

Whether you're licensing the right to use copyrights, trademarks, patents or design rights, you need the widest rights proposition you can get:

✔ **Extent of rights:** Licensors like to reserve as many rights as possible so that they can license different licensees for different channels (for example, music rights may be licensed separately for digital transmission by streaming, download, mobile phone or physical sales such as compilation albums and mail-order use).

See whether you can negotiate to add a right to different channels of sale subject to approval – at least this gives you an opportunity to get the conversation started in relation to extending your rights.

You may also find that the licensor wants to exercise strict control and approvals over other aspects of your exploitation (such as your packaging, the credit information you include on products, the way you use its trademark to sell the products, your marketing plans, any edits or alterations to products and so on).

This request can be annoying: like a chef exercising control over which dish you eat and how you eat it. If you can, limit these control rights to a right of consultation only, which gives you more freedom of action. If you have to give approval rights, make sure that you set a time limit for the licensor's approval and that if you don't hear anything within that period, the usage you want to carry out is deemed approved. This stops licensors thwarting your endeavours by endlessly delaying approvals.

✔ **Territory:** The issues here are the same as in agreements for retail sale to consumers. Work your way to the section 'Getting it all: Contractual rights for retail products' earlier in this chapter.

✔ **Exclusivity:** License agreements are traditionally non-exclusive. Given that they frequently involve the licensing of intellectual property rights, the licensor wants to reserve the right to license many different parties to the same product.

Try to negotiate exclusive windows within the term during which the licensor at least doesn't license other related business channels, so that your channel has the chance to shine. The licensing of movie rights has traditionally been organised in this way, with different channels (such as pay per view, satellite and cable, DVD and terrestrial TV) having an exclusive 'window' of their own after cinema release. This system gives licensees in each window more chance of exploiting the product successfully. The advent of widespread illegal copying over the Internet almost immediately after a film is released to cinema has rather disrupted this carefully constructed rights flow.

✔ **Term:** License agreements are usually relatively short (from one to three years), giving the licensor the opportunity to pick another licensee if you don't perform as well as expected.

Give yourself a right in the agreement to extend the term if you haven't recouped your initial advance payment at the end of the term – or an option to extend if you hit royalty targets during the term.

✔ **Licensing or assigning rights:** Read the section 'Bringing home the bacon: Contractual rights for distributed products' earlier in this chapter for the importance of not agreeing to restrictions on your ability to license or assign your rights.

You can also find that a licensor seeks the right to terminate the licence if your business experiences a change of control, arguing that you may find yourself acquired by a competitor of it.

Licensors having this right is dangerous, because a change of control may well occur when you take in extra investment. Rights owners suddenly withdrawing rights when you raise new money is pretty unpalatable – like eating lumpy mashed potato when you're hungry.

Shifting responsibility: Contractual obligations for licensed products

Whether you're licensing the right to reproduce photos, pharmaceuticals or phone covers, be clear about each party's obligations:

✔ **Product:** Make sure that you acquire everything you need for the licence (for example, if you're licensing book rights, you don't just want the manuscript but also the artwork, credit information, photos, right to use the author's name and biography, publicity materials and so on). You want all the filling for your steak pie, not just the pastry.

✔ **Format of delivery:** You may require licensed materials to be in a certain physical format and films or graphics in a certain digital format so that you can manufacture them yourself. Put any of these technical requirements in the contract.

✔ **When and where:** Timing can be crucial. For example, to exploit the Christmas selling period you may need items delivered by the previous 30 June, so that you have time to sell the products to your own retail customers and get everything manufactured and ready to ship. Address this priority in the licence agreement.

✔ **Placing orders:** Normally a licence is for a right to use a pre-defined set of materials and so you don't need to place orders subsequently. But if you're likely to need to add to those requirements, give yourself the right to place further orders subsequently (say, if you need more parts or components from the licensor with which to manufacture products).

Rolling in it: Contractual rewards for licensed products

Payment terms need to be agreed whether you're licensing the right to produce fishhooks, fasteners or fire guards:

✔ **What's being paid?** License deals are often constructed on the basis of payment of a *royalty,* expressed as a percentage of the retail price or the price at which you sell on to other business customers (the *dealer price*). Alternatively, you may have to pay a percentage of what you receive from sales to your own customers to the supplier.

The licensor may try to bring other sources of your revenue into account as well (such as digital advertising on your site or sponsorship monies that you receive for your site). The market for digital licences is still emerging and you can find licensors trying to hedge their bets by saying that the royalty payable to them is the greater of a certain amount per unit or a share of the revenues you receive from your own exploitation. Try and resist so that you're certain what you're paying to the licensor.

✔ **Deductions from payment:** Deduct VAT or sales taxes you receive from your customers from your sale price *before* you account to the licensor – otherwise you're paying the licensor for a share of taxes that you have to pay to HMRC. Often you can also deduct from royalties payable to licensors amounts for free goods that you have to give away to generate further sales. Equally common is deducting the value of discounts that you give as a licensee from the price at which you account to the licensor, as well as the value of returns you receive from your customers.

For royalty calculation, the supplier is likely to want to cap the amount of free goods you can give away, the levels of discount you grant and the amount of returns you can deduct by reference to a percentage of the goods you sell.

✔ **Changes in payment:** The licensor may seek to charge you for higher royalties over time, reasoning that the deal becomes worth more to you over the duration of the term.

This reasoning may or may not be true, and so the best way to deal with this request is to negotiate royalty escalations based on sales success. That way you're paying increased royalty rates when you know you can afford them. Make sure that any escalations are only prospective (apply only for the future, not retrospectively) and that they apply only to sales above the sales target(s) you agree.

✔ **Any extras?** The licensor may try to charge you for the cost of preparing delivery materials for you, such as manufacturing parts. Try and make this the licensor's cost or at least share it.

✔ **Any upfront payments?** To license a product, often you have to pay an upfront amount against your potential revenue from future sales. If so, ensure that it's an *advance* against future royalties, so that you can deduct it from the future royalties you'd otherwise have had to pay. This method is much less risky than paying the sum as a *non-recoupable* payment, which has to be recovered from your own margin and paid to the supplier on top of any royalties.

✔ **Any other payment commitments during the term?** As with distribution agreements, sometimes you're asked to commit to a certain marketing spend so that your licensor knows that you're committed to spending money on promoting its product. Make sure that any such commitments are variable and linked to the sales performance of the product (for example, 10 per cent of your gross receipts less VAT from sales of the product is a safer marketing commitment than £x thousand per year).

✔ **Any back-end payments?** You may be asked for a guarantee that during the term you'll generate a certain amount in royalties for the licensor. If you don't, at the end of the term you have to pay the difference to the supplier between what was achieved by way of royalty payments and what you guaranteed.

Although guarantees can be irksome, they do have an advantage for you over advances, because they're normally not settled till the end of the term. This delay conserves your cash and by the time the guarantee falls due, you may be able to roll it generally into a conversation about extending the term with your licensor.

✔ **Accounting for payments:** If you're paying royalties, give yourself as long as possible to send sales reporting statements and make payments. This applies to the length of the accounting period and the number of days after each accounting period by which you have to account. For example, annual accounting (with statements due 90 days after the end of the year) is better for you than monthly accounting (with statements due 30 days after the end of each month). (When you take ice-cream out of the freezer, waiting a while is much more satisfying than rushing to eat it all crunchy.)

Your licensor may well pressure you for faster accounting (say, quarterly). In the online world, payments move quickly and licensors can expect monthly payment of royalties under digital licensing agreements.

✔ **Audit rights:** Check under the earlier section 'Sweeping success: Contractual rewards for distributed products' for audit tips.

De-risking your bets: Contractual precautions for licensed products

The earlier 'Spreading the risk: Contractual precautions for retail products' section discusses allocating risk in licensing agreements.

Chapter 11

Contracting with Suppliers for Services

In This Chapter

▶ Spreading your wings with SaaS

▶ Taking flight with affiliate agreements

▶ Cruising with introducer contracts

*O*ne way to grow your business is through contracts with different suppliers of services to you – if you get those agreements right.

As with product agreements (which I look at in Chapter 10), a whole range of different service agreements are available (check out Chapter 5 to read about personal consultancy agreements for services). You may even say (well I do, anyway) that you have an entire drinks cabinet of possibilities to choose from (just don't get squiffy from drinking this chapter's 100 per cent proof information). I look at three kinds of service agreement: Software as a Service, affiliate agreements and introducer agreements. They're all very different cocktails with different flavours. As with Chapter 10, I review each agreement using the 4 Rs (rights, responsibilities, rewards, risks).

I examine these agreements from your point of view (as the beneficiary of these services) rather than the supplier's. If you're a supplier in these arrangements, just reverse the 'Tips', 'Warnings' and 'Remember' information and apply them in your favour.

Drinking in Software as a Service Agreements

Software as a Service (SaaS) agreements involve a supplier providing software through Internet access (and not members of the British Army operating dangerous missions, armed only with an elastic band and a bunch of grapes). Software as a Service agreements are therefore different from the software agreements I cover in Chapter 9, where a developer provides the software to you and you download, install or copy it and operate it from your own machine. Those agreements cover you owning or licensing the software from the developer.

In an SaaS agreement, you don't put software on a computer or copy it at all. The software sits on the supplier's computer and you merely access it through the Internet – you get a service in an SaaS deal, not the software itself. The supplier just uses software to provide the service.

Internet Service Providers are effectively SaaS providers: they use their software to give you access to the Internet rather than giving you the software itself. Other large SaaS providers are Google apps, Facebook, Twitter and Flickr, but in your everyday business you encounter many smaller software service providers who support your business.

Now that as clear as a glass of Evian's finest, I look at rights, responsibilities, rewards and risks in SaaS agreements.

Staring at the Cloud

Software as a Service providers normally use the Cloud either to store your user data that's created from using their services or to provide their applications. *The Cloud* isn't that fluffy rain-sodden thing hanging perpetually over Scotland; it's the network of connected servers that enables all these services to be delivered because it's so huge – 1 Exabyte huge apparently. That's the same amount of storage as 4.2 million Mac hard drives . . . way bigger than what could be stored in all the Himalayas or even the biggest beer belly in the world.

The ease of Cloud storage and the fact that these services can be supplied remotely means the costs of IT can fall for businesses, because they no longer have to develop their own bespoke software applications and store them on their own servers.

Granting rights in SaaS agreements

Suppliers of SaaS are by definition offering the same service to many different customers, and so the draft agreement is usually issued by the supplier and may not be open to much negotiation.

The granting of rights is usually fairly simple and short – like a vodka shot. The supplier grants you, as the customer, the right to access the software, usually from a designated website. The right is restricted to the number of users for which you pay. That's it, really.

Dividing responsibilities in SaaS agreements

The responsibilities in an SaaS agreement are a bit more complicated than the rights in the preceding section. SaaS may be intoxicatingly easy to use, but you need to drink responsibly.

Here are your obligations:

- **Password protection:** The supplier gives each permitted user a password to access the software. As the customer you must ensure that you change the password regularly, in accordance with the supplier's guidelines, and keep any password(s) secure.

- **User lists and audits:** You have to keep up-to-date records of the identities of your permitted users, and supply that list to the supplier when asked so that it knows that you haven't exceeded your allowance of users.

- **Protecting the software:** You can't behave like an out-of-control drunk, causing mayhem and disruption in a bar. You must make sure that you don't introduce any Trojans or viruses into the software, and you can't try to copy the software or re-create it for your own use.

- **Providing the right infrastructure:** You're responsible for making sure that any networks, systems and telecommunications links you use to access the software work properly and comply with any specification the supplier gives you.

Software as a Service obligations aren't all one-way traffic, however, and so make sure that the supplier takes on some responsibilities too:

- The supplier must supply you with the necessary documentation and/or training so that you and your paid-for users can access the software and use it properly.

- ✔ The supplier must back up your user data (in case it gets lost in the Cloud). Therefore, pay particular attention to how often that happens (weekly, daily, hourly?). Your requirements depend on how much critical data you can afford to lose at any one time. If it's only one hour's worth, ensure that the supplier's back-up policy matches your needs.

- ✔ The supplier has to provide you with support services in case the software doesn't work. This kind of clause is very similar to the kind of clause I discuss in Chapter 9 in relation to maintenance agreements. The clause refers to service levels for fixing faults to which the supplier must adhere, a procedure for notifying such faults and a remedy if the service levels are breached (normally 'credits' against payments that you'd otherwise have to make to the supplier as part of your usage fees for the SaaS).

If you're using a normal-sized SaaS provider (rather than a big gorilla such as Google), see whether it'll agree to make 'time of the essence' (that is, agreeing that if it doesn't deliver its services in a timely way that amounts to a breach of the agreement) with regard to these maintenance obligations. It may be a stretch but is worth a try.

Earning rewards in SaaS agreements

The payment rewards in SaaS agreements are all for the supplier, just as in the drinks industry the money flows inexorably to the bartender:

- ✔ **Subscription fees:** Normally the payment structure is linked to your usage. The more of the service you use, the more you pay. Payments are usually linked to a number of permitted users and you pay an annual subscription fee for each permitted user. You agree a maximum number of permitted users at the beginning of the agreement, but you can normally add extra users by paying extra subscription fees.

Software as a Service agreements may operate with you selling on the SaaS to others (rather than just consuming the service yourself). In this case, you're more likely to pay the SaaS supplier a percentage of what you're paid by your own customers, or retain a commission out of such sales revenue for yourself and remit the rest back to the supplier. Alternatively, because the supplier still hosts the service, even in respect of your sales, the supplier may receive the cash directly for your sales and account to you for your commission instead.

If you're a customer under an SaaS agreement and instead of paying subscription fees you're asked instead to pay a flat fee amount per year for using the SaaS, something's going wrong – usually the supplier thinks it can get more out of you that way than by charging you on an actual usage basis.

- **Storage fees:** Suppliers also require payment for additional storage of your user data over and above the limits that they set.

  Watch out for this aspect and make sure that the proposed storage limits are adequate for your needs. If you don't understand the jargon around storage capacity, get an expert to help explain it.

- **Increases:** The supplier may try to build in a right to increase these fees during the course of the agreement, in which case make sure that you apply the kinds of limitation I describe in Chapter 10 (limiting increases to the lesser of an agreed percentage or the rate of inflation).

- **Failure to pay:** If you don't pay on time, the supplier gives itself the right to switch off your access – just like a pub turning off the beer tap.

Allocating risks in SaaS agreements

Suppliers try to limit their risk for service failure in a number of ways in SaaS agreements.

It all starts off quite innocently, with the supplier assuring you in the agreement that the service will be performed substantially in accordance with the documentation supplied and with reasonable care and skill. The agreement also says that the supplier will use 'commercially reasonable efforts' to make the service available on a 24/7 basis other than for planned maintenance (between certain hours) or unplanned but necessary maintenance, for which it will try to give you reasonable notice.

Things go downhill from here, however, with the supplier then introducing a number of disclaimers and liability limitations, such as the following:

- The supplier isn't responsible for loss of your data and only has to use reasonable efforts to try to restore it for you.

- The supplier isn't responsible for failure to perform its services because of anything contained in its own agreements with Cloud service providers such as Amazon (who effectively 'rent out' space in the Cloud to SaaS providers).

- The supplier doesn't promise that the provision of the service will be uninterrupted or error free.

- The supplier limits its legal liability to responsibility only for death or personal injury caused by its negligence (which must be a pretty rare result of using a software service) or fraud. All other liability is excluded (and the clause may go on to give a tedious list of such exclusions, including for all contractual and economic loss, tort – see Chapter 15 – and all warranties).

For good measure the clause then normally limits the supplier's loss for anything that gets through the rather small eye of this legal needle by saying that in no event will it have to pay you more than £*x* in compensation (often the same amount that you've paid by way of subscription fees). Enough to sober up even the most hardened drinker.

Take heart though – all is not lost. Sure, as a business you aren't as well-protected as a consumer against unfair terms in contracts (see Chapter 12). The law expects businesses to be able to look after themselves a bit better. But limits still apply to the extent to which businesses (such as SaaS suppliers) can exclude liability against other businesses. Under the Unfair Contract Terms Act:

- A business can't exclude liability for 'negligence' unless doing so is reasonable (*negligence* is not taking reasonable care in performing a duty that you owe to somebody).

- In a contract for sale, a business can't exclude liability for 'title' (in other words, it can't exclude liability if it turns out that it doesn't own what it's selling).

- In a contract for sale or hire, a business can't exclude liability for the quality, description or fitness for purpose of its goods or samples, unless doing so is reasonable.

- The burden is on the supplier to show that any of the above exclusions are 'reasonable'. When deciding what's *reasonable,* the courts consider factors such as the information available to the buyer at the time the contract was made, whether the buying business had bargaining power to negotiate better terms and whether the term was included in a standard form contract.

As long as you add words to the effect that nothing in the supplier's disclaimers is intended to deprive you of your statutory rights, these pieces of protective legislation can look after you when dealing with even the most brutal standard terms. I think that calls for a drink. Bottoms up!

Gulping Down Affiliate Agreements

Affiliate agreements are those in which a supplier (the affiliate) provides you with online introductions by providing a link from its site to yours. If traffic from the supplier site to your site results in a commercial benefit for you (such as a sale), you reward the supplier with a commission.

Affiliate agreements work best when the two sites share a common target audience but each one provides a different service: for example, an accountancy firm dealing with small businesses linking to a law firm dealing with small businesses. The arrangement encourages users of the accountancy site (who're after, say, tax advice on a share transaction) to visit the legal site and then buy something complementary to their needs for accountancy services (such as legal documents for that share transaction). Often affiliate agreements are reciprocal – the supplier sends sales leads to your site and you send sales leads to its site, like regularly buying a round for each other.

Here are some key features of affiliate agreements, organised by the 4 Rs of rights, responsibilities, rewards and risks.

Making friends quickly: Rights in affiliate agreements

The affiliate is granted the right to use your link and logo on its site in order to send traffic back to yours. The positioning of the link and logo and the wording around it on the supplier site are negotiated between the parties – the supplier doesn't want the size and positioning of your offering to outshine its own and equally you don't want to be buried on page 121 of its 122-page website.

These rights sometimes continue for a fixed period or (more commonly) can be terminated by written notice by either side (of say 1–3 months). Apart from this, of course, each side has the usual rights to terminate if the other side commits a breach or gets into financial difficulties (refer to Chapter 10).

Falling into line: Responsibilities in affiliate agreements

In the agreement, ensure that the affiliate fulfils the following obligations:

✔ Copies your link exactly and doesn't change that link or any graphics that you supply

✔ Makes sure that any information it displays about your site is accurate

✔ Promises that its site will be functional and accessible at all times for users (apart from reasonable maintenance downtime and factors beyond its control, such as fire, earthquakes and attacks by viruses, worms or other slimy creatures)

Try to get your affiliate to agree to some marketing commitments on your behalf. For example, it can notify its customer database of its affiliate partnership deal with you or include in its customer newsletter details of any special offer you've agreed to make available to visitors from the affiliate site. This arrangement helps your partnership stand out and encourages a bigger flow of traffic from its site to yours – like adding some spice to what would otherwise be just a tomato juice.

Your responsibilities are as follows:

- ✔ Promise that you'll continue to make the products or services advertised on the affiliate site available during the term of your agreement.
- ✔ Promise that you'll process properly all user orders from customers who are visitors from the affiliate site.
- ✔ Track the origin of all visitors to your site from the affiliate site and track the products or services which those visitors select from your site and the revenues they pay for them.
- ✔ Make full reports to the affiliate of all such information in relation to each visitor from the affiliate site.

Technology solutions such as Omnistar (www.osiaffiliate.com) can help you track and count information about visitors to your site from affiliate sites on an automated basis. Or you can do it manually using your fingers and toes and a pencil and paper if you find that easier.

The intervals at which you account to your affiliate are a matter for negotiation. You want the intervals to be as long as possible for reasons of cash flow and because reconciling accountings takes time; you may want to account 30 days after each month end. The affiliate supplier will be much more impatient and may ask for weekly accounting.

Eyeing the prize: Rewards in affiliate agreements

The affiliate receives a payment in return for the traffic it sends, which you need to negotiate. The affiliate can be paid only for the number of people who click on the link to your site, but you want those visitors to buy something for the link to be worthwhile. Therefore, affiliates often get paid a percentage of the price you receive for anything its visitors buy at your site. This percentage typically ranges from 5 to 25 per cent – the more marketing effort the affiliate puts in on your behalf, the higher percentage it deserves.

Take any appropriate deductions off your receipt before you account to the affiliate on a sale – for example, if the customer pays you VAT on top of the sales price, deduct that VAT before paying the affiliate, otherwise you end up paying commission on a VAT receipt that's not usable revenue for you. Equally, if you have automatic payments you have to make to third parties out of that receipt (such as payment provider charges to PayPal) that figure should come off the top too.

Put a time limit or cap on what the affiliate can receive from the introduction; otherwise, you can end up overpaying for it. Over time the value of the referral fades. For example, the referred visitor coming back to your site a second or a third time and making a repeat purchase is less down to the initial referral from the affiliate and more because that visitor likes your product or service. If the visitor pays for a subscription to your site, the value of the initial introduction in his mind is far less after six months of that subscription than when he first visited your site.

For this reason, try to limit the commission to a certain percentage of the net price received from the visitor concerned within, say, one month of his first visit to your site. Or you can limit the commission on any one visitor to no more than a certain amount; therefore, if the visitor pays you for an upfront subscription, not all that subscription value is taken into account in calculating the commission. The best way to avoid crying over spilt milk is not to spill too much of it.

Skirting danger: Risks in affiliate agreements

As long as the term of the affiliate agreement is quite short or can be terminated with a short notice period, neither side has too much risk, because if the relationship doesn't work, either of them can easily end it.

Here are some risks, however, you want to protect against:

- ✔ The affiliate may well ask you to promise that you fully own or have cleared any content or logo you give it to use on its site. It doesn't want to pick up the tab if you give it any infringing materials – that would be a bitter lemon to swallow.

- ✔ You want to make sure that you don't have to pay commission unless you can track the sale by the visitor from the affiliate site: no proof of sale equals no commission.

- ✔ Make sure that you have to pay commission only on sales where you actually receive the money from the referred visitor. If the visitor defaults on payment or is entitled to a rebate, you don't want to have to pay the affiliate commission for that sale.

Gently Sipping Introducer Agreements

In an *introducer* agreement, you appoint someone to find sales leads for your goods and services. Unlike the affiliate agreements of the preceding section, introducers tend to operate in the physical rather than the online world. They cover sales where you reach agreement over a handshake and a whiskey and soda, instead of at the click of a button.

Guess what . . . I look at introducer agreements using the 'rights, responsibilities, rewards, risk' structure. I'm not addicted to this particular tipple . . . I can stop anytime I want. I'll just have one more.

Meeting and greeting: Granting rights in introducer agreements

You secure the right to sales introductions made by the supplier. Usually the supplier has a 'black book' of contacts in your sector, which means that it can secure sales introductions for you. This right applies during the agreed term – perhaps a fixed period or just running on until either side terminates by giving a certain period of written notice (say 30 or 60 days).

Sometimes your rights are restricted to a particular territory in which the introducer is active and knows the market.

You can make the agreement *exclusive* on the supplier, meaning that it can't introduce sales leads to anybody else in your sector during the term. But if you do include an exclusivity provision preventing it from making introductions to others, it's exactly the sort of thing that turns a 'contractor' agreement into an 'employee' one (flip to Chapter 5 for details of this tricky area).

Make sure that the agreement isn't made exclusive on you (and you can't appoint other introducers). You don't want only one introducer, any more than you want only one bottle of wine in your wine cellar.

In return for making successful introductions, the supplier gets a right to a payment (see the later 'Splashing the cash: Rewards in introducer agreements' section).

Playing it straight: Responsibilities in introducer agreements

The supplier has an obligation to provide a written list of potential contacts for you to approve before it makes contact. You may have tactical or timing reasons why you don't want it to approach all the contacts at once. This list is normally refreshed regularly during the term (say, monthly).

You can ask for a minimum quantity of introductions each year or during the term as a whole.

When the target list of potential customers is approved, the supplier's obligation is to provide *qualifying introductions* for you, which are those on which the supplier gets commission. Usually a number of qualifying conditions apply, such as the following:

- ✓ The supplier must provide you with full contact details for the introduction.

- ✓ The introduction must be to a customer not already known to you (which should be obvious to you, unless you've had one too many sherbets).

- ✓ The introduction must be at a level of seniority that can make purchase decisions within the introduced organisation (you don't want to be paying for sales leads to the nightwatchman unless you happen to be in the sales-to-nightwatchmen business).

- ✓ The introduction must result in a contract with you for a sale from that customer entered into during the term (or within a few months of the term ending, to allow for completion of paperwork).

- ✓ Your responsibility is to confirm to the supplier in writing when a qualifying introduction has been made, with details of the date of the contract, how much is due to the supplier for the introduction and when you'll pay.

Splashing the cash: Rewards in introducer agreements

The introducer receives a reward for making qualifying introductions. The reward can be a flat payment for each qualifying introduction, a bonus payment or even a crate of the supplier's favourite cocktail (a Margarita, a Brooklyn, a Planter's Punch, but please, no Cosmopolitans. A sour vodka? Do me a favour.). More conventionally, the supplier receives a percentage commission related to the revenue generated for you by the qualifying introduction. The commission applies to any qualifying introduction made during the term.

Take off those revenues any necessary deductions (such as for VAT, discounts you had to give the customer to close the sale and any other expenses arising from the sale). Also make sure that the commission is capped, through one of these two possible methods:

✔ **Cap the commission over time:** If someone makes a qualifying introduction, you don't want the commission to go on to infinity and beyond. For example, maybe the commission only applies for the first year of the sales contract arising from the qualifying introduction, or until 12 months after the end of the term of the introducer agreement.

✔ **Limit the commission by amount:** For example, no more than '£x' in relation to any particular contract from a qualifying introduction, or no more than a total of '£y' over the term of the introducer's contract. As with affiliate agreements (see the earlier 'Eyeing the prize: Rewards in affiliate agreements' section), the logic for this capping is that the value of the introduction recedes over time – the customer is increasingly buying your goods or service delivery in his own right.

Pay commission only on monies you actually *receive* from the introduced customer: no revenue received equals no commission. If the customer pays in instalments, split up the commission based on each instalment you receive, instead of paying any commission upfront.

Treading carefully: Risks in introducer agreements

From your point of view, you want to protect yourself against the following risks in the agreement:

✔ **Your supplier entering into agreements on your behalf or making commitments on your behalf without your approval can give you a real hangover.** The supplier making introductions is one thing, but you must remain in sole control of contractual negotiations with any prospective customers; only you can decide whether to enter into an agreement with a prospective customer.

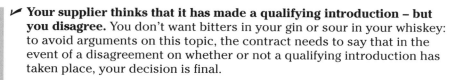

✔ **Your supplier thinks that it has made a qualifying introduction – but you disagree.** You don't want bitters in your gin or sour in your whiskey: to avoid arguments on this topic, the contract needs to say that in the event of a disagreement on whether or not a qualifying introduction has taken place, your decision is final.

✔ **Your supplier makes bribes to get you contracts.** In the UK, the Bribery Act, 2010 is a criminal offence. As a limited company or partnership you can face unlimited fines (crikey!) and as an individual you can be liable to ten years' imprisonment (strewth!).

You can be guilty for offering, promising or giving a bribe, or for requesting, agreeing to receive or accepting a bribe. A limited company can be liable for failing to prevent bribery taking place on its behalf. This offence doesn't just apply to failing to control your employees; you can also be liable if an 'associated person' (a consultant or introducer) makes the bribe. Introducer agreements therefore contain strict prohibitions against the supplier carrying out any activity that would be an offence under the Bribery Act.

The introducer agreement normally also contains the usual clauses enforcing confidentiality (because the introducer may well receive confidential information from you in order to facilitate sales) and clauses in relation to termination for each contract partner's breach or financial adversity (refer to Chapter 10).

The supplier's main risk is that you don't pay it for commission it has earned from a qualifying introduction. For this reason, suppliers request rights of audit of your financial records concerning qualifying introductions. If you have to agree to audit rights, limit them as I suggest in Chapter 10.

Chapter 12

Creating Legal Contracts with Consumers

*I*n Chapter 6, I discuss the importance of creating a robust set of Terms and Conditions for your website and considering how the legislation impacts them (for example, the Data Protection Act, 1998, Electronic Commerce Regulations, 2002, Consumer Products Act, 1987 and Consumer Credit Act, 1974). But even if you comply with Chapter 6 word for word, you're not out of the woods in your dealings with customers.

In this chapter, I describe another layer of issues you need to address in your contracts with consumers, which apply *offline* as well as online. I also cover consumer complaints and how to create binding contracts with customers. Some of this information may be a bit of an education, but if you pay attention to the blackboard and don't stare out of the window, you gain a good grasp of how to deal with consumer contracts.

Minding Your Step in the Legal Minefield

Right, listen carefully at the back – Molesworth, I've got my eye on you! Here are the legislative tripwires that you don't want to trigger, because they can blow up in your face like a stink bomb.

I cover here only aspects that are in addition to the text on online trading in Chapter 6. For example, for details of legislation on defective products and offering credit, check out that chapter for the necessary curriculum.

Playing fair: Avoiding unfair trading practices

The Consumer Protection from Unfair Trading Regulations, 2008 contain a general ban on unfair commercial practices, specific prohibitions against misleading and aggressive practices, and a blacklist of 31 automatically unfair commercial practices (for the details, see https://www.gov.uk/government/uploads/system/uploads/attachment_data/file/284442/oft1008.pdf).

A practice is covered by the general ban if it breaches the requirement to act with professional diligence, doesn't meet the standard that can be reasonably expected and is likely to distort materially the behaviour of the average consumer.

Misleading and aggressive practices are also prohibited and include: providing false information, omitting important information, creating confusion with a competitor's products, failing to follow the rules of a code, and harassing, coercing or exerting undue influence.

The 31 specific practices outlawed automatically include the following:

- **Bait advertising:** Luring the consumer with attractive advertising around special prices when such products aren't available

- **Bait and switching:** Promoting one product with the intention of selling another

- **False free offers:** Describing a product as free or without charge if the consumer is required to pay a fee other than that applicable to delivery

- **Pressure selling:** Creating the impression that a consumer can't leave the premises until a contract is formed

- **Aggressive doorstop selling:** Ignoring a consumer's request not to visit or to leave her home

- **Limited offers:** Falsely stating that a product is only available for a very limited period of time or only available on specific terms, in order to obtain an immediate decision from consumers and so deprive them of the opportunity to make an informed decision

- **Targeting of children:** Advertising that directly encourages children to purchase a product or persuades their parents to do so

> ✔ **Inertia selling:** Supplying products without being asked and proceeding to require payment for them
>
> ✔ **Running bogus competitions:** Includes pyramid schemes

You wouldn't dream of doing any of these things, would you? Splendid.

Ensuring that the price you see is what you pay

The Price Marking Order, 2004 requires you to indicate the selling prices of all products offered for sale to consumers (except those offered in the course of the provision of a service, those sold by auction, works of art or antiques, or products made to order). It applies only to sales between traders and consumers (see http://eradar.eu/the-price-marking-order-2004/).

Here are the two key requirements:

> ✔ The shown selling price must be the final price including VAT and other taxes.
>
> ✔ Prices must be 'unambiguous, easily identifiable and clearly legible'.

In addition:

> ✔ Consumers shouldn't have to seek assistance to be able to see a price.
>
> ✔ You must display the unit price for goods sold from bulk or mark the quantity of pre-packaged goods, as required by the Weights and Measures (Packaged Goods) Regulations, 2006.
>
> ✔ Prices must be in sterling. If you're prepared to accept a foreign currency, you must also give further specific information about exchange rates and commission.
>
> ✔ You can show prices on the goods on a notice near to them or grouped together with other prices in a list or in catalogues in close proximity.

> ✔ To reduce the price of a product, you can indicate the final selling price by displaying a general notice that the product is for sale at a reduced price, but the details of the reduction must be prominent, unambiguous, easily identifiable and clearly legible.
>
> ✔ Window or other displays must display selling prices on products in line with the above requirements. An exception applies to jewellery or items of precious metal priced above £3,000.

A detention if you don't comply with all these requirements.

Breaking up is hard to do: Avoiding defective products

The Consumer Protection Act, 1987 requires that all products must be safe for their intended use. Under the Act, manufacturers, distributors, suppliers and retailers can be held liable for any injuries caused as a result of their products or any component parts being defective. Fortunately the Act was introduced after I'd given up woodwork at school and was no longer distributing dangerous pencil boxes to unsuspecting grandparents. A product is *defective* if it doesn't meet the legitimate expectations of the customer taking into account:

- All aspects of the marketing of the product
- The use of any mark in relation to the product
- Any instructions and warnings supplied with the product and what may reasonably be expected to be done with the product at the time the product was supplied

The Act introduces *strict liability* for damage caused by defective product. Therefore, a customer only needs to show that the product was defective and the defect caused the injury – whether it was your fault or not is irrelevant. So no shortcuts please: you only need one thing to go wrong and you can face heavy-duty financial damage, not to mention reputational damage when disgruntled customers take to the social media airwaves.

The basic limitation period for claims under the Act is three years from the date of damage or injury, with a further limited period covering claims that don't immediately become apparent. Anybody who puts her name on a product or holds herself out as being a producer of the product can be liable. If a product is manufactured outside the EU, the importer can be held liable as can the supplier if it doesn't respond to a request to identify the producer of a defective product it supplied. Retailers aren't usually held liable under the Act unless they fail to identify the producer or importer when asked to do so by an injured party.

Giving something for nothing: Complying with Consumer credit rules

The Consumer Credit Act, 1974 requires you to get a licence if you want to allow consumers to pay for goods on credit. Since April 2014, the Financial Conduct Authority (FCA) handles regulation of consumer credit (http://www.which.co.uk/consumer-rights/regulation/consumer-credit-act). To operate consumer credit activities, you must register with the FCA and apply for authorisation. The FCA can refuse, revoke such licences and impose prosecutions and fines if you offer credit without a licence. So there.

At least one individual in the business must be 'approved' to perform 'controlled functions' on behalf of your firm. The test applied is whether the person is 'fit and proper' to perform these functions considering her honesty, integrity, reputation, competence, capability and financial soundness. High-sounding words given that bankers are supposed to comply with the Code too.

If a licence is granted, you must provide specific information to the consumer before entering into a credit agreement, including:

- ✔ Rate of interest and how such charges are calculated
- ✔ Annual Percentage Rate of interest (APR) (a broader calculation of the cost of the credit, taking into account frequency of interest payments and other expenses such as arrangement fees)
- ✔ Total amount payable
- ✔ Timing of the repayments
- ✔ Total charge for credit

A licence isn't needed to allow consumers to pay for goods bought in four or fewer instalments within a year from the date of sale.

Compelling selling: Working within the Consumer Rights Act, 2015

What was your least favourite school food? Mine was Mulligatawny soup. You may find the Consumer Rights Act, 2015 equally unappetising. This Act attempts to clarify and codify numerous existing pieces of consumer protection legislation and applies to all applicable consumer contracts entered into from 1 October 2015. It replaces the Sale of Goods Act, 1979 and the Supply of Goods and Services Act, 1982.

The Act says that contracts have a number of terms 'implied' into them (whether the contract contains those terms or not). A qualifying contract is one that's:

- ✔ A contract for sale
- ✔ A hire agreement

  ✔ A hire purchase agreement

  ✔ A contract for the transfer of goods

The following terms are implied for transactions involving the sale and supply of *goods:*

  ✔ Traders must have the right to transfer/sell the goods.

  ✔ Goods must be of satisfactory quality.

  ✔ Goods must be fit for a particular purpose.

  ✔ Goods must match the description, sample or model that the customer sees or examines.

  ✔ Goods must be installed correctly.

If the goods provided don't meet these requirements, the consumer has a number of remedies against you, including the following:

  ✔ **Reject goods that are faulty or not as described:** This short-term right allows customers to return and obtain a full refund within 30 days (unless goods have a short shelf-life).

  ✔ **Repair or replacement:** Consumers can request that faulty goods or ones not as described are repaired or replaced even after the 30-day right to reject period has ended. The business must bear the costs of postage, labour and materials and must do so within a reasonable period of time and without significant inconvenience to the consumer.

  ✔ **Price reduction:** Consumers have the right to a reduction in the price after one unsuccessful repair or replacement. You may be entitled to make a deduction in respect of any use the consumer has made of the goods before they're rejected.

For transactions involving *services* all the three following terms are implied into any sales contract:

  ✔ The service must be performed with reasonable skill and care.

  ✔ The price for the service must be 'reasonable' if not agreed.

  ✔ The service must be performed within a reasonable period if not agreed.

Statutory remedies

If you fail to provide a service with reasonable care and skill, consumers have both the following rights:

✔ To require repeat performance of services that aren't performed with reasonable care and skill or in line with information provided by you. If that's not possible or done within a reasonable time, they have the right to a price reduction.

✔ To receive a price reduction if services aren't performed within a reasonable time.

So, if you're considering ignoring these requirements, go and write out 100 times 'I must comply with the Consumer Rights Act, 2015'.

These remedies for consumers aren't available to them where any defects or breaches of the implied terms were brought to the consumer's attention by you prior to the conclusion of the contract, or if the consumer had examined the goods before purchasing them and the goods are of such a type that any defects would've been identifiable on inspection.

Delivery of goods

The Act also says that unless you and the consumer agree otherwise, the contract includes an obligation on you to deliver the goods to the consumer without undue delay, and in any event not later than 30 days after the date on which the contract was entered into.

Avoiding unfair contract terms

As well as observing the prohibitions in the earlier 'Playing Fair: Avoiding unfair trading practices' section, you also have to do further homework in the commercial practices area. The Consumer Rights Act, 2015 prohibits 'unfair terms' in consumer contracts and the unfair limiting of liability.

The Act defines a term as *unfair* if 'it causes a significant imbalance in the parties' rights and obligations to the detriment of the consumer'.

Any clauses you include that the Act regards as unfair aren't enforceable. Many businesses have blanket waivers of liability in their terms and regard that as 'job done' in terms of protecting themselves. Not so.

Here are some key clauses likely to be considered 'unfair'; before Skools Out you need to have learned them by heart:

✔ Any term that's very difficult to understand, perhaps because of the obscure language or tiny print size

✔ Any term that tries to prevent consumers from carrying out their legal rights – for example, their right to a refund for faulty goods

- ✔ Any term that tries to prevent the consumer from taking you to court
- ✔ Any term saying you aren't responsible for a death or injury caused by something you have or haven't done
- ✔ Any term saying you aren't responsible for delays, even ones that are your fault
- ✔ Any term saying you aren't responsible if you don't do what you should do under the contract
- ✔ Any term that tries to prevent consumers from keeping back payments when they have a genuine complaint about goods or services
- ✔ Any term that tries to make consumers pay more than needed to cover your losses if they cancel the contract
- ✔ Any term hidden from consumers until after they sign the contract
- ✔ Any term giving you wide cancellation rights but not giving the consumer the same rights
- ✔ Any term giving you the right to change the contract to your benefit after it has been created
- ✔ Any term that makes ending a contract very difficult for consumers; for example, making them pay high termination charges or give a long notice period
- ✔ Any term that allows you to determine the price after the contract has been formed

So, you have to be nice to consumers in your contracts, got it?

Other requirements include the following:

- ✔ Price/subject matter contract terms are only exempt if they're *transparent* (in plain and intelligible language) and *prominent* (brought to customers' attention in such a way that the average well-informed, observant and careful customer would be aware of the term).
- ✔ All written terms of a consumer contract must be transparent and the main points, including price, must be clear.

You can't exclude or limit liability for including unfair terms.

Here are a couple more warnings (it's worse than the School Rules: no running, shouting or swearing – and that's just to control the teachers):

- ✔ Rules on unfair terms in consumer contracts also apply to *consumer notices,* broadly defined as ones relating to rights or obligations between you and the consumer, or ones that restrict your liability (say, a notice in your shop or on your premises). The definition also includes oral communications and announcements. In effect, the Act treats consumer notices in the same way as contract terms: ensure that your notices comply with the fairness requirement too.

✔ A spoken or written voluntary statement made by you, and about you or your service can be deemed a binding term of the contract. This applies where the consumer takes the statement into account when deciding to enter the contract or making any decision about the service after entering into the contract. So, take care: the more you say, the more you give away.

If you aren't complying with these requirements on fairness in your contracts, you must try harder. See me afterwards.

Complying with the Consumer Contracts Regulations, 2013

Taking in more regulations after reading through the preceding section probably sounds about as appetising as a ten-mile cross-country run organised by a sadistic gym master followed by a cold school shower – but I'm afraid it's even worse than that!

The Consumer Contracts Regulations may *sound* just like the Consumer Rights Act, 2015 (refer to the preceding section), but they're different. The fully and memorably named Consumer Contracts (Information, Cancellation & Additional Charges) Regulations, 2013 replace the former Distance Selling Regulations and govern all applicable consumer contracts entered into after 13 June 2014 (for help, visit http://www.lawsociety.org.uk/support-services/advice/practice-notes/consumer-contracts-regulations-2013/).

The Regulations apply to the sale of goods or services involving no face-to-face contact with the consumer and where the sale occurs at a distance: by mail-order, over the Internet, and by telephone, fax or text message. Potentially, therefore, they cover a mixture of online and offline sales.

Failure to comply with the information and other requirements in this section can result in you being seen to be in breach of contract and consumers not being bound by particular contracts or not having to pay for goods/services. Consumers may also get an extension of cancellation rights for up to 12 months or you may face enforcement action by Trading Standards officers, including fines and a smacked bottom.

Exclusions from the Consumer Contracts Regulations

The Regulations exclude the following products and services (I have no idea why these particular ones): financial services; gambling; package travel; residential lettings; construction of new buildings; supply of food, beverages or other goods intended for current consumption; certain time-share or long-term holiday products; purchases from vending machines; and single telecom connection (payphones/café Internet connection).

The Regulations also don't apply to contracts between businesses, which are covered by the Electronic Commerce Regulations (refer to Chapter 6), or to a one-off distance sale made in response to a consumer request. But they do apply if your business is set up to deal with such requests on a regular basis.

To ensure compliance, your website's Terms and Conditions (Ts and Cs) must refer specifically to these Regulations as well as to other relevant parts of the website, including provision of a model cancellation form, updates to confirmation emails and the ordering process.

Key points

Bear in mind these points when dealing with consumers:

- ✔ Most products and services fall within the scope of these Regulations, with the limited exceptions in the nearby sidebar 'Exclusions from the Consumer Contracts Regulations'.

- ✔ The rules protect consumers based in the UK and apply regardless of the country in which a supplier or trader is based.

- ✔ Strict pre-contractual information requirements apply. You must provide this information (including the following) to consumers in a clear and comprehensible way so that they're bound by the contract:

  - Main characteristics of the goods, services or digital content

  - Identity of the trader

  - Total price inclusive of tax, delivery or other charges

  - Minimum duration of any obligation and how to cancel or terminate

You must provide this required information on a 'durable medium' – by paper or email or in any other way that fulfils all the following:

- Allows information to be addressed personally to the consumer

- Allows consumers to store the information in an accessible way for future reference for a period that's long enough for the purposes of the information

- Allows copying of the information stored

Providing this information through a link to a website is *not* sufficient and the information is only regarded as having been made available if the consumer can reasonably be expected to know how to access it.

✔ Obligations exist in relation to payments. You must ensure that a consumer explicitly acknowledges that placing the order brings with it an obligation to pay. Any ordering mechanisms such as order buttons must be clearly labelled and must be 'unambiguous . . . indicating that placing the order entails an obligation to pay'.

Pre-ticked charging options or hidden charges aren't binding on a consumer. Consumers must expressly agree to any such charges.

A button marked 'Pay now' suffices.

✔ If you operate a telephone helpline that consumers can use for assistance regarding their contract, the cost must be provided at a basic rate and not at a premium. You must refund any costs in excess of a basic rate to the consumer.

Cancellation rights and information

You must include cancellation rights and information. The right to cancel (the *cooling off* period) is 14 days from delivery of the goods, during which consumers are entitled to change their minds, cancel the contract and receive a full refund, regardless of the reason and without incurring any liability. Even if they want to cancel their order for a purple cardigan because it brings Aunty Irene out in hives – that's a good enough reason.

Any ancillary contracts into which consumers enter, such as warranties or insurance cover, are automatically cancelled when they exercise this cancellation right. The provision of a model cancellation form is now mandatory and consumers must be given information about their cancellation rights, laid out *exactly* as required by the Regulations.

Certain contracts are exempt from these cancellation requirements, including the supply of goods that are liable to deteriorate or expire rapidly (for example, food) and personalised goods (for example, a personally monogrammed purse).

You must reimburse the consumer within 14 days of you receiving back the goods or notification that they've been sent. You must refund the total price – including the delivery charge.

The Regulations clarify that you need to refund only standard delivery charges in the event of cancellation. You're also allowed to make a deduction from a refund for any reduction in value of the returned goods due to handling that 'goes beyond the sort of handling that might reasonably be allowed in a shop'.

When you're providing a service, you mustn't begin the supply of it before the end of the cancellation period unless consumers expressly ask you to do so. If they request that the service commence before the cancellation period, they have to pay for such services and can't cancel them.

After the cooling-off period, the consumers' cancellation rights end. But if goods have been incorrectly described or are faulty, the consumer can return them for a refund within six months of the goods being supplied.

Delivery of a contract for the sale of goods must be made to the consumer without undue delay and within 30 days after the contract is entered into, unless you and the consumer agree something else. If you're providing services, you must start providing the service within this time frame. The goods remain at your risk (for instance, of damage or loss) until they come into the physical possession of the consumer.

These cancellation rights also apply to digital content, unless you obtain specific consent and acknowledgement from the consumer that the digital download will start before the end of the 14-day cancellation period. Digital content providers must provide information about functionality, interoperability and compatibility with hardware and software.

As you can see, following the Consumer Contracts Regulations properly is like adhering to the strict instructions for school exams – 'use a ruler to draw lines; pencil not allowed; illegible handwriting, smudges and spelling mistakes will be penalised'. If you take on-board this section at one sitting, well done. Award yourself an 'A Star' in GCSE in consumer legislation.

Making It Stick: Creating Binding Consumer Contracts

The guidance I give in this chapter and Chapter 6 means that you know what needs to be in your consumer contracts. Great. But how do you make sure that your contracts are binding on your customers?

Any contract requires *an offer* from one person, clear *acceptance* of that offer by the other and *consideration* (which means that each party must receive a tangible benefit in return for whatever she promises to do under the contract).

Getting consumers to accept a price is one thing, but you also need to get them to accept all the other clauses as well. How you do that depends, but this section provides some practical and helpful answers.

Some businesses argue for the implication of their standard Ts and Cs into the sales process by 'custom and practice', but this is a stiff test to pass. Such custom and practice must be universally accepted within an industry and must be established, long-standing and followed by the parties over a long period of time. You must also show that the term is 'notorious, certain and reasonable'. Rely on this route and you can end up as the class dunce.

Other businesses rely on implying terms into the transaction that favour them based on a 'previous course of dealings' between the parties. Again, the 'pass mark' for this test is very high. You must show that the parties have a frequent and consistent recurring relationship. In reality, this relationship is only likely to occur where both parties are commercial organisations with a history of dealing with each other. If you're dealing with a consumer, the courts expect you to have given explicit notice of your Ts and Cs if you want to rely on them.

Tying up physical, face-to-face or postal sales

For physical or face-to-face sales, if you want to *incorporate* (include) Ts and Cs into the sales contract, you have to ensure that a customer is given notice of them before the contract is concluded. Consumers aren't deemed to have accepted such terms unless you've given adequate notice and taken reasonable steps to bring the terms to their attention.

For example, a sale in your retail shop is governed by your specific Ts and Cs, as long as a sufficiently obvious and clear notice at the premises is brought to the attention of the consumer. A notice printed in small letters or at a distance from where the purchase is made doesn't amount to 'adequate notice'. Equally, if your Ts and Cs are on the back of a document (say, a sales docket or a receipt) that may not be sufficient to fix the consumer with notice, unless a statement on the front of the document states that the contract is made subject to the terms printed on the reverse.

For postal sales where Ts and Cs are 'shrink-wrapped' to a package (for example, on the box containing computer software), the terms are normally assumed to have been sufficiently brought to the attention of consumers to constitute 'acceptance', unless when they made their buying decision no mention was made to them that these other Ts and Cs would apply.

Securing your online sales

In the case of online sales, you must properly bring the terms to the attention of consumers before they can be bound by such terms. Just placing the terms on your website doesn't help you pass any exams.

To ensure that the terms are legally binding, make consumers scroll through all the Ts and Cs and then click an 'Accept' or 'I agree' button before they're permitted to place the order.

To reduce the number of pages in the purchasing process, and because this isn't very user-friendly, many sellers place a link on the purchasing page to a separate page where the Ts and Cs are displayed (a *browse-wrap* agreement), without requiring a click on this link.

Don't use this solution – and if currently you do, correct it as soon as possible. These agreements have been held unenforceable in the US, because they don't bring the relevant terms to the attention of the buyer before the contract is made and therefore aren't binding on the buyer.

Instead, use a more prudent option, such as displaying the terms as follows:

- ✔ In a prominent place on the homepage
- ✔ In a separate scroll-down window on the website, which consumers are forced to view before placing the order

If you include your Ts and Cs as a separate page in the sales process, make sure that consumers have to acknowledge that they've read and agree to be bound by them by ticking a clearly marked 'Agree' or 'I accept' button *before* placing the order. If you accompany the button with a prominently displayed warning of the existence of your Ts and Cs, it should amount to sufficient notice to allow effective incorporation of the Ts and Cs.

Drawing the Sting: Dealing with Complaints

Even if you run a perfect business, you're bound to receive complaints from time to time. Create heaven on earth and someone will complain that it's too peaceful, for sure.

Complaints are increasingly dangerous for businesses, because many disgruntled customers are more than happy to broadcast their grievances on social media, ensuring that one unhappy customer can turn into lasting reputational damage. You're being too cool for school if you think you can ignore complaints.

Taking it on the chin: Running a complaints policy

Make sure that you have a formal complaints procedure, which you apply consistently. A proper complaints procedure does the following:

- ✔ Gives customers a chance to let off steam safely.

- ✔ Is more cost-effective and less stressful than dealing with difficult complainants who've become even angrier because you ignored their initial complaint.

- ✔ Gives you the chance to turn a situation around. If you handle a complaint quickly, efficiently and sensitively you can turn an unhappy customer into a champion for your business.

- ✔ Helps you improve your customer service and eliminate similar problems arising in the future.

An effective complaints system contains certain elements. Go to the top of the class if yours provides the following:

- ✔ **Accessibility:** Clear information is available on how to pursue a complaint that's easy to access (clearly available on a website or in the retail space). The policy allows for the complaint to be made in writing (including by email) or in person.

- ✔ **Fairness:** All customers are treated fairly and with respect, and a consistent approach is applied to resolve all complaints. You make no charge to the complainant when dealing with the matter.

> ✔ **Timeliness:** You lay down a time limit within which the complaint is addressed, together with a time frame for keeping the customer informed.
>
> ✔ **Remedies:** A range of remedies is available if the complaint is found to be justified.

Even if you don't fancy implementing a complaints policy, certain regulatory requirements in your business sector may require you to do so. For example:

✔ **Financial services:** The Financial Services Authority (FSA) requires firms working in the financial services sector to comply with rules on complaint handling. You must handle complaints free of charge, identify a senior individual as responsible for complaint handling and deal with complaints fairly and not dismiss them when they're first made. You may not get the cane if you get this wrong, but the Financial Ombudsman Service can give consumers financial awards when such policies are breached and/or impose financial penalties on you.

✔ **Telecommunications:** Ofcom is the Regulator for complaint handling for telecommunications businesses. It has a duty to ensure that providers have procedures in place for the handling of complaints in line with the Communications Act, 2003. A minimum set of obligations are set out in the Ofcom Code of Practice, including that procedures are transparent, accessible and effective, and that they facilitate appropriate access to alternative dispute resolution.

✔ **Property:** Ofcom also deals with complaints regarding businesses in some other sectors, including those involved in the property sector (surveyors, estate agents, letting agents and valuers).

✔ **Energy businesses:** Firms providing gas and electricity must meet the requirements laid out in the Consumers, Estate Agents and Redress Act, 2007. The Act says that consumers and small business consumers of energy companies have the right to take certain complaints to the Ombudsman if the firm fails to resolve the problem.

Providing a mediation option

The Alternative Dispute Resolution for Consumer Disputes (Competent Authorities and Information) Regulations, 2015 (try saying that with your mouth full) took effect from 9 July 2015. The aim is to encourage the use of alternative dispute resolution (ADR) among traders in relation to consumer disputes, and they impose a minimum level of consumer protection. Check out the details at `https://www.gov.uk/government/uploads/system/uploads/attachment_data/file/377522/bis-14-1122-alternative-dispute-resolution-for-consumers.pdf`.

The Regulations require you to provide a mediation option for sorting out disputes. Mediation involves the appointment of a neutral mediator who tries to facilitate the settlement of a dispute. The regulations apply to online and offline consumer contracts (flip to Chapter 15 for more on mediation).

Businesses dealing with consumers that have exhausted their internal complaint handling procedure must do the following:

1. **Inform the consumer in writing that they can't settle the complaint.**

2. **Provide the name of an ADR entity that's competent to deal with the complaint (if the consumer wants to use ADR).**

3. **Say whether they're prepared to submit to such an ADR procedure.**

Although the parties aren't obliged to use ADR and both must agree, the obligation to direct consumers to a certified mediation scheme is mandatory. This process also makes good business sense, because mediation is generally faster, less complicated and less expensive than court proceedings and therefore beneficial to both consumers and traders.

Chapter 13

Saying Bonjour, Ciao, Hola, Ni Hao to Trading Abroad

- -

In This Chapter

▶ Buying into overseas trading structures

▶ Exporting with all due dispatch

▶ Shoring up your understanding of local legal issues

- -

*I*f you export or import as the sole focus of your business, you need to be aware from day one of the dos and don'ts of trading abroad. Even if you begin focusing only on your home territory, when things start going well your mind may turn to expanding into other countries. However you come to it, trading overseas is potentially an important way to grow your business.

Here I look at different structures for organising your trade offering overseas and the legal and regulatory concerns you have to bear in mind. Each of these factors can affect the others (for example, currency restrictions in a local territory can influence what kind of operations you want to conduct in that country).

I also take into account the array of worldly advice available from the countries you may be trading with. For a start, if you're operating abroad, 'don't have tomatoes on your eyes' (German expression for 'missing things that are obvious to other people').

So pack your toothbrush for a whistle-stop trading tour of the globe, including a legal samba in Brazil, a contractual bhangra in India and a short Highland reel in Scotland.

Reviewing International Trading Structures

You can use a number of different structures when you trade abroad. Each one suits different businesses. Make sure that you consider the possibilities and 'Don't do something with the French whiplash' (sounds kinky, but it's just a French idiom for 'Don't rush into things'):

- ✔ **Direct exporting:** Literally selling and shipping your finished goods to your customer in another country. This approach works well for a one-off order or a series of one-off orders, but you don't know what your customer then does with the goods or for what price it sells them, and so you have no control.

- ✔ **Appointing a distributor:** Contracting with a local business to receive your goods and then market/sell and distribute them on your behalf in the local country. You have more transparency and control over your customer with a distribution agreement. I look at the legal ingredients of distribution contracts in Chapter 10.

- ✔ **Appointing a licensee:** Granting a licence to a local business to manufacture, market and sell goods on your behalf. This relationship gives you some control over your trade partner, but because you aren't manufacturing and supplying the goods you have less control (and responsibility) over that part of the supply chain. I discuss the contractual elements of licence agreements in Chapter 10.

- ✔ **Operating a joint venture:** Creating a partnership with another enterprise in order to promote and run a business. You can expect a bigger share of the rewards and the risks from overseas expansion by developing through joint ventures. Chapter 17 reviews how joint ventures typically work.

- ✔ **Franchising:** Agreeing that a local entity can operate a branded version of your business strictly in accordance with the style and manner set out in the franchise agreement. I look at this option in the next section.

- ✔ **Setting up a subsidiary:** Creating a local company that you own and that's part of your own corporate structure (see the later section 'Creating and running your own subsidiary').

Appointing a franchisee

A *franchise* agreement is a common route to achieve rapid expansion overseas – McDonalds, Subway, KFC, Kwik Fit, Hertz Car Rentals and Hilton Hotels are among many brands that operate franchise businesses.

Franchise agreements give you lots of controls over the way your business partner operates locally, but they only work where you have an established brand and business model and a way of running your business that you can franchise. This section describes the key ingredients of a franchise agreement.

Rights

You grant a package of rights to your franchisee, including to: operate your business model; use your business's trademarks, trade name and intellectual property; operate any systems or software that underpin your business; and use your manual or 'style guide' (that sets out detailed procedures and guidelines for running the business). You retain ownership of these rights and grant them for a limited term and territory.

You may or may not grant rights to the franchisee exclusively (oh that certain fast-food restaurants confined themselves to one branch per territory).

Responsibilities

You must supply to franchisees all the materials that they need to run the business locally: for example, your manual, logos, equipment, advertising materials, training for staff and advice on setting up the local business.

The franchisee must operate the business strictly in accordance with the agreement, using only approved marketing and advertising materials, approved products and approved packaging and stationery.

The franchise may operate from approved premises (think of a particular pub), in which case the franchisee must take care of all tenant obligations, keep the place clean, fix all approved signage and operate agreed opening hours.

The franchisee must use its best efforts to promote the business (for example, applying an agreed percentage of its receipts on advertising and marketing). The franchisee must also run the business responsibly (for example, paying all debts and making sure that its contractors comply with the franchise agreement).

Rewards

Rewards are a matter of negotiation, but commonly the franchisee pays you an initial fee as an entry payment to become a member of your franchise. After that you receive monthly payments of a percentage of gross receipts from the franchise operation (allowing for the franchisee to cover its costs of overhead, marketing and so on and still make a profit for itself). Or perhaps the franchisee keeps the local gross receipts after paying you a management fee every month. Sometimes the franchisee has to meet certain minimum monthly revenue targets, so that you know that the business is going to grow.

If the franchisee is small, you can require a personal guarantee to back up these payment obligations.

Risks

You don't want the franchisee competing with you during or after the term, and so include restrictions on this activity. To avoid the franchisee poaching your customers or employees post-term, include restrictions on this for a limited period (say, one year post-term).

The franchisee must operate in accordance with a strict confidentiality clause. This is important when two people know each other's secrets – or, as they put it in Thailand, when 'the hen sees the snake's feet and the snake sees the hen's boobs'. Hmm . . . a bit unseemly. The franchisee must keep accounting records and allow you to audit them, and no doubt you want to include strict termination rights if the franchisee breaches its obligations.

Creating and running your own subsidiary

A *subsidiary* is a local incorporated company that's part of your overall corporate group. Your UK company can own it, or you can create a parent company that owns all your subsidiaries (including your company in the UK). Millions of companies operate subsidiaries all around the world, from Sony to Google and many small companies too.

The advantages of running your own subsidiary are as follows:

- ✔ You get to keep all the rewards of running the business. No need to share with local partners as you do with licensing, distribution, joint ventures or franchise agreements.
- ✔ You have financial visibility of exactly what revenues and costs are being generated locally.
- ✔ You have complete end-to-end transparency and control over the operation of the business.
- ✔ You have a permanent structure in the country in which you're trading, which can be helpful if you're in it for the long term.
- ✔ You can improve local consumer perceptions of your business if you're present on the ground employing local people.
- ✔ You may gain taxation benefits locally and within your corporation.

Here are the disadvantages of a subsidiary:

- ✔ You require knowledge and compliance with local laws, including corporate, employment, environmental and tax laws.

- ✔ You have to take care with marketing and advertising to ensure that you respect local sensitivities, including censorship rules and restrictions relevant to minors – you don't necessarily have a local partner to help you with such knowledge.

- ✔ You have to spend more time on the ground, because ultimately nobody's responsible for the local business except you.

Examining Expert Exporting

If you choose to export directly or distribute to a local entity (or possibly if you joint venture or franchise too – refer to the preceding section), you're going to be sending goods from the UK overseas. If so, you need to be clear about a number of legal technicalities.

Shipping goods overseas isn't a straightforward task – it's not a 'roll with butter' as they say in Poland. If you're going to export, you need to clarify the following aspects in any contract:

- ✔ The nature of the contracting party; that is, whether you're dealing with a direct-end customer or an agent.

- ✔ Who bears responsibility for insuring the goods on their journey.

- ✔ Who's responsible for obtaining relevant export and import licences and paying duties.

- ✔ Details of payment methods, time frames and currency.

- ✔ When *title* (ownership) of the goods passes; for example, do you retain title until payment is received?

- ✔ What law applies – for example, if you're exporting to Timbuktu and something goes wrong, do England's laws apply or those of Timbuktu? (I say 'England' rather than 'the UK' deliberately; to see some differences between English and Scots law, read the later section 'Trading Abroad . . . with Scotland'.)

- ✔ What happens if a dispute arises: where do you have to litigate – in the UK or in Timbuktu? Or are you using an alternative procedure for settling your disputes, such as arbitration (see Chapter 15)?

In this section, I describe some of these and other aspects of exporting, including getting export licences, customs clearances, tax requirements, paying local duties, conventions on trading terms and government support and subsidies for export.

Getting export licences

You can export from the UK the vast majority of goods without an export licence, but certain goods are *controlled* and need an appropriate licence. These items include military or paramilitary goods, technology, artworks, plants and animals, medicine and chemicals, and *dual-use* goods (software and technology normally used for civilian purposes but that may have military applications).

The Export Control Organisation is the Regulatory Authority for export licensing of controlled goods. It provides an online Goods Checker Resource, which you can use to establish whether items are controlled and require a licence (visit www.ecochecker.bis.gov.uk).

The government can impose trade sanctions on particular countries at certain times. If a sanction or embargo is set, exports to that country are prohibited or may require a licence. You can find these countries at http://www.gov.uk/government/organisations/export-control-organisation.

Complying with customs clearance requirements

To export goods out of (and import them into) the EU, you need a Single Administrative Document (SAD) (form C88), which you submit to customs to enable clearance of the goods (for more info, visit http://www.gov.uk/guidance/declarations-and-the-single-administrative-document). This form is also required for moving non-EU goods within the EU. (This document is probably called SAD because it's so miserably laborious to fill in.)

You must ensure that you have an Economic Operator Registration and Identification (EORI) number with customs – a unique number valid across all Member States (see http://www.gov.uk/guidance/eori-supporting-guidance). When you're EORI-registered, you can download SADs through the Her Majesty's Revenue and Customs (HMRC) service. Whether you use an agent or handle customs entries yourself, you have a legal responsibility to ensure that the information provided on the SAD document is accurate as per the Community Customs Code (Regulation No 2913.92). Incorrect classification can lead to delays in processing goods, overpayment of duty and possible penalties.

A correct tariff code must be assigned to the goods: it determines the import duty rates. Access these codes through the EU TARIC database (`http://ec.europa.eu/taxation_customs/customs/customs_duties/tariff_aspects/customs_tariff/index_en.htm`), which provides details of the duty rates on products. You may also require a Certificate of Origin when exporting from the EU to countries outside the EU. It must accompany the SAD declaration and state where the goods were made and whether wholly or partially produced in the EU.

As long as you comply with these intricate customs requirements, 'There's no cow on the ice' (Swedish for 'Nothing to worry about').

Remembering individual country customs requirements

As well as the over-arching requirements (refer to the preceding section), you also need to observe individual countries' regulations. I can hear you saying now 'Stop ironing my head' (Armenian for 'stop annoying me'), but you do need to familiarise yourself with these local requirements. Here are just three examples:

- ✔ **Certificates:** To export to some countries and territories, you need a certificate. For example, you require an Arab-British certificate to identify the origin of goods being exported into 19 Arab League States. You can obtain it from a local chamber of commerce.

- ✔ **Clearance documentation:** Certain countries require additional customs paperwork. For example, in Saudi Arabia all goods must be accompanied by a Certificate of Conformity from an authorised inspection agency. This form is needed to ensure customs clearance and confirmation that the goods comply with relevant Saudi regulations.

- ✔ **Licensing:** Some countries have highly complex legal regulations. For example, in China many products must be certified or licensed by the relevant Chinese authority before you can sell them in China. Strict regulations also apply to foreign exchange and the movement of currency – many verification procedures are required. Local taxes and import duties are also complex, and intellectual property protection requires separate registration in China. I talk more about exporting to China in the later section 'Doing your local homework'.

The Authorised Economic Operator (AEO) certificate is an internationally recognised quality mark available to businesses in an international supply chain taking part in customs-related activities. Although AEO status isn't mandatory, it brings many commercial benefits, including simplified customs arrangements and the ability to track consignments and move them quicker through customs controls. HMRC is responsible for processing AEO applications (www.gov.uk).

The following criteria determine whether such status is granted:

- ✔ Record of customs and tax compliance
- ✔ Satisfactory system of managing commercial records
- ✔ Appropriate financial security
- ✔ Appropriate security and safety standards

Valuing VAT

Value-Added Tax (VAT) is the main tax charged on exports from the UK. If you're selling within the EU to another VAT-registered business, the sale can be *zero-rated* (no VAT is payable but a VAT declaration is required).

I'm not going to 'walk around hot porridge' (Czech for 'beat around the bush'). All VAT-registered businesses must provide details of transactions with other EU Member States on their VAT returns. If the value of goods you export reaches a certain threshold, you must submit an additional monthly supplementary declaration called an *Intrastat declaration* (the EU system for collecting trade information) to HMRC.

The threshold is reviewed annually and currently is £250,000 for dispatches (exports) in a calendar year.

If you're selling to a *non-VAT-registered* business or a consumer, VAT is charged at the normal UK rate. If these sales in any EU country exceed that country's VAT threshold, your firm must register to pay VAT in that country.

Businesses providing digital services to consumers in the EU are required to charge VAT at the rate applying in the consumer's country under the *place of supply* rules. Digital services include music, gaming, apps, radio and television programming, and other e-services. The VAT Mini One Stop Shop (VAT MOSS) allows you to submit such VAT returns and payments online (https://www.gov.uk/register-and-use-the-vat-mini-one-stop-shop).

VAT isn't charged on sales outside the EU and can be zero-rated, as long as you keep records as proof that goods have been exported outside the EU.

Dabbling in overseas duties

International taxes such as import duties may be payable in the country to which you're exporting the goods. Who's responsible for paying these taxes depends on the agreement you enter into with the customer or supplier. To minimise the risk of disputes, many businesses use one of the internationally recognised Incoterms (see the following section).

As the exporter, you're normally responsible for clearing goods leaving the UK; the customer is responsible for handling overseas customs and taxes. You can hire agents or freight forwarders to handle customs clearance and transport (but as the seller you're responsible for information provided on the SAD declaration – refer to the earlier section 'Complying with customs clearance requirements').

You can find reputable freight forwarders through the British International Freight Association (at www.bifa.org).

Agents or freight forwarders acting on behalf of the seller are classed as indirect or direct representatives:

- ✔ **Indirect representative:** An agent signs the customs declaration in his own name and on behalf of the exporter. The agent and seller are jointly and individually liable for any customs duties.

- ✔ **Direct representative:** The agent signs the declaration as a representative acting in the name of and on behalf of you as the exporter. You're liable for any duties and the agent can't be held liable.

Listen carefully and make sure that 'your ears aren't lined with ham' (as they say in Italy). Take care when dealing with agents, because liability can arise for their actions if the agreement doesn't clearly specify responsibilities and limit their authority to act on the exporter's behalf. The Commercial Agents (Council Directive) Regulations, 1993 can also apply to these arrangements. These Regulations provide a minimum level of protection for commercial sales agents that can't be excluded (for example, how and when they get commission and what compensation they get if the agency is terminated).

Don't just sleepwalk your way into an agency relationship. As the Russian saying goes, 'Your elbow is close yet you can't bite it' (meaning 'Things aren't always as simple as they seem').

Incorporating Incoterms

The useful and internationally recognised standard terms of trade – International Commercial Terms (Incoterms) – are used in export contracts. Incoterms help traders to avoid misunderstandings by setting out the duties, costs and risks involved in the delivery of goods from the seller to the buyer.

The Rules are created and published by the International Chamber of Commerce (at www.iccwbo.org) and essentially provide clarity for the buyer and seller regarding the following:

- ✔ Cost of transporting the goods and who's responsible, including insurance, taxes and duties
- ✔ Where the goods will be picked up and transported to
- ✔ Who's responsible for the goods during each step of the transportation process

Here are just two commonly used Inconterm terms and structures:

- ✔ **EXW ('Ex Works'):** The seller makes the goods available to be collected at its premises and the buyer is responsible from that point onwards for transportation, insurance, taxes and duties and all other risks. This term puts the most obligations on a buyer.
- ✔ **DDP (Delivered Duty Paid):** The seller is responsible for delivering the goods to a named destination in the buyer's country and covers all costs (transportation, insurance, taxes and duties). This term is the most onerous for exporters.

Numerous other example structures exist, in which responsibility for the tasks mentioned is shared between seller and buyer.

Accelerating exports: Support and schemes

Exporting can be a tricky business. Therefore, you may appreciate knowing about some useful resources to help you grow your business overseas. If you're very busy, you'll no doubt be 'willing to borrow a cat's paws' to help you (ask the Japanese; I don't get it either):

- ✔ **UK Trade & Investment (UKTI)** (www.ukti.gov.uk): Government department that assists UK-based businesses seeking to expand in global markets. Services include country guides and support for first-time exporters and small and medium-size enterprises (SMEs), including an online export advice service, a guide to trade fairs and missions and an export credit agency.

- ✔ **British Chamber of Commerce (**www.chambers.org.uk**):** Supports and advises businesses on international trade. Also gives UK exporters advice and assistance on dealing with export documentation, training, market research and letters of credit.

- ✔ **Export Marketing Research Scheme (**http://www.gov.uk/export-marketing-research-scheme**):** Free independent advice on exporting to new markets and how best to deliver products and services. Financial support is also available to businesses with between 5 and 250 employees who have products or services with a proven track record of at least two years.

- ✔ **Market Visit Support (**http://www.gov.uk/market-visit-support**):** Assists SMEs (with up to 250 employees) with market research, trade fair visits and meetings with potential distributors.

- ✔ **Open to Export Programme (**http://opentoexport.com/**):** Information and advice on exporting products from the UK for SMEs through events and trade opportunities in emerging markets.

- ✔ **Passport to Export Service (**http://www.gov.uk/passport-to-export-service**):** 12-month export assessment and support programme for SMEs.

- ✔ **UK Export Finance (**www.ecgd.gov.uk**):** The UK's official export credit agency offering a range of products and services, including the export insurance policy, bond support scheme, export working capital scheme and the foreign exchange credit support scheme. These schemes are specifically targeted at SMEs.

Looking at the Local Legal Terrain

The legal landscape of the country in which you're planning to operate has a big bearing on which trading structure you end up with.

The more complicated the local legal environment, the more you may be tempted to shy away from structures that give you a lot of on-the-ground responsibilities (such as running your own subsidiary) and the more you may be tempted by looser links (perhaps directly exporting or running a remote relationship such as a licensing agreement). I discuss these structures earlier in this chapter in the section 'Reviewing International Trading Structures'.

Taking on additional complications

Here are some important issues to consider – I'm not 'casting a brick to attract jade' (Chinese for 'just throwing ideas out there'):

- **Currency exchange restrictions or taxes:** On payments to foreign countries (withholding taxes).

- **Local tax regime:** For example, is a double-tax treaty in place, which means that if you pay tax locally you don't have to pay tax on the same revenues in the UK.

- **Local product regulations:** Say for labelling or product certification.

- **Other local trading laws:** For example, relating to the environment, employment or bribery (I discuss the UK Bribery Act in Chapter 11).

- **Ownership:** Rules on ownership of any local subsidiary and/or regulations concerning protection of intellectual property.

Doing your local homework

Here are some country-specific examples of local legal complications. Of course, it's not exhaustive – similar issues apply in many different countries. I just hope to give you an idea of the sort of issues you can encounter in markets where the path isn't always straightforward.

China

I start with China, the second largest economy in the world (after the US) and a potentially enormous market for UK firms:

- Compulsory Certification (CCC) is an essential quality and safety mark required for a wide variety of manufactured goods before they can be exported to or sold in China.

- China wants to restrict foreign ownership of companies in China. The Wholly Foreign Owned Enterprise (WFOE) is a limited liability company but complex and costly to set up in comparison to joint ventures or a representative office and only available if the business activity isn't restricted under local government rules.

- Strict rules exist on the movement of foreign exchange.

- ✔ Taxation and import duties vary in all regions.
- ✔ Intellectual property rights must be registered on a worldwide basis to be afforded protection under Chinese law.

The China British Business Council (at www.cbbc.org) provides detailed guidance and information on setting up and trading in China.

Saudi Arabia

Don't tie one hand behind your back – bear these local requirements in mind if you want to prosper in Saudi Arabia. As the Arabic saying goes, 'You can't clap with one hand':

- ✔ Licences are required to do business and must be obtained from the relevant government ministries.
- ✔ Physical presence is required to be actively involved in the buying and selling of goods in Saudi Arabia.
- ✔ All businesses must comply with employment law rules that require all businesses to employ a certain quota of Saudis.
- ✔ A Certificate of Conformity is required for goods sold in Saudi.

The Saudi British Joint Business Council (at www.sbjbc.org) provides advice on regulatory requirements specific to Saudi Arabia.

India

You need to consider the following local issues in India:

- ✔ You have to comply with the Import Export Code (IEC) to import or export out of India. Available from the Directorate General of Trade, this Code is mandatory.
- ✔ Know Your Customer (KYC) documentation is required by the Central Board of Excise and Customs for import/export shipments to and from India to verify the identity of the shipper.
- ✔ The Bureau of Indian Standards requires certification for certain items, including food and electrical goods, before you can export them to India.
- ✔ The Ministry of Commerce requires all pre-packaged commodities for direct sale to be labelled with the name of the importer, name of product, net quantity and maximum retail sales price.
- ✔ Intellectual property must be registered in India to be afforded protection from infringement.

> # Qualifying to trade in India
>
> Whether you can conduct a business through a wholly owned subsidiary or require an Indian investor depends on pre-approval under the Foreign Direct Investment (FDI) Policy. At least one director must have stayed in India for 182 days or more in the year. Alternatively, you can set up a *liaison office* primarily for marketing purposes, though it can't trade directly or generate revenue. Or you can create a *branch office,* which can trade but not manufacture. Both these options require approval and permission from the Reserve Bank of India.

The UK India Business Council (ukibc.com) promotes trade and investment between the two countries. It organises networking events, partnerships, sector-specific delegations to India, market research services, mentoring and training schemes, and also assists with incorporating and establishing a business correctly in India.

Brazil

Here are some local legal issues that come up in Brazil:

- Importer/Exporter Registration is required with SECEX (Chamber of Foreign Trade) as is registration with RADAR, an electronic system operated by the Brazilian Revenue Service, along with registration with the Brazilian Central Bank.

- Under the Brazilian Customer Protection Code, product labelling must include quality, quantity, price, origin and any risks to consumers' health and safety. Imported products must also bear a Portuguese translation.

- Brazil has a complex taxation system with different regimes at federal, state and municipal level. Withholding tax is due on payment of Brazilian source income to most non-residents, such as service fees, royalties, capital gains and so on; tax is at the highest rate because no double-tax treaty exists with the UK.

- You must register funds being sent into or out of Brazil with the Brazilian Central Bank. You can't transfer the Brazilian Real outside Brazil or hold foreign currency accounts. Strict controls exist on the repatriation of capital in a foreign currency.

> ✔ All employers (with few exceptions) must employ Brazilian citizens in a proportion of at least two-thirds of their overall staff, both in terms of numbers and total remuneration. A raft of labour legislation is favourable to employees, coupled with strong unions.

The Brazilian Chamber of Commerce provides assistance to businesses exporting to Brazil (`brazilianchamber.org.uk`). Also check out the different but equally useful guides at `brazildoingbusinessguide.co.uk` and `http://www.gov.uk/government/publications/exporting-to-brazil`.

Trading Abroad with . . . Scotland

I know this heading sounds a bit strange, like I'm 'blowing little ducks' (Latvian for spouting nonsense), but from a legal point of view, doing business in or with Scotland is a bit like trading abroad. To a certain extent Scotland uses English Law (for example, the intellectual property regime is identical), but it has also developed its own. (The law in Northern Ireland also has differences from the rest of the UK.)

I hope you won't be too 'fair puckled' (an old Scottish saying for out of breath) after going through this (far-from-exhaustive) list of some examples of the differences:

> ✔ **Contract law:** Forming contracts is different from English law. In Scotland, as soon as the essential terms are agreed and both parties intend to create a legal relationship, a contract is formed, even if all the details haven't been agreed:
>
> • You don't have to provide *consideration* (money or money's worth). You can make a binding promise to another party without any reciprocal obligation.
>
> • The general principle under Scots law is that only the contracting parties are entitled to enforce the contract. (The Contracts [Rights of Third Parties] Act, 1999, which gives rights to third parties in the rest of the UK, doesn't apply.) A special process in Scotland (*jus quaesitum tertio;* third party right of action) decides how other people can acquire rights under an agreement to which they aren't a party.
>
> • The phrase 'subject to contract' doesn't have any particular meaning in Scots law (in the rest of the UK, it distinguishes between mere discussions and binding obligations) and it doesn't prevent a court from finding that a contract has been entered into.

✔ **Commercial leases:** The Landlord and Tenant Act that applies in the UK doesn't apply in Scotland:

- No statutory protection of occupation exists for commercial tenants to renew their lease (as in the rest of the UK), which is enough to make you 'chow the chafts' (gnash your teeth). (One small exception does exist in Scotland for shop tenants, though, who do have a limited right of renewal.)

- Leases ordinarily end only if the landlord or the tenant gives written notice (not less than 40 days) to avoid the lease continuing automatically (even if a date is specified).

- Authorised guarantee agreements on assignments to another tenant aren't a feature of Scots law.

✔ **Registration:** Only commercial leases for longer than 20 years must be registered in the Land Register of Scotland (in the rest of the UK, the trigger is a lease of more than 7 years).

✔ **Company law:** All UK companies are incorporated under one single company law regime – the Companies Act, 2006 – though Companies House operates in three separate jurisdictions: England and Wales (in Cardiff), Scotland (in Edinburgh) and Northern Ireland (in Belfast). A company doesn't have to be registered in the part of the UK in which the registrant lives. To verify where a company is registered, Companies House maintains a public register (at wck2.companieshouse.gov.uk).

✔ **Corporate insolvency:** The majority of the provisions of the UK's Insolvency Act, 1986 apply equally to Scotland, but some different procedural rules apply under the Insolvency (Scotland) Rules, 1986 (check out Chapter 16 for more on these terms):

- Receivership in Scotland has its own system.

- Administrative receivership is the only type of receivership.

- A company registered in Scotland must be wound up in Scotland.

- If a company is registered in Scotland, resolutions regarding liquidations must be advertised in the *Edinburgh Gazette*.

- The Accountant in Bankruptcy (aib.gov.uk) is the Scottish statutory body responsible for administering corporate insolvencies and personal bankruptcies. It maintains an insolvency register.

✔ **Claims:** Scotland has a separate and distinct civil court system, and its court procedures, timescales and enforcement differ substantially from the rest of the UK:

- Normally, less complex and lower value claims are brought in the local Sheriff Court and more complex claims in the Court of Session.

- Scotland has a unique *caveat system*. This offers protection if a third party attempts to seek an *interdict* (injunction or urgent remedy) against the party in whose name the caveat is lodged, because the court must first contact the party and allow him to state his case. This acts as an early warning system for those who maintain caveats lodged with the local Sheriff Court and the Court of Session.

Good luck with these subtle intricacies and 'Lang may yer lum reek' ('Long may your chimney smoke', or 'Live long and prosper' if you're speaking with Mr Spock, who I don't think ever visited Scotland, boldly or otherwise).

Part IV
Staying in Business – Legal Pitfalls

Top Five Tips for Dispute Management

- **Prevent contractual problems from escalating:** Don't ignore or inflame them!

- **Know what you're entitled to claim:** Any legal claim must have a legal basis – what's yours? Contract? Tort? Misrepresentation?

- **Work out in advance what it's going to cost you:** Bringing or defending a claim costs time, money and stress. Is it really worthwhile, even if the other side has got you really mad?

- **Manage the legal process efficiently:** It's complicated, but you have to get it right or you're wasting time and resources. Using good lawyers is a help, not a hindrance.

- **Remember the alternative ways to sort out disputes:** Mediation may be quicker and cheaper than litigation, and arbitration ensures that your case is decided by an industry expert, not a doddering old fool – sorry, esteemed judge.

Check out the online article to see whether you know the nuts and bolts of minimising your business risks. You can find it at www.dummies.com/extras/lawforsmallbusinessuk.

In this part . . .

- ✔ Take the precaution of checking your customers for creditworthiness.

- ✔ Use the protection of discounting your invoices to smooth out your cash flow.

- ✔ Surround the vulnerable parts of your business with insurance policies.

- ✔ Discover how to avoid, defend and win legal disputes.

- ✔ Stay safe when dealing with potential insolvency.

Chapter 14

Managing Your Legal Risks

In This Chapter

▶ Carrying the shield of credit control

▶ Armour-plating yourself with insurance

As the singer Bjork put it, 'If you never take any risks you never have any treats'. Certainly if you're an entrepreneur, you take risks on a daily basis. (If you want a safe, unadventurous life, don't run a small business!) But if you're comfortable with risk – and feel that 'ships are safe in harbour, but that's not what ships are built for' – set sail on the high seas of business, knowing that you'll encounter storms as well as gentle breezes.

Of course, a big difference exists between acknowledging risk and doing nothing to minimise it. In this chapter, I look at some of the legal steps you can take in two areas to reduce your level of risk as your business grows: controlling credit and ensuring that you have the right insurance.

Giving Credit Where Credit Is Due

Lack of cash flow is the most common cause of failure among small businesses – many small enterprises with great ideas, products and staff go under because they run out of cash. At best, not having enough cash reduces your growth and productivity, but at worst it can cause you reputational damage from not paying your bills on time.

One good way of minimising your risk in this area is to make sure that you have a robust policy in place for credit control. *Credit* is money that another business owes you for goods and services that you've supplied, but which hasn't been paid for yet. Here are some key elements of a successful credit control policy.

Filling out a credit form

You don't want your house to be made out of straw, do you? No, of course not – not by the hairs on your chinny-chin-chin.

Start by getting your customers to fill out a credit application form when they begin doing business with you. It needs to include all the following:

- ✔ Business's name

- ✔ Registration number (if registered with Companies House)

- ✔ Legal status of the enterprise (sole trader, partnership or limited company)

- ✔ Details of the person(s) responsible for the day-to-day running of the business

- ✔ Amount of credit being sought and the agreed amount of credit you're prepared to allow

- ✔ Full contact details of the person responsible for dealing with payment issues

- ✔ Address to forward invoices to if different from the delivery address

- ✔ Bank details, including account and sort code numbers

- ✔ Trade and banking references

Ascertaining creditworthiness

When you have a completed credit application form from the customer, you can check the information provided by referring to the following sources (and so ensure that your house isn't made out of sticks):

- ✔ **Register of Judgements, Orders and Fines (**www.trustonline.org. uk**):** This public register details County Court Judgements, orders and fines imposed on businesses and individuals. You can search it to ascertain whether a potential customer has a history of bad debts or a poor payment history. All such orders remain on the register for six years unless satisfied in full or set aside. The Registry Trust Limited operates the Register of County Court Judgements on behalf of the Ministry of Justice.

- ✔ **Insolvency Registers (**www.insolvencydirect.bis.gov.uk**):** The Insolvency Service maintains the public Register of Individual Voluntary Arrangements (IVA) and the Bankruptcy Public Search Room (BPSR).

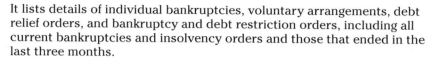

It lists details of individual bankruptcies, voluntary arrangements, debt relief orders, and bankruptcy and debt restriction orders, including all current bankruptcies and insolvency orders and those that ended in the last three months.

Check these registers at this web address when you're dealing with an individual, such as a sole trader.

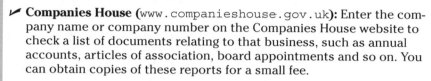

✔ **Companies House (**`www.companieshouse.gov.uk`**):** Enter the company name or company number on the Companies House website to check a list of documents relating to that business, such as annual accounts, articles of association, board appointments and so on. You can obtain copies of these reports for a small fee.

If a company has only recently got into difficulties, such as in the last six months, this information may not yet be available at Companies House: financial reporting normally lags behind events.

✔ **Bank references:** If you can, obtain a bank reference about your intended customer. You can only get one if the bank has the written permission of its customer, and normally you're charged a fee.

✔ **Trade references:** Taking up multiple trade references about the potential customer is a good idea. Doing so helps you to glean valuable information about the customer, such as whether it has paid promptly in the past, maintained long-standing relationships with its suppliers and met Terms and Conditions (Ts and Cs), especially in relation to high-value orders.

✔ **Status reports from credit agencies:** If you don't fancy carrying out these tasks yourself, many credit reference agencies perform searches on prospective trading partners and can provide quite detailed reports. Information provided includes any County Court Judgements registered, a comparison of how the business has dealt with past invoices against other firms of that size, potential credit limits and details of information registered with Companies House. Agencies can provide this information online and so you can access it quickly. A fee is payable and usually ranges from £10 to £50, depending on the level of detail required.

Creating clear Terms and Conditions

To help keep the Big Bad Wolf from your door, make sure that your business's Ts and Cs support your credit control policy by covering the following points:

✔ **Clear credit terms and limits:** How long does the customer have to pay and what's the maximum amount it can owe at any time? Bring these terms to the attention of the customer and get it to agree clearly in writing.

From that point on, reaffirm those terms in all order acknowledgments, invoices and statements of account.

✔ **Retention of Title clauses:** These clauses provide that ownership of goods remains with you until the purchaser has paid for them. They also allow you to enter the customer's premises and recover them:

- *Simple* clauses apply to goods supplied under a particular invoice only.

- *All monies* clauses apply to all goods supplied to the purchaser until all monies owing are paid.

Make sure that your goods are easily identifiable by a serial number, particular packaging or branding or other prominent marking that clearly identifies them as belonging to you and not another supplier. To make this system work, include an obligation to store your goods separately from those of other suppliers and also include a prohibition on selling the goods on until they've been paid for.

Retention of title clauses can be difficult to enforce and so they aren't a silver bullet to keep that wolf from your door, but to help make them work include these clauses in your terms and conditions.

✔ **Termination clauses:** Give you the right to terminate the agreement with your purchaser if you believe the purchaser is about to become insolvent. They can maximise your chances of receiving payment or recovery of the goods, because if the customer is already in administration or a winding-up procedure has commenced (see Chapter 16), recovering payment may be too late.

Building your house of stone with late payment clauses

The Late Payment of Commercial Debts (Interest) Act, 1998 and the Late Payment of Commercial Debts Regulations (2002 and 2013) give you a legal right to claim interest on late payments from other businesses (see www. gov.uk/government/uploads/system/uploads/attachment_data/ file/360834/bis-14-1116-a-users-guide-to-the-recast-late- payment-directive.pdf).

A *late payment* is where the agreed credit period you've given to your customer has expired. If no credit period has been specified, the Act provides a default period of 30 days. After that time, interest accumulates and runs from when the goods are delivered or the service performed or the day the purchaser receives notice of the debt.

The 2013 Regulations also allow you to recoup reasonable costs incurred in recovering the money and provides that businesses have 60 days to pay invoices (unless a longer period is negotiated) and public authorities have only a 30-day period to pay. The applicable interest rate is the Bank of England base rate that applies during the period in which the debt falls due plus a hefty 8 per cent (the rate is set every six months).

Small businesses often don't know about this right or, if they do, are often reluctant to exercise it and claim such interest, because they fear that doing so antagonises or jeopardises relationships with larger customers. But given the culture of late payments and the consequent damaging effects on businesses, many are now stating at the time the contract is entered into that they will exercise this right if payment is late or overdue.

Maintaining effective debt recovery

Be a smart little piggy and have a procedure in place to stop credit and recover debt. If customers subsequently default, no amount of huffing and puffing by the Big Bad Cash-flow Wolf can blow your house down:

✔ When an account becomes overdue, employ a set timetable of actions, including regular contact by phone, email and letter. Inability to contact a customer can be a warning sign that the business is in trouble. If a genuine problem exists, a rescheduling of payment terms can help to solve the problem for both parties.

✔ If that doesn't work you can hire a business that specialises in debt collection to act on your behalf and recover outstanding debts. Use a reputable firm to ensure that debts are pursued in a professional manner and via lawful means. You can check the Credit Services Association to make sure that an agency is registered and has signed up to the relevant Code of Practice (www.csa-uk.com).

The cost of this service is typically 10 per cent of the amount being sought, though one-off collection cases tend to be more expensive.

✔ If all else fails you can issue a *statutory demand* for the debt. This remedy (in the Insolvency Act, 1986) is a formal written demand for a debt in excess of £750 (from a company) and £5,000 (from an individual) and is effectively a precursor to insolvency proceedings. If your customer (the *debtor*) doesn't pay within 21 days of receiving the demand, you (the *creditor*) can apply to the court to request bankruptcy (for an individual) or a winding up (for a company) if the debt isn't paid.

You can only issue a statutory demand for undisputed debts and only where a debtor lacks a genuine defence and has assets (so not as good as boiling that Big Bad Wolf alive in a cooking pot). But it's a useful debt recovery tool, because the mere threat of a winding up or bankruptcy petition can be enough to force action and settle the amounts owing.

Statutory demand is a relatively quick and inexpensive way to work out whether your debtor will pay the debt owed. Chapter 16 has more details on statutory demands (and how to defend yourself if one is served on you).

Cashing in your invoices

When you invoice somebody you naturally hope that the invoice is paid promptly and in full. But the time lag between issuing the invoice and receiving payment can create stresses and strains for your business.

Invoice discounting and *invoice factoring* are two ways to help reduce your business risk, because they enable you to obtain funding secured against the value of your invoices that have yet to be paid. Typically, the provider can advance 80 per cent of the value of invoices. This approach is better for managing this risk than waiting to be saved by the bell (traditionally, a phrase related to the coffins of people who were scared of waking up after burial and wanted something to ring so that they could be dug up).

Here's how each type works:

- ✔ **Invoice discounting:** The business remains in charge of managing credit control. The costs involved with invoice discounting are normally lower than for factoring and allow you to keep the condition of your business confidential, because customers aren't aware of the arrangement. Because you stay in control of the credit collection process, the requirements for obtaining invoice discounting are more demanding and may include a high annual turnover, (say £500,000) and regular auditing of the books to verify that credit control procedures are adequate.

- ✔ **Invoice factoring:** All credit control is outsourced to the factoring provider who's responsible for chasing any outstanding invoices. Thus it involves surrendering more control of your business. The payment provider may want to pre-approve potential customers and you may not have complete control over ending the arrangement. One version of invoice factoring, called *non-recourse factoring,* is where the payment provider assumes responsibility for bad debts (non-payment of the invoice by your creditor), but this costs you more in fees due to the increased level of risk.

Going the whole nine yards with court action

I used to think that the phrase 'going the whole nine yards' came from American football, because that's the farthest distance anybody seems to move before yet another time-out. But actually it refers to the fact that World War II fighter pilots were given nine-yard long ammunition chains and it meant to discharge all your ammunition during your mission. So now you know.

Court action is the ultimate way to go the whole nine yards and control your credit risk, but it brings risks of its own. Peep nervously at Chapter 15 to find out more about managing disputes (including debt disputes).

Check out organisations such as Urica (`https://urica.com/`) and Market Invoice (`www.marketinvoice.com`) for more on early payment solutions.

Inoculating Yourself with Insurance

Your business faces all sorts of risks and for many of them insurance is the answer. A policy exists for almost every contingency you can think of. 'We cover you from the cradle to the grave' boast some insurers (or 'from the womb to the tomb' or 'from the sperm to the worm' – that last one hasn't quite taken off yet).

Insurance isn't the most riveting of subjects. As doctors often say, 'For people who need sleep we have Mogadon, and for complete insomniacs we have insurance policies'. But even if reading an insurance policy sends you to sleep in seconds, the risks of not insuring really can keep you awake at night. In this section, I describe some common insurance policies to reduce your risks that you need to think about. In all cases:

✔ Shop around for quotes.

✔ Be aware of possible exclusions for particular risks (like a hospital gown, an insurance policy never covers you as much as you think).

✔ Be mindful of any *excess* – an amount of damage that the policy doesn't cover in any event (for example, the first £1,000 of damage). The higher the excess, the more exposed you are.

Covering your workers: Employers' liability insurance

You have no option here: employers' liability insurance is the only type of business insurance required by law. Under the Employers Liability (Compulsory Insurance) Act, 1969, any business that employs workers *must* obtain employers' liability insurance (even for part-time workers). This insurance is designed to protect a business against claims by employees who're injured in the workplace or suffer a work-related illness.

Here are the key points to note in relation to an employer's liability:

- **Level of insurance cover:** Required minimum level of protection is set at £5 million.

- **Certificate of insurance:** Must be displayed prominently at all workplaces, but can be available in electronic form if employees have access to it.

- **Keeping records and previous certificates:** A requirement, because claims may arise at a future date or in respect of former employees.

- **Using an authorised insurer:** Insurance of this variety can be provided only by an 'authorised insurer' as per the Financial Services and Markets Act, 2000. The Financial Conduct Authority maintains a Register of Authorised Insurers at www.fca.org.uk.

- **Status of workers:** Legislation applies to any employer who:

    - Deducts National Insurance and income tax contributions

    - Controls where and when the employees work and how they work

    - Supplies work materials and equipment

    - Has a right to any profit that workers make

    - Requires employees to deliver the work and the applicable employee can't provide substitutes

Some very limited exceptions exist to this mandatory requirement:

- Family businesses employing close family members (as long as they're not incorporated as a limited company). All employees must be closely related to the owner.

- A company employing only the owner where that employee also owns the majority of the share capital of the company.

The appointment of even one employee creates a duty to purchase employers' liability insurance, as does a company with two directors.

✔ Volunteers, unpaid students and those on training programmes (though informing the insurer of their presence is advisable).

✔ Genuine independent contractors (refer to Chapter 5).

✔ Employees normally based abroad, unless they spend more than 14 days continuously in the UK.

The Health and Safety Executive (HSE) enforces the law on employers' liability insurance. Inspectors can ask to see a business's certificate of insurance so that they can verify that an approved insurer provided it and that the cover meets the minimum threshold of £5 million. Significant penalties exist for non-compliance, including severe fines and criminal liability (you can go to jail for 14 years).

In addition, if an insurer believes that your business has failed to meet its legal responsibilities for the health and safety of employees, the policy may enable it to sue your enterprise to reclaim the cost of compensation if this failure leads to such a claim. Scary stuff. It can start 'raining cats and dogs' if you get this one wrong (apparently, this phrase dates to the Middle Ages, when heavy rain brought dead cats and dogs floating down the gutter. Ah, the good old days. . . .).

Compliance with the statutory duties outlined in the Health and Safety Act, 1974, in particular the requirement to 'ensure the health, safety and welfare of employees' through a written health and safety policy and risk assessment, helps to avoid any such claim. (Scurry safely to Chapter 7 for all your health and safety responsibilities.)

Protecting the public: Public liability insurance

Public liability insurance provides you with protection against claims made by members of the public for injury or property damage and any associated legal costs. This insurance isn't a legal requirement, but don't throw caution to the wind (though throwing caution against anything would seem tricky). Any business that regularly has members of the public on its site or premises needs this kind of policy (which is also sometimes referred to as *third-party insurance*). The *public* includes anybody who isn't an employee – such as customers, visitors and clients.

Consider these important aspects of public liability insurance:

✔ **Cost-determining factors:** A number exist, including:

- Nature of your business (high-risk industries such as construction attract a higher premium).

- Number of employees of the business.

- Level of business turnover.

- Previous claims history (whether you have any skeletons in your closet). If you do, why? Is it something to do with that delightful and not-at-all irritating US import, Halloween?

- Demonstrate your compliance with the Health and Safety Act, 1974, a clear policy on health and safety, and a completed risk assessment, because these items mitigate risk and help you negotiate a competitive rate.

✔ **Establishing required level of cover:** Tends to start at a £1 million threshold. The UK is an increasingly litigious environment – another US import – and so you have to be covered even for fraudulent or spurious claims without merit. Certain companies or local authorities may insist that you have a certain level of public liability cover before contracting with them (usually up to £10 million).

✔ **Reviewing cover:** As your business expands, you may need to increase the level of protection. Equally, check your policy to ensure that any exclusions or terms don't specifically exclude certain business activities that leave your business without adequate cover.

✔ **Saving costs:** Combining a policy with employers' liability insurance (see the preceding section) or other insurance as part of a flexible insurance bundle can provide overall cost savings.

Taking care of your directors with liability insurance

Directors' liability insurance (or *Directors' and Officers' liability insurance* – D&O) protects directors if they're sued in their personal capacity. You can also obtain this policy for non-executive directors, company secretaries, senior managers or other officers of the company.

Here are the key reasons why this policy is becoming more popular for small companies:

✔ The directors of many smaller and medium-size companies without in-house legal counsel or a dedicated human resources department to guide their board can feel exposed.

✔ Although directors of incorporated companies benefit from the concept of limited liability, this doesn't protect them if they're sued in their personal capacity.

✔ Directors carry an increasingly onerous burden, and they can get things wrong. They must exercise care and skill, comply with numerous statutory obligations, act in good faith and comply with an ever-changing and complex legislative landscape (see Chapter 1).

✔ The Companies Act, 2006 generally prohibits a company from indemnifying a director against her liability for negligence or breach of duty in relation to the company. But the legislation specifically allows companies to maintain D&O insurance, which can be wider in scope than the very limited indemnities permitted in the Act.

As a result of these factors, many directors demand such coverage as a condition of their employment, and/or outside investors or financiers may impose this requirement before providing funding to a business. Bite the bullet and get this insurance. Other features of these policies include the following:

✔ **Cost of the premium:** Dependent on a number of factors:

　• Type of business and industry and the extent to which it's regulated

　• Number of directors covered

　• Turnover of the company

　• Previous claims history

✔ **Side A and Side B cover:** Although D&O policies vary, most cover directors for their own liabilities *(side A cover)* and provide separate cover for the company itself in respect of its indemnification of the directors *(side B cover)*.

✔ **Common exemptions:** Deliberate, fraudulent or illegal acts, damage to property, personal injury, criminal and regulatory fines and possessing an offensive doughnut aren't covered (spot the made-up one).

✔ **Defence costs:** Policies need to cover the legal costs incurred in defending the claim as well as damage arising from the claim, because these sums can be significant. This is often a source of contention with insurers. (Some policies require repayment of defence costs if the director is found guilty of an offence and not merely negligent.)

✔ **Presumptive indemnification clauses:** Watch out for these clauses in your policy. They mean that the company is presumed to have indemnified the director to the fullest extent permissible by law, and therefore the insurance policy only needs to cover the director for any liability *over and above* what the company should have covered. If the company fails to indemnify the director to the maximum extent permissible by law, the director is in trouble – I believe the expression 'Going to hell in a handbasket' covers it (or similar expressions involving malodorous creeks and paddles).

✓ **Claims-made basis:** Directors' liability insurance policies are usually written on a *claims-made* basis, and so only cover claims made during the term of the policy (the next section has more info).

✓ **'Aggregate' basis of claim:** An overall limit per year is likely on the amount that can be recovered and any claims made are deducted from that total amount. This stipulation can be problematic if a number of directors are subject to a claim or if more than a single claim arises.

✓ **Run-off cover:** Make sure that the cover continues for a sufficient period of time after a director retires or leaves – generally six years (see the next section).

Looking after yourself: Professional indemnity insurance

Professional indemnity (PI) insurance (sometimes known as *professional liability* or *errors and omissions insurance*) covers the costs associated with you compensating clients for loss or damage arising from negligent advice or services provided by your business or an individual, including loss of data.

Here are some key pointers on this type of insurance:

✓ **Professional requirement:** Although PI cover isn't a legal requirement, some businesses only contract with you if you have this cover in place (especially in the IT sector). Equally, the professional body or regulator of certain professions require that you have PI insurance and set minimum levels of cover, including:

- Accountants
- Architects
- Chartered surveyors
- Certain healthcare professionals
- Financial advisers
- Solicitors

✓ **Amount of cover:** Depends on the nature of the business, the client (the larger the client(s), the greater the likelihood of requiring increased cover), and the value and budget of the project(s) engaged in. The lowest level of cover usually available is £50,000.

- ✔ **Basis of claims:** Usually offered on a *claims-made basis* – an insurer only covers claims made during the term of the policy. A claim made after the policy expires isn't covered (even if the incident occurred while the policy was in place).

   Given that under UK law claims of this nature can be made for up to six years after an alleged negligent act occurs, you need to be aware of this potential gap. If you're starting a new policy (or changing insurers), make sure that your new policy covers claims made during the course of that new policy even though the incident may have arisen during the six years before it started (called *retroactive cover*).

- ✔ **Run-off policy:** Purchase if your business is ceasing to trade or you're retiring; it protects you against claims brought after the policy expires.

- ✔ **Any one claim and annual aggregate:** Check the policy limits cover as follows:

    - *Any one claim* cover pays out the maximum full amount on any number of claims.

    - *Annual aggregate limit* is the maximum amount that the policy covers for one year, and so the more claims, the less you get for each claim. This option is normally a bit cheaper, because it carries less risk for the insurer.

Placating your inner pessimist: Other forms of insurance

You can take out a number of other types of insurance to mitigate your risks:

- ✔ **Product liability:** Protects you if a product causes injury or damage to people or their property. Consider this protection if your business manufactures products, sells its own branded products, alters or repairs products, or imports products from outside the EU.

   Strict liability exists under the Consumer Protection Act, 1987 (check out Chapter 12). You don't need to have been negligent as manufacturer or supplier – if a defect in your product causes injury or loss, you're liable.

- ✔ **Business interruption:** Provides cover for loss of income during a period when you can't conduct business as normal due to an unforeseen or unexpected event, such as fire, storm, flooding or the breakdown of essential equipment. Normally only covers incidents where the business is affected due to damage to the premises.

Check on the list of exclusions – for example, fallout from fights between rival Transformers isn't usually covered. The policy can be offered as an optional extra to a buildings and contents insurance policy.

✔ **Credit risk:** Protects a business against the risk of non-payment by credit customers and minimises the risk of bad debts and disruption to cash flow. Generally you need to demonstrate that you have an effective credit control system in place (see the earlier section 'Giving Credit Where Credit Is Due').

Drawbacks to such cover include the following:

- Obtaining it is often difficult for new companies.

- Insurers may cancel or alter the limit of credit approved on particular customers.

- The policy doesn't cover disputed debts.

✔ **Key person:** A form of life assurance policy on a key employee on whom the continued successful operation of the business is dependent. For example, you! Many small- and medium-size businesses rely heavily on their founder to drive the business, find customers, raise money, fix the toilets and challenge office rodents to unarmed combat. This policy provides financial protection for the business if you suffer a major illness, injury or death (after being bested by a particularly feisty rat).

Chapter 15

Winning Disputes (When You Can't Avoid Them)

Disputes are an inevitable part of doing business, though the reasons for them vary. Sometimes contracts aren't worded clearly enough and create differing points of view. Sometimes they don't even exist – allowing disagreements to fill the vacuum. Occasionally the parties fail to anticipate events and argue about the consequences. At other times, a firm deliberately creates a dispute by breaching a term in a contract, judging that the financial risk of doing so is favourable compared to continuing to spend, or lose, money under the arrangement.

But disputes don't relate only to contracts. Accidents can happen at work and people can infringe your intellectual property rights (for pursuing such claims, refer to Chapter 8) or behave in ways that negatively affect the reputation of your business. Some people just thrive on the energy of confrontation. World War II General George Patton suggested that 'Battle is the most magnificent competition that human beings can engage in'. He'd have enjoyed litigation and plenty of people like him simply love a good scrap.

No matter how they arise, disputes sap your business of energy, time and money – and can be very stressful. The poet Robert Frost remarked that 'The only successful lawsuit is that worn by a policeman'. Hear, hear!

In this chapter, I look at avoiding disputes where possible and managing them effectively when they do arise, using the wisdom of great generals to help you. Sorry that this chapter is quite long, but there's a lot to say. As Napoleon pointed out, 'There are so many laws now that nobody is safe from hanging'. Even if that fate isn't on your radar, you do need to know the legal niceties of disputes.

The best approach to disputes is to avoid them, and the best way to do that is not to get worked up by the inevitable disagreements that arise in business. As the little French Emperor said, 'A true man hates no one'.

Handling Claims Relating to Contracts

As the Chinese general Sun Tzu put it 2,500 years ago: 'The supreme art of war is to subdue the enemy without fighting', and so you want to avoid combat where possible. Contractual disputes are likely to be the most common that you face in your business. Here are some tips for avoiding or minimising them:

✔ **Have a contract:** Amazingly, many people think that winging it is okay when dealing with their major business arrangements. But if you don't have a written agreement or just rely on emails you're asking for trouble. Falling out is much easier when the parties have no agreed terms of reference to fall back on.

✔ **Be thorough in your agreements:** In Chapter 10, I introduce you to some new friends: the 4 Rs (rights, responsibilities, rewards, risks). Make sure that you cover those elements in any written agreement.

For each responsibility, ask yourself the following:

- What's the obligation?
- On whom does it fall?
- Where must the obligation/action take place?
- When must it happen and how?
- Do any other factors affect the performance of the obligation?

Ensure that you provide for answers to all these questions in the drafting of the agreement's terms. Easy-peasy.

✔ **Be clear in your agreements:** You win no prizes for impressive sounding words or for quantity. Make sure that you mean what you say. Sentences written in plain English are much less likely to confuse each other than sentences written in lawyer jargon.

✔ **Cover remedies in the agreement:** For the obligations, write down what happens if a party doesn't do what it's supposed to. If a person is supposed to make a payment at a certain time and doesn't, include a clause that interest runs until the date the payment is made. If someone is supposed to deliver at a certain time and doesn't, include a clause that if he doesn't correct that failure within 30 days of you telling him about it, you can terminate the agreement.

These kinds of clause discourage people from committing breaches of the agreement in the first place, encourage them to put things right when they go wrong and give everybody an answer that doesn't involve suing each other.

Preventing contractual disputes from escalating

Despite your best efforts with your contract drafting, disputes can still develop. They usually involve the other side's actions:

- ✓ **Not doing what it said it would:** For example, not delivering or buying something, or not having the rights it claimed it had.

- ✓ **Doing what it said it wouldn't:** For example, trading with someone else when it promised that you had an exclusive arrangement.

- ✓ **Doing something at the wrong time:** For example, paying you late.

- ✓ **Not doing something in the way it said it would:** For example, delivering a smaller quantity than promised or the wrong type of goods.

Although you may be tempted to lash out and crush your enemies into the dust, ensure that you aren't over-reacting and creating a dispute where one needn't arise. As Napoleon astutely put it, 'If they want peace, nations should avoid the pin pricks that precede canon shots'. The point is not to rush to the battlefield before you've tried other methods of sorting out the problem. Here are three suggestions:

- ✓ **Speak to the other side rather than firing off aggressive emails.** Emails have a habit of escalating problems rather than creating solutions, partly because they're in black and white (and leave no room for nuanced communication) and partly because people tend to be tougher in emails than in a conversation. Face-to-face is best, but phone and Skype are definitely better than email.

- ✓ **Negotiate before you confront.** Negotiation can save you a lot of time and trouble in dealing with difficult situations and difficult people. Yet few people practise negotiation or work to a coherent framework when negotiating. Gallop to Chapter 21 for some hints and tips on how to negotiate effectively.

- ✓ **Include provisions in the contract that encourage negotiation before either side starts chucking missiles.** This approach is common in IT agreements. For a customer issue, the agreement can say that the customer must first speak to your customer relationship manager. If the issue isn't resolved within, say, seven business days, the matter is referred onto the head of sales in your team and the head of procurement in the customer's team. Those two parties then have a further seven business days to resolve the dispute, failing which the matter is passed up the chain to the chief operating officer of each party. Only after all such avenues are exhausted is either side free to pursue other legal options.

Terminating agreements

When a negotiation isn't going well, you may have to consider suspending or terminating the agreement. If you covered failure by the other side in your contract, you should have a right to terminate the agreement for its particular breach.

Often this right arises after a period during which the other side has a contractual opportunity to cure its breach. You give it notice of the breach and if it hasn't cured the breach after a set period (usually between 7 and 30 days of receipt of your notice), you can automatically terminate the agreement by a further notice. During that cure period you may also have the right to suspend performance of your own obligations.

Make sure that you comply with the notice provisions in the agreement. If you send a notice to the wrong person (say, the Operations Manager when a notice to the Chairman is required), or by the wrong method (say by email when registered post is required), your notice is invalid.

Unfortunately, you can't possibly itemise all possible breaches in the contract. Therefore, for those that aren't listed, you have to consider exactly what action to take following a default by the other side.

Be very wary of terminating an agreement as a result of the dispute when you aren't legally allowed to do so. If you do, *you* can be in breach of the agreement for wrongfully terminating, because not all breaches of contract give you an automatic right to terminate. Instead, your ability to terminate the agreement depends on the status of the breached term.

Contractual terms can be classified into three types:

✔ **Conditions:** A term that goes right to the heart of the contract. In general, condition breaches come in two types:

- **Repudiatory:** A very serious breach of the condition that in effect deprives you of the benefit of the entire contract and so can entitle you to terminate the agreement.

- **Material:** A serious breach but not quite as bad as a repudiatory one.

Imagine that you love duck eggs and you agree that Farmer Giles is to deliver you 8,000 duck eggs in return for $8,000. If he doesn't deliver any eggs, that's a *repudiatory* breach, entitling you to terminate the agreement. If he sends 6,000 duck eggs rather than 8,000, that's probably a *material* breach, for which you can terminate only if the contract allows you.

For that reason, contracts often refer to 'material' terms as a general category of breaches for which termination is allowed. Unfortunately no legal definition exists of what 'material' means, and so arguments often revolve around whether or not a breach is sufficiently serious (material) to allow termination.

✔ **Warranty:** A contractual term that doesn't go to the root of the contract. Therefore, a breach of warranty by the other side doesn't allow you to terminate the agreement.

Imagine that Farmer Giles warrants that the majority of the eggs would have 15 speckles on the shell and yet 3,999 eggs have 15 speckles and 4,001 eggs have 14 speckles. Not only have you wasted an entire day counting speckles, but also you'd conclude that you aren't entitled to terminate for such a minor breach.

✔ **Innominate:** Terms that can be either conditions or warranties. The decision depends on the effect that the breach causes on the innocent party. If the breach deprives you of substantially the whole benefit of the contract, it may be a repudiatory breach. If not, it's classified as only a warranty breach (which doesn't allow you to terminate).

If Farmer Giles sends only 1,000 eggs out of 8,000 and that was the only quantity you ordered, the breach is pretty serious (a repudiatory one). But if your family are big duck-egg eaters and you ordered 1,000,000 duck eggs off him over the previous year, a 7,000 duck-egg shortfall is a less serious warranty breach.

Knowing what you can claim

You can claim for breach of contract in a number of ways, as I describe in this section. Under contract, you have six years from the date on which the contract was breached to bring a claim.

Action for an agreed sum

An *action for an agreed sum* is fairly straightforward and relates to when a specified amount owed under the contract hasn't been paid. So, for example, if Farmer Giles delivers all 8,000 of your ordered duck eggs and you fail to pay him $8,000, he can claim that amount as a debt.

Damages claim

Damages are a measure of compensation for what you've lost as a result of a contract breach. You can calculate damages in two ways:

- **Expectation loss:** The most frequently applied measure of damages, it puts you in the position you would've been in had the defaulting party properly performed the contract.

- **Reliance loss:** Puts you in the position you'd have been in if the two parties hadn't entered into the contract. In other words, you get back all the expenditure incurred in relation to the contract. Reliance loss is sometimes preferred as a way of quantifying loss, because calculating the amount of your loss isn't always easy. In these cases, recovering the amount invested is more practical.

Say that Farmer Giles was supposed to deliver de-shelling equipment with your duck eggs so that you don't have to crack open 8,000 eggs by hand. If the equipment doesn't work, you may find that claiming for the cost of the equipment (reliance loss) is easier than working out your losses from cracking open the eggs manually (expectation loss).

Generally, you're free to choose which measure of loss to pursue, but the following three limitations do exist on any type of damages:

- **Mitigation:** A legal requirement that you must always try to minimise your loss. If Farmer Giles lets you down and delivers 6,000 instead of 8,000 eggs, you have a duty to minimise your loss by trying to get the eggs replaced elsewhere. If the replacement eggs cost more, or take longer to arrive, you can use that cost as a measure of your damages.

  You have to act reasonably in doing what you can to reduce your losses. You can't recover any loss that you could've avoided by taking such reasonable steps.

- **Remoteness:** How foreseeable the damage from the breach was. Essentially, under the remote rule, a claimant can recover losses that fall within the scope of two categories of loss:

  - **Direct loss:** Any loss that happens as a natural result of the breach or 'in the ordinary course of things'.

  - **Indirect (or consequential) loss:** Any other loss that the parties can reasonably expect to have anticipated at the time they entered into the contract. In other words, any special loss that isn't an ordinary loss but that both parties are aware of when they make the agreement.

  Any loss that doesn't fall within either of these two categories isn't recoverable, because it's considered too 'remote'. If Farmer Giles delivers only 6,000 duck eggs and you have to pay extra for the other 2,000 from somewhere else, that's direct loss. If you were going to give some of those eggs to Aunty Irene, and instead you have to buy her more expensive ostrich eggs, because no duck egg suppliers are within 500 miles of her remote Scottish village, that extra cost is indirect loss. You can recover that loss if Farmer Giles knew all about your plan and the lack of suitable duck-egg suppliers near Aunty Irene. Otherwise, your loss is too remote.

Parties often try to restrict their potential exposure for damages by seeking to exclude liability for all forms of indirect loss in the contract. The list may include loss of business, revenues, anticipated savings, opportunity and reputation, or goodwill. Avoid the other side imposing these restrictions on you if you can.

✔ **Restitution:** Instead of compensating you for the loss you've suffered, the aim here is to prevent the defending party from being unjustly enriched, by requiring it to pay back the amount of the unfair benefit it received. So if you paid Farmer Giles upfront for the eggs and he didn't deliver any, you can seek restitution of the amount you paid.

If you also agreed that you'd both erect a new barn to house the eggs and Farmer Giles would contribute £2,000 to its cost, you can also claim for the work you carried out in reliance on this payment (called a *quantum meruit* claim – 'as much as he deserves').

Specific performance

The remedy of *specific performance* involves the court issuing a decree to a party to perform its contractual obligations. Normally, the refusal of one party to perform its obligations to you, as agreed under a contract, allows you to bring a claim for damages. But in certain circumstances, damages alone don't provide an adequate remedy to you.

For example, if the particular duck eggs you wanted from Farmer Giles were the only ones in the country with a large 3-centimetre circumference, you may find that tracking down alternatives is very hard. So you can seek an order for specific performance that Farmer Giles has to keep to his bargain and deliver those eggs to you.

Specific performance isn't available in certain situations, including those in relation to contracts for personal service. So you can't seek an order for specific performance in order to make someone stay and work for you. That's why footballers who sulk because they feel their club doesn't pay them enough normally end up being sold in the end.

Injunctions

Like specific performance, *injunction* is another remedy only available where damages wouldn't be adequate. It comes in two delicious flavours:

✔ **Prohibitory injunctions:** The most common type, which prevent a party from doing something.

✔ **Mandatory injunctions:** Require parties to do something.

If Farmer Giles is about to sell your promised duck eggs to somebody else, you may be able to get a prohibitory injunction if they were the product of an extremely rare breed of duck and very hard to replace with an order from somewhere else.

Injunctions can be granted as a final remedy *(perpetual injunctions)* or on a temporary basis to stop some harm from occurring before a final hearing or trial takes place *(interim injunctions)*.

An injunction is an *equitable* remedy, and so the court refuses to grant it if doing so would be unfair on the other side. Here are the typical situations for refusing to grant an injunction and why:

- ✔ **You delay too long in seeking the injunction:** The damage isn't that serious or urgent.

- ✔ **You behaved badly yourself:** You don't deserve the injunction.

- ✔ **The injunction would cause disproportionate harm to the other side:** Granting an injunction wouldn't be fair.

- ✔ **You're unable to agree that you'll compensate the other side in damages if the decision to grant you an injunction proves to be wrong later:** You can't afford an injunction.

Paying Attention to Negligence Claims

Negligence is one of a category of *torts* (wrongs) that are done to a party independently of any contractual relationship. *Negligence* claims arise because you have a duty to take reasonable care not to harm certain people you may affect with your actions. A number of overlapping elements make up a negligence claim: establishing a duty of care, proving a breach of the duty of care and demonstrating loss.

You have six years from the date on which the damage was suffered to bring your claim (or, if harm is unknown at that time, three years from the date you know or ought to have known all facts about the loss, the identity of the defendant and that you were able to bring a claim).

Deciding whether a duty of care exists

To establish a *duty of care,* three criteria must be met:

- ✔ **Damage must be reasonably foreseeable:** Similar to the remoteness rule in relation to contractual damages (refer to the earlier section

'Damages claim'). The test of reasonable foreseeability is whether a reasonable person in the defendant's position would've reasonably foreseen the damage occurring (not whether the defendant knew or didn't know that it would occur).

Imagine that while delivering 8,000 duck eggs to you, Farmer Giles drives his tractor at pace into the side of your barn and it falls down, killing three of your prize heifers. Could he have foreseen that crashing into your barn at speed would lead it to fall down and harm some of your animals? Probably, yes.

✔ **Sufficient closeness or 'proximity' of relationship must exist between the defendant and the claimant:** A business can't be held responsible for the fate of every single person that may, in some way or another, be affected by any (negligent) act or omission. The field of people to whom a duty can be owed is therefore narrowed by this second criterion looking at the nature and closeness of the relationship between the claimant and the defendant.

With your destroyed barn, sufficient proximity exists between you and Farmer Giles. If, unknown to Giles, your batty aunt had stored valuable Persian carpets in the barn and they got damaged in the crash, probably too little proximity exists for her to bring a claim.

✔ **Imposing a duty of care on the defendant must be fair, just and reasonable:** A policy issue and one of proportionality. In relation to the barn, this condition is met and Giles is in trouble.

Breaching a duty of care

If a duty of care is established, the next stage is to decide whether it has been breached. A key aspect is whether the defendant exercised a reasonable level of care or not. In determining what's *reasonable* you have to place yourself in the position of the hypothetical, average, 'reasonable' person – 'the man on the Clapham omnibus' as the Courts used to call him, quaintly.

If Farmer Giles were driving his tractor at 60 miles an hour, he probably wasn't exercising reasonable care and is in breach. If he was creeping along at 5 miles per hour (as farmers always do when you're following in your car on a narrow country road) that sounds reasonable.

Claiming damages for breach of duty of care: Loss

When a breach is confirmed, you have to show that the defendant's breach of duty caused you to suffer loss.

If your negligence claim is successful, you can claim damages as for a breach of contract, although the damages are calculated in a different way. For negligence, the goal of damages is to put you in the position you would've been in had the duty of care been properly fulfilled.

In the Farmer Giles case, you can claim for the cost of repairing your barn, replacing your heifers, and maybe even the pain and suffering you went through, because they were prize heifers you were very fond of.

One exception applies to the general rules on recovery for negligence, centred on what's called *pure economic loss.* If items are damaged or an injury is sustained as a result of negligence, and either case causes financial consequences, you can recover the resulting financial loss. Where no accompanying harm is suffered, however, economic loss alone isn't recoverable under negligence. The reason is that traditionally the domain of contract law is to deal with pure economic loss. The general rule is that no recovery exists under negligence for pure economic loss.

Suing for negligent misstatement

In certain cases, people make statements to others that are relied upon and used in relation to certain decisions or actions they take. In these circumstances, the law states that where a sufficiently close relationship exists between the parties, the maker of the statement owes the claimant a duty of care and can be held liable for resulting financial loss suffered by the claimant as a result of a statement negligently made.

For *negligent misstatement,* the test for the existence of a duty of care is adapted. Here are the requirements:

- ✔ Existence of a 'special relationship' between the parties
- ✔ Claimant places reliance on the statement (and this is the defendant's intention)
- ✔ Reasonable foreseeability that reliance will be placed on the statement

Negligent misstatement is particularly relevant when your business is seeking advice from third-party professionals, banks, surveyors and so on.

Say that troublesome Farmer Giles is a leading authority on duck eggs and you're a beginner. If he tells you that you can keep the duck eggs safely in your barn for several weeks, when in fact all 8,000 need to be kept in your fridge (even if that means you have no room for your pots of fromage frais), you can sue him for negligent misstatement when all the eggs go off.

Defending negligence claims

If you do bring a claim for negligence, a defendant can raise several possible defences against your claim:

- ✔ No duty of care existed in the first place.
- ✔ Damage wasn't reasonably foreseeable.
- ✔ You assumed a degree of risk voluntarily.
- ✔ Defendant's actions didn't cause the damage (maybe your heifers had a disease and were about to pop off anyway).
- ✔ You contributed to your loss (called *contributory negligence*), perhaps by building your barn out of cardboard rather than bricks, so that it was likely to fall down anyway.

Alleging Defamation

Like negligence, *defamation* is a legal tort. It refers to publishing statements that negatively affect a person's reputation, and covers *slander,* which is defamation in transient form (such as spoken comment or gestures), and *libel,* which is any lasting form of publication (printed or placed online).

The Defamation Act, 2013 updates the tort of defamation, raising the bar for people who want to bring defamation claims. The requirements for a defamation claim are as follows:

- ✔ **The statement must be defamatory:** It must lower somebody's reputation. When Napoleon said that 'In politics, stupidity is not a handicap', on the face of it that seems a defamatory statement about politicians. But under the Defamation Act, you have to show that the statement caused or is likely to cause 'serious harm' to your reputation. This is likely to rule out claims by most politicians, as well as claims by 'z'-list celebrities over tittle-tattle in the gossip columns (which the Act is designed to prevent).

   In relation to a business, the test of 'serious harm' means that the statement must have caused or be likely to cause the organisation serious financial loss.

- ✔ **The statement must refer to the claimant:** Not difficult to satisfy if the claimant is named in the statement. But if the claimant is identified by some other means, the test is whether a reasonable person would understand that the statement refers to the claimant. An individual can even bring a successful claim for defamation in relation to a statement about a particular group or class of people of which the person is a member where it would be understood that the statement refers to each member of that group.

- ✔ **The statement must have been published:** This refers to publishing to a third party, and the defendant needs to publish, or be responsible for publishing, the statement. In the case of publication on the Internet, each time a user requests the information (that is, the user downloads material containing the statement or sends a request to a web server to send a web page containing the statement), a separate publication has occurred.

Remedies for defamation are damages, an injunction and orders for removal of the offending statement (see 'Knowing what you can claim' earlier in this chapter).

The Defamation Act sets out a number of defences that can defeat a claim of defamation:

- ✔ **Truth:** If a statement is true, this fact provides a full defence to any claim, because although the claimant's reputation is affected, that reputation is deserved. If you say that Farmer Giles was a careless driver after he negligently drove into your barn and killed your heifers, it would be true. If you add that he drinks the blood of babies, that wouldn't be true (unless you know something I don't).

- ✔ **Honest opinion:** If you provide an opinion that's honest (based on existing or supposed facts) and you hold such an opinion, you also have a defence to defamation.

- ✔ **Public interest:** Commenting on matters of public interest is a defence, as long as you reasonably believe that publishing the statement is in the public interest. If you write an article in the *Farming Bugle* about the increase in cases of damage done by speeding tractors, and you refer to Farmer Giles's example, that can count as commenting on a matter of public interest.

- ✔ **Defences for operators of websites on which statements are posted:** Relevant, of course, to social networking sites and any websites that allow individuals to express opinions on any content or issues. If the claimant can't identify the person responsible for making the defamatory comment, however, and as a result makes a complaint to the website operator in connection with the statement, the operator has to take appropriate steps to respond to such a complaint. Failure to do so makes the defence unavailable.

A defamation claim can only be made within one year of the date on which the defamatory statement was published.

Making Claims in Court

You have to follow certain rules when you get to the stage of making a formal legal claim. This point is where the bombardment begins: 'Hard pounding, gentlemen, let's see who pounds the longest' was the Duke of Wellington's no-nonsense approach to battle commencing.

Legal hand-to-hand fighting is (slightly) more civilised and the litigation process is governed by a strict set of rules known as the Civil Procedure Rules (CPRs), which apply to all civil claims brought in England and Wales. You can find the CPRs at `https://www.justice.gov.uk/courts/procedure-rules/civil` or in hard copy in what's familiarly termed 'the White Book'.

The CPRs are accompanied by *practice directions,* which explain the rules in further detail and provide supplementary rules and guidelines for the parties to follow. The CPRs are underpinned by Part 1, the 'Overriding Objective', which is to deal with cases justly and at proportionate cost. The parties to a dispute are required to help the court achieve this overriding objective (Rule 1.3), which means following the CPRs, complying with any orders of the court and generally co-operating with the court and the other parties involved in the claim so that the process can be conducted as efficiently as possible.

In addition to the rules and practice directions, you also have pre-action protocols accompanied by a practice direction on pre-action conduct.

Preparing for court action

Commencing formal legal proceedings is a big step that involves the use of public funding and a potentially significant amount of the court's time and other resources, and so before starting any proceedings the parties are expected to have made a genuine effort to resolve their dispute. Accordingly, the CPRs include a preliminary section that sets out the nature of the action that the court expects the parties to have taken to avoid litigation, together with further advice and guidance in relation to such pre-litigation action. You can be punished with costs if the court feels that you ignored these requirements.

Here are the steps involved in pre-action conduct:

1. **The parties enter into correspondence with each other.** The aim is to identify clearly the problem and try to see whether an alternative way exists to settle the dispute.

2. **The claimant writes to the defendant setting out details of the claim, including:**

   - An explanation of the basis on which the claim is made (for example, failure to deliver goods by a certain date, services not provided as required under the contract and so on)

   - A summary of all facts relevant to the claim

   - Details of exactly what the claimant is seeking from the defendant

3. **The defendant responds to the claimant, including the following:**

   - Confirmation that the claim has been accepted, in full or in part

   - Explanation as to the reasons why the claim isn't accepted, or which parts of the claim aren't accepted

   - Explanation of why any facts in the claimant's letter are denied

   - Whether the defendant wants to make any counterclaim (that is, bring its own claim against the claimant)

4. **The defendant must respond to the claimant's letter within a reasonable period following receipt.** The pre-action conduct practice direction suggests that this period can be from 14 days (in the case of simple claims) to three months when the dispute is very complicated. In both cases, the parties should also send to each other any evidence that they have supporting their claim or defence. The letter sent by the claimant is known as a *letter of claim* (or a *letter before action*).

Following the formal process

The details of starting and running a legal procedure are set out at `http://hmctsformfinder.justice.gov.uk/HMCTS/GetForm.do?court_forms_id=338`. I don't want to burden you with all one million pages of the White Book, but here are some helpful hints.

Legal claims are allocated to one of three *tracks*. Allocation is generally dependant on the value and complexity of the claim:

- ✔ **Small claims track:** Usually handles claims of up to £10,000 (or £1,000 in the case of personal injury claims).

- ✔ **Fast track:** Usually handles claims of no more than £25,000 where the trial is likely to last for no more than one day and expert evidence is limited.

- ✔ **Multitrack:** For more complicated cases involving larger sums of money.

Claims allocated to the small claims and fast tracks are heard in a county court. Multitrack claims are usually heard in the more senior High Court.

Get your case into the small claims track or the fast track if you can, where the process tends to be streamlined and cheaper (£90–900, comprising claim fees, court fees and hearing fees). Getting your costs back is harder in the small claims court (even if you win), but the amounts you pay out in the first place are much smaller.

For claims for money worth less than £100,000, you can opt for an alternative service to settle disputes called *Money Claim Online,* where claims are submitted online. The particulars of the claim must be included in the claim form and be of limited length. Defences to claims can also be made electronically. For further details, go to http://www.moneyclaim.gov.uk/web/mcol/welcome.

To claim any interest on the amount of a claim, you must set out this fact in the particulars of the claim at the beginning of the process. You can claim interest in several ways: as a result of a specific term in a contract, under statute (the Late Payment of Commercial Debts [Interest] Act, 1998) or under the court's discretion. Interest can't be awarded unless you claim it.

No section on legal proceedings is complete without a few warnings:

- ✔ **Follow the deadlines to serve documents to the other side:** Otherwise you run the risk of your case being struck out. Take care: the rules for calculating time in the CPRs involve *clear days* (the dates of sending and receiving documents aren't included in the specified period).

- ✔ **State specifically whether you're denying any claims made against you:** Unless the issue is dealt with elsewhere in the defence, you're assumed to have admitted the allegation.

- ✔ **Watch out for costs:** Court action can be very expensive, especially in superior courts. You may think that you have the most brilliant case in the world, but you can still lose. Costs for lawyers' time, instructing expert witnesses, gathering evidence and preparing case files, as well as court fees, all add up. Apart from in the small claims court, 'the loser pays the winner's costs' (subject to the court's discretion), and so you can lose your shirt (not to mention your unmentionables – oh, too late) if you lose the case.

  Even if you win, the court normally awards costs on a *taxed* basis – that is, it assesses the rate at which you should recover your costs. This is normally a lower rate than the actual rate you paid for them. So, even if you win the case, you're still out of pocket on costs.

Choosing Alternative Dispute Resolutions

The pre-action conduct practice direction (check out the preceding section) stresses that you're to see litigation as a last resort. The court expects parties to consider alternative methods to help resolve disputes and so avoid litigation. Even during it, you should always consider finding a settlement. Here I look at two other forms of dispute resolution: mediation and arbitration.

Mediating: The nonviolent solution to legal battles

Mediation is an option open to disputing parties at any time. The parties use the services of an independent third party (the *mediator*) whose role is to facilitate constructive dialogue with the aim of enabling the parties to reach a settlement that's satisfactory to them both.

Advantages

'Invincibility lies in defence; the possibility of victory in the attack' wrote Sun Tzu. Lots of potential advantages exist to mediation as a peaceable alternative:

- ✔ **Costs:** Mediation is relatively cheap. The parties normally split the cost of the mediator (typically £1,000 for a day) and any associated expenses (such as hiring meeting rooms). Contrast this cost with the heavy bills associated with long court cases.

- ✔ **Time:** Mediation is normally over within one day, in contrast with the enormous delays often associated with court litigation.

- ✔ **Stress:** Mediation is normally less stressful than giving formal evidence in court or facing cross examination.

- ✔ **Empowerment:** The mediator doesn't decide the case – that's up to the parties. They can agree any solution they want or choose not to agree, whereas in court the judge makes the decisions for you.

- ✔ **Confidentiality:** Mediation is confidential – court proceedings aren't.

- ✔ **Relationships:** Few relationships survive the brutality of the courtroom. In the capsule of mediation, however, the parties can work through their differences and emerge with their relationship intact.

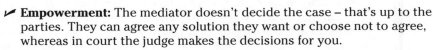

- ✔ **Success:** A 2014 audit for the Centre for Effective Dispute Resolution (CEDR) shows that just over 75 per cent of cases heard by mediators in the UK settled on the day of the mediation, and another 11 per cent settled shortly after (see http://www.cedr.com/docslib/TheMediatorAudit2014.pdf).

Mediation isn't right for every dispute – for example, where parties to a contract are relying on case law to support their claim or an injunction is sought as a remedy – but it's definitely worth considering as an alternative to court action.

Insert a mediation clause in your agreements, requiring parties to attend mediation before taking further legal action to resolve a contractual dispute.

Process

You need to appoint a mediator to hear the mediation (check out `www.civilmediation.justice.gov.uk` for a list). Alternatively, certain organisations, such as the Ombudsman (`http://www.ombudsman-services-b2b.org/meet-our-neutrals/`) or CEDR (`www.cedr.com`), can recommend a suitable mediator and a mediation process.

The mediator usually contacts the parties in advance of the mediation to discuss certain formalities and ensure that no other matters require attention before the mediation takes place. The two parties sign a mediation agreement that sets out the basis on which the mediation is conducted. Typical clauses cover the confidential nature of the discussions, allocation of fees for the mediation and formalities relating to settling the dispute.

At the mediation, the mediator takes both sides through the process and explains the purpose of the mediation and his role. He invites each side to make a short opening statement, setting out its position and drawing attention to the principal areas of dispute. The mediator summarises the issues and establishes a process to follow. You can represent yourself in a mediation or you can engage lawyers to speak for you.

Some lawyers belong to the General Patton school of conflict management: 'Nobody ever defended anything successfully. There is only attack, attack and attack some more'. If you use a lawyer, make sure that the person is collaborative rather than confrontational.

The mediator takes the two sides to separate rooms for private sessions. He passes between the two rooms as each side considers its position, listening to the respective concerns and encouraging them to think about ways in which they may arrive at an understanding with each other. The discussions are confidential, and the mediator doesn't reveal any content of a private discussion with one side to the other party unless consent is specifically provided. The whole point of the private sessions is that frank discussions can take place with the mediator without the risk of any negative feeling being communicated to the other side, which can have a serious impact on settlement negotiations.

After exploring the issues and assessing the parties' positions, the participants are encouraged to start making concrete offers of settlement. The mediator can move between the rooms with offers and counter-offers or the two sides can reconvene together and negotiate directly. If negotiation is successful, the parties formalise any deal in writing.

Draft a settlement agreement at this time to avoid any possibility of further dispute later about its exact terms. The mediator oversees the drafting of the terms and both sides sign the agreement. If litigation has commenced, the mediation document sets out how it's to be ended.

Arbitrating: Halfway to paradise

Unlike mediation, *arbitration* is an alternative to litigation – you choose one or the other. In addition, instead of the emphasis being on facilitating a process of negotiation, as with mediation, the role of the arbitrator is to hear the dispute and rule on it. So it's more like litigation, the difference being that arbitrators are usually experts in the subject matter of the arbitration.

Advantages

The advantages of arbitration over litigation are as follows:

- ✔ **Expert decision-making:** You don't have to rely on a judge who knows absolutely nothing about your business sector (or a dodderer who thinks that an iPad is something you apply to tired). You can appoint an arbitrator who's a business expert from your industry.

- ✔ **Privacy:** The arbitration is heard in private and the details remain confidential.

- ✔ **Flexible process:** Arbitrations held in England and Wales are subject to the Arbitration Act, 1996, which sets out the rules. The Act is divided into *mandatory* provisions (must be applied in all arbitrations) and *non-mandatory* provisions. So arbitration is a more flexible option: the participants and/or the arbitrator are free to decide the procedures to adopt. (For example, the arbitrator may decide to relax the formal rules of evidence that apply in court cases for the purpose of the arbitration.)

- ✔ **Timing:** Arbitration can be quicker than litigation, because the arbitrator doesn't have the same constraints on his time as the courts (where you can wait months before a case is scheduled).

- ✔ **Venue-neutrality:** The sides choose the *seat* of the arbitration (the national law supervising it), and so it can be different to the law of the countries in which the participants are based. This aspect can be a good way of avoiding cases being decided in countries where the local court procedure is difficult or favours local residents.

- ✔ **Ease of enforcement:** The Convention on the Recognition and Enforcement of Foreign Arbitral Awards, 1958 (New York Convention) says that an arbitration award made in one contracting state is automatically enforceable in all other contracting states. The convention covers 149 countries, and so an arbitration award can be much easier to enforce than a judgement from a national court. (The latter involves seeing whether the awarding country has a treaty or convention in place with the country in which enforcement is sought, and what action is required under the terms of that treaty or convention; or, if no such convention is in place, bringing a new claim in the country of enforcement.)

Process

Arbitration can be one-off and self-contained or an institutional process, in which case the rules of the chosen institution must be followed. Two well-known institutions that preside over arbitrations are the London Court of International Arbitration (LCIA; www.lcia.org) and the International Chamber of Commerce (http://www.iccwbo.org/products-and-services/arbitration-and-adr/).

The two sides can decide to arbitrate rather than commence litigation proceedings, or they may be required to arbitrate under the terms of a contractual agreement. An *arbitration agreement* is a set of terms that you can include in a contract under which parties agree to use arbitration rather than litigation to solve disputes.

If you're going to include a clause in your contract requiring arbitration, you need to be clear about a number of issues, including which contractual issues can be arbitrated, which country's law applies to the supervision of the arbitration, how many arbitrators are going to be appointed and whether any procedural rules of an institution govern the process (such as LCIA).

To commence the arbitration, one side usually serves a written notice on the other to arbitrate, referring to the arbitration clause in the contract (if that exists) together with the list of possible arbitrators to choose from and an explanation of the dispute. If the two sides can't agree on an arbitrator, you can apply to the court to appoint one. Difficulties in selecting a preferred arbitrator mean that arbitrations often have three arbitrators. Each side chooses one arbitrator and the two selected can then appoint a third arbitrator. Alternatively, an institution can appoint the third, or all, arbitrators. Institutions such as the Central Institute of Arbitrators (www.ciarb.org) provide lists of accredited arbitrators.

When selected, the arbitrator arranges a *preliminary meeting* with the participants, where they discuss and agree an agenda. Section 34 of the Arbitration Act sets out matters to be decided by the arbitrator, unless the participants otherwise agree, including time and place of the hearing, appointment of experts, which rules of evidence apply and how costs will be treated. Also covered is whether written statements of claim will be used, the form they should take and the date by which they need to be supplied, as well as how disclosure of documents to the other side will be managed and in what format.

Under section 40 of the Arbitration Act, the two sides must do 'all things necessary for the proper and expeditious conduct of the arbitral proceedings'. This includes complying, without delay, with any decision of the arbitration tribunal as to procedural or evidential matters, or with any orders or directions of the arbitrator.

If either side is responsible for any 'inordinate and inexcusable delay', the arbitrator has the right to dismiss the claim, although the two sides can agree to amend this and other powers of the arbitrator.

The arbitrator issues copies of correspondence to both sides and usually requires correspondence sent to him also to be copied to the other side.

Although an arbitrator's role and powers are similar to a judge's, at times the court has to intervene in the arbitration. For example, to enforce an arbitrator's order, remove one who isn't acting impartially or (in limited cases) decide on a point of law. The arbitrator must comply with Section 33 of the Arbitration Act in that he must 'act fairly and impartially as between the parties, giving each party a reasonable opportunity of putting his case and dealing with that of his opponent'. He must also ensure that the 'procedure is fair and suitable to the circumstances of the case, avoiding unnecessary delay or expense'.

Following the hearing, the arbitrator makes a decision on the issues. He delivers an 'award', which is normally in writing and signed by the arbitrator, together with the reasons why it was made and its date. Unless the two sides agree otherwise, the arbitrator can award interest on any monetary award he makes. The general rule for arbitration, as for litigation, is that costs 'follow the event' (the loser pays the winner's costs). But this isn't mandatory: if a term in an arbitration agreement states that one side is to be responsible for the costs of the arbitration before the dispute has arisen, this clause is disregarded by the arbitrator in making his decision on awarding costs.

Arbitration costs can be very expensive (arbitrators can charge £25,000 or more). An ICC calculator helps you to project the likely cost of your arbitration, given the amount claimed (`http://www.iccwbo.org/products-and-services/arbitration-and-adr/arbitration/cost-and-payment/cost-calculator/`). Also, although quicker than litigation, the process is still time-intensive and likely to involve costs for lawyers, experts and preparing documents. Finally, unlike mediation, arbitration is still an adversarial intellectual battle that can be very wearing. Napoleon tartly remarked that 'you don't reason with intellectuals, you shoot them', but unfortunately this remedy isn't available to you.

Chapter 16

Coping with Liquidation and Insolvency

*A*ll entrepreneurs start off with the highest of hopes for their business, wanting it to change the world, or their own or other people's lives. Their ambition drives them through the pressures, challenges and dark moments that assail any growing business. Unfortunately the stats on survival aren't too good: according to the Small Business Association, half of small businesses don't survive beyond the first five years.

Therefore, you need to know what to do if your business gets into trouble (statistically you'll face that situation at some point). If it happens you don't want to be a rabbit in the headlights – or even a dead one. You want to be a rabbit that avoids the wheels of the car and goes on to create dozens of new bunnies with pretty ears and fluffy tails. Ahhh. . .

In this chapter, I introduce you to insolvency law and cover a number of different states that can apply to a limited company or a Limited Liability Partnership (LLP) in trouble. I describe in each case the most miserable financial conditions you can face as a company (receivership, facing statutory demands, liquidation) as well as rescue procedures that offer a ray of hope (company voluntary arrangements, schemes of arrangement and administration). I also discuss the tricky area of creditor prioritisation. Be prepared, it's laugh-a-minute stuff.

I also deal with individual bankruptcy, where you can see the steady rain of bankruptcy giving way to the intermittent showers of an individual voluntary arrangement and the patchy sunshine of Debt Relief Orders.

Getting into financial trouble with your enterprise can seem like a terrible defeat, but it's no disgrace. Often it occurs through no fault of your own and you couldn't have foreseen the problems: in business, the rear-view mirror is always clearer than the front windscreen. So don't be too hard on yourself; as Winston Churchill put it, 'Success consists of going from failure to failure without losing enthusiasm'.

Understanding the Law in Relation to Insolvency

'The safe way to double your money is to fold it over once and put it in your pocket', wrote Frank Hubbard. Like any small business, you carry the risk of it starting to lose money, which is why you need to know about the laws of insolvency in the following pieces of legislation:

- ✔ **Insolvency Act, 1986:** Sets out the procedures for when a limited company or LLP is unable to pay its debts as and when they fall due *(cash-flow test)* or its liabilities are greater than its assets *(balance-sheet test)*. The Act also prohibits directors from the following:

    - Misapplying or retaining company funds

    - Transactions defrauding creditors (people it owes money to)

    - Granting a preference (an advantage to one creditor over another)

    - Entering into a transaction at an undervalue prior to a liquidation (leap to the later section 'Lining up a Liquidation' for all about liquidation)

    - Disposing of company property made after a winding up has started (see 'Catering for compulsory liquidation' later in this chapter for more on winding up)

- ✔ **Companies Act, 2006:** Contains duties that are relevant to limited companies and their directors (and LLPs as well, because the same insolvency regime applies to LLPs as to limited companies – bear this in mind as you read through the rest of this chapter):

- One of the key duties of directors is to promote the success of the company for the benefit of its shareholders as a whole. But if a company is approaching insolvency, the directors are required to act in the interests of the company's creditors.

- The Act prohibits a company from continuing to trade while insolvent.

- The definition of *wrongful trading* is in the Insolvency Act and occurs where a director has failed to take every step to minimise potential loss to the company's creditors where she knew or ought to have concluded that no reasonable prospect existed of the company avoiding insolvent liquidation.

✔ **Company Directors Disqualification Act, 1986:** Directors can be held personally responsible for wrongful trading, which can result in a director being disqualified under this Act. Furthermore, a court can make a compensation order against disqualified directors, requiring them personally to compensate creditors of an insolvent company who, as a result of their misconduct, suffered an identifiable loss.

Readying Yourself for Receivership

Receivership normally arises where you have a loan that you can't pay back. As Earl Wilson remarked, 'If you think nobody cares if you're alive, try missing a couple of payments on your car'. Your borrower, whether it's a bank or some other institution, is all over you very quickly.

Introducing receivership

Here are the basic elements of receivership:

✔ *Receivership* grants an enforcement right to the holder of the loan to get the loan back, which usually results in the company's business being sold and the company itself going into liquidation.

✔ The process can move quickly, with a company being served with a demand for repayment, followed by an appointment of a receiver shortly after that.

✔ A company can also invite a *charge-holder* to appoint a receiver, hence the expression 'calling in the receivers'. A *charge* is a security interest that a creditor takes over property to protect against non-payment of a debt (such as a loan). If the debtor doesn't pay the debt, the creditor has the right to take the property. Refer to Chapter 4 for a description of different types of charges, including fixed charges and floating charges.

✔ If at the end of the receivership, the assets are insufficient to pay the charge-holder in full, no funds are available for unsecured creditors (who don't have a charge).

✔ If funds remain after the charge-holder has been paid, they're usually passed over to a liquidator to distribute.

Fixing Up a fixed charge receiver

Two types of receivership exist under UK law: administrative receiverships and fixed charge receiverships. *Administrative receivership* is now fairly rare, because it's an option only for those with a floating charge, which dates back to pre-2003, and so I look at fixed charge receiverships in this section.

Fixed charge receivership is also known as the Law of Property Act receivership, because it's governed by the Law of Property Act, 1925. It provides an enforcement mechanism that a holder of a fixed charge (see Chapter 4) can use to sell the asset and repay the holder.

Keep in mind these key points regarding fixed charge receivership:

✔ Generally, fixed charge receivership is only used to sell land or single fixed assets (such as equipment) over which a charge exists.

✔ Fixed charge receivership is a relatively cost-effective way for the lender to take control of assets, because the lender can make the appointment and no court action is required.

✔ The fixed charge receiver must stop acting if an administrator is appointed (flip to the later 'Activating Administration' section).

✔ The fixed charge receiver doesn't need to be a licensed *Insolvency Practitioner* (a specialist in insolvency matters licensed by a body such as the Institute of Chartered Accountants for England and Wales).

Lining Up a Liquidation

Liquidation is the process of winding up a company's affairs. It's a termination or end-game procedure when the company (or LLP) has run out of road. The notoriously extravagant actor Errol Flynn said, 'My problem lies in reconciling my gross habits with my net income'. Liquidation is what happens when you find yourself in that position. Here are the key ingredients:

- ✔ Liquidation involves turning the company's assets into cash and then distributing them to creditors and shareholders (a process called *realising* assets).

- ✔ When the liquidation is completed, the company is dissolved and ceases to exist – normally at the end of a three-month period following receipt by the Registrar of Companies of a return from a liquidator (or an administrator – see 'Activating Administration' later in this chapter) setting out that the winding up has finished.

- ✔ The liquidator is concerned with ending the company and so is unlikely to become involved in the trading of the business.

- ✔ If a liquidator believes that creditors can achieve a better result by placing the company into administration instead of liquidation, an application can be made to the court to achieve that end.

As I discuss in this section, liquidation can be compulsory or voluntary.

Catering for compulsory liquidation

In a *compulsory liquidation* the company is wound up by order of the court. Compulsory liquidation provides for a *moratorium* (suspension of activity for a specified period of time) by stopping any action or proceedings from being started against the company without permission of the court.

Compulsory liquidation is commenced by the filing of a winding up petition to the court. Usually a creditor (or group of creditors) owed at least £750 presents a petition, although it can also be presented by the directors, the company itself, a shareholder, or an administrator or receiver. Directors may start a compulsory liquidation to avoid incurring liability for wrongful or fraudulent trading.

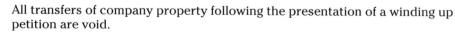

In practice, compulsory liquidation is the only insolvency procedure that a creditor can initiate regardless of the company's desires. In every other procedure, the company has to participate to some extent.

All transfers of company property following the presentation of a winding up petition are void.

The petitioner must demonstrate that the company is unable to pay its debts, which is assumed to be the case when one of the following applies:

- ✔ A judgement against the company remains unpaid.

- ✔ The value of the company's assets is less than the amount of its liabilities *(balance-sheet test)* – the court assesses the company's balance-sheet position.

✔ The company has failed to respond to a statutory demand (it has failed to pay a debt of at least £750 within 21 days of service of a demand; refer to Chapter 14 for more details and `http://www.gov.uk/statutory-demands/forms-to-issue-a-statutory-demand` for the form to fill in to make a statutory demand).

✔ The company is unable to pay debts as they fall due *(cash-flow test)*, which can be satisfied by the existence of an unsatisfied statutory demand.

Responding to a statutory demand

Receiving statutory demands can be scary. A company only has 21 days to respond to a statutory demand, and so immediate action is required when you receive one. Don't ignore it or fuss about other aspects of the company that you prefer to prioritise: 'Do not worry about your beard if you are about to lose your head'.

If you receive a statutory demand:

✔ Seek independent advice from an insolvency expert.

✔ Pay the due debt if you can, reduce it to less than £750 or set it off against a debt the creditor owes you, so that you come beneath the £750 threshold.

✔ Consider the following if you can't pay the debt:

- Emergency loan

- Invoice factoring or discounting (Chapter 14 has the info)

- Payment on any outstanding invoices

- Informal agreement with the creditor to pay the debt at an agreed future date

- Alternative procedure, such as a company voluntary arrangement or administration (see the sections 'Clearing up with a company voluntary arrangement' and 'Activating Administration', later in this chapter)

✔ Place the company into a creditors' voluntary liquidation if none of these options is viable, allowing the directors to retain control over the liquidation process (see the next section)

A further option is to challenge the validity of the debt – a winding up order can't be granted following service of a statutory demand unless two conditions are satisfied:

- The amount of the debt is at least £750.

- The debt isn't disputed. If a genuine dispute exists about whether the debt is due, the statutory demand can't lead to a winding up.

Facing a winding up petition or order

If you fail to deal with a statutory demand, or the company can't pay its debts for one of the reasons I set out earlier in this section, a winding up order can be granted against it. Now you face a real battle to survive.

A granted winding-up *petition* allows the court to liquidate the company and repay the creditors. This invariably leads to the making of a winding-up *order* against the company. If a petition is received or a company becomes aware that a creditor is about to issue such a petition, immediate action is required. Here's why:

- You have only *seven days* from the date the petition is *served* (given notice of) to try to avoid the petition being advertised in the Government's insolvency register, the *London Gazette*. This zany, fun-busting official publication of the Department for Business, Innovation and Skills (BIS) makes formal announcements concerning companies.

- Banks, debt collection agencies, Her Majesty's Revenue & Customs (HMRC) and other creditors monitor the daily *Gazette*. If a petition is advertised in it, the company's bank usually freezes the company account. You then require a *validation order* from the court to authorise the bank to release funds and that's normally only granted if you can show that the petition will be dismissed; in other words, that the company is solvent or is likely to reach agreement with its creditors to reschedule its debts.

- When the petition is on public record, other creditors of the company are likely to become aware of it. They may seek to support the petitioning creditor, or if the company pays the petitioning creditor they can *adopt* (take over) the petition with the court's consent.

- Continuing to trade from this point on is extremely difficult. The petition can also trigger breaches in the company's other banking and financial arrangements – certain contracts may contain termination/default clauses that are activated when a petition is presented against the company. In addition, the costs associated with dealing with such a petition at this stage are significant, because legal representation is required.

- After a petition is presented, the company can no longer place itself in voluntary liquidation.

When you're involved in a fight, Sun Tzu advises 'Move swift as the wind and closely formed as the wood. Attack like the fire and be still as the mountain.' If you can't manage that, here are some other tips for dealing with the presentation of winding-up petitions:

- ✔ Stopping a winding up-petition at the early stage is easier and less costly, ideally before the petition is advertised in the *Gazette*.

- ✔ Seek immediate advice from a licensed Insolvency Practitioner; these people have seen it all before and can provide you with reassurance as well as practical help.

- ✔ See whether you can negotiate an agreement to repay the debt to the creditor over time.

- ✔ Examine the possibility of a company voluntary arrangement or administration (see the later sections 'Clearing up with a company voluntary arrangement' and 'Activating Administration').

If the debt is disputed, notify the creditor that you'll seek an injunction to stop the presentation of the petition and seek costs for making that application. An injunction is granted *only* if you can show that the petitioner is abusing the court process; that is, the debt is disputed or unfair or your company has a genuine cross-claim or set off (for example, you're owed part of the debt by the creditor or are dissatisfied with goods/services it provided).

If a petition has been already been advertised, the only option is to seek an *adjournment* of the hearing; this could enable a settlement arrangement to be put in place or allow a decision to be made about the debt if it's disputed.

If the winding-up order has been granted, you have only three ways to reverse the order:

- ✔ **Rescind (cancel):** You can make an application to rescind the order if the court didn't have all the relevant facts when making the order. Your application must be made within seven days of the order.

- ✔ **Appeal:** You can appeal within four weeks of the order being made.

- ✔ **Stay (stop):** An application to stop liquidation proceedings can be made by the liquidator, the official receiver, a shareholder or creditor at any time after the order has been made.

Any of these actions has significant cost implications and no guarantee of success. If a creditor is persuaded to withdraw the petition, its legal costs and possibly interest and late payment charges may have to be paid. If a petition has been advertised, substantial damage to the commercial reputation of the company has already occurred.

Veering towards a voluntary liquidation

Voluntary liquidation is a slightly softer option than compulsory liquidation, but only insofar as a cricket ball landing on your head is softer than a brick.

Two types of voluntary liquidation exist, which start by the company passing a resolution at a meeting of members:

- ✔ **Members' voluntary liquidation (solvent liquidation):** The company's directors can make a statutory declaration of solvency.
- ✔ **Creditors' voluntary liquidation (insolvent liquidation):** No such declaration can be made.

In a creditors' voluntary liquidation or a compulsory liquidation, the liquidator is responsible for investigating the directors' conduct and prior transactions. This doesn't apply in a members' voluntary liquidation.

Minding a members' voluntary liquidation

Here are the key aspects of a members' voluntary liquidation:

- ✔ The majority of directors must swear a *statutory declaration of solvency*. This means that they've made a full inquiry into the affairs of the company and have concluded that it'll be able to pay its debts, together with interest, within 12 months of the declaration. The directors have to swear this declaration not more than five weeks before the shareholders meeting I mention in the next point.

- ✔ At a general meeting, the company passes a Special Resolution (by a 75 per cent majority) to wind up the company and appoint a liquidator who must be a licensed Insolvency Practitioner.

- ✔ A copy of the resolution must be delivered to the *London Gazette* within 14 days and to the Registrar of Companies within 15 days, together with the statutory declaration.

- ✔ The appointment of the liquidator must also be notified to the *Gazette* and to the Registrar within 14 days and advertised in a newspaper local to the business.

- ✔ The process requires no approval by creditors and no court involvement.

- ✔ The liquidation is solvent and so it generally results in all creditors being paid in full.

A company may consider a members' voluntary liquidation for various reasons, including the following:

✔ Key directors or shareholders want to retire.

✔ An unresolvable disagreement exists between shareholders and directors.

✔ A group of companies want to close a *dormant* (non-trading) company.

✔ Directors and shareholders want to end a solvent company, because it's a tax-efficient method of doing so. All distributions of income made to the shareholders are classed as distributions of capital rather than income and so are subject to the lower rate of Capital Gains Tax rather than income tax.

If, during the course of a members' voluntary liquidation, a liquidator forms the opinion that the company is unable to pay its debts in full, the liquidation can be converted to a creditors' voluntary liquidation.

Co-ordinating a creditors' voluntary liquidation

This kind of liquidation (which is normally less expensive than applying to the court for a compulsory liquidation) applies when a company is insolvent or the directors aren't willing to give a declaration of solvency. So if your company is having an out-of-money experience, it may be right for you. Here are the main features:

✔ The directors initiate this process by passing a resolution requiring meetings of the shareholders (members) and creditors for the purposes of placing the company into liquidation.

✔ The directors nominate a liquidator who must be a licensed Insolvency Practitioner.

✔ The directors must prepare a *statement of affairs* for review at the creditors meeting (and provide it to the liquidator when appointed).

✔ Shareholders must approve a resolution to wind up the company by a 75 per cent majority.

✔ The creditors' meeting must be held within 14 days of the shareholders resolution and at least 7 days' notice must be given to creditors. The meeting of creditors must be advertised in the *Gazette* and other ways that the directors think appropriate.

> ✔ At the creditors' meeting, the creditors by a majority can confirm the appointment of the liquidator appointed by the shareholders or nominate another of their own choosing.
>
> ✔ The liquidator's appointment must be notified to the *London Gazette* and to the Registrar within 14 days and (at the liquidator's discretion) may be advertised in a local newspaper.

Relying on Rescue Procedures

Wouldn't it be great if instead of dealing with the death of your company or LLP, you could rescue it when it runs into troubled waters? Well, options are available, and they're the subject of this section.

Warren Buffett knows a thing or two about money (he's apparently worth US$72 billion at the last count). He points out that 'Predicting rain doesn't count. Building Arks does.' Here are a few more hopeful tips for managing your financial difficulties in order to avoid the flood.

Your rescue vessel is most likely to be the process of a company voluntary arrangement or a scheme of arrangement (I discuss another option, administration, in its own section 'Activating Administration', later in this chapter). Fortunately, you don't have to share any of these rescue Arks with numerous pairs of animals getting up to all sorts.

Clearing up with a company voluntary arrangement

The process for implementing a company voluntary arrangement (CVA) is set out in the Insolvency Act, 1986. The *company voluntary arrangement* enables a company in financial difficulties to propose a restructuring scheme for (delayed) payment of (some or all) its debts to its creditors. The statute doesn't require the company to be insolvent.

Here are the CVA's main elements:

> ✔ The CVA can be used to avoid or supplement other insolvency procedures and the procedure must be supervised by a licensed Insolvency Practitioner.

✔ The CVA must be approved by more than 75 per cent in value of the company's creditors and more than 50 per cent in value of the company's shareholders. If approved, it binds all the unsecured creditors (whose interest isn't backed up by a charge).

In the event of a difference of decision between the creditors and the shareholders, the creditors' decision is decisive.

A CVA has a number of advantages:

✔ It's a flexible tool for restructuring the finances of a company that's in financial difficulties but remains viable as a business.

✔ It allows the directors to remain in control of the company and minimises disruption to the business.

✔ It's less expensive than other more formal insolvency procedures because of minimal court involvement and no statutory reporting requirements.

✔ The company isn't required to indicate on its documents that it's subject to a CVA procedure.

✔ The conduct of directors isn't investigated under this process.

✔ It's recognised under the EC Regulation on Insolvency Proceedings, 2000 and therefore can be used in cross-border situations (a revised version of the Regulations is due to come into effect in 2017).

✔ Creditors are likely to agree to a CVA proposal if it's fair, reasonable and provides a greater return than liquidation.

The following limitations apply to the CVA process:

✔ No proposal can alter the rights of secured or preferential creditors without their consent (see the later section 'Prioritising Creditors' for a definition of these creditors).

✔ A creditor can challenge the process in court within 28 days on grounds of unfair prejudice or material irregularity in the process.

Normally, no automatic *moratorium* exists (a period of time where creditors are prevented from taking action or invoking another insolvency procedure). However, an exception applies for a qualifying small company that meets two or more of the following criteria in its preceding financial year:

- Turnover of not more than £6.5 million

- Balance sheet not more than £3.26 million

- Not more than 50 employees

If this test is satisfied, a partial moratorium is available for 28 days (and can be extended for a further two months by shareholder consent). This gives the company some breathing space while it sorts itself out.

Sorting out with a scheme of arrangement

A *scheme of arrangement* is a settlement arrangement between a company and its creditors allowed under the Companies Act, 2006. Here are the main elements and advantages:

✔ Solvent and insolvent companies can use it – the former to reorganise a group of companies or for acquisitions, and the latter to restructure their debts, get a waiver of their debts (debt forgiveness) or enable them to swap debt for shares in their company.

✔ All classes of creditors affected must approve the scheme, with at least 75 per cent approval required (in value) from each class of the members or creditors who vote on the scheme, who must also be a majority in number in each class.

If this majority is reached, the court must approve this arrangement.

Although making every reasonable effort to give creditors notice of the scheme is necessary, an approved scheme binds all creditors even if they haven't received notice (useful when the location or views of some creditors is uncertain). It's also a key difference to a CVA, where creditors who don't receive notice may challenge an arrangement within 28 days on the grounds of unfair prejudice or material irregularity.

The following limitations apply to a scheme of arrangement:

✔ The process is more complicated, expensive and time-consuming than a CVA due to court applications and the need to hold meetings of various classes of shareholder.

✔ No moratorium is available under this arrangement, and so it doesn't stop other creditors applying for other remedies.

✔ Unlike a CVA, it isn't recognised under the EC Regulation on Insolvency Proceedings, 2000.

Activating Administration

Administration allows reorganisation of a company or LLP or the sale of a company's assets while it's under protection of a *statutory moratorium,* which protects the company or LLP from any creditor action during a specified period. This time gives the business respite from its creditors.

The Insolvency Act, 1986 introduced the concept of administration as a rescue procedure for companies that are, or are likely to become, insolvent. The Enterprise Act, 2002 revised and streamlined the process: a company or its directors can now appoint an administrator without involving the court.

Appointing an administrator

An administrator is appointed in one of three ways:

- ✔ **By court order:** A company, its directors or one or more creditors can apply to the court to appoint an administrator. The court does so only if satisfied that the company is, or is likely to become, unable to pay its debts and that the administration order is likely to achieve one of the three objectives I outline in the next section.

- ✔ **By the company or directors:** A company or its directors can appoint an administrator *without a court order,* as long as no history of administration exists within the previous 12 months.

- ✔ **By the holder of a qualifying floating charge (QFC):** The floating charge (refer to Chapter 4) must be over the whole or most of the company's property. A qualifying floating charge-holder must be given five business days' notice of any out-of-court appointment and can 'trump' this appointment by appointing its own administrator during this period. This administrator must act in the interests of *all creditors,* not only the floating charge-holder.

Understanding the objectives of administration

Whatever the entry route to administration, an administrator must be satisfied that one of the following three objectives can be achieved:

✔ Rescuing the company as a going concern

✔ If that isn't reasonably achievable, getting a better result for the company's creditors as a whole than would be likely if the company were wound up (without first being in administration)

✔ If that isn't reasonably achievable, disposing of property in order to make a distribution to one or more secured or preferential creditors (which I define later in 'Prioritising Creditors')

Working with an administrator

Here are the important points about the administrator:

✔ The administrator must be a licensed Insolvency Practitioner.

✔ The administrator owes her duties to the company and the creditors.

✔ The administrator takes over management and control of the company and its directors must provide her with a statement of affairs.

✔ The administrator must then (within eight weeks) prepare proposals for managing the affairs of the company for approval by the creditors (who must be given two weeks' notice of the proposals and meet within ten weeks of the company entering administration).

✔ The administrator must send regular progress reports to the creditors, the court and Registrar of Companies every six months until the administration ends (including details of receipts and payments).

✔ The administrator's appointment automatically ends after 12 months unless extended by the court or with approval of the creditors. Under the Small Business and Enterprise Act, 2015, however, an administrator's term can be extended for up to a year by consent without the need for a court application.

✔ The administrator has the power to bring wrongful or fraudulent trading claims against directors (until 2015, only liquidators had this capacity).

Balancing the pros and cons of administration

No doubt you're wondering about the advantages of administration:

✔ Directors can appoint an administrator without having to go to court.

✔ It's preferable to liquidation if the company has a prospect of recovery.

- A moratorium exists on creditors' actions as soon as a company is placed into administration, and so they're prevented from trying to place the company into liquidation.

- No one can take legal proceedings against the company while it's in administration.

- The company avoids being wound up and can continue as a going concern.

- An appointed administrator takes over the management of the company, relieving the directors of taking critical decisions and so minimising any risk of liability for them from that point.

With anything, of course, disadvantages always accompany advantages:

- High costs due to the frequency and depth of reporting required of the administrator.

- Directors' management powers usually cease when an administrator is appointed – they can exercise only managerial functions with the express consent of the administrator.

- Administration is a public event. The appointment must be advertised in the *London Gazette* and all company documentation must include 'in administration' after the company name, and so it's not great if you're trying to keep your financial plight quiet.

- Administration can be a lengthy process and is often extended beyond its initial one-year period (see 'Working with an administrator' earlier in this chapter).

- The administrator often sells company assets, and so it may not 'emerge' from administration and get back on an even keel.

Concluding an administration

The exit from administration depends on the objective sought at the outset. Generally, administration results in one of the following:

- The company trades its way out of its difficult position. Hooray!

- The administrator sells the company's assets and distributes the proceeds to creditors and shareholders (see the later section 'Prioritising Creditors' for the order of creditor priority).

- A scheme of arrangement or CVA is put in place.

- Liquidation and the dissolution of the company. Boo!

Being prepared: Pre-packaged administrations

With a *pre-packaged* (pre-pack) administration, a company is put into administration and its business and assets sold under an arrangement agreed *before* the administrator is appointed. It usually results in the former company's liabilities being left behind so that the creditors don't get paid. The following advantages exist to this kind of administration:

- ✔ It can limit the destructive effect of an insolvency procedure.
- ✔ It's generally a speedy process.

Pre-packs have their critics too, for the following reasons:

- ✔ Pre-packs aren't provided for insolvency legislation.
- ✔ The sale may not put the interests of creditors first.
- ✔ Companies may be sold back to the original owners and suspicion sometimes arises that the sale occurs to allow *asset stripping* (that is, selling off key assets of the company regardless of its future well-being) and avoidance of company debts. Naughty, naughty.
- ✔ The company (or *newco*) may gain an unfair market advantage, because it's allowed to leave its unwanted debts behind.

For the government's response to such criticisms, see the nearby sidebar 'Tightening up on pre-packs'.

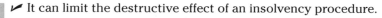
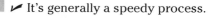
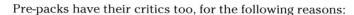

Tightening up on pre-packs

In 2009, the government published new guidelines on pre-packs through its Insolvency Service: administrators now require a *Statement of Insolvency Practice* (SIP 16) on pre-pack sales. Under SIP 16, an administrator must provide creditors with background information on the purchaser, which assures them that the sale is being made in good faith.

These requirements encourage the administrator to inform the creditors as soon as possible after the appointment. In addition, failure to comply by an administrator can result in regulatory or disciplinary action, and directors who misuse the administration process to disadvantage creditors or for personal gain can be subject to disqualification proceedings and compensation orders under the Small Business Enterprise and Employment Act, 2015.

If you go for a pre-pack, be careful if you intend to reuse the company name or a similar name to that of the liquidated company without gaining court approval. The Insolvency Act, 1986 prohibits such use except in limited circumstances. Any person in contravention can be held personally liable for the relevant debts of the new company.

Prioritising Creditors

Creditors are repaid in a descending order dependent upon the funds available when a company or LLP is placed into administration or liquidation (as I describe in the earlier sections 'Activating Administration' and 'Lining Up a Liquidation', respectively). The administrator or liquidator is under a duty to make such distributions in accordance with this *statutory* order of priority (for definitions of fixed and floating charges, pop over to Chapter 4):

- ✔ **Secured fixed charge creditors:** These top-of-the-heap creditors have a charge over specific assets owned by the company and are entitled to receive the proceeds of sale of the assets in priority to any other class of creditor (minus the costs of realising the assets). If more than one such creditor exists, the date the charge was registered at Companies House applies, with the charge registered earliest ranking first in priority.

- ✔ **Expenses of the liquidation/administration:** Next come the liquidators' fees and expenses, which have priority over preferential creditors and floating charge-holders.

- ✔ **Preferential creditors' claims:** In third place and in bronze medal position come preferential creditors – usually employees who can recover limited amounts relating to the four months prior to liquidation (capped at £800 per employee), outstanding holiday pay and outstanding contributions to pension schemes.

- ✔ **Prescribed part:** An amount the administrator or liquidator must set aside for unsecured creditors. It's calculated as a proportion of the amount of assets, which are subject to any floating charge.

- ✔ **Proceeds of floating charge assets:** Fifth in priority, these proceeds go to floating charge-holders.

- ✔ **Unsecured creditors' claims:** Unsecured creditors don't have a security interest in the debtor's assets and such creditors normally rank *pari passu* (equally) unless they're subject to a binding subordination agreement (which gives priority to current claims over those made at a later date). Unsecured creditors include anybody else who's owed monies by the company, including trade creditors, utilities, council tax, HMRC (for PAYE/National Insurance contributions, Value-Added Tax [VAT] or corporation tax) and loans to directors that aren't secured.

✔ **Shareholders:** Any surplus left after that little lot is paid out to shareholders in accordance with the company's Articles of Association.

Banking against Bankruptcy

This chapter's preceding sections concern insolvency in companies and LLPs, but you also need to consider the uncomfortable subject of personal insolvency: *bankruptcy*. This possibility can become relevant to you if you guarantee any of your company's debts, you're a sole trader or you're a partner in one of the old-style General Partnerships I look at in Chapter 1 (as opposed to one of the LLPs). The primary legislation governing personal bankruptcy is in the Insolvency Act, 1986.

Here I describe the three ways in which a person can be made bankrupt and the available resolutions.

Courting bankruptcy

Here's what happens if you ask the court to declare you bankrupt:

✔ You have to pay a court fee of £180 and a deposit of £525 towards the cost of administering the bankruptcy.

✔ You have to complete court forms detailing all assets and liabilities.

✔ The court may decide that a Debt Relief Order is more appropriate (see the later 'Relieving bankruptcy' section).

✔ Alternatively, an Insolvency Practitioner may be appointed if an Individual Voluntary Arrangement (IVA) is more suitable (if assets are above £4,000 and debts are below £40,000). Check out the later section 'Defaulting your way into bankruptcy' for more on IVAs.

✔ If the court declares you bankrupt, the Official Receiver or an Insolvency Practitioner acting as a *trustee in bankruptcy* takes ownership of all your assets (including your house), which are then sold and distributed to creditors. You can keep only those assets necessary for your basic needs and employment. In addition, you may have to continue to make payments from future income to creditors for up to three years.

✔ After 12 months you're normally *discharged* from bankruptcy, and any remaining debts you have are 'written off' with a few exceptions (criminal fines, matrimonial orders and of course that absolute essential . . . your TV licence fee).

✔ You don't have to pay any further income to people other than income orders agreed during your bankruptcy.

✔ Unsold assets aren't returned to you at this stage – they remain in your *bankruptcy estate*, though your house may be returned if not sold within three years of your bankruptcy.

Apart from the practical financial difficulties and embarrassment, some further disadvantages exist to being made bankrupt:

✔ During the bankruptcy, you can't borrow more than £500 without disclosing your bankruptcy.

✔ If self-employed, you can't promote, form or manage a limited company without court permission.

✔ You can't trade in any business under any other name unless all persons concerned with the bankruptcy are informed.

✔ Your bankruptcy remains on your credit file for six years from the date of the bankruptcy.

✔ The Individual Insolvency Register lists all current bankruptcies and those discharged from bankruptcy in the last three months.

If a person declared bankrupt has behaved culpably, recklessly or fraudulently, the court can impose a Bankruptcy Restrictions Order (BRO) (for example, if you concealed assets or continued to borrow with no prospect of repayment). The BRO can last from 2 to 15 years and you can't act as a company director, trade under a different name or borrow in excess of £500 during that period.

Demanding bankruptcy

You can be made bankrupt if a creditor or group of creditors owed more than £5,000 personally serve a statutory demand on you. The process and the ways of dealing with it are similar to those I outline for a company or LLP earlier in this chapter in 'Responding to a statutory demand'.

Defaulting your way into bankruptcy

If you enter into an Individual Voluntary Arrangement (IVA) and then breach it, the Insolvency Practitioner can apply to the court for a declaration of bankruptcy against you:

- ✔ An IVA involves a formal proposal to creditors in respect of your debt, which an Insolvency Practitioner must draft.

- ✔ A majority of the creditors totalling more than 75 per cent (in value) of those voting must vote in favour of the proposal. If they do, the IVA normally lasts up to five or even six years and you must adhere to it during that period.

Although it removes the immediate threat of bankruptcy, an IVA does have some disadvantages:

- ✔ The IVA appears on the public Individual Insolvency Register and remains on file for six years.

- ✔ Your credit rating is affected during this period.

- ✔ Creditor approval is required for an IVA (unlike going into bankruptcy) and the IVA can't be altered without creditors' agreement.

- ✔ If you have equity in your home, you may be asked to remortgage it in order to release further funds for the IVA.

- ✔ The IVA lasts longer than bankruptcy (which is normally over after a year).

- ✔ Any subsequent debts aren't included and must be paid.

Despite these issues, an IVA can be a better alternative than bankruptcy:

- ✔ All creditors are bound by the agreement.

- ✔ It's more flexible in nature than bankruptcy – for example, you may be able to negotiate payment breaks with your creditors.

- ✔ You have a bit more control, because influencing the Insolvency Practitioner may be easier than influencing the court-appointed trustee in bankruptcy.

- ✔ You avoid the rather scary process of bankruptcy.

- ✔ You may keep your home if all creditors agree, whereas in bankruptcy it goes to the trustee, who tries to sell it.

Whether you go bankrupt or enter into an IVA, any *secured debts* (with a charge) aren't covered by the process and you still owe them.

Relieving bankruptcy

You can obtain relief from your creditors by applying to the Official Receiver for a year-long Debt Relief Order (DRO; see `https://www.gov.uk/government/publications/debt-relief-orders`) in the following circumstances:

- A DRO is suitable only if you have few assets and a relatively low level of liabilities.
- You must owe less than £20,000 and have less than £1,000 in assets (not including your car if it's worth less than £1,000).
- The remedy isn't available for home owners (even if your property is in negative equity).
- You must have disposable income of no more than £50 per month (after living expenses).
- You must live in England, Wales or Northern Ireland or have been resident or carried on business there at any time in the last three years.
- A DRO isn't available if you're involved in any other formal insolvency procedure.
- Certain debts are excluded: student loans, child maintenance arrears, TV licence arrears (why is it so important?), criminal fines and damages for personal injury ordered by a court.

Here are the disadvantages of DROs:

- Getting a DRO appears on the public Individual Insolvency Register.
- A DRO affects your credit rating and remains on file for six years.
- If you seek credit above £500 during a DRO, the lender must be informed of the DRO.
- During the course of the DRO you can't act as a company director.
- You can't create, manage or promote a limited company without the court's permission.

✔ You can't manage a business without informing those who you trade with of the DRO.

✔ If you haven't given an honest account of your financial affairs before or during the DRO, A Debt Relief Restriction Order (DRRO) for between 2 and 15 years can be enforced against you.

The DRO process has these advantages:

✔ Involves lower costs as an alternative to bankruptcy (£90 fee).

✔ Doesn't involve a court appearance.

✔ Avoids creditors pursuing debts or interest on those debts during the 12-month period, and at the end of that period if your financial circumstances haven't changed your debts are written off. Yippee!

Consult only licensed Insolvency Practitioners, those regulated by the Insolvency Service and who subscribe to the 'Insolvency Ethical Code', when seeking debt advice (at `http://www.nidirect.gov.uk/the-insolvency-practitioner-directory`).

Part V
Exiting Successfully – Legal Secrets

Top Five Tips for Selling Your Business

- ✔ **Choose the right buyer:** Is this a trade sale, a sale to a player who wants to get into your sector or a sale to a private equity institution?

- ✔ **Talk to at least two interested parties at the same time:** Doing so keeps a little bit of fear in the deal for potential buyers and stops them dragging their heels or messing you around on price.

- ✔ **Prepare thoroughly for due diligence:** Make sure that you have no holes in your business boat.

- ✔ **Understand different methods of valuing your business:** You don't want anyone pulling the wool over your eyes as to what it's worth.

- ✔ **Get out as cleanly as you can:** Keep earn-out periods and warranties to a minimum.

Try your hand at the quiz in the online article to test your expertise at raising institutional finance: www.dummies.com/extras/lawforsmallbusinessuk.

In this part . . .

- ✔ View the options available for growing your business skywards.
- ✔ Understand the agreements and pitfalls of joint ventures.
- ✔ Pick the right investor and get your business match-fit.
- ✔ Acquire other companies like a seasoned business mogul.
- ✔ Get the best deal when selling your business.

Chapter 17

Lifting-Off to Further Business Goals

. . . .

In This Chapter

▶ Entering joint ventures

▶ Acquiring new investment

▶ Purchasing other companies

. . . .

*W*hen your business reaches a certain level of maturity and you've been running it for several years, your hope is to have a successful undertaking with a solid trading history. Your turnover is increasing and your brand is acquiring a reputation. You've reached a break-even point and net profits are growing.

Such a profile doesn't go unnoticed, however, and your business may start attracting interest from third parties. If so, the time has come for you to think about the various ways in which you can build on your strong start and take your business to the next stage. You've been hanging around in football's lower divisions long enough – now you want promotion to the Premier League or to win the FA Cup (or at least the Johnstone's Paint Trophy). (Apologies if football isn't your thing, but this chapter is about achieving goals!)

Here I set out your options: joint venturing with other businesses, obtaining more investment, acquiring or merging with other firms, being bought-out or even listing on the Alternative Investment Market (now that's something to *AIM* for – sorry!).

Jumping High with Joint Ventures

A *joint venture* (JV) isn't a legal term and has no formal status under the law (as a limited company or a partnership does). It's simply a commercial arrangement that two distinct economic entities enter into as a specific business undertaking.

Passing on the pros and cons of joint ventures

Working with another business allows you to complement your own firm's strengths and bridge any gaps to help fulfil your goals. Unlike when raising investment, you don't have to give up ownership or control of your business or give away (further) shares in your company. You don't have to put a new director on your board or be restricted from taking decisions (over which an investor may negotiate a right of veto).

More specifically, you may want to enter into a JV arrangement for the following reasons:

✔ **Natural operational efficiencies *(synergies)* exist between you and another business:** For example, your firm manufactures certain products while another provides expert services in relation to products of the same kind. By working with the other business and creating deals combining the two offerings, you potentially attract more customers.

This increased customer base allows you to cut margins on both sides of the business, making you more competitive while leading to an overall increase in operating profits. Imagine your football team playing a big strong striker and you bring in a smaller, mobile one – they're more effective working off each other than operating on their own for different clubs.

✔ **To target other markets:** Perhaps you want to sell your product or services in other markets, nationally or abroad, but don't have the resources to do so. By teaming up with a partner already operating in that market, you have access to a ready-made resource and can make use of its experience and expertise to develop in that new locality.

✔ **Two heads are better than one:** Not always of course – two similar players on the pitch can get in each other's way. But when they work collaboratively, they have double the know-how and experience to apply to any problem . . . 'You'll Neeeeeever Walk Alone'.

✔ **Reduce competition:** 'If you can't beat 'em, join 'em'. Powerful reasons can exist for working with another business rather than competing against it. (This is different from the old Leeds United adage of, 'if you can't beat 'em, kick 'em'.)

✔ **Cost and resource:** Sometimes, you simply don't have the resources in place to achieve the kind of growth that you're targeting without having a partner to share the load.

Joint ventures have disadvantages too and often fail because:

✔ The two partners aren't aligned in their aims or values.

✔ One partner puts more into the JV than the other and it becomes unbalanced.

✔ Operational disagreements between the partners paralyse the business. If some members of a football team are playing one formation and the rest insist on playing a different formation at the same time, that team isn't going to win many matches.

Forming joint ventures

Joint ventures can take a number of forms, ranging from a simple contractual agreement to work together to the establishment of a new limited company structure in which both parties invest and to which they transfer existing business assets. In between these extremes, partnerships can provide some level of integration without the organisational rigidity of a limited company.

Whatever structure you decide on, you need to consider the following issues in a *Joint Venture Agreement* (that is, a written agreement that sets up and regulates the way that the JV runs):

✔ **Object of the JV:** Be clear on your aims and objectives for entering into the venture. Clearly define the nature and scope of the business activity to be carried out, whether that's in a *Shareholder Agreement* (if you're setting up a JV limited company) or a simple *Co-operation Agreement* (if your JV is just a collaborative operational agreement between your enterprise and another).

✔ **Obligations and responsibilities:** Key to a productive relationship. Both parties have to understand their roles in the JV and what's expected of them. Who's doing the marketing? Who's doing the selling? Who's responsible for running the finances of the JV?

A JV Agreement also sets up details of the management of the new business (for example, whether the JV has a limited company structure, powers of each party to elect people to the board). If the business is to have its own executives (seconded from the partners or hired-in), you need to complete service agreements for them.

✔ **Investment:** In addition to the taking of shares in a JV company (if a limited company structure is chosen), the partners have to decide whether any assets are to be transferred to the JV, such as intellectual property, software or a database. These transfers have to be put in place with appropriate documents (for example, licences from the applicable partner into the JV).

✔ **Profit and liability sharing:** How are profits and losses between the partners to be divided – equally or more in favour of one partner than the other?

  Agree whether and to what extent one partner can act on behalf of the other in incurring costs on behalf of the JV, to avoid confusion on this issue.

Dealing with deadlock

Often a JV is a 50:50 venture where both participants take equal shareholdings in the JV limited company and have equal representation on its board of directors. But the competing interests of the participants can cause 50:50 tackles in relation to decision-making. Here are some ways to resolve this problem without anybody getting hurt:

  ✔ At board level, you can give the chairman of the Board meeting an additional deciding vote by contract or under the Articles of Association of the JV company. Although this alone would provide an unfair advantage to the chairperson's participant business, you can rotate chairmanship of Board meetings between the two parties.

  ✔ An independent party can be elected as a non-executive director to avoid any deadlock, though finding a person acceptable to both parties may be hard.

  ✔ For shareholder deadlock, you can appoint an expert to help resolve certain issues on which the parties have difficulty agreeing.

  ✔ Agree an escalation procedure in which disagreements are referred up the chain until they reach the desk of the chairperson or chief executive of each partner. The threat of referring matters to the highest echelons can focus the minds of those in disagreement and provide the necessary impetus to find a breakthrough.

Terminating and getting out

The ultimate possibility in the case of deadlock (refer to the preceding section) is to terminate the JV. In a Co-operation Agreement, you can include standard termination provisions (termination by notice, for material breach, insolvency and so on). For a JV limited company, termination is dealt with in a Shareholder Agreement; the partners can agree in the JV Agreement that termination can be implemented by the winding up of the JV company.

If you're winding up a JV company, you need to decide what happens to any assets in the business. Are they simply transferred back to the partner that sold or brought them into the JV? If so, at what price?

One side wants to leave

Where only *one* JV participant wants to exit the JV, the partners have to consider provisions relating to the sale of the departing partner's interest or shares to the other partner. If the JV is a company, the remaining JV participant almost certainly wants to have the first right to purchase the exiting partner's shares, and a procedure may exist for that to happen. In any event, the JV Agreement may contain restrictions that prevent a participant from selling its shares to a competitor of the JV. You need to include a method of valuing the interests of the exiting partner in the JV Agreement.

To cater for one JV participant wanting to sell the JV when the other doesn't, you can include a clause saying that if you want to sell and you get a genuine offer you can 'drag' the other partner with you and make it sell at the same price (though such a clause can also be used against you).

Both partners want out

Sometimes, both participants want the JV to end but both are potentially interested in carrying on the business of the JV without the other (as opposed to winding it up). Various methods exist of breaking this deadlock by requiring one partner to sell its interest to the other. I take a look at two here that apply to a limited company JV. They have the exotic names 'Russian roulette' and 'Mexican shoot-out' to make them sound enticing, though they have nothing to do with making decisions with guns. Shame, really – it would liven up the negotiations no end.

In a *Russian roulette* scenario, one partner of the JV can serve notice on the other in which it takes one of the two following options:

- ✔ Requires the other partner to *purchase* all its own shares in the JV company at the price quoted in the notice.
- ✔ Requires the other partner to *sell* all its shares in the JV company to it, again at the price in the notice.

The other partner can then accept the offer (whether buying or selling all the shares) or decline the offer, in which case the offer is automatically reversed. If declined, the partner who initiated the offer now has to decide whether it wants to buy or be bought.

The point of this exit arrangement is that it forces the vendor or purchaser initiating it to fix a fair price for the shares. The possibility of the positions being reversed means that: setting too high a sale price for its own shares would cause it to overpay to purchase the other partner's shares (when the positions are reversed); and setting too low a purchase price for the other partner's shares causes it to be short-changed (when the positions are reversed and it has to sell its own shares instead).

A *Mexican shoot-out* (also known as a *Texan shoot-out*) is a variation on the Russian roulette exit method. Again, one partner serves notice on the other, this time offering to buy the shares of the other JV party (but not to sell them) at a set price quoted in the notice. The other partner can accept the purchase offer or, alternatively, it can offer to buy the shares of the partner serving the notice of purchase but at a higher price.

The partner that served the original notice can accept this new offer or buy the other partner out at the higher price now proposed. Alternatively, the partners can then enter into a system of sealed bids and the highest bidder wins (gets the right to buy the shares of the other partner).

If you aren't confused by that, consider using your remarkable superhero powers as 'Never Confused Man' or 'Clear Thinking Woman'. It may be a nice additional revenue stream for your company.

Aiming High by Acquiring New Investment

At some point you may need to think about growing your business through further investment, perhaps to finance additional salespeople, management, manufacturing facilities, IT development, international expansion or product diversification.

At different stages of your company's business development, you can have different funding rounds:

- **Seed funding:** Normally covers up to the first £1 million of funding (dribble your way to Chapter 3 for details).
- **Series A funding:** Covers the next £1 million to £10 million (follow a long ball to Chapter 4 for more).
- **Series B funding:** For £10 million and more (Chapter 4 again).

You can go on to Series C funding and beyond if you're really pushing for promotion.

Funding growth with institutional investors

You can go for series A funding as you begin your upward business growth path or you can wait until your business growth is truly underway. Either way, you're going to need more money than is likely to be available from seed investors.

If you were a football club, you'd look around for a wealthy overseas entrepreneur, preferably with a dodgy past or ideally a criminal record, and get the person to invest millions in your business. For most businesses that isn't an option, which is where institutional players such as private equity or venture capital funds arrive on the scene.

Private equity

Private equity refers to investment in shares that are not publicly traded, and so, basically, it covers all private companies (limited by shares). Private equity firms are run by experts in corporate finance whose purpose is to seek out investment opportunities that have the potential to realise large profits. They set up funds, which are structured as limited partnerships, and then find other organisations to invest money into the fund, which is then used to invest in companies.

The private equity firm is the *general partner* of the fund and its job is to manage the fund and make all the investment decisions. The investors – mostly pension funds, insurance companies and banks, together with some corporates and wealthy individuals – are *limited partners*. Their job is to put up the money.

In general, private equity firms:

- ✔ Invest in established enterprises that aren't performing to their potential and restructure them to optimise their performance and investor returns
- ✔ Focus their investment in a single undertaking at a time, often through an outright purchase
- ✔ Often invest through a mixture of shares and loans

Venture capital

Venture capitalists are a specialist form of private equity fund. They

- ✔ Invest in early-stage companies showing high-growth and/or significant potential returns on investment
- ✔ Are associated with highly innovative companies in the technology sphere
- ✔ Are characterised by their high-risk investments
- ✔ Tend to spread that risk across multiple investments
- ✔ Invest normally only through shares (equity) rather than through loans

Preparing for institutional investment

You can choose from a large number of private equity and venture capital firms.

Asking the right questions

Here are some factors to consider when appraising firms to deal with:

- ✔ Is the industry (or industries) in which the firm specialises a match with yours?
- ✔ Do the amounts of money that the firm usually invests in businesses align with your investment requirements?
- ✔ What about geographical focus? Does the firm invest in local businesses, those operating internationally or in certain developing markets?
- ✔ How long has the firm been going?
- ✔ Can you find any financial information on the businesses in which the firm has invested?
- ✔ For what period does the firm generally invest in businesses? Is it likely to want to stay involved for as long as you want to or is its track record one of quick sales? It's more likely to be interested in making a quick profit than the long-term potential of your business (which is your priority).

- ✔ Do you have any contacts in the firm? You can just send in your business plan and hope for the best, but you're far more likely to get its attention if you know somebody at the firm or are introduced by someone who does.
- ✔ How many funds does the firm operate?
- ✔ How much experience does it have of investing in this particular market?
- ✔ How are its investments performing?

- ✔ How many founders of companies in which the private equity firm has invested are still at those companies? This concern is important, because institutional investors can get involved and then rather ruthlessly remove the founder (you!).

Assembling a crack squad

Having researched your potential investment targets, you engage with them in a similar way to when approaching angels (as I describe in Chapter 3), including getting a confidentiality agreement in place, submitting your business plan narrative and numbers, and pitching your business.

Be prepared for a stiffer challenge though. These firms are tough and have no problem with committing the intellectual equivalent of professional fouls and two-footed challenges if it suits them.

If you're going to deal with institutional investors successfully, you need the right kind of advisors around you:

- **Non-executive directors (refer to Chapter 5):** With experience of dealing with institutional investment and possibly a network of contacts in that field.

- **External financial advisers:** To get your past financial records and future forecasts 'match fit' for the scrutiny they have to go through.

- **External lawyers:** To ensure that your corporate records are tickety-boo.

- **(Probably) a corporate finance advisor:** To help you structure your offering and gain introductions to institutional investors. Don't underestimate their expertise in modelling businesses and 'selling' to the private equity firm the investment opportunity your business represents. They also know how to combat institutions' dirty play.

Corporate finance advisors don't come cheap, and so check their terms:

- **They may want a retainer per month:** Can get very expensive – avoid or cap it if you can.

- **They may want a percentage of the amount you raise:** Up to 5 per cent is normal. Sometimes, however, they ask for this percentage even if you find the money from a different source that they have nothing to do with – cheeky, huh? Yellow Card! They may also seek that percentage if the investment money is found by you for up to a year after their engagement ceases (arguing that their efforts made you investable). Red Card!

- **They may want shares in your business:** Be very careful about agreeing. You have to give shares to the institutional investors when they invest, and they drive a hard bargain. You don't want to have to give away more shares than you must to anybody else and run the risk of feeling as sick as a gang gang cockatoo or a peach-faced lovebird (okay, sick as a parrot then).

Agreeing a term sheet with institutional investors

Following initial discussions, if a private equity fund or venture capitalist wants to invest in your business, it draws up a document that sets out the key terms of the investment. This *term sheet* (or *heads of terms*) isn't usually legally binding except for some specific terms – such as ones relating to confidentiality and exclusivity (and sometimes costs).

The point of the term sheet is to summarise the principal terms of the future agreement so that both parties are clear about the basis on which they're proceeding. Although not a legally binding agreement (it doesn't carry the force of law), the term sheet is an agreement in principle and an important and significant step on the way to concluding a full agreement.

The term sheet must therefore be completed carefully and ideally drafted by lawyers. Typical terms of a term sheet include the following:

- **Details of the investment:** Covers the amount of capital to be provided from the institutional fund and details of the equity (shares) to be given in return for that capital injection: how many shares, type of shares, when the money will be made available to the business, whether it will be provided all at once or in two or more slices (called *tranches*).

- **Conditions precedent:** Conditions that have to be fulfilled before any legal agreement can come into force. Examples include:

  - Satisfactory results of due diligence (the investor doesn't want to receive a 'hospital pass' from you).

  - Agreements are in place for additional funding from third parties (for example, a bank loan).

  - All necessary internal and regulatory approvals have been secured.

- **Terms of the investment relationship:** Includes information in relation to the following:

  - Appointment by the institutional investor of directors to the board of your business.

  - Signing of new service agreements (employment contracts) by members of the management team.

  - Payment to the institutional investor for its advisory services (yep, you probably have to pay it to do its job).

- **Details of warranties and indemnities:** Provided by your business and the current management/founders to the investor (not an exhaustive list at this stage). Chapter 18 has more on warranties.

- **Exclusivity or 'lock-out':** You can't approach other firms or individuals with a view to securing investment of any kind during the period between the signing of the term sheet and either the conclusion of a legal agreement between the parties or the lapse of this period. So you can't sell the investor a dummy and then talk to someone else.

- **Confidentiality:** This obligation covers any matters arising out of the proposed investment, including the existence of the term sheet.

Types of shares investors may want

The most common type of share that an investor in your company may want to acquire, apart from an ordinary share (see Chapter 4 for a definition), is a preference share. A *preference share* normally carries a preferential right to a fixed annual dividend (or payment), which is usually expressed as a percentage of the nominal (or *par*) value of the share. For example, a 10 per cent preference share, whose nominal value is £1, attracts an automatic dividend payment of 10 pence each year to its owner on all distributable profits of the company – no more and no less. Preferential dividends are usually *cumulative:* in the event of insufficient profits to pay the dividend in one year, the dividend rolls over to the following year (and so on) until you get all your Christmases at once and it can be paid. The dividend is paid ahead of any dividends paid to any holders of ordinary shares (as are the proceeds available for distribution on a winding up – see Chapter 16) and preference shares are usually not accompanied by a right to vote.

Other types of share to look out for in the term sheet are *convertible shares,* which come with a right to convert from one share class to another, on a fixed date or at the option of the shareholder. For example, a preference shareholder may insist that its preference shares are convertible into ordinary shares if the company starts doing well and the shareholder thinks that it'll get a higher dividend from ordinary shares than from the 'fixed' dividend payable for its preference shares.

Redeemable shares are capable of being bought back on the basis of a pre-agreed price formula and on a particular date by either the company or at the option of the shareholder. The latter can be great for an investor (who's assured of getting its money back at a certain date) but may end up being of concern for you: your company may have to find the proceeds to repay the investor on the date when the investor is allowed to require the repayment.

Stepping Up through Acquisition

You may decide that the best way for your business to grow is to acquire another company lock, stock and barrel. This way you can take advantage of having another ready-made operation with all its resources and expertise without the hassle of working with a partner in a JV (refer to the earlier 'Jumping High with Joint Ventures' section). At the click of your fingers you get new channels to market and new customers, as well as the opportunity to save costs and maximise revenues by sharing functionalities (say, IT or sales). Think of it as dipping into the transfer market to bolster your team with a strategic purchase – a flying winger, a stopper centre half, a box-to-box midfielder or whatever you lack.

Any business that naturally complements yours doesn't just generate its own income (as before your acquisition). The pooled resources and leveraged strengths of your current operations result in the new combination of businesses achieving greater success than the sum of its parts. You can share intellectual property and know-how, 'rationalise' staffing (that's jargon for letting people go) and achieve further savings to other assets, such as plant and machinery, and business premises. It sounds great – you shoot, you score!

Thinking through buying another business

Although acquiring another business is certainly an attractive proposition in theory, it's a large undertaking with built-in headaches:

- ✔ You may need to raise institutional finance so that you can afford your target firm (refer to the earlier section 'Aiming High by Acquiring New Investment').

- ✔ Individuals in the enterprise you acquire will be used to working in a particular environment, following the culture or systems of the target business. If that culture is a strong one, they can have great difficulty adjusting to working life in your business – culture clash and dressing room unrest often follows.

   Overlooking the well-being of employees in acquisitions can have disastrous consequences for the purchaser. When you invest in a business, you're investing in its people, and if they aren't happy they may not hang around to help you drive the growth you were expecting.

- ✔ At board level, disagreement between the new and old guards can make reaching agreement on matters a lengthy, frustrating experience.

The whole acquisition process is relatively lengthy, like a slow-motion replay of an entire football game. It takes up a significant amount of time and energy and can prove a large distraction for your business, placing a greater burden on you and your management team. You have to make sure that your players keep their eye on the ball as well as cope with the competing demand of looking into the acquisition process.

Pursuing acquisition

An acquisition can take place in two main ways, and you need to decide which one is right for you:

 ✔ **Share purchase:** You acquire the target business's shares. A share purchase is often cleaner for the seller, because of the clean break.

 ✔ **Asset (or business) purchase:** You purchase the business itself (comprising a collection of assets) as a going concern.

Share purchase

The acquired company itself doesn't change in any way, only its ownership (via the share transfer) alters. The firm continues its business operation as before, trading as the same entity with its customers and suppliers. From an ongoing administrative perspective, therefore, much less change is required than in the case of an asset purchase.

The problem of a share purchase for you as a buyer is that you're stuck with all liabilities and obligations of the acquired company. This includes any debts the acquired company owes to third parties under agreements it made, as well as unprofitable agreements into which it had entered. You need to watch out for this risk.

Asset purchase

The collection of assets the target company sells moves to the purchasing company: plant and machinery, intellectual property rights, premises, receivable cash from customer contracts, 'goodwill' (reputation) in the business and any other asset that you're proposing to buy.

The main advantage of an asset purchase is that you can choose what assets to take on. Being able to 'cherry-pick' means that you can leave behind any of the target company's liabilities and undesirable assets.

You have to alter all contracts with third parties, however, because they're now contracting with an entirely new company (yours). You need to give notice to all such parties and, depending on the complexity, a formal transfer of contracts to your company has to occur. Also, transferring employees after a sale of business assets isn't straightforward (I deal with this aspect in Chapter 18).

Reaching for the Sky: Listing on AIM

You may decide to grow your business by seeking the benefits of being a public company, such as additional investment and liquidity. Obtaining a listing on the main market of the London Stock Exchange (LSE) is difficult, however, because of rigorous entry requirements (for example, 25 per cent of the shares must be in public hands and your company must be worth [currently] a minimum of £700,000).

So in 1995 the LSE set up the Alternative Investment Market (AIM), which significantly lowers the barriers to entry on a regulated exchange. For example, AIM has no lower limit on the number of shares in public hands, no minimum valuation requirement and no minimum period for which the company must have been trading. Therefore, AIM allows people to invest, and trade shares, in smaller businesses, passing on the benefits to the smaller companies and helping them to raise their profile.

Requesting a transfer to AIM

In order to be admitted to AIM, a company still has to meet a defined set of eligibility requirements. You can't go from playing in the Vanarama National League to playing at Wembley without having to make some adjustments to your playing style.

These requirements, together with all continuing requirements of AIM-listed companies, are set out in the 'AIM Rules for Companies' (http://www.londonstockexchange.com/companies-and-advisors/aim/advisers/aim-notices/aimrulescompaniesmay2014.pdf). You need to have a broker and a nominated advisor, and produce an admission document. The nominated advisor is called a *nomad* (which doesn't mean the person has to wander the desert herding goats, although it doesn't mean that he can't either, if goats float his boat).

The need for listed companies to nominate and retain a broker at all times is to address one of the concerns of creating a market for trading shares in smaller companies: it doesn't provide sufficient levels of liquidity to enable institutions to invest in them. In other words, too few shares exist to buy or sell, leading to a lack of activity on the exchange – which also cancels out the potential benefits gained by the listed companies.

The broker's job is to keep the markets flowing *(liquid)* by finding buyers and sellers of shares and matching them up. The broker can also be the nomad of the AIM-listed company (see the nearby sidebar 'Herding companies towards suitability' for more details).

Herding companies towards suitability

The nomad is an accountancy firm, corporate finance outfit, investment bank or broker who's approved by the LSE. Its job is to guide the company through the admission process and advise it on its responsibilities as a member of the exchange. Nomads have their own set of rules that they must follow, known as the 'AIM Rules for Nominated Advisors'. Their duties under these rules include assessing the suitability of a company for listing on AIM.

In order to fulfil its duty, the nomad appoints third parties, such as lawyers and accountants, to perform a due diligence exercise on the company, as well as conducting its own research to ensure that the company's affairs are all in order and no material issues may affect its application for listing. When satisfied with the status of the company, the nomad has to provide a written declaration to the LSE confirming suitability for listing.

The information the nomad collects during its due diligence (to check a firm's suitability for AIM listing) forms the basis of the admission document. The document must include the following information:

- A description of the business of your company
- Details of its board and management
- An accountant's report on the trading history of the company
- Detailed information on share capital, Articles of Association, share option schemes, working capital statement and various other details

Signing for the AIM club

The LSE doesn't check the admission document, but the nomad has to state that the document complies with the required AIM Rules. Ten days before the scheduled admission date, the company has to send the LSE an announcement with prescribed information. At least three days before the scheduled admission date, the company has to submit to the LSE a completed application form, an electronic version of the admission document and the nomad's declaration. No extra time if you're late.

You also have to pay an admission fee, which depends upon the *market capitalisation* of the company (the total market value of its shares). The admission only becomes effective when the LSE issues what's known as a *dealing notice* confirming the admission.

You can find further details on admission to AIM, continuing obligations and guidance at www.londonstockexchange.com/companies-and-advisors/aim/aim/aim.htm.

Listing on AIM is very exciting: if your company is successful you can take a lot of cash off the table (initially when the shares go on the market or later as they increase in value). But before you launch a jubilant pitch invasion, bear in mind that AIM is a public forum. Expect everything you do from now to be subject to market scrutiny and that your value isn't just influenced by your own efforts but also by market sentiment.

Markets don't always behave rationally, and so your value can go down as well as up due to factors over which you have no control: for example, bear markets, interest rates, tittle-tattle by ill-informed analysts. (Don't ask me why people call a downward market a *bear market* and an upward one a *bull market* – apparently bears tend to swat downwards with their paws when they attack and bulls swing their horns upwards; all sounds a bit abstract to me.)

Another problem with liquidity on AIM is that going back to the market for further equity funding can be difficult; follow-on funding is much less attractive to investors than an initial funding, unless the company has been outstandingly successful as an AIM company. And moving up to the main LSE is often too big a leap. As a result, AIM can become a cul-de-sac for a company, so that the only way for it to develop is to be acquired and taken off the market.

Chapter 18

Cashing In: Selling Your Business

. . . .

In This Chapter

▶ Negotiating with potential buyers

▶ Thinking about knock-on tax effects

▶ Flogging the firm's assets

. . . .

Merry Christmas: presents, silly hats, drink and food, mistletoe (but not when tipsy Aunty Sheila has been at the sherry), and all the paraphernalia of the country's favourite winter blowout. That's what it should feel like when you achieve your dreams and sell the business you guided from start-up. You no longer have to worry about finding money, selling new products, managing staff, dealing with disputes or keeping up-to-date with legislation. 'Let it snow, let it snow, let it snow . . .'.

But to make sure that Christmas falls on whichever day you complete the sale, you need to get the contractual issues right. Therefore, in this chapter I guide you through the sale negotiations, tax implications, and asset valuations and depreciations. Most of this information applies to limited companies, because that's the most likely type of business to get sold (Chapter 1 helps you set up your legal structure).

After selling your business successfully, you simply have to decide what you're going to do next: perhaps travel the world, or get drunk and lie on the sofa all day (that's my 8-year-old's career plan). Or maybe, like many entrepreneurs, you want to see whether you can do it all over again. . . .

Dealing Successfully with a Buyer

If your business is profitable, growing and has a good brand, you may well find that suitable buyers start to find you. If not, you can look for them in the following places:

> ✔ **Your own market sector:** Players looking to expand within your section through acquisition.

- ✔ **Related market sectors:** Players looking to expand into your sector through acquisition – for example, if you're a financial services company, a service company in the insurance sector may be interested in snapping you up.

- ✔ **Technology players:** If technology underpins your business, a technology company may want to acquire your platform to bolt it on to its existing offering or repurpose it for other sectors it supports.

- ✔ **Private equity funds:** They may be interested in purchasing you if your market and financial performance align with their objectives (check out Chapter 17 for more details on institutional investors).

When you've identified a willing buyer (or preferably two, because that gives you a better chance of securing a higher price), you can move on to the formalities of reaching agreement.

In this section, I deal with selling shares in your company. To read about selling your firm's assets, check out the later section 'Selling Your Business's Assets' (Chapter 17 has more on this distinction).

Experiencing due diligence

Any potential buyer of your business wants to conduct due diligence to check out what it's getting (just as you kick the tyres on a used car lot before buying one). I look at due diligence when someone invests in your business in Chapter 4, but you can expect a buyer of your business to pay closer attention to it, and so I provide more detail on the process here.

Due diligence is equally relevant if you take on extra institutional funding and is also required if you're thinking of acquiring another company (see Chapter 17 for both processes). Therefore, the information in this section applies equally in those cases (though if you're acquiring, you're doing the due diligence rather than undergoing it).

Due diligence questionnaire

Whoever's carrying out the due diligence sends a *due diligence questionnaire* (or *information request*) to you. Think of it as a bit like its Christmas list for Santa – too long and rather dull to read after a while.

The questionnaire lists all the information and accompanying documentation that the potential buyer of your business needs to conduct its due diligence review:

✔ **Company details and structure:** Includes registered address and company number, places of business, other contact details, whether the group has other companies, and details of all company directors and senior staff. The buyer also needs incorporation documents, including Articles of Association and any changes of name.

✔ **Share capital:** Covers all information relating to your business's shareholding structure: allotted and issued shares; number of shareholders; names, addresses and details of individual shareholdings, including class of shares; details of *buybacks* (rights for your company to buy back shares), *share options* and *warrants* (existing rights for other people to acquire shares); details of any shares used as security for a charge (such as a loan); any limitations on disposing of shares (such as pre-emption rights, rights of veto, consents required under your Articles) and any Shareholder Agreements.

✔ **Financial accounts:** Copies of annual accounts and reports going back at least three years, plus any other financial information, such as auditors' reports, management accounts and a balance sheet, as well as up-to-date details of the business's tax position.

✔ **Current contracts:** Details of all current agreements in place with third parties (suppliers and customers), including duration, termination provisions and any restrictions on assignment and liability provisions.

✔ **Assets:** Information on all the assets your company owns, along with all paperwork evidencing ownership, including valuations and how they're determined, plus details of any charges or other restrictions to which the assets are subject. The list of assets is long and can include property (the purchaser is interested to know details of your rights and obligations) and intellectual property (the purchaser wants to know what you own and how well it's protected).

✔ **Employment:** Lists of employees, positions, salaries and duration of employment and pension arrangements, as well as consultants, agents and any other representatives of your company – plus copies of their contracts of employment (or consultancy agreements) along with any staff policies and the employment handbook.

✔ **Litigation and disputes:** Details of any current or threatened litigation or disputes of any other kind (including employment grievances); claims against your company are a risk and may have an effect on its market value.

Data room

Thanks to technological advances, this process is now done almost exclusively electronically, instead of sending millions of bits of paper.

As the seller, you set up a *virtual data room* and add all requested documents to it. You choose the provider and foot the costs of the service. A well-arranged data room with easy-to-locate files helps the buyer conduct a smoother review and gives reassurance about the state of your company.

When the documentation in the data room has been reviewed, the buyer's advisors compile a due diligence report. The goal of the review is to locate any issues that can put a halt to the deal or cause problems for the buyer if not attended to, and to ensure that the buyer, if the purchase goes ahead, isn't paying over the odds for your business.

Agreeing a price

The due diligence report initially impacts on the negotiation of the price for your company. If the report reveals some problems or risks, you can expect the buyer to want to knock the price down, whether as a result of missing contracts, lack of regulatory approvals, outstanding claims against you or holes in your numbers. If the due diligence report shows that you're on the Naughty List, you can expect less valuable presents for Christmas. (The report also affects the warranties in the purchase agreement; see the later 'Providing warranties and indemnities' section.)

Apart from due diligence, how is the price of your company assessed? At the early stage of your company's development, valuations are often a question of guesswork (refer to Chapter 4), but as the company matures buyers can employ the more established ways that I describe in this section. (You can also use these methods when taking in institutional investment or buying another company.)

If you're selling shares, three common methods are used to value your company: discounted cash flows, market multiples and net asset value. Some of this discussion is quite technical, and so you may be tempted to take your post-Christmas-lunch nap right now.

Discounting cash flows

All refreshed? Great. The *discounted cash flow* (DCF) method works by estimating future cash flows and discounting them to come up with a value in today's terms, because the value of money changes over time. (One pound today is worth more than one pound in one, five or ten years' time, because you can invest it at a given rate of annual interest to produce a larger amount at a point in the future.) Instead of taking your forecasts of future cash at face value, the DCF method applies a discount to reflect what could've been earned with that money over the same period.

To work out discounted cash flows, you look at the estimated amount of cash made by your company each year in the future for a certain number of years and apply a discounted value to come up with the value of that cash in today's market (called a *present value*).

I hope you're still with me, because things get more indigestible from here, just like when you pile Christmas cake and brandy snaps on top of turkey, stuffing and bread sauce. The discount that's applied to each cash flow in future years is determined by the *weighted average cost of capital* (WACC), which is the amount of return required by any investor or debtor of the company. Imagine, for example, that a shareholder requires a 10 per cent yearly return on her investment in your firm while a bank requires a 6 per cent annual interest on a loan that it provided to you. The cost of capital is therefore 10 per cent for the equity investor and 6 per cent for the debtor, or an average cost of capital of 8 per cent.

The ratio of equity to debt in a company is unlikely to be equal, and so a weighted average must then be employed to work out an average figure for the cost of capital (the WACC). So if, continuing the example, your company is financed by 40 per cent equity and 60 per cent debt, the calculation for weighted average cost of capital would be:

(40 per cent × 10 per cent) + (60 per cent × 6 per cent) = 4 + 3.6 = 7.6 per cent

For each additional year into the future, the present value for discounted cash flow is smaller, because a larger discount has to be made. When the calculation has been applied to your future projected cash flows, you end up with a present day valuation of the company.

Multiplying earnings

The *market multiple approach* takes an estimated value for future earnings of the company over a specified period of time and multiplies it by a certain number. The multiple chosen is produced by looking at other publicly listed companies in the same sector – multiples tend to be higher for fast-growth sectors such as technology than for lower-growth traditional sectors (such as manufacturing).

A number of different types of multiples can be used when valuing a company. One of the most common is the *price-earnings ratio* (PE). Read the nearby sidebar 'Working Out your PE' for the calculations.

Other multiples used for this purpose include those derived from the *enterprise value* of your company, which is based on your EBIT (profit Earnings Before Interest and Tax).

Working Out your PE

To find the price-earnings (PE) ratio, first you work out the earnings per share for your company by taking the profit after tax of the company and dividing it by the number of ordinary shares in issue at the time the profit was made. Here's an example:

✔ If your business makes £10 million in one financial year and 8 million shares were issued during the same period, the earnings per share is £10 million/8 million = £1.25.

✔ You then divide the current price of a share in the company by this earnings per share number. In this example, if the current price of a share is £6, the PE would be £6/£1.25 = 4. You then use this PE multiple and apply it to your present profitability (or your future forecast of profits) to work out the current (or future) value of your company.

Whatever way the multiple is worked out, a range of likely outcomes exists. A multiple of three times your profits is at the low end, a multiple of 6 to 8 times your profit is good, and sometimes you get very high multiples of 20 or more for companies that are burning hot and in a fast-expanding sector.

Valuing net assets

You determine the *net asset value* by valuing all your business's assets and deducting the value of all its liabilities. This method is more relevant where a company is being broken up and sold off (as part of a liquidation) rather than when you're selling the business as a going concern. But people still sometimes use it to help come to a valuation of a business.

Getting the money

After shaking on the price, you need to agree how it's paid. This involves how benefits to you on the sale are going to be taxed (see 'Thinking Through Taxing Issues' later in this chapter) and (my subject here) whether you get paid all the money straightaway.

If you have visions of collecting all the cash from the sale in a large suitcase and jetting straight off to the Caribbean to live out a life of riotous luxury, put them on hold – your buyer may not see it that way. Typically a buyer wants to pay some of the cash upfront but keep back as much as possible for an earn-out.

An *earn-out* is a deferral of some part of the purchase price, with the exact amount that's paid subsequently determined by the performance of your company after its acquisition. The most common reference point for the earn-out is the profits made by the target business in the two to three years following the purchase.

From a buyer's perspective, an earn-out is an excellent way to structure the share purchase. In addition to reducing payment of the initial purchase price, the final amount paid is linked directly to the performance of the company over a sustained period (the earn-out period). What better way of keeping your nose to the grindstone.

Clearly earn-outs have disadvantages for you as the seller:

✔ They're dependent on future performance, which means that you can't walk away from your business after you sell the shares and you have to continue to participate in it for the earn-out period before you can see your deferred monies. No fair! Like waking up Christmas morning to be told that you're going to get most of your presents in a couple of years.

✔ The amount that you reap from the sale depends (in part) upon the future performance of the business, and so you aren't able to rest on your laurels and coast through the earn-out period. Instead you have to continue to work hard for your money. The clean break that was so attractive to you originally is no longer an option.

✔ You have little control over the future profitability of your former company. The buyer decides future strategy and may not listen much to your views. Plus you're placing yourself at the mercy of general economic conditions, risking decreased profits in the earn-out period that arise from no fault of your own. Sometimes buyers even skew the numbers so that the future profitability of the company is understated for the purpose of calculating your earn-out. This is tough to fight because you have no control over the way those numbers are calculated and presented.

✔ The combination of feeling that you now have little control over the business, and that the new owner is preventing you from maximising your earn-out can quickly lead to frustration and frayed tempers between you and the buyer – like the annual family argument over the Christmas Day game of Monopoly. Frequently this friction results in a negotiated settlement, where you leave the business early but with a reduced pay-out, which you resent because it doesn't represent the full value of the earn-out.

Providing warranties and indemnities

Apart from giving you a good kicking on price, the buyer also tries to limit its risk by making you agree to *warranties* – promises you make in the purchase agreement about the state of the company.

You want to reduce their impact, but you can expect the warranties to be stiffer when you're selling the company compared to raising seed funding (refer to Chapter 4). This section also applies if you're just taking in investment (rather than selling) or you're buying a company yourself.

These warranties are unpleasant to look at – just like that hideous Christmas sweater Aunty Mabel gave you last year. Here are the typical promises covered by warranties:

- ✔ You've correctly identified all share owners and they own all shares in the business.

- ✔ The company's accounts give a true view of the state of the business, and make any proper reserve for bad debts or future liabilities. If a gap exists between due diligence and the signing of the purchase agreement, nothing untoward has happened to affect the accounts since then.

- ✔ The company owns all its own assets and no charges exist over them.

- ✔ The company has complied with all relevant laws relating to the carrying on of the business.

- ✔ You've disclosed all material trading contracts of the business, and none of them have strange or onerous terms.

- ✔ You own all intellectual property rights in the business or all required licences for those rights are in place. Any registrations required (for example, for trademarks) have taken place.

- ✔ You've fully disclosed all employment agreements.

- ✔ No current or threatened litigation proceedings exist, including in relation to employee disputes.

- ✔ You've delivered and made all tax returns and payments.

- ✔ The company has full records and has complied with all corporate notification and accounting requirements.

- ✔ All the company's insurance policies are in place and up-to-date.

- ✔ If you lease premises, you've disclosed all terms, all payments are up-to-date and you've complied with all obligations under the lease.

- ✔ The company isn't involved in any insolvency proceedings or restructuring agreements with its creditors.

The purchase contract may also contain *indemnities* – a promise to reimburse the buyer for all costs associated with claims in relation to warranties. For example, in case the company has infringed copyright prior to the sale and the buyer subsequently gets sued for that infringement, you can expect to have to indemnify the buyer against all costs and expenses associated with that claim (including legal expenses).

Typically, an indemnity also applies in relation to liability for tax payments. This issue is usually dealt with in a tax indemnity (or *tax covenant*), which is contained in the purchase agreement or set out in a separate deed of tax.

Reducing the effect of warranties and indemnities

To avoid being trussed-up like a Christmas turkey, here are some ways to reduce the impact of the warranties in the preceding section.

Warranty and indemnity insurance cover is now potentially available in the insurance market and can be a good way of reducing any risk for you from warranties and indemnities in your purchase agreement.

Admitting all

You can provide a Disclosure Letter in relation to the warranties before the purchase agreement is signed. In this letter, you disclose to the buyer all the matters contained in the warranties that *aren't* correct. For example, if a warranty applies that all your significant trading contracts have been signed and disclosed and you don't have a third-party contract for a particular trade partner because it has been lost, say so.

You may think that revealing this kind of weakness is counter-intuitive – like confessing to Santa in his Grotto that you've been a bad girl all year. But when you disclose against a warranty, the buyer can't sue you for breach of warranty in relation to the matter disclosed, because it already knew about the problem before the sale and bought the company anyway.

If you disclose, disclose fully, so that no doubt exists that the buyer knew about that problem. Or you can include a clause in the purchase agreement saying that where only brief details of a matter are disclosed, the buyer is deemed to have received full details of such matter and it's agreed that it won't need any further details of the matter to be disclosed.

Don't be surprised if a buyer tries to counter this by including a clause saying that matters are regarded as disclosed only if they're 'fairly disclosed with sufficient details to identify the nature and scope of the matter disclosed'.

Using qualifying wording

You can reduce your legal and commercial risk under warranty provisions by qualifying them by referring to *awareness*. To do so, you insert words in each warranty along the lines of 'The Seller warrants that, *so far as it is aware . . .*'. Then, if the warranty turns out to be untrue, you're only liable for any resulting loss suffered by the buyer if you had knowledge that the warranty wasn't true. If you were unaware of a problem at the time, you can't be held responsible when it subsequently emerges.

Of course, the use of this 'awareness' wording can, effectively, allow you to plead ignorance in relation to every warranty, and so the buyer often inserts a term imparting a level of knowledge to you that you'd have 'after making due and careful enquiry' or 'reasonable enquiries'. Such enquiries can include asking other directors or professional advisers of the target business about the subject matter of the relevant warranties.

Using time limits

To limit your risk under the sale agreement, you can place an express time limit on warranty claims (I touch on this briefly in Chapter 4):

- ✔ If you place no time limit on the making of warranty claims, the buyer legally has six years from the agreement's date to bring them.

- ✔ Although most issues are discovered in the first year after completion, some go unnoticed for longer. So insert a limitation period for claims that's less than the statutory default period.

- ✔ In relation to non-tax warranties, the period agreed between the parties is usually 18 months (two years max), which allows the purchaser to run the business for a year and produce one set of accounts before the warranty claim window closes.

- ✔ In respect of tax warranties, the limitation period is usually six or seven years, due to the ability of Her Majesty's Revenue & Customs (HMRC) to reopen a company's tax affairs up to six years after the end of the accounting period in which the issue arose.

- ✔ In addition to the time limit for bringing a claim, ensure that the buyer is also required to notify you of any claim promptly and to commence any proceedings within a specified period following notification of the claim.

- ✔ You can also specify a procedure that must be followed in order for the claim to be valid, such as setting out details of the claim in writing and specifying the amount claimed.

Using financial limits

You can limit the amount of financial loss that the buyer can recover in several ways. Here are the most common:

- ✔ **Overall limit:** Cap (limit) your liability to an amount not exceeding the purchase price. If you can limit it further, great! Or you can vary the limit of liability depending on the type of warranty in question.

- ✔ **Lower limit for individual claims:** A minimum *(de minimis)* limit prevents the buyer from making individual claims that don't meet a certain financial threshold. Where the buyer accepts, the threshold usually represents a small percentage of the total consideration.

- ✔ **Lower limit for aggregated claims:** A minimum *total* financial threshold that must be met before any claims can be made (when individual claims are added together). The buyer then usually insists on being able to recover the full amount of the claim (not just the amount in excess of the aggregate threshold).

- ✔ **Prevention of double recovery:** Ensure that the buyer can't recover twice in respect of the same loss. For example, a *price* adjustment made following the drawing up of completion accounts prevents the buyer from also bringing a *breach of warranty* claim against you in respect of the accounts.

- ✔ **Conduct of claims:** Include a provision in the purchase agreement allowing you take control of any proceedings or threatened proceedings by third parties, where the subject matter of the claim relates to an event for which you're liable under the warranties. Although not a financial limitation on the buyer, it may well help you successfully limit your liability where a claim is threatened.

When you're selling your business with other shareholders, consider how to divide up liability for issues between you. The buyer usually requests that the sellers are 'jointly and severally' liable for any warranty loss arising from the share sale. This means that the buyer is able to bring the whole claim against any one or more of the sellers for any loss it suffers. You can find yourself paying the total cost of a claim despite being only a part shareholder in the business.

To avoid this scenario, draw up a *contribution agreement,* in which you agree, along with the other selling shareholders, how to divide up liability among yourselves. The standard allocation agreed is an amount equal to the percentage of the total consideration that you each receive.

Beware of some shareholders not wanting to provide warranties for certain reasons (for example, smaller shareholders or those who don't participate in the business). Check how this may affect the extent of your relative liability to the buyer.

Thinking Through Taxing Issues

Tax is a boring subject, of course, but it's a bit like watching the Queen's speech on TV on Christmas day – dull but an important part of the ritual. Here are some pointers on tax when selling your business.

You definitely need the advice of a good accountant to help you avoid your sale price being worth less than a partridge in a pear tree!

Most likely, you'd prefer your consideration for your shares to be in cash. I would. But different payment options exist and the buyer of the shares may well want to use one of them. The most common types of consideration are shares and *loan notes* – evidence of a debt and a promise to repay that debt. Either, or both, of these types of consideration are frequently combined with cash payments.

Considering tax implications

When thinking about how you want to be paid, take into account the way that different types of payment are taxed:

- ✔ **Consideration consists of shares:** No *taxable gain* arises (you have to pay no tax) at the time and any gain and payment of tax on account of such gain is only calculated after you sell the new shares.

    If this deferral of any capital gain is viewed as a means of tax avoidance, however, you have to pay tax on the shares straightaway.

- ✔ **Consideration consists of loan notes:** As with shares, any gain is calculated after you receive payment on the loan notes.

- ✔ **Deferred consideration arises:** The way in which gains are taxed depends on whether the amount of deferred consideration is ascertainable at the time of the sale or unascertainable:

    - • **Ascertainable consideration:** The whole amount is taxed upfront. This case arises for a formal system of post-acquisition instalment payments set out under the agreement and when a single portion of the consideration is held back. Taxation of the full amount even applies where the payment (or any part of it) is conditional in any way. The nearby sidebar 'Using completion accounts to finalise the price' has more.

Using completion accounts to finalise the price

The price is frequently adjusted post-sale under a *completion accounts* mechanism, where the actual purchase price of the acquisition is determined by drawing up another set of accounts following the purchase. The buyer uses completion accounts to verify the financial standing of your business at the time of completion, instead of relying on a valuation based on the latest set of audited accounts. As well as providing a more accurate reflection of the current value of the business, completion accounts also help to highlight the strength or weakness of any assumptions on which the sale price was calculated.

The purchase agreement provides a mechanism by which the price can be adjusted upwards or downwards according to what the completion accounts reveal. However, any potential price adjustment isn't taken into account at the time of sale for tax purposes. Instead, the sale price is treated as the actual price. The seller's tax liability can then be adjusted at a later date following the price adjustment.

✔ **Unascertainable consideration:** You're treated as making two disposals for tax purposes. The first one takes place on the actual sale of the shares, at which point you're treated as receiving an amount equal to the market value of the *right* to receive deferred consideration later.

The second deemed disposal occurs when you receive the deferred consideration. If this amount is *greater* than the value attributed to the right to receive the deferred consideration, a further tax charge is due on the additional gain. If the amount of the consideration received is *less* than the value attributed to the right to deferred consideration, it can constitute an allowable loss, which you can set off against any chargeable gain made on the sale of the shares (that is, the part of the consideration that wasn't deferred).

Working out what tax rate applies to you

If you sell your shares, you're subject to Capital Gains Tax (CGT). Under current tax rules, the rate is 18 per cent of the gain below the basic tax rate for income and 28 per cent of the gain above that limit. You have a tax free allowance each year for CGT of (currently) £11,000. For information on how this works in practice, go to www.gov.uk/capital-gains-tax/work-out-your-capital-gains-tax-rate.

You may also be able to apply for *entrepreneurs relief*, which isn't turning off the TV during a painful interrogation on *Dragons' Den,* but taking your tax burden down from 28 per cent (or 18 per cent) to 10 per cent. To qualify for this relief, you must fulfil the following criteria for at least one year before the date of disposal of the shares:

- ✔ You must have owned at least 5 per cent of the ordinary shares and voting rights in the company.

- ✔ You must have been an employee or director of the company.

- ✔ The company in which the shares were held must be a trading company (and not carry out non-trading activities such as investing).

Selling Your Business's Assets

As I discuss in Chapter 17, buyers can acquire assets (as well as shares) in a firm. Here are some of the issues to bear in mind when selling your business's assets.

Valuing assets

In an asset sale, your company sells a collection of assets to the buyer as a going concern, whether stock, equipment, ten lords a-leaping or eight maids a-milking. Therefore, instead of fixing a value for shares, you attribute values to the sold assets. How do you do that?

As a starting point you can take the *book value* of the relevant assets, which is the amount stated in the latest accounts. You calculate this value by taking the value of the asset when purchased and then applying depreciation that reflects the reduced price due to its use.

This method doesn't apply to intangible assets, including intellectual property that you own and goodwill (reputation) in the business. Unlike tangible assets, such as machinery, the overall value of an intangible asset can go up, but such increases in value can't be represented on a company's balance sheet under current accounting rules. Comparisons with similar sales in your sector may be hard to find. As a result, in this area your negotiation skills are particularly important.

Undergoing asset due diligence

The buyer's due diligence review in respect of an asset purchase fulfils a similar purpose as it does for a share purchase, and raises many similar issues (take a look at the earlier section 'Experiencing due diligence'). But it's more limited, because the buyer is able to choose which assets to purchase and which ones to leave behind in your business.

Receiving an asset price

In an asset sale, you face much less chance of a deferred consideration compared with a share sale (check out the section 'Getting the money' earlier in this chapter). But the buyer may want further security from you to prevent it from being left out-of-pocket if any of the warranties you provide turn out to be untrue and the assets aren't worth what it paid for them. One way of achieving that is to place a sufficient amount of the consideration in a retention account, which it can then use to settle any warranty claims.

If some of the purchase price *does* have to be held back in a retention account, the amount shouldn't exceed 5–15 per cent of the total consideration. Make sure that the buyer can hold the retention only for a limited period (say six months or one year), after which any unused portion is released to you.

Handling debtors and creditors

When a purchaser buys the shares in a company, all debts and creditors of the company are transferred with the shares. When the assets of a company are bought, however, you need to negotiate what happens in relation to existing debtors and creditors. For example, who's to collect existing debts: you or the purchaser? If you, the purchaser restricts you from litigating or harassing those debtors for at least three months after the asset sale, so that the goodwill in the company (for which the purchaser has just paid) doesn't suffer. If the purchaser (and not you) is collecting the debts as your agent, you want to make sure that it does so speedily and efficiently (preferably at no cost to you) and must pay you quickly when the debts are received.

In relation to existing creditors (who the company owes money to), are you or the purchaser responsible for paying these? Whoever is doing it, the other party wants protection that the payments are going to be made quickly, so that its reputation (and that of the business) doesn't suffer because either side drags its feet.

Making warranties on asset sales

The buyer wants your company to warrant that it owns the assets being transferred, and that no charges or other competing interests hang over the assets. Where you don't own the assets, the buyer wants to know that it can use them after it purchases the business. So, it seeks warranties in relation to existing licences and requires you to attempt to secure approval from the licensor to transfer the licence over to it. Failure to obtain such consent may lead to a reduction in the purchase price.

You want as many liabilities as possible in relation to the assets to transfer to the buyer – you don't want to be haunted after the sale by the Ghosts of Christmas Past. You can't, however, transfer certain liabilities, including most rights under occupational pension schemes, criminal liability and responsibility for pay as you earn tax (PAYE) and National Insurance contributions (NICs) up to the transfer date.

You also want contractual protection in respect of any claims brought against you that relate to any liabilities arising *on* or *after* the transfer.

The transfer of intellectual property rights that you own involves certain administration and results in additional costs (for example, you must update the details for your registered trademarks if you want to assign trademark ownership). You can expect to have to agree that you'll do everything required of you to 'perfect' the transfer of rights to the buyer. But make sure that the buyer pays for all such work.

The buyer will want a warranty that it can freely use the assets without any interference. Therefore, when you're selling only part of the business, you may have to consider whether you'll require use of any of the transferred assets following the sale: for example, your IT systems. You need to sort out how that ongoing access is going to be achieved.

Transferring employees

When you sell your business, or part of it, you have to be very careful about what happens to your employees (one of the firm's most valuable assets). You can't simply bring their contracts to an end. The Transfer of Undertakings (Protection of Employment) Regulations (TUPE) provides special protections to employees of a business when that business is transferred to a third party.

The principal protection measure under this piece of law essentially requires a buyer of a business to 'step into the shoes' of the seller. The result is that the employees transfer over to the buyer, as do their terms of employment. Therefore, all obligations and liabilities that you had under that employment contract also transfer to the buyer.

This principle means that if you dismiss an employee because of the transfer (or if the transfer is the main reason for the dismissal), that dismissal is automatically unfair and the employee is able to bring a claim against you (the company) for unfair dismissal. In addition to this general principle, as seller of the business you have an obligation to inform and consult the employees who may be affected by the transfer. If you don't do so in the correct way, you again risk being liable to compensate the affected employees.

As a result of TUPE, specific indemnities apply under an asset purchase in relation to employees, because the buyer wants protection against any such liabilities that have arisen, or do arise, prior to the transfer. Equally, you need to seek protection against the buyer threatening to breach its requirements under TUPE after the date of the transfer.

Take particular care with a sale of only part of the business. In such instances you have to distinguish between those employees who form part of the section of the business being transferred and those who don't. Due to employees performing various duties across departments and various other issues, this task isn't always straightforward.

Reducing your tax bill on sold assets

In asset sales, the company itself is disposing of the assets, not the shareholders. Accordingly, the tax benefits and reliefs to consider are those accruing to the company (and not to you personally):

- ✔ **Allowable losses:** This relief allows you to set off any loss on the sale of an asset against any chargeable gains made on the sale of other assets. But you have to reduce any allowable loss by the amount of any capital allowances that you've already claimed.

- ✔ **Balancing allowance:** If you sell any assets for less than their *written down value* (their value after a period of use including depreciation), this creates a *balancing allowance,* which you can use to set against business income or chargeable gains made on the sale of these assets.

- ✔ **Other tax reliefs:** Consider carefully how to apportion the purchase price among the various assets being sold, because the sale of assets of different categories provides different accompanying reliefs. For example, you may prefer to increase the amount of the sale price allocated to *fixed assets* (those that provide continuing economic benefits to the business) if you have capital losses that you haven't yet used, and against which you can set the tax otherwise payable on the sale of those fixed assets.

  Be careful: HMRC has a right to reapportion the consideration among the assets if it's not done in a 'just and reasonable' manner.

Part VI
The Part of Tens

the
part of
tens

For ten ways to beat the business bullies, head to www.dummies.com/extras/
lawforsmallbusinessuk.

In this part . . .

- ✔ Avoid ten legal pitfalls that catch out others.
- ✔ Become familiar with the necessary legal documents.
- ✔ Negotiate like a pro, with ten hush-hush tips.
- ✔ Know ten things a good lawyer should do for you.

Chapter 19

Top Ten Legal Bear Pits to Avoid

In This Chapter

▶ Tracing the ten most common legal mistakes

▶ Seeing the results if you do make them

▶ Avoiding falling into the traps

*H*ello there, pop-pickers, and welcome to your chart of the top ten legal pitfalls to avoid. Each one is guaranteed to cause a smash for your business if it happens to you – and I don't mean a smash hit!

Deciding Not to Bother with Lawyers or Contracts

You'll definitely be staying at 'Heartbreak Hotel' if you're guilty of this error. Dispensing with lawyers is often tempting – some of them can be expensive, slow and difficult to understand. But they aren't all like that. In Chapter 22, I cover what you're entitled to expect from a good lawyer. One of those can be incredibly valuable to your business, as a trusted guide and guardian angel (well, a guardian anyway).

You can also be tempted not to bother with contracts. They're so very boring to draft and cause tensions in the relationship. Anyway, you get on well with your trading partner and you both trust each other, right? Who needs a contract?

The answer is, you do. If I had a pound for every time I've picked up the pieces in this situation I could buy Disneyland. Well, perhaps buy several flights to Disneyland. Or even somewhere I'd like to go. My experience is that all too often Shareholder Agreements, licensing agreements, software agreements, employment agreements and contractor agreements aren't written down at all or exist in a disconnected string of vague, ambiguous emails that are difficult to enforce. If this sounds like you, you're on the 'Road to Nowhere'.

When people do fall out the custard really hits the fan, because no agreed framework exists for sorting out who's accountable for what. In Chapters 10 and 11, I detail the 4 Rs (rights, responsibilities, risk and rewards): no contract means that you face much more difficulty in working out your rights, the other side's responsibilities, who's taking which risk and how the rewards in the contract are calculated. Do yourself a favour and put proper contracts in place.

Forgetting to Sign Your Contracts

How often have you gone to the trouble of getting a draft contract agreed, only to find that one side or the other never gets round to signing it? Or maybe it's not dated (which is sometimes required to give it legal effect).

Sometimes people fight like cat and dog over the wording of the draft agreement and then lose interest in completing the contractual paperwork as their business moves on. You're on the 'Highway to Hell' if you don't complete the contractual process.

Sure, agreements can be oral or inferred from emails and conduct, but doing that is much harder than having a fully signed agreement that provides evidence of the parties' intentions. If you're relying on oral contracts, you're into the murky world of evidencing who said what to whom, whether the parties intended to contract and whether the terms were certain enough to be capable of enforcement.

Often the difference between success and failure within small companies is having the rigour to see initiatives all the way through to the end. That rigour applies as much to getting contracts signed as to any other project you're involved with.

Failing to Read Your Contracts

Come on, you know better than not reading contracts. I know that they can be dull and confusing to read. As a result, many people have signed off on legal agreements without bothering to read the small print – especially if you're dealing with contracts you perceive as 'standard'. This category can include contracts from banks or other funders, service providers or big websites (Google, Facebook, YouTube and so on). As a result you can commit yourself to all sorts of hidden charges, liabilities and exclusions without realising it.

Did you know that eBay can sell your children online to recover commissions you owe? Or that at its discretion PayPal can suspend your payments and hold on to all your monies without giving any reason for up to six months after it collects them? I made up only one of those examples.

Maybe you can't negotiate changes with the other side, especially if it has a lot of bargaining power. But at least you need to know what you're letting yourself in for. Plus, when dealing with entities that aren't corporate monoliths, you may be able to negotiate. In any event, if you don't take the sensible precaution of reading before you sign, don't come complaining to me later that 'Heaven Knows I'm Miserable Now'.

Omitting to Monitor Your Contracts

How often do the contract partners negotiate a contract fiercely, only for the signed version to end up in a drawer (or more likely carefully hidden in a place so special that nobody can find it again)? In some ways that's a good thing – you don't build much of a climate of trust if you're forever whipping out the contract and pointing out the small print to your contract partner. On the other hand, if you never look at the contract again you risk making mistakes.

Rarely are all the obligations in a contract to be carried out in the first five minutes. If you're not paying attention to the contract terms as you go along, you risk the following:

- ✔ **Missing an option date:** For example, to acquire more rights.
- ✔ **Missing a renewal date:** So that the term of your rights expires.
- ✔ **Missing a payment date:** Putting you in breach.
- ✔ **Sending contractual notices in the wrong way:** So that they're invalid.
- ✔ **Failing to fulfil ongoing commitments:** For example, in relation to marketing or packaging.
- ✔ **Losing out on approval rights:** For example, by not responding within the time limits set out in the contract.

You may well 'Cry Me a River' if that happens, but it'll be too late.

Being Remiss about Protecting Your Intellectual Property

Intellectual property (IP, refer to Chapter 8) includes your copyrights, trademarks, patents and design rights, and they're an enormous potential source of value for your business.

These rights are slightly abstract but don't assume that they aren't as important as tangible things, such as raising money, making products and marketing. To make raising money, building products and marketing worthwhile, the more you focus on your IP the better.

If anybody invests in you or wants to buy your business, your IP is likely to be a key component of your valuation that they focus on. Don't assume that you have no IP – you can potentially trademark everything from a logo to a smell. You may have design rights in anything from the shape and colour of your bottles to the graphic designs on your website. You may have copyright in everything from a photo to an app.

If you don't look after your IP, other firms may punish you. They can register as a trademark a brand that you've been using and then stop you using it. They may create something that would've breached your copyright, if only you'd realised that you had a copyright or known how to enforce it. Sounds harsh, doesn't it? 'Welcome to the Jungle'.

Letting Your Understanding of Employment Legislation Slide

Employment legislation is a highly regulated area of the law (as I discuss in Chapters 5 and 7), and the range of laws you have to comply with is ever-increasing – a rising tide of red tape. (Not literally, of course. Maybe I should say a 'rising bloom of jellyfish' – yes, that's what a group of jellyfish is called.)

Like jellyfish, the range of employment laws is often not visible to the innocent swimmer, but can give you a nasty sting. The dangers of compliance-failure are high. If a disgruntled employee brings a case against you in the Employment Tribunal for Unfair Dismissal or Discrimination, bear in mind that between 2013 and 2014 the maximum individual award was £162,000 for a Racial Discrimination case, £168,000 for a Sex Discrimination Case and £3,000,000 for an Unfair Dismissal. Extreme examples, but you get the point. The average award in that year in each of those categories was between £10,000 and £14,000, which is plenty for an SME.

If you breach Sections 2–6 of the Health and Safety at Work regulations, you can be fined £20,000 or face six months' imprisonment, leaving you wandering around a concrete yard crying 'Where Have All the Flowers Gone?' Don't put yourself in that position.

Ignoring Legal Problems

In this ostrich strategy, you pretend nasty arguments aren't happening and try to avoid dealing with them by sticking your head in the sand. But arguments are like weeds: they're easier to remove when they're small. When grown they're much harder to eradicate and they strangle the rest of your garden too. Go on . . . grasp the nettle and give it a good yank.

Don't ignore emails, letters or forever be 'in a meeting' when people ring you. Arguments aren't normally as bad as you fear – except when they fester. Then they can go litigious, and become stressful, bruising, time-consuming and costly. This is what it sounds like 'When Doves Cry'.

So, when that outrageous email or claim clatters into your inbox, don't just file it in 'B for Bin'. Pick up the phone to the person on the other side and talk it through.

Getting on the Wrong Side of HMRC

Her Majesty's Revenue & Customs (HMRC) is an organisation you don't want to irritate. Get your returns in on time and pay any outstanding amounts promptly. If you don't pay your tax, HMRC can investigate your affairs – going back 6 years if it thinks you've been careless with your returns and 20 years if it believes you've been deceitful.

It can charge penalties of up to 100 per cent of the tax owed, plus interest. HMRC can also commence proceedings against you in the Magistrates Court or the County Court for sums that you owe. Alternatively, or in addition, it can send representatives to your house, take your possessions and sell them to fulfil the debt that you owe (a jolly process known as *distraint*). Plus, it can commence bankruptcy proceedings against you or, if your company owes money, start proceedings to have it wound up.

The tax regime became tougher as the recession forced the government to find extra tax revenues. So at the end of every business month, don't just 'Say a Little Prayer' – keep enough revenues to one side to pay tax.

Neglecting to Complete Your Corporate Documentation

As I discuss in Chapters 1 and 2, you have numerous obligations to file paperwork with Companies House. Serious consequences await if you don't deal with these issues. For example, if you file your company accounts more than six months late, you can face a fine of £1,500. If you repeat the offence in the next financial year, the fine doubles.

The Registrar of Companies also has the right to strike your company off the record for late filing of returns. If you're a director, you can be subject to criminal charges for late filings, resulting in fines and permanent damage to your reputation. Just to rub it in, when you go to sell your enterprise your prospective buyer is likely to engage accountants and lawyers to crawl all over your books. If they find that your company records are littered with missing documents and missed filing dates, it reduces the buyer's confidence in your business and may result in no sale at all, or a sale at a reduced valuation.

Don't leave yourself 'Blowin' in the Wind'. Take care of this kind of detail or pay someone to take care of it for you.

Wasting Time on Fighting Disputes

Without doubt you're going to come across people in business who treat you badly. You'll suffer injustice. You'll encounter situations that make you very angry, and people who're dishonest or who let you down.

I provide a whole array of tips and hints on managing litigation in Chapter 15, but my advice is, wherever possible, to avoid getting bogged down in legal battles. Legal action is a distraction, a strain and a money pit. The only way to guarantee coming back from court with a small fortune is to commence proceedings with a much larger one.

I know that you may want to fight 'on principle', but sometimes you have to choose between 'being right' and 'doing what's best for the business'. They aren't always the same thing. Litigation is also risky. As Mark Twain put it: 'October . . . is one of the particularly dangerous months in which to speculate. . . . The others are July, January, September, April, November, May, March, June, December, August and February'.

Negotiate, mediate and put legal pressure on the other side by all means. But do me a favour and don't start legal proceedings unless you really have to: 'You Can't Always Get What You Want' . . . .

Chapter 20

Ten Documents You Need to Get Signed

In This Chapter

▶ Signing ten crucial legal documents

▶ Seeing why they're so important

I look at many different types of agreement in this book, but I know that you're a busy entrepreneur – and when you're under pressure, you take the least boring route. You believe that you get a much better return on your time if you spend it on building a product, and marketing or selling that product, rather than by concentrating on contracts. Anyway, getting legal documents in place is high on your list of boring chores, along with talking to people who can't help your business, listening to other people tell you about their business and doing your VAT return.

But you don't want your business to turn into a Hammer horror film (even if your business is producing horror movies), which is what happens if you fail to get these ten important documents signed when doing business.

Avoiding Future Problems with Shareholder/Partnership Agreements

You're setting yourself up for a bit of an *Amityville Horror* if you don't get agreements signed with your shareholders (or partners, if you're operating through a partnership). Consider the following questions. If you can't answer them, you need an agreement that can.

✔ How do you know who's responsible for what?

✔ How is decision-making to be organised between you?

- What happens if you have a dispute – how is it to be resolved?

- What happens if one of you dies, wants to exit or sell up, or wants to give shares to a spouse (or does so and then gets divorced)?

- Are voting rights the same for all shareholders and for all issues?

- What happens if you need to issue new shares or a new shareholder comes on board?

- If one of you ceases to be a shareholder, can the person immediately set up in competition with the company?

I get into the details of partnership and shareholder agreements in Chapter 2.

Protecting Yourself with Contractor Agreements

If you use contractors/consultants/freelancers and you don't get them to sign a contract, you're going to have a *Texas Chainsaw Massacre* on your hands. What exactly are contractors supposed to do for you? How will you measure their success? What standards do they have to reach? What are their deliverables?

Here are some more burning questions that may be too hot to handle:

- How long are they going to work for you?

- To what extent are they allowed to work for other people?

- Can they work for a competitor at the same time as for you?

- What happens if they deliver their work for you late, their work isn't satisfactory or it's unlawful – for example, because it infringes somebody's rights? Do you have any protection if that happens?

- Can you remove them? If so, on what basis?

- Is it clear exactly what they're paid and when?

- If they create work for you, do you own it automatically? What happens if they assert that they own it instead?

- Are they really contractors at all or are they in fact employees?

The central question is, 'Do you have an agreement in place for all your contractors?' Check out Chapter 5 for all you need to know about the value of proper contractor agreements.

Sorting out Employee Agreements

It's *Question Time* again, and, unlike the Prime Minister, you can't give evasive answers or choose to answer a different question. If you don't have an employment agreement:

- How do you know exactly what duties your employees are supposed to be carrying out?

- How do you go about changing their duties?

- What are they paid exactly, and how do you handle discretionary payments such as bonuses without any contractual format to guide you?

- How long is the agreement for, and what notice provisions exist if you terminate? For what reasons can you terminate?

- What happens if somebody leaves – can she just take your customers, staff and commercial secrets with her? What happens if she's a director of the company or has share options?

- How can you demonstrate your compliance with the important legislation I discuss in Chapters 5 and 7, and regulations concerning pensions, sick pay, holidays, maternity pay and leave, and so on?

You can get yourself into some scary situations if you don't get your employment agreements in place. So don't *Don't Look Now,* but do look now at Chapters 5 and 7, to realise that you need signed agreements with your employees (and a staff handbook incorporated into them).

Staying Alive with IP Documentation

Your business's intellectual property (IP) – copyrights, trademarks, patents or design rights – contains potential value to your business and can mean a lot to investors or potential purchasers (refer to Chapter 8).

Here are the questions of the day:

- Do you know what copyrights you have? If not, how are you going to protect them?

- Are you sure that you own all software, videos, designs and databases that others have created for you?

✔ What trademarks can you protect? In which classes would you apply for trademark protection? What would you do if somebody asserted that you can't use your trading name, because he has a competing trademark, or somebody else started using your trade name and you hadn't protected it?

✔ Have you created a technical process that's innovative enough to entitle you to apply for a patent?

✔ Does your business use any protectable designs – graphics, logos, shapes? If so, what are you doing about that? If you haven't done anything about it yet and somebody else registers those designs, what are you going to do about it?

Getting your IP documentation in order is important, whether through applications or registrations. If you're not attentive to protecting these rights, you can create an enterprise that looks vibrant to you from the inside but is dead to outsiders: in other words, a *Night of the Living Dead* (not to be confused with a *Day of the Living Dead,* a *Return of the Living Dead,* a *Dawn of the Dead* or a *Zone of the Dead,* which all have completely different plots). Don't turn your business into a zombie.

Keeping Schtum with Confidentiality Agreements

Confidentiality agreements can have real value (refer to Chapter 4). Don't listen to the cynics who say that they're difficult to enforce: if you don't try to protect the confidentiality of your information and ideas, people have even less incentive to stop taking them from you. You can also insert confidentiality clauses into all sorts of agreements, from distribution agreements to joint ventures to Shareholder Agreements.

Without a confidentiality agreement in place, you may have no recourse if someone steals information from your business plan, copies your strategy document, tells someone else how to copy your technology software, reveals your script, screenplay or book, or usurps your technology know-how.

These people must be stopped. They're stealing the lifeblood of your business. Don't tolerate an *Invasion of the Body Snatchers*; make them sign confidentiality agreements instead.

Considering Online Ts and Cs

You need to have online Terms and Conditions (Ts and Cs) in order to regulate your relationship with your customers (flip to Chapters 6 and 11). Use appropriate documentation online and get your customers to agree to it. Otherwise, you face problems:

✔ How can customers know what products and services you promise to deliver and what you don't?

✔ How do you set your standards of delivery for customers? What technical standards are you required to meet? If the website goes down, are you liable for that?

✔ What are the limits of your liability to customers? If you've imposed limits, are they enforceable?

✔ What standards of behaviour do your customers have to meet if they use your site? Can they import viruses or post illegal content?

✔ How can you show that you're fulfilling your statutory obligations in relation to the various statutes I mention in Chapters 6 and 11?

✔ How can you ensure that customers are bound by any online terms you deploy?

Don't be a *Psycho* or it'll all end in tears – not to mention fines and other penalties. Make sure that you comply with your online responsibilities.

Ensuring You Have Supplier Agreements

You need to put agreements in place with your suppliers of products: for example, manufacturers, wholesalers, distribution suppliers or licensees (refer to Chapter 10). You can't just ignore the job of getting these agreements in writing – verbal agreements, handshakes or scrappy emails don't do the job. If you skimp on these agreements, how do you know what rights you have in the products your supplier delivers and whether you need any approvals before exercising those rights?

✔ How long do your rights last?

✔ Can you resell outside the UK or not?

✔ What does your supplier have to deliver and when?

✔ What quality standards does the supplier have to meet, and what happens if it delivers late, the wrong amount or a faulty product?

 ✔ What happens if your supplier doesn't have the rights to give you the product?

 ✔ Who pays for the cost of shipments to you?

 ✔ How are returns dealt with?

 ✔ What are the payment terms? Do you get any discounts? Can you deduct any of your costs from what you have to pay a supplier or licensor?

 ✔ What accounting obligations do you have?

Your business is your child, and it needs protecting if it's to grow up into a strong healthy adult. Don't turn it into *Rosemary's Baby* by taking shortcuts with your product supply agreements.

Looking after Service Agreements

In Chapter 11, I set out the value of putting in place proper agreements with suppliers of services to your business (including Software as a Service providers, affiliates and sales agents). A question mark hovers over your business if you don't take care of these agreements – in fact, several question marks:

 ✔ How do you know what standards of service you're entitled to?

 ✔ Is the service provider making any guarantees to you about introductions or revenues?

 ✔ What happens if a service-level failure occurs? How does it get fixed and does it cost you extra money to fix it?

 ✔ What does your service provider get paid and by when?

 ✔ What are your accounting obligations?

 ✔ Can you stop using the service provider if you aren't happy? Do you have to pay any penalties if you do stop?

 ✔ Is the service provider properly insured? What happens if it's not and something goes wrong and causes you damage?

Some rather spooky things can go bump in the night if you don't pay attention to getting these agreements signed. If that starts happening don't blame it on the *Poltergeist* (or even the *Poultrygeist* from *Night of the Chicken Dead*) – blame it on yourself.

Adventuring Safely Overseas

Trading abroad is a big step to take. Apart from the differences in culture, language and customs, you have to be familiar with the local legal framework too, as well as understanding what business structure suits you best (check out Chapter 13 for loads more). If you don't put in place enforceable legal documentation with your trading partner(s), you open up yourself to a number of worrying ambiguities that the documentation would otherwise flush out:

- ✔ What's the legal relationship between you and your trading partner? Are you licensing, franchising, distributing, selling, joint venturing? Are you aware of the differences between these different legal relationships?

- ✔ Is what your trading partners have to do, how often and by when, clear?

- ✔ What are the payment terms? What currency do you get paid in?

- ✔ Are any exchange controls or withholding taxes involved? How are your revenues in the local territory taxed? Who's responsible for paying local customs duties?

- ✔ Who's responsible for complying with local product and packaging laws?

- ✔ If you're setting up an entity, does it require a local presence as a shareholder or board member?

Plenty of horror movies demonstrate that odd, scary things can happen abroad. In *Dead Snow* (which I believe is based on a true story), a group of Norwegian medical students unexpectedly encounter a battalion of frozen Nazi zombie soldiers. Don't risk your overseas experiences turning into a bloodbath. Get the right agreements signed with your overseas trading partners.

Insuring Your Business against Horrifying Events

Insurance agreements are a great way of protecting your business against legal risks (refer to Chapter 14). For example, what do you do if you're liable for a claim with a trading partner? Here are some types of insurance to help you deal with and fund otherwise disastrous situations:

- ✔ **Employer liability insurance:** If a staff member is injured on your site

- ✔ **Professional indemnity insurance:** If you face a claim of negligence

 ✔ **Public liability insurance:** If your van injures a pedestrian

 ✔ **Product liability insurance:** If one of your products injures a child

 ✔ **Life assurance:** If you fall critically ill

Insurance policies can feel like an unnecessary expense and, yes, they can trip you up with small print. But as with horror classics *Cockneys vs Zombies, Leprechaun 3* and *The Cuckoo Clocks of Hell,* don't underestimate their value. Put your insurance documentation in place and you won't be doing *The Howling* when things go wrong.

Chapter 21

Shush! Ten Secrets of Negotiation

In This Chapter
▶ Finding your personal negotiating style
▶ Achieving what you want from negotiations

*A*s an entrepreneur, almost all your revenues and costs are likely to derive from deals that you negotiate: for funding, manufacturing, software, sales, marketing, distribution, services, consulting, employment, property, acquisition, merger, joint ventures and so on.

Yet despite its significance, most people don't use any framework when they negotiate. Instead, they negotiate by instinct, maybe imitating what they learned from their boss, their peers or by watching successful business leaders on television. As a result, whether it works or fails, they don't know why. So they trudge on, never getting exactly what they want.

When I wrote *The Yes Book: The Art of Better Negotiation* (`http://www.amazon.co.uk/The-Yes-Book-Better-Negotiation/dp/0753541092`), I used You Gov to conduct a study of 1,000 British businesses, asking them how they negotiate. Economists at the Centre for Economics and Business Research then analysed the respondents' results. They worked out that British business loses £9 million an hour from poor negotiation – a horrifying sum. They also calculated that the average business can increase its profits by 7 per cent per year through better negotiation – a figure not to be sneered at.

Here are ten essential secrets for negotiating that you can apply yourself.

Bringing the Right Attitude

How you feel on the inside and what you project on the outside make a big difference in any negotiation. Here are four common attitudes that negotiators display:

- **User:** A self-centred negotiator who takes advantage of the other side and uses pressure tactics. This approach is very common but not recommended. All the research shows that users make getting deals done harder for themselves, because they provoke resentment. Some people refuse to deal with users at all and others want to take revenge on them later (nobody likes to be pushed around).

- **Loser:** Believes that the other side's needs are more important or doesn't think he can succeed in the negotiation. Typical loser outlooks are 'I always do badly at negotiating' and 'as long as I keep you happy, there won't be any arguments'. This approach is as common as the user and equally destructive. If you project a losing attitude, the other side picks it up (consciously or otherwise). Even if they're nice people they won't be able to resist pushing you harder, because they know that you won't stand up to them.

- **Confuser:** Makes snap judgements about what's going on in the negotiation. If you judge a book by its cover, you can make serious mistakes. For example, you may believe that the other side has bad motives (when it doesn't) or that only two points are worth discussing (when the potential pie is much larger). Alternatively, you may assume that the other side wants 'x' (when it, in fact, wants something completely different), or you exaggerate the impact of past or present one-off events. Confusers start the negotiation on the wrong foot, and set off in the wrong direction. When they do so, getting back on track is very difficult.

- **Fuser:** Addresses the agendas of both parties in the negotiation – fusing them together to create common currency. As a fuser, you're confident about your own aims, but recognise that you get more out of a deal if you address the aims of the other side too. This modern approach suits the current interdependent, interconnected world.

In case you haven't realised, fuser is the way to go.

Preparing Is Everything

The business world is hectic, full of meetings, phone calls, texts and emails. As a result, the possibility of thinking in advance about a negotiation may seem like a waste of time. Many people do their deal preparation in the lift on the way to the meeting!

In my experience, however, if you miss out on preparation, you're preparing to miss out. This is especially true of team negotiations, where you need to put in the spade work to ensure that all team members are equally prepared, or risk being disunited and exploited by the other side.

Here are some of the areas to consider when preparing:

- Who's on your team and what roles are they going to play (speaker/listener/authorised to make concessions and so on)?

- Who's on the other side and what roles will they play?

- Any previous history between the parties?

- Any additional expertise or materials required for the negotiation (for example, spreadsheets, accounts, market reports)?

- If a negative attitude is likely on the other side, what steps can you take to change that?

- What's each side's ideal opening position in relation to organisational wants such as price, delivery date and quantity?

- What's each side's likely acceptable position and bottom line?

- What easy concessions are available on each side that have high value to the other party, because they meet an underlying need?

- What are the best and worst alternatives available to getting the deal done?

- How do the projected terms stack up against the risks that the deal (if done) may not work? (Many deals don't work, and so you always need to consider this risk.)

Understanding Your Aces

The balance of bargaining power on both sides is crucial. How many aces does each side have? These aces are rarely all stacked in favour of one side – you normally have more bargaining power than you think:

- **Authority power:** From reputation or title.

- **Expertise:** For example, the degree of technological expertise you have if operating in the tech sector.

- **Information:** The expression 'information is power' translates very well to negotiating.

- **Market power:** Not just market share, but also niche market power, exclusivity or ability to create market scarcity, through, for example, only making an offer available for a certain period of time or to a certain number of customers.

- **Network power:** The power to access a network that someone else finds desirable, or the power of being a 'node' in a network who controls access to a certain person or position.

- **Numbers:** Of people you have involved in the negotiations.

- **Personal power:** The total of your negotiation skills and expertise.

- **Power of standards:** The law, rules, regulations, custom or practice, or other standards that apply in your favour.

- **Referral power:** The power to refer to someone for a decision who isn't at the meeting means that you can't be forced into agreeing to something that you don't want to concede.

- **Relationship power:** The power of having an existing relationship in place. Humans are creatures of habit and prefer negotiating with someone they already know instead of starting again with someone brand new. That's why sales reps are always so keen to cultivate a relationship with you – they hope that you'll come back again next time as well as buy something now.

- **Scale or weight:** Some evidence exists that physically big negotiators have an advantage over physically smaller ones (what a surprise!). So, if you aren't a large negotiator you need to compensate by ensuring that your voice, gestures and physical presence make you seem bigger that you are.

Managing the Climate

You need to manage the climate (or negotiating atmosphere) and normally have four options:

- **Warm:** Open and friendly
- **Cool:** Objective, formal and data-driven
- **Hostile:** Pressurised and fast-moving
- **Cheeky:** Unusual, provocative or surprising

Different climates suit different people and different kinds of negotiation, and so make a tactical choice about which climate is most appropriate for the deal concerned. Whichever one you choose, always make sure that you cover the following issues at the climate-setting phase:

- What's the agenda?
- Where's the venue?
- What are the timescales for the negotiation?
- How much negotiating authority does each side have?

For example, you can see why this is important to sort out early on: if I think the negotiation is going to last two hours and you think it's going to last three months, after three hours I'm getting very irritated while you're feeling that the negotiation has barely started.

As the song says, 'always take the weather with you'.

Asking Why People Need What They Say They Want

Many deals get stuck because most negotiations focus only on what people want (price, delivery date, quantity and so on) instead of the reasons *why* they want those things. People can ask for the same thing (for example, a certain price) for many different reasons: because it makes them feel they've achieved something or they're more respected, they believe that they can trust you or it solves a desperate need.

If they want a certain price and you can work out *why,* maybe you can discern other ways apart from price to meet that need. This knowledge gives you far more options to work with in sorting out a deal.

For example, if you have a need for reassurance, I may be able to meet that need through transparent, regular and trustworthy accounting – at which point you may not need to focus so much on a high price to give you that reassurance. Or if you have a need to achieve something, I may be able to come up with an innovative deal structure that appeals to you but doesn't just depend on price.

Two sisters were fighting over the last orange in the bowl and couldn't decide how to divide it. So they cut it in half and shared it 50/50. Only afterwards did they realise that one sister needed the juice of the orange to make a drink and the other needed the rind of the orange in order to bake a cake. If they'd bothered to explore each other's needs first, they could've done a much more effective deal for both of them.

Finding Your Coinage

Coinage is king. This tip follows on from the preceding section on exploring the other side's needs. Can you make any concessions that are of low value to you (hence the term *coinage* – they feel like loose change), but meet a high value need or motivation on the other side?

If someone has a reassurance need, maybe you can give him comfort by offering him testimonials from his peers about your priorities or commitments that have nothing to do with price, but give him the same level of comfort as if you had offered a higher price. This costs you nothing to give, but you can then get something you want in return (for example, a lower price in exchange for offering that coinage).

Bidding Like You Mean It

When you're making offers in a negotiation, be direct – 'I want, I need or I require' are much better than 'Could I possibly have. . . ?' or 'How would you feel about. . . ?' People often try to 'soften' their bids in these ways to make them sound more palatable, but in fact it just sounds like you don't mean it, allowing the other side to take the bid less seriously.

Young children are the world's most natural bidders, because they just demand what they're after: 'I want a bar of chocolate'. Their approach isn't particularly polite, but it's effective because the adult has to take it seriously and stand up to it or negotiate. When you're bidding, remember what it was like when you asked for something as a child.

Cracking Deadlocks

Deals often get deadlocked in the bargaining stage. The parties are unable to resolve their differences, which harden into positions of 'principle'. Getting the deal done becomes very difficult. These deal 'blockers' are often the same the world over.

Parties can get stuck in a positional negotiation based solely on what they want: this price, that delivery date, this number of units and so on. Positional negotiations are bad news, because they don't give the parties any flexibility. If I want to buy something for £50 and you want me to pay £1,000, no obvious way exists of resolving the disagreement without one of us disappointing the other. This situation is frustrating for everybody and the negotiation becomes marked by bad feeling. If you attack my position, I can feel as though you're attacking me personally.

In order to address deadlocks, go back to focusing on underlying needs rather than surface 'positions' (check out the earlier 'Asking Why People Need What They Say They Want' section).

Also, take breaks in a negotiation. Many people plough on with negotiations for hours, but this is a recipe for trouble if deals get stuck, because the participants get more and more exasperated with each other. Taking a break can avoid this problem, giving people a chance to calm down and reconnect with a proper perspective on the problem. It gives people the chance to re-energise and come up with creative solutions.

Taking a break also offers the chance for informal sidebar conversations, which often lead to breakthroughs – in informal corridor conversations people may be a bit less guarded than when under pressure in a formal negotiating session.

If you're getting stuck:

- **Change the pattern in the negotiation.** Change the layout of the room, the venue, the teams, the speakers, the time of day you meet, the agenda or the type of clothes you wear (something informal instead of formal). A change in the energy of the negotiation can make all the difference in shifting people's views.

- **Offer people more than one option to solve a dilemma.** If you offer them two options (each of which you're equally happy with), often they pick one of them rather than just rejecting both.

- **Question your own assumptions.** Often you get stuck in a negotiation because you assume what the other side wants or needs, or what you think he ought to want, or what you think he deserves. Often those assumptions have no basis in reality. When you're stuck in a negotiation, don't assume it's the other person's fault. Your own assumptions may be the biggest enemy.

Applying the Appropriate Behaviour

You have 16 different behaviours available to you as a negotiator, and the perfect negotiator uses them all as he needs them. Yet most people have a favourite behaviour or two, and they tend to concentrate on them whatever the situation and the personalities on the other side.

Employ different behaviours at different stages and to deal with different people. The seven billion people in the world are all different, and the same behaviour working with them all would be surprising.

You don't need to be a psychologist to spot the many different types of behaviour. You do, however, need to be able to adapt your behaviour and work with the characteristics of the person you're dealing with, instead of going against his grain, to give yourself the best chance of being persuasive.

Here are just some examples of those different types:

- ✔ Some people love making decisions; others prefer to avoid them.
- ✔ Some people love the big picture; others focus on the detail.
- ✔ Some people are *associated,* that is, animated and in-the-moment when they negotiate; others are disassociated or distant.
- ✔ Some people love having lots of options; others prefer a linear approach with a clear path.
- ✔ Some people love to rely on the advice of experts or other people to give reinforcement; others are internally referenced and don't need anybody else's approval.
- ✔ Some people are natural *matchers* who look for things that are 'right' about a situation; others are *mis-matchers,* always looking for the problem or the thing that's wrong.

Work out whom you're dealing with and then deploy behaviour that suits that person. If you do so, the person feels that you're 'speaking his sort of language' or are 'his type of person', and you're more likely to persuade him to agree with your point of view. For example:

- ✔ If someone likes the big picture, *visualisation* works well (painting a positive image to inspire him). But if the person prefers detail, you need a more objective behaviour, such as 'proposing with reasons', with lots of data and information to focus on.

✔ If someone is associated, a sociable behaviour such as sharing problems or solutions works well. If he's disassociated, give him space – for example, lots of breaks and the use of silence so the person has the opportunity to think.

✔ If someone likes moving towards a solution, use collaborative behaviours such as 'focusing on common ground'. If he avoids solutions, you need to use 'incentives' (which seem more attractive than staying in the problem) to get him off the fence.

Closing the Deal

Remarkably, negotiators often fall at the final hurdle of getting the deal closed. Sometimes, this is because people take their eye off the ball as the negotiation enters its final stages and it grinds to a halt. Sometimes, people become over-competitive about winning those last extra points, even though they don't really need them, and so a stand-off develops.

Be careful about missing the closure moment. If you delay too long, the other side can get deal fatigue, change strategy or review their budget and no longer need a deal with you. Alternatively, a key sponsor on the other side that supported doing a deal with you may leave, or the other side may find a competitor of yours that they prefer to deal with.

If you sense that the other side is ready to close and you've achieved the objectives you set at the preparation stage, get on and finalise the deal. Make sure that the key points are summarised ('Are we all agreed that. . .?' is a good phrase to use) and ensure that paperwork is completed swiftly (without allowing intermediaries such as . . . ahem . . . lawyers to drag their feet or spin the process out).

A good way of spotting that the other side is ready to close is when they start talking about the future and how the deal is going to work in practice, rather than focusing purely on issues that still divide you.

Chapter 22

Ten Ways You Can Expect Your Lawyer to Behave

In This Chapter

▶ Getting good value from your lawyer

▶ Receiving the right service for your needs

*O*ne of the reasons for the prevalence of anti-lawyer jokes is the perception that lawyers don't give value for money. Of course, I'm not talking about all lawyers – just the 99 per cent that give the rest a bad name. (Sorry, I'll flag all anti-lawyer jokes with a warning from now on.)

The reality is that, as in all professions, some lawyers don't give good value for money. Plus, the legal profession isn't really structured to give small businesses legal help in the way they need it. Small firms want quick, practical, affordable advice that's easy to understand. Lawyers are used to giving considered advice, which takes time to assemble and is therefore more expensive. Such advice is often quite complicated, because it embraces many different theoretical possibilities.

One way for small firms to avoid a mismatch between their expectations and the service they subsequently receive is to be aware of their entitlements when dealing with lawyers. Many of the problems that arise are already covered by regulatory requirements for lawyers and you can avoid others by simply asking the right questions upfront.

'Lawyers' is a term that includes *barristers* (who largely undertake dispute-related litigation and court work), *notaries* (who specialise in authenticating and certifying documents) and *solicitors.* When small businesses use a lawyer, they normally deal with a firm of solicitors, the bulk of whose practice is non-litigation matters. Therefore, solicitors are likely to deal with most of the topics I discuss in this book (contracts, share agreements, intellectual property protection and so on).

So, when I use the word 'lawyer' in this chapter, I'm talking about what you can expect from your solicitor.

Receiving a Quote Upfront

Under the Solicitors Regulation Authority (SRA) Code of Conduct, clients must be given the best possible information about the cost of their matter, at the start of the retainer and throughout. You have the right to expect lawyers to be clear about how much they're likely to charge you and to explain clearly the final bill.

The Law Society provides examples of what a lawyer can include when discussing your anticipated bill with you:

- The basis for the fixed fee or the relevant hourly rates and an estimate of the time to be charged
- Whether rates may be increased during the period of the retainer
- Expected extra expenses (called *disbursements* – for example, photocopying) and likely time frames for them being due
- Potential liability for paying others' costs, where relevant (for example, if you lose a court case)
- Your VAT liability

Lawyers should also discuss whether the potential outcome of your case is likely to justify the risk involved, particularly the risk of paying the costs incurred by someone else's fees. They should do this upfront, before the meter starts ticking. If your lawyer is acting for you and you haven't had an upfront estimate, make sure that she doesn't do anything else until she's given you a proper quote.

Getting a Fixed Price

Lawyers aren't obliged to give a fixed price for their work, which often creates a problem. They can give an initial quote, which sounds okay, but then the matter takes longer to resolve than expected or veers off in a new direction. At the end, you get a nasty surprise – with a much higher bill than you were initially quoted.

Make a lawyer be clear about what work the quote covers. If it's an hourly rate, how many hours does she think the matter will take? If it's 'fixed', does it include all anticipated charges? Are any extra charges likely (say, the cost of stamp duty tax if you're buying shares)? Are any hidden costs not apparent in the fixed total? For example, some lawyers charge extra for answering your queries on the phone, or the cost of that time eats into the hours they've quoted for, leaving insufficient time for meaningful activity. Some lawyers bill in units of six minutes, and so if something takes three minutes its cost is rounded up to six minutes.

Sometimes lawyers tell you that predicting the overall cost of a matter is hard, which may be true, because the other side can be difficult or raise unexpected or complicating points. Even in these instances, though, lawyers can at least give you a range of expectation as to the final cost (between £x and £y). Alternatively, you can agree a fixed cost for each stage of the matter, so that they aren't allowed to exceed the cost for each stage without your approval.

Achieving an Affordable Price

A long-standing perception exists that lawyers charge too much for the value they deliver. A 14th-century poem written during the reign of Edward II warns that lawyers 'will beguile you in your hand unless you beware/and speak for you a word or two and do you little good/get silver for naught and make men begin what they had not thought'.

But generalising is difficult, because different lawyers at different firms charge different rates for the same work. For example, some big city firms charge a Partner's time at £650 per hour – not quite as much as Ronaldo, but certainly not to be sniffed at. Other law firms outside London may have more 'reasonable' rates of, say, £250 or £200 an hour.

Online legal firms that don't carry the burden of a big partnership structure and physical overheads are likely to be cheaper than more traditionally organised physical firms. With the latter, you can expect one-third of the bill to go towards paying for the partnership structure of the firm (including those partners who aren't working on your case), one third towards overheads (buildings, marble hallways, mahogany desks, secretaries and so on) and one third to the lawyer doing the billing. Online law firms have more room for cost-effective pricing, because generally they don't have to cover the first two categories of cost.

No regulatory limit applies on what you can be charged, though lawyers do have a duty under the SRA Code of Conduct to ensure that they treat clients 'fairly' and that their fee agreements are 'suitable to the client's needs and take into account the client's best interests'. Therefore, take into account all the circumstances when you consider a quote – perhaps one law firm charges more than another for genuine reasons (for example, it puts a more senior lawyer on your matter, it has greater expertise in a particular matter or the matter is genuinely complicated).

Here are my best tips:

- ✔ **Shop around.** Don't go to just one law firm, any more than you'd get a quote from one builder for doing work on your home.

- ✔ **Negotiate.** Many law firms have come under pressure with their charging structures as a result of the recession, and they can be more open to negotiation on price than you may think.

- ✔ **Check whose time you're being charged for.** Sometimes the law firm seeks to charge you a 'Partner' rate when in fact an experienced, well-qualified but junior lawyer is doing some or most of the work for the Partner. If an Associate is doing most of the work and the Partner is rubber-stamping it, perhaps you can reduce the cost.

- ✔ **Look for an over-the-top charge.** If it looks and feels like an over-the-top-cost, it probably *is* an over-the top-cost. This is usually readily apparent to a small business, used to scrapping for every penny of cost. As a result, some bigger law firms have more affordable initial rates for small company clients (for example, for an initial shareholder agreement or bundle of documents). But they revert to charging higher rates when the initial work is concluded and they feel they've 'won' the client. So, watch out that the rates don't spring back to the firm's normal high levels after the initial, affordably priced work is completed.

Charging Only for Work Done for You

Many legal situations come up time and again. The individual circumstances may differ slightly, but the overall context is very similar: a business wants a distribution agreement, a new Shareholder Agreement, a software development agreement and so on.

Therefore, when you ask for something to be done for you, the law firm often has an existing precedent it can use. Sure, it may need adapting to suit the circumstances of your particular case, but rarely does a law firm have to generate the whole document from scratch. If 70 per cent of the job has already been done before (for someone else), and it needs to generate only the extra 30 per cent for you, make sure that you're not charged as though 100 per cent of the job was being done for you.

Lawyers say they're entitled to charge you an increment for the expertise and experience that goes into preparing the precedent in the first place (as well as the time spent on your matter). Fair enough, but how many times does that same expertise need to be charged for before its cost has been recovered? Not infinitely, to every client, for sure.

A good question to ask when you're discussing quotes with lawyers is 'Are you using an existing precedent?' If the answer is 'yes' (and it normally is) that's a good reason for your bill to be reduced; they should charge only for the work being done just for you.

Explaining Things in Plain English

Lawyers have a reputation for making things more complicated than they need to be. Cynics say that this is deliberate – the more mysterious the language of the law, the more you need an expensive expert lawyer to translate it for you.

Certainly the legal profession does itself no favours with its reliance on archaic language and jargon or expressions that lawyers understand but normal human beings don't. The problem is that these expressions and linguistic mouthfuls have become so ingrained that lawyers go with the flow instead of rewriting everything in plain English.

Believe it or not, the Law Society *does* advocate use of simple English. Plus, the SRA states that 'it is important that clients can understand the information they are provided with and that significant information is highlighted to them and explained clearly'.

Many lawyers are aware of the problem and strive to communicate more simply – they may even claim to use 'plain English' in marketing communications. However, lawyers do genuinely have difficulty stepping away from the professional jargon they use with other lawyers every day. It's a bit like asking doctors to explain medical conditions and treatments without using jargon; the flesh may be willing, but the tongue is weak.

Be assertive about what you want. You have a right to understand the documents that you're asked to sign and the legal advice given to you. If lawyers start to bamboozle you with legal language or complicated drafting, insist that they simplify it. You don't have to be squeamish about doing so; the lawyer's job is to communicate with you in a way that you find comfortable and yours isn't to understand legalese dating back to Norman times, or to pretend that you do.

Doing Things Quickly

Lawyers have a reputation for dragging things out, in part because they see potential problems whereas clients want only outcomes. The lawyer feels duty-bound to solve all the potential problems that may arise from the client's proposed outcome, even if they're theoretical or unrealistic. If they don't address those hazards and a problem arises later, lawyers think that they'll be blamed for not addressing that issue, even though the client hadn't thought or didn't care about it at the time and was simply focused on the outcome.

Of course, the lawyer for the other side doesn't always see those problems from the same point of view, and may have other issues to raise for her own client. And so the debate turns into the legal equivalent of the Battle of the Somme, with lawyers hurling explosive letters at each other and the matter getting stuck in the mud.

Insist on regular communication from your lawyer. This minimises the likelihood of frustrating delays, because the communication process you set up doesn't allow for issues to sit still for long. You have an ally here in the Law Society, which provides law firms with examples of the service standards they may want to agree to, including the timetabling of phone or written updates, and regular updates on future timescales and changes in those timescales.

By insisting on tight timelines for regular communication, you don't allow momentum to slow or give lawyers the chance to get stuck on points that may be important to them, but are of minor relevance to a successful outcome for you.

Producing Documents of a Practical Length

Some people say that lawyers deliberately produce longer documentation because they can get paid more – and it's not a new problem. People complained about the fact that Roman notaries were paid by the line!

Sometimes this problem is down to lawyers with good intentions trying to cater for every contingency, however remote, in their documentation, and ending up adding pages to the draft that the other side has to amend. By the time both sides have had two or three attempts, the document has doubled in length. You can add to this the many general legal clauses and recitals that get inserted into agreements out of habit rather than because they're necessary or ever likely to be invoked.

Lawyers tell you that you take risks by leaving all this stuff out of any agreement, but an equal risk is making the documents too long: the more content exists, the more to argue about, and the more opportunity for mistakes and confusion by lawyers or clients on both sides. You may even reach the point of despair where you stop reading the documents you're given because their size and complexity is so daunting.

Make your lawyers justify the length of their documentation. Ask them to state the practical consequences of not addressing the apparent problem that's taking up pages of text to resolve. Ask whether they've ever had to rely on a general clause they're fighting so hard to add to the agreement, which seems to add no practical value. You're the client, and part of the lawyer's service to you is to put the minimum required number of correct words in the right order to do the job effectively.

Producing Documents that Reflect Your Business

Sometimes lawyers use legacy documents from other transactions combined with traditional clauses and phrases that pass into the agreement without being questioned. As a result, the agreement ends up not reflecting your particular business priorities or circumstances. The practical outcomes you desired get lost as lawyers produce documents that suit them instead – the legal tail wagging the dog. As a client, you have a right to insist that documentation produced for you reflects what you want to achieve for the business, instead of what lawyers are used to seeing in documents of this kind.

Sometimes clients are too squeamish to question the documentation that the lawyer produces, feeling that the document must be right because an expert produced it and it's costing a lot. But don't be nervous. Quite possibly a lawyer using a traditional document with ritualised language has missed the business point of the exercise.

I like to write out the phrase I'm constructing in everyday English first and then add on any legal conventions needed to customise it for my profession. You can get your lawyer to work the same way, by writing a script of your ideal outcome, written in conversational English language, and then insisting that the lawyer stick to that when drafting.

Sending You Their Terms

No regulatory requirement says that lawyers have to set out terms of business, but law firms usually send you a Client Engagement letter and/or terms of business. The SRA insists that lawyers must tell their clients about the following:

- ✔ Details of fees and costs, how they're calculated, when they're paid and whether the client may have to pay interest on unpaid bills
- ✔ Service levels
- ✔ Contact details and status of the lawyer dealing with and/or supervising the matter
- ✔ Firm's regulatory status
- ✔ Any limits on the firm's liability to the client (for example, for loss of client profits)

The Law Society maintains that good business practice is to send terms of business. Its 'Practice Direction' (guidelines to lawyers on best practice) covers some of the above requirements and additional ones, including:

- ✔ Information on *professional indemnity insurance* (the cover lawyers must maintain against the possibility that they make mistakes when doing your work; currently, a minimum of £3 million).
- ✔ Data protection issues (Chapter 6 has lots on data protection); lawyers must comply with the Data Protection Act.
- ✔ Storage of documents and any related costs (how long the lawyer retains the file and what happens after that).
- ✔ Outsourcing of work (for example, if the law firm uses another agency to do any of your work).
- ✔ Processes for the client and the lawyer terminating the retainer.
- ✔ Client due diligence the lawyer has to undertake (to check that you're not a money launderer or terrorist).
- ✔ Payments of a fair rate of interest to you on any of your money held in client accounts.

Client Engagement letters and terms of business are often very long and difficult for laypeople to follow. But make sure that you receive them and that they cover the minimum points for your own protection.

Having an Effective Complaints Procedure

The SRA requires that lawyers have in place a Complaints Procedure and notify clients about it. You must also be informed, in writing, at the time of engagement and at the conclusion of any complaints procedure, of your right to complain to (and full details of how to contact) the Legal Ombudsman and the time frame for doing so.

This aspect is often dealt with in the Client Engagement letter (refer to the preceding section). Lawyers must also make you aware of your right to challenge, or complain about, your bill, including of your right to complain to the Legal Complaints Service or to apply to the court for assessment of the fairness of your bill under the Solicitors Act, 1974.

The Complaints Procedure must be open, fair, easy to understand and effective, and law firms aren't allowed to charge for handling your complaints. Make sure that your Client Engagement letter has a complaints procedure like this; if not, demand to see it upfront.

Index

• *U* •

• *V* •

About the Author

Clive Rich has been a lawyer for over 30 years, originally qualifying as a Barrister. He's also a CEDR-qualified Mediator and a CIArb-qualified Arbitrator.

Over the years he has worked for many large corporations, such as Sony, Warner and Bertelsmann, where he ran legal departments in the UK and Europe and digital and TV divisions. He has also worked with hundreds of small companies as a lawyer, shareholder, negotiator and investor.

Clive has run two companies of his own, and so he's familiar with the challenges that small companies face on a daily basis, as practitioner and entrepreneur. Rich Futures is his professional negotiation company, from which he has provided deal-making and coaching services all over the world, as well as creating a negotiation app ('Close My Deal') and writing *The Yes Book* – a modern guide to the art of negotiation.

He also founded and now runs LawBite, an online legal service providing 'Simple Law for Small Companies' (www.lawbite.co.uk). LawBite provides a range of easy-to-understand, affordable online documents and contracts, a suite of editing, sharing and e-signing tools, and a virtual law firm wrapped around its platform. It uses only qualified, insured lawyers, but by using technology to democratise the law, it charges 50 per cent or less than normal law firms.

Dedication

To my wife Joanna for her unwavering support – exactly what every entrepreneur needs most of all, but nobody ever writes about. And for my children Tabitha, Felix, Hugo and my stepdaughter Emily – all impressive (though terrifying) Barrack Room lawyers in the making.

This book is also for all those lawyers who believe in keeping small companies safe and sound at a price they can afford, and to all those lawyers dedicated to the little-known legal art of explaining things simply.

Author's Acknowledgments

My grateful thanks to Adam Werth and Julie Bowe for all their research and assistance to me in the writing of this book.

Publisher's Acknowledgments

Executive Commissioning Editor: Annie Knight

Project Manager: Michelle Hacker

Development Editor: Andy Finch

Copy Editor: Kerry Laundon

Technical Editors: Jonathan Loake & Simon Newman (Barrister)

Production Editor: Siddique Shaik

Cover Photos: ©iStockphoto/Pali Rao

Take Dummies with you everywhere you go!

Whether you're excited about e-books, want more from the web, must have your mobile apps, or swept up in social media, Dummies makes everything easier.

Visit Us

Like Us

Follow Us

Watch Us

Join Us

Pin Us

Circle Us

Shop Us

FOR DUMMIES®

A Wiley Brand

BUSINESS

978-1-118-73077-5

978-1-118-44349-1

978-1-119-97527-4

MUSIC

978-1-119-94276-4

978-0-470-97799-6

978-0-470-49644-2

DIGITAL PHOTOGRAPHY

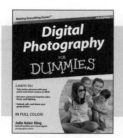

978-1-118-09203-3

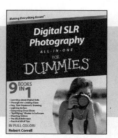

978-0-470-76878-5

978-1-118-00472-2

Algebra I For Dummies
978-0-470-55964-2

Anatomy & Physiology For Dummies,
2nd Edition
978-0-470-92326-9

Asperger's Syndrome For Dummies
978-0-470-66087-4

Basic Maths For Dummies
978-1-119-97452-9

Body Language For Dummies, 2nd Edition
978-1-119-95351-7

Bookkeeping For Dummies, 3rd Edition
978-1-118-34689-1

British Sign Language For Dummies
978-0-470-69477-0

Cricket for Dummies, 2nd Edition
978-1-118-48032-8

Currency Trading For Dummies,
2nd Edition
978-1-118-01851-4

Cycling For Dummies
978-1-118-36435-2

Diabetes For Dummies, 3rd Edition
978-0-470-97711-8

eBay For Dummies, 3rd Edition
978-1-119-94122-4

Electronics For Dummies All-in-One
For Dummies
978-1-118-58973-1

English Grammar For Dummies
978-0-470-05752-0

French For Dummies, 2nd Edition
978-1-118-00464-7

Guitar For Dummies, 3rd Edition
978-1-118-11554-1

IBS For Dummies
978-0-470-51737-6

Keeping Chickens For Dummies
978-1-119-99417-6

Knitting For Dummies, 3rd Edition
978-1-118-66151-2